JOURNEY
TEMP

Book Two

Journeyman Chronicles of the

American Revolution

Frank A. Mason

NOVEMBER 1, 1788

Will Yelverton took in the smell of the river, the marsh, and the odor of wooden ships – a mixture of wood rot, hemp, tar, salt, rotting fish, mud. The smell cast him back ten years to his first visit to Savannah, Georgia. The river still had that strange copper color, and it still moved with the same slow pace to the sea. Snags still bobbed in the shallows, the current eddying around them. A couple masts still stuck out of the water, visible tombstones of ships sunk in 1776 and again in 1779 to block the enemy vessels from coming upriver. The river was still alive with energy and promise.

The river and Georgia were alive, but Samuel Elbert was dead. Signal guns fired in the distance. Closer, the crash of another brace of signal guns echoed the pop of the distant guns. The vessels in the harbor all hauled their colors to half-staff. Will turned to look at the government buildings near the waterfront. Their colors were all being lowered to half-staff. The near flag caught the strong sea breeze blowing across the harbor and its rampant thirteen stars and thirteen red and white stripes snapped into the breeze.

Samuel Elbert: Major General of the Georgia Militia, Brigadier General of the United States Army, former Governor of Georgia, hero of the American Revolution, and Will Yelverton's friend. Sam Elbert was dead at 48. And Will Yelverton was bereft.

Will's wife put her hand on his arm, and he touched her fingers with a gentle brush of his hand. Will looked at her and, through his tears, saw her in her youth. He smiled at her.

She said, "You loved him, didn't you?"

"Yes. He was a great man. He changed my life, as have so many others before and after him. But he was so important in who I am. Like others, he believed in me with only a little information to go on."

"Of course he did," she murmured.

Will heard the guns and saw the flags, the honors rendered to a great man, yet his mind ranged to the night he met Sam Elbert in a tavern in Sunbury, Georgia. Will smiled as he remembered threatening Elbert with a pistol. It seemed like only a moment ago.

He smiled through his tears when he thought about how he had been honored to stand next to General Samuel Elbert at Yorktown as British General Charles O'Hara surrendered his sword to General Benjamin Lincoln. Of many other candidates, Elbert had invited Will to join him for the surrender. On Elbert's other side stood Marie-Joseph Paul Yves Roch Gilbert du Motier, Marquis de La Fayette.

This is the story of Will Yelverton's Revolutionary War in Georgia.

PART I: THE COAST

CHAPTER 1 – LATE FEBRUARY 1778

The *Beatrice* rode the rolling North Atlantic Ocean like a lusty woman straddling her lover. The communication between ship, wind, and water created in a reverie that defied understanding by those who were not mariners. Scent of salt spray, wet hemp, canvas, wood, and tar. A sailing vessel in its element at sea. Smooth, rhythmic, sensual, questing, passionate. The reason ships were always considered feminine.

Nineteen-year-old Will Yelverton stood in the forecastle, the bow, of the *Beatrice*, a three-masted sloop of war, his feet planted wide apart. After a nearly a fortnight aboard Captain Obadiah Dawkins' privateer Will had his sea legs and was comfortably at home, his balance perfectly attuned to the rise and fall of the *Beatrice*. Never before a sailor, Will had surprised himself and Dawkins by quickly adapting to the rhythms of the ocean.

In the near distance an elegant, two-masted sloop pounded its way on a similar southerly heading to *Beatrice*. Captain Dawkins had adjusted course to bring the ships closer together, *Beatrice* pursuing. Dawkins' intent was to take the sloop as a prize.

Turning aft, Will made his way to the quarterdeck where Captain Dawkins stood placidly beside the helmsman, Mr. Sneed. In his days aboard the *Bea*, Will had learned to watch his footing, dodge swinging booms that held the sails, and listen to

4

the hum of the wind in the rigging to gauge the ship's motion and anticipate tacks – turns – ordered by Dawkins to sail the ship to its best advantage.

Will, a master gunsmith, saw the *Bea* as akin to one of the beautiful rifles he made. The *Bea* was a carefully assembled collection of finely tuned parts that, taken as a whole, were beautiful and superbly effective in doing exactly the thing it was intended to do – glide efficiently through the sea, safely carrying crew and cargo to their destination. Will understood implicitly that the *Beatrice* was the culmination of thousands of years of human learning about the sea, vessel design, sail technology, and dozens of other elements that coalesced to make an eighteenth-century sailing vessel.

Beautiful, smooth, slightly dangerous. *Beatrice* was a New Jersey privateer. The sloop running three points off the starboard bow was quarry. Will wondered what cargo or other valuables the sloop might be carrying? *Beatrice* had letters of marque from the New Jersey State Government, signed by the governor. Detaining and plundering another vessel on the high seas was therefore not an act of piracy. Rather, it was the legitimate business of the fledgling United States and the State of New Jersey. Never mind that *Beatrice* and her quarry were now off the coast of Georgia.

Will stepped up to the ladder and called out, "Permission to come on deck?"

Captain Obadiah Dawkins' grinned, exposing his few stubs of brown teeth and said, "Permission granted!"

With that, Will quickly bounded up the ladder to stand beside Dawkins. As Will gained his footing on the quarterdeck, *Bea* took a particularly nasty wallow in a trough.

"Steady as she goes, Mr. Sneed."

"Aye, Captain, steady on heading Sou Sou-West."

To Will Dawkins said, "You're getting to be quite a sailor for a landlubber."

"I think this is great fun, Sir."

"We'll see how much fun you think it is when the prize shoots back."

Will murmured, "Aye."

The two small ships they had taken as prizes in the past several days had been unarmed and had given up without a fight. The sloop that was now some 400 yards off the starboard bow was bigger, faster, and seemed more prepared for a fight than the other prizes had been. Still, she was smaller than *Beatrice*.

Dawkins handed Will the spyglass. "Have a look, will ye?"

"Aye, Captain. Thank you."

Will expanded the glass and ran it bow to stern across the sloop. Several things stood out immediately. First, there was more of a crew than the smaller prizes, and the crewmembers Will could see seemed more professional at their duties. They went about the ship with purpose. Will thought he saw a cutlass hanging from one man's hip. A lookout high in the rigging had a musket.

Next, there were two bow chaser guns – perhaps six pounders – one on either side of the bow, and there were four gunports visible on the near, port, side of the sloop. Will concluded there were probably four similar gunports on the starboard side. Two swivel guns were mounted on either side of the after deck where the captain and helmsman were stationed. Assuming each gunport hid a cannon, and Will had no reason to believe otherwise, the sloop mounted the same number of guns as *Beatrice*, in roughly the same configuration. That was not good. If there was a fight, then the two ships were closely matched. Will considered that in the privateering trade overmatching your potential prize was most desirable.

As Will adjusted the spyglass he brought the two men at the helm into view. One, the helmsman, was unremarkable. But the captain was tall, had a fore and aft hat with a plume, a blue uniform coat with braid, and a sword hanging from his left hip. To Will this man looked like an officer of the crown and not just some merchant ship's captain. The captain was training a spyglass on the *Beatrice*.

A chill ran up Will's spine. "Was he looking at me?"

7

Will swung the glass further aft and noted there was no flag flying. On the transom – the rear of the sloop – the name *Rebecca* was written in gold-leaf script.

It was not really a surprise that *Rebecca* had not streamed her colors. *Beatrice* had not yet hoisted her own red, white, and blue striped flag marking her as a United States ship.

Will closed the spyglass and looked at Dawkins. Dawkins raised an eyebrow in query.

Will reported, "Sir, I believe that ship may be near as well armed as we are. I also believe the crew are skilled and armed. The captain appears to be more than just an ordinary sailor. He is wearing what looks to be an officer's coat with braid and a sword. The ship is the *Rebecca*. She bears no colors, but I believe she could be a British privateer."

"Aye, Will. We'll make a sailor of you yet. I agree with your report. What shall we do?"

"Run."

Dawkins spat over the rail into the foaming Atlantic. Running the back of his hand across his mouth, he said, "Aye. Run we will."

"Mr. Sneed, come about to steer south south-east. Sailing master! Put on all sail, we're tacking to port! Mr. Childers, have your gunners load, but do not run out the guns."

Each of the three junior officers set about their tasks. Will watched closely as Mr. Childers, the master gunner,

8

oversaw bringing of powder from the magazine and the loading process. The powder was stored in silk bags in special wooden boxes to keep it dry and to avoid sparks that might ignite the powder and potentially explode the magazine. The cannon balls – 12 pounders – were brought on deck. The crews for the eight guns set about loading powder bag, ball, and wadding.

The master gunner removed large flintlock firing locks from their protective boxes and carefully screwed them in place over the touch holes of the guns. The use of a flintlock mechanism was a shipboard innovation that kept the gunners from having to use a burning linstock which might accidentally set off the powder. Will had seen linstocks, long burning matchs wrapped around metal tongs on the end of a wooden rod, used as a matter of course for artillery on land at both the Battle of Moore's Creek Bridge and at Brandywine. Here, linstocks were dangerous. The flintlock firing mechanism was affixed to the touchhole of the cannon and attached to a long lanyard which the gunner pulled to trigger the cock holding a piece of razor-sharp flint to fall on a pan filled with gunpowder. The flint would spark the powder which would ignite the main charge in the breech of the cannon.

The guns on *Beatrice* were carronades. These were stubby British naval cannon that made up for lack of long range by throwing a large projectile with considerably more force than most cannons. This was because the ball fit the carronade's barrel tightly as opposed to other cannons where the ball was more loosely fitted. Mr. Childers had explained to Will that the stubby carronades were found on a good many British merchantmen, and these had been taken off a prize just a few months ago. Naval combat was at close quarters and a large projectile slamming into a wooden hull would have devastating effect. The carronades were also capable of firing cannister shot. Cannister was designed to spray small balls like a shotgun and was terrible in its ability to kill and maim the enemy crew. Will noticed the master gunner was loading cannister shot in the starboard guns. The port guns were loaded with ball.

The ship steadied up on its new heading that was slightly East of South. Will noticed that *Rebecca* followed suit and was now tacking more easterly.

Will said, "Captain, the *Rebecca* is staying in one spot. I mean, when I look at her without having moved my place, she is staying in one spot relative to that cleat on our gunwale."

"Aye. And what d'ye think that might mean?"

"Uh, well, uh, if we don't turn, she'll hit us."

"Aye. She's on a collision course. What d'ye think that means?"

"She's chasing us now."

"Aye. I'll wager she's the British privateer and a man named John Mowbray is her skipper. Hails from Saint Augustine."

"Where's that?"

"Florida, Laddie. British East Florida." Dawkins lifted his chin to the south, "that a way, Sonny. About 40 leagues. All British, too. They're not minded to revolution."

At that moment, the red flag of the British Atlantic fleet with the Union Jack in the corner snapped out from the halyard at the stern of *Rebecca*. Nothing subtle about the flag, either. It was some twenty feet across.

Dawkins spat over the side of *Beatrice*. "Thought so. Will, take our flag and run it up. Do it smartly so that it snaps."

It was the last day of February 1778, and the fight was on.

CHAPTER 2 - THE CHASE

The flag snapped out into the wind, its thirteen red, white, and blue stripes bright against the gray of the Atlantic sky. The flag's blue field of thirteen white, five-pointed stars arrayed three, two, three, two, three had just recently been added to replace the British Union Jack that had filled the upper corner of the flag. The naval flag was different from the striped Continental flag Will had seen at Brandywine. The Continental Army flag had been alternating red and white stripes while the naval flag had red, white, blue stripes repeating and ending with a red stripe at the bottom to make thirteen. Will looked at it the flag streaming out and thought about what it symbolized. Thirteen states all united in a quest for liberty and the pursuit of happiness.

Will thought about how his pursuit of liberty and happiness had been delayed by the war to keep them. "I was doing just fine before the war," he thought. "My liberty was almost cut short by Major Banastre Tarleton in New Jersey, and I could have been dangling at the end of a rope. That certainly would have ended my happiness. Perhaps my happiness still lies on the frontier?"

A cannon ball howled through the air, interrupting Will's musing. It splashed into the sea about 100 yards in front of the *Beatrice*, jetting a thirty-foot geyser of water into the air.

Will glanced at Captain Dawkins.

Seeing the look, Dawkins said, "Aye, that's a warning shot, Sonny. He means business."

"What will we do now?"

"He plainly wants us to heave to and be boarded. That won't be happening, so we're going to pile on more sail and see if we can get to nightfall without being in a close fight."

"What are our chances?"

"He has a faster hull and a good crew. I can tell that by the set of his sails. And that cannon round was well placed. We have a fight on our hands."

Will asked, "Permission to go below?"

Dawkins looked at Will inquiringly but nodded.

Will walked quickly to the main hatchway and down to the hold where Molly was in her makeshift stall. Stroking Molly's neck and giving her a carrot, Will quietly said, "I'll get you out of this, girl. I know this is not good for you to be caged up here."

Molly whickered softly and nuzzled Will's hand. She moved some, stamping her feet in the limited space she had. Nodding her head, she snuffled and rolled her eyes.

"I know." Will said, "I know, girl." Will checked Molly's hay and water. Patting her neck again, Will turned and quickly went up the ladder. He walked with purpose to the cabin he shared with Childers.

Will stepped onto the main deck and paused at the ladder to the quarterdeck.

"Permission to enter the bridge?"

"Permission granted."

Dawkins looked Will over. Will had changed from linen shirt and loose trousers to his hunting shirt and breeches. His belt held Uncle Ewan's surgically sharp Scottish dirk. Across his shoulders he wore his shot pouch and powder horn. Tucked into his belt was the Brander pistol Will had taken from Major Banastre Tarleton during his frantic escape from British custody in New Jersey. Strapped across his back was his 69 caliber English dragoon carbine. In his hands Will carried a deer hide case that was some five feet long.

Dawkins' grin made his hatchet face look even more like a cadaver. "I see ye'er ready for the fight."

"Aye, Captain. If this is going to turn into a fight, I want to be useful."

"Well, if it's scarin' 'em with a bunch o' weapons ye're after, ye've done that! Look at *Rebecca*, now."

Will turned to look at *Rebecca*. Dawkin's pursuer had come closer and signal flags were now flying.

"What do the flags say?"

"What you'd expect. Heave to and prepare to be boarded."

"What shall we do?"

"I've ordered Mr. Childers be ready to repel boarders with the canister shot in the starboard guns. When the ship gets closer, I'll order the crew armed with cutlasses and muskets. Right now, I think we should prepare a surprise for Captain Mowbray."

"What kind of surprise?"

"How good are ye with that fancy rifle?"

Will said, "I usually hit what I'm aiming at."

"Good. Then, perhaps ye'll put on a bit of a demonstration for yonder crew to make 'em think twice about their current enterprise." Dawkins' face pulled to a point, his eyes glinting.

"You want me to shoot at them?"

"No, I want you to kill one of them."

Will swallowed hard. "I'm not in the habit of killing someone for sport."

Dawkins' eyes went flinty hard. "This ain't sport, Sonny. If they take this ship, we'll all be wearin' chains or maybe swingin' from the yardarm. D'ye see that sand Mr. Childers has thrown about the gundeck? That's so's when it's runnin' with blood you don't slip and fall. If they board us, the fight will be

15

bloody and close quarters, and that sand will be full of blood. You'll be one of us. Maybe it'll be your blood. So, the only difference between that kind of fight and what I'm asking you to do is just the distance between you and the man trying to kill you."

Will looked out toward *Rebecca*. 200 yards. Rolling sea. Pitching and tossing of both ships.

"If I hit anybody it'll be pure luck."

"I don't care. A near miss might give 'em pause. I'm not going to run the carronades out early because that'll tip our hand that we have 'em. Them short-barreled carronades are hell in a close fight, and we'll clear his decks with the first broadside, if ye can call four guns a broadside. I want the carronades to be a surprise for Captain Mowbray should he get close enough to enjoy their attention."

The short-barreled carronades are hell in a close fight, and we'll clear his decks with the first broadside, if ye can call four guns a broadside. I want the carronades to be a surprise for Captain Mowbray should he get close enough to enjoy their attention."

Will drew Josie, his .40 caliber rifle, from its deerskin case. Josie was exquisitely made. Will had spent the better part of a year at Alexander Kennedy's gun factory in Bear Creek, North Carolina, hand building the gun. Josie was Will's masterpiece – the presentation piece of work that earned him the paper he carried certifying him a master gunsmith.

16

Engraved in a small piece of coin silver inlet on the top of the stock were the initials *WBY*, William Branch Yelverton. A small conceit.

Abigail Kennedy had made the deerskin gun case for Josie. Eighteen-year-old Abby had sandy hair, nearly the same color as Will's. She also had the same English coloring with blue eyes that smiled in merriment, especially when Will was present. Will had learned too late in his apprenticeship at the Kennedy's that Abby had strong feelings for him.

Will's judgement had been clouded by his infatuation with Martha Black, daughter of the wealthiest merchant in Will's adopted hometown of New Bern, North Carolina. Martha had unceremoniously dumped him when he returned from the year at Kennedy's. She ran off to sea with one of Charles Black's rough-and-tumble merchant captains.

Now, each time Will touched the soft, supple deerskin gun case he thought of Abby. Abby who had shyly said that something as hard and long as Josie needed a soft case to protect it. Abby of the smiling eyes and warm touch.

Shaking off his memories of Abby, Will carefully loaded Josie. The range was some 200 yards, so resting the butt plate against his foot, Will added a small amount of powder to the normal charge of finely ground powder kept exclusively for Josie. He poured the powder charge down Josie's barrel, the sharp stink of fresh, dry gunpowder wafting into his nostrils, tasting it in the back of his throat. Then, he carefully wrapped the .40 caliber ball in a small patch of linen and pushed it into the bore, using the small hardwood dowel he kept for that purpose. Then, Will used the horn-tipped hickory ramrod to smoothly seat the ball against the charge. Will tapped the ball gently with the ramrod to be sure it was fully seated. He had seen other rifle shooters jam the ball in place and then slam the ramrod against the ball. Will knew this might deform the lead ball and harm the accuracy of the shot, so he was cautious to avoid that bad behavior.

Will slid the ramrod into its pipes under Josie's long, octagonal barrel. He lifted Josie and flicked open the priming pan where he added a small measure of powder and clicked the pan closed. A quick look at the flint told Will he was ready to shoot.

The ship rode the rolling sea with some regularity. Will stood at the rail watching the motion of the ship, gauging the period between troughs and peaks. He watched *Rebecca* as she rode the same rolling waves. Will had not been schooled past the 6th grade, but he was natively intelligent and understood innately the eccentricity of the complex motion of *Beatrice* and *Rebecca*. Each ship moved to its own rhythm. Will would have to gauge when to shoot so that *Beatrice* was steady, and *Rebecca* was on her way up. Ideally, the ball from Josie would arrive just as *Rebecca* paused for an instant at the crest of a wave. Looking for the swing in *Rebecca* from trough to peak helped Will to approximate how far to lead his target.

"Not a chance I can hit anything with precision," Will thought with a wry grin. He looked at Dawkins and nodded.

Dawkins said, "Can ye shoot the lookout?"

Will looked at *Rebecca* and located the man atop the rigging. That man held a musket and would surely be shooting down at *Beatrice* when they came close enough. "Fair enough. He's standing in the way of my pursuit of happiness," Will thought wryly.

Will had built Josie with two triggers, a regular trigger, and a set trigger. The set trigger's job was to move the internal catch for the hammer to a much lighter position. Once the set trigger was pulled the regular trigger only required the slightest touch to cause the hammer to fly forward, strike the pan and fire the rifle. Will pulled the set trigger and cocked the hammer. Josie was now a killing machine with a hair trigger.

Will leaned against the bulkhead and rested Josie on the rail. Will carefully lined-up the sights. Target sitting atop the front blade site front blade site squarely between the buckhorns of the rear site. Ordinarily, a 200-yard shot was a bit of a test, but not overly so. Today, with *Beatrice* riding the waves, *Rebecca* tossed by the same rollers, and the target was the lookout atop a mast that was swinging several feet side to side with each roll of the sea, the shot was more than a bit of a test.

Will set the sights ten feet above and about the same number of feet ahead of *Rebecca*'s forward progress. Up. Down. Up. Down. Gently, Will touched the trigger. WizCRAAAK!

19

A moment later Dawkins exclaimed, "Jesus, Mary and Joseph! You hit him!"

Will waived away the smoke that eddied in his face to see the lookout caught in the rigging, dangling by one foot, head down. His musket must have fallen to the deck below or into the sea. The lookout's arms were lifeless, and his body swung with the motion of the ship.

Dawkins said, "My God! And Captain Mowbray is throwing a fit! Damn if he didn't just draw his sword and start waiving it around. Well, that son-of-a-bitch is next!"

Will asked, "Is it fair to shoot the captain of another ship?"

"All's fair out here, Sonny. They'd shoot me right now if they could. But they can't 'cause I've got a secret weapon! You!"

Dawkins' hatchet face cracked into a wild-eyed deathshead grin. "Load 'er up Sonny! Let's see if ye can make 'em think twice about chasin' ol' *Bea.*"

Rebecca's bow chaser guns opened fire. A ball whizzed through the rigging in front of the main mast, clipping one of the sheets and setting a sail flapping. The second ball, probably a six-pounder, skipped harmlessly across the water.

Dawkins said, "Can't shoot the gunners. They're behind the rail and them gun ports. Let's take a crack at the skipper."

"Captain, you know that was quite a lucky shot?"

"I don't give a damn what kind of shot it was, Sonny. You clipped that lookout good, and that gave ol' Mowbray something to consider. That's why he opened fire with them bow chasers. He didn't expect to do shit with them, but he was mad as a wet settin' hen. So, he cut loose just to show off. Showed his ass, more like."

Will had reloaded Josie and leaned against the bulkhead, resting the rifle on the rail once again. The range was now about 150 yards and Will was beginning to be able to discern details on *Rebecca*. This time the rise and fall was the same, but the range made the lead less.

Will caressed the trigger. WizCRAAAK! Dawkins jumped up and down and bent double with laughter.

Will said, "What happened?" The smoke was still wafting and obscured his vision.

"Why, Sonny, you shot his damn hat off! He's dancin' a fair jig and waivin' around that sword like he's in a duel with the Devil himself. Only, there ain't nobody there to stick."

Will breathed a sigh of relief that he had not killed yet another human being. He understood that they'd kill him without hesitation, but still, shooting another person from a distance seemed so...impersonal and murderous.

Dawkins said, "Load 'er up, Sonny!"

Rebecca's bow chasers fired again. This time, the first ball flew through the rigging doing no damage, but the second ball shattered railing in front of the mid-ships boat davit and sprayed splinters all around. The sand on the deck got a workout because one of the gunners took a foot-long splinter in his forearm, spraying blood like a small fountain until Mr. Childers threw his belt around the arm as a tourniquet. The splinter stuck all the way through the sailor's arm and twitched with each beat of the sailor's heart. Childers used another splinter as a lever to twist the tourniquet tight, and another crewman took the injured gunner below decks to sickbay.

There was no ship's doctor, so the cook would serve as surgeon. The cook had a table to place a wounded man on and sharp knives to cut him with.

Will thought, "God help that poor man. The cook's miserable at making food, I can't imagine he would be any good as a surgeon."

Will had already seen plenty of death and gore in this war. There had been some terrible wounds, mostly for the Loyalists, at Moore's Creek, and the Patriots at Brandywine had died in a bloodbath of hundreds. Something about the suddenness with which the gunner was injured and the spray of red blood against the white of the sand and the smoothness of the deck caused Will to recoil.

As he reloaded Josie, Will thought, "We're in it now, Josie."

A spent musket ball thumped against the rail. Harmless, but a harbinger of worse to come. *Rebecca* was getting into range for small arms.

Will located the musketeer who had fired the shot. Josie jumped against Will's shoulder, and the musketeer spun around and disappeared behind the rail. Will stepped behind the bulkhead and reloaded Josie. Another musket ball smacked against a bulkhead behind Will. This time, *Rebecca* was closer, and that ball had some force.

Dawkins quietly told the helmsman to prepare to turn toward *Rebecca*.

"Mr. Childers, we're going to give them a taste of the carronades! Open the gun ports and prepare to fire!"

"Captain we still have cannister loaded."

"Aye, I plan to rake them from stem to stern with cannister."

"Very well, Captain!"

"Will, can you spot the sailor who's shooting at us with that musket?"

"Aye, Captain."

Will shot at the musket wielding sailor, splintering a rail just inches from his face and causing him to duck below *Rebecca*'s port rail. Will reloaded Josie.

Dawkins shouted, "Sailing master! Prepare to come about to starboard."

Thirty seconds later, Dawkins ordered, "Mr. Sneed, hard a' starboard. Cross their bow. Mr. Childers you may fire when the target is in view. I want to rake her with that canister!"

Sneed spun the wheel, and the sailing master shouted orders to sailors to reset the sails for the tack. *Beatrice* heeled hard over to starboard and her sails luffed briefly before filling. *Beatrice* shot forward crossing *Rebecca*'s bow, and the carronades began firing with an amazing roar. One after the other, each of the four 12-pound short-barreled guns crashed and slammed back against its carriage, sweeping the *Rebecca's* decks with hundreds of deadly musket balls, buzzing as they shattered railings, ripped into the masts, tore holes in sails and killed crewmen.

Dawkins shouted, "Prepare to come about and let 'em have it with the port guns!"

The gunners quickly ran from the starboard guns to the port battery. They opened the gun ports and ran the carronades into position. The gunners cocked the flintlock firing mechanisms and stood by with the lanyards, braced against the coming hard turn.

Nodding at Sneed, Dawkins shouted, "Hard a port! Mr. Childers, you may open fire when the target is in view!"

Mowbray must have seen the turn coming because he too turned hard to port. This brought both ships broadside to one another. *Rebecca's* four starboard guns were run out into firing position, and they cracked as *Beatrice* came alongside. One ball nicked *Beatrice's* foremast and another other ball shattered the yawl boat that was mounted amidships. Blood spewed in a vertical fountain as a sailor was decapitated by the ball that shattered the yawl.

Rebecca's other two guns fired when she was heeled over in the turn and the balls flew wild. Will breathed a deep breath, but his relief did not last long.

Mr. Childers shouted, "Number one gun, Fire! Number two gun, Fire! Number three gun, Fire! Number four gun, Fire."

One after the other *Beatrice's* carronades boomed a crashing broadside hurling solid balls crashing into *Rebecca*. *Rebecca's* rail shattered and one of her guns was blasted out of its mount. A ball flew wild and tore loose the mainsail's boom. A fourth ball flew harmlessly over the deck to splash into the sea beyond *Rebecca*.

Dawkins shouted, "Sailing master! Prepare to come about to starboard."

After a minute for the crew to be ready, Dawkins shouted, "Hard a starboard, Mr. Sneed! Make your heading west southwest. We're going to run for the Medway River."

Rebecca lost way. Her mainsail was flapping uselessly, its boom shot away. *Rebecca* turned to point her bow at the receding *Beatrice*, and her bow chaser guns boomed out. One ball skipped across the water. Out of energy, it thumped harmlessly into *Beatrice*'s hull. The other ball howled overhead.

Dawkins said, "Steady as she goes on this heading, Mr. Sneed."

"Steady as she goes, Aye."

Will asked, "Are we going into a port?"

Dawkins said, "Aye, we're going to Sunbury, Georgia. 'Tis a bustling port town and solidly in Patriot hands, last I heard. We need to repair the rail, bury our dead, get medical care for the man with the injured arm, and I need a shipwright to look at the foremast. That nick in it won't stand bad weather."

Will asked, "Will *Rebecca* come after us?"

Dawkins said, "Maybe. He might be able to repair that main boom and get his mainsail back in operation. If not, he'll have to put into port to make repairs. When we come out of port, he might be waiting for us. We won't know until we come out in a few days."

Rebecca receded in the distance. Soon, she was just a sail on the horizon. Then, nothing.

CHAPTER 3 – SUNBURY

It was late in the day when *Beatrice* approached the coast.

Will asked, "Where are we?"

Dawkins said, "That land off the starboard beam is Ossabaw Island. On the port beam is St Catherine's Island. Straight ahead is the St Catherine's Sound and the Medway River. It looks safe, but the sound has shoals, especially on the north end of St Catherine's."

Dawkins paused and looked at Will with friendly eyes, "Ye'll want to be gettin' off here?"

Will said, "I need to get Molly on dry land. She was not doing well this morning when I checked on her. I have not been down to the hold since the fight, but I'm sure she was quite shaken by all the gun fire."

"Aye. Molly's a fine horse. Ye have earned yer keep, Will Yelverton. I won't take yer ten Spanish dollars, and ye'll have a share of the prize money equal to the junior officers' shares. Though we haven't sold the prizes yet, I calculate the value as a year's pay. Junior officers' pay is $20 each month. So, unless you want to wait for the auction of the prizes, I will give you $240 for your share."

Will said, "That's quite generous."

"No, it's not. I don't know what the two ships we took will bring at auction. It could be a good bit more if they had good cargo. Even after the costs of repairs to *Beatrice*, we could make more than what I'm offering."

"Aye. I see that," Will said. "But I must get Molly on land and let her recover from the voyage. Then, I should go home to North Carolina. That's quite a journey from Georgia. The $240 will help with my plan to go to the frontier."

"Very well, I'll give ye the money when we dock in Sunbury."

"Thank you, Captain."

"Nay. Thank ye for the entertainment of watchin' ol' Mowbray get his hat blowed off and then dancin' a jig flinging that sword around. Damn near killed his first mate, I'll own!"

With that, Dawkins laughed, bending double until a gargling cough made him nearly retch.

Will, his personal items packed and ready to go, stood on the bridge of the *Beatrice* watching Dawkins go about his business of skippering the ship with the quiet competence of an expert. Dawkins stood next to Mr. Sneed quietly giving commands as *Beatrice* cleared the bar entering St Catherine's Sound, Georgia. The wind was light, but enough to fill *Beatrice*'s sails for the relatively short trip up the Medway River to Georgia's second busiest seaport, the thriving town of Sunbury.

As the greenish gray water lapped at the hull, Will noticed an odor he had never smelled. It was the salt marsh of Georgia. The heavy smell of oysters, mud, salt water, pine trees, and rotting leaves on the floor of the oak forest in the distance wafted across the water. A fresh wind rippled across the vastness of the marsh grass making it look like a sea of molten gold.

Dawkins explained that this reach of the Medway was called Blackbeard's Creek. Will supposed that was from the famous pirate of the same name. Will smiled to himself. Perhaps there was treasure buried hereabouts...

The Medway was wide, but there were treacherous shallows on the south side of the river. Dawkins ordered turns that tacked northerly and then northeasterly before swinging west to run the channel. Ahead, Will could see the water had spots where the surface was more glossy than other parts. Dawkins said these were shoals, and they must be avoided.

A leadsman on the bow of the *Beatrice* swung a lead weight on a line and flung it ahead of the ship. When the weight hit bottom, the leadsman would call out the depth indicated by the marks on the line. Will did not envy the leadsman his job. The weight was heavy, and the work tiresome. Worse, the early March weather in was cold, even in Georgia. The Medway water temperature was probably 50 degrees, and the line was wet the leadsman's hands.

The leadsman called, "Mark four!"

Dawkins explained this meant there were four fathoms, 24 feet of water, beneath the ship.

"Mark Ta-Ree!" Will could see the lead line was wet at the three-fathom mark – three leather strips woven into the rope.

"Quarter Less Ta-Ree!"

The leadsman continued calling slightly shallower marks.

Dawkins ordered a slight turn of three points to port. Then he shouted, "Sailing master! Reduce sail to the top sails and the mainsail. I want to keep pressure off the damaged mizzen. Prepare to drop sail as we approach the dock."

"Aye, Captain. Reducing sail," came from the Sailing Master.

The leadsman shouted, "Mark Twaaaain..."

Dawkins grinned at Will. "Mark Twain means safe water – 12 feet below us. My chart says it'll be that way to the dock after we pass these last shoals."

Dawkins ordered another two points to port and then 5 points back to starboard as *Beatrice* threaded the shoals on the north side of the Medway. Dead ahead was an island and to its southeast Will could see docks. To the south of the wharves and the buildings of Sunbury, Will could also see a dirt fortification.

"Mark Twaaaain..."

Will asked, "What fort is that?"

"I'm not sure of the name, if it has one, but 'tis been here for perhaps two years. This is my third visit in the past three years, and it's been here since about '76."

Dawkins brought *Beatrice* alongside the wharf and ordered the mainsail dropped. The crew threw lines to waiting dock workers who hauled on the lines to bring the ship close to the wharf and make it fast with large hawsers and spring lines to keep the ship from swinging. A gangplank was brought from the dock and affixed so that Dawkins, Will and the ships officers could disembark.

Dawkins went to inquire about a doctor for the injured sailor and to arrange funeral services and burial for the dead seaman. As he left, Dawkins said, "Sailing Master, kindly find a ship fitter to look at repairing the mizzen mast as well as that rail. We'll do without the yawl until we get back to Jersey."

Dawkins and Will, along with *Beatrice*'s other officers, stood in line at the bottom of the gangplank as the bosuns mate blew a piping whistle. As the notes died six sailors solemnly carried the shrouded stretcher bearing the body of the man killed in the battle down to the dock. A small wagon awaited the body to take it to the graveyard up the sloping bluff to the west behind Sunbury. A stiff-necked Congregationalist preacher stood before the wagon holding a bible. Once the body was loaded, the preacher turned to lead the small procession to the

31

graveyard. The crew walked quietly behind the wagon into the setting sun that filtered through Georgia's coast maritime oak forest.

Beards of gray moss hanging from the trees swayed in the light breeze as the preacher read the service. Will learned the dead sailor was named John Watkins. Will felt sorry for Watkins who left a wife and two small children. When the hat was passed to gather a collection for Watkins' widow, Will put ten continental dollars in and hoped that was acceptable. Will hoped that others would care for him in this way should he be killed. It occurred to Will that being killed was a real possibility. After all, *Rebecca's* four-pounder ball randomly struck the yawl and then Watkins. It could have been Will, the captain, or any one of the other men of the *Beatrice*. Will understood that the Congregationalist preacher was a Calvinist at heart. The preacher would have said Watkins' death was preordained. Either way, Watkins was dead, and his widow had children to feed. Will reflected that this encounter with *Rebecca*, like Moore's Creek and Brandywine, as well as many other battles, was one more fight in what promised to be a long war.

The crew was in a more upbeat mood on the walk back to the ship. The two taverns in Sunbury would be busy tonight. After all, even if they had lost a man and had another one seriously wounded, the voyage had been a success with two prizes sent back to Jersey. This afternoon they had cheated Mowbray and *Rebecca* out of a prize. Money would flow from the upcoming auction, and rum would flow tonight.

Will gathered his belongings and went to supervise the crew taking Molly out of the hold. As when she was loaded, Molly was placed in a sling and, using the ship's crane, winched up onto the deck. Molly stood blinking in the twilight. Will led her down the gangplank onto the dock and then out to a large grassy patch near the wharf. He tied her to a tree and got her a bucket of water which she drank greedily. Molly nuzzled Will's hand and then began to crop grass.

Wiping his wet hand on his pants, Will smiled. Molly was happy to be out in the fresh air and cropping grass in the fresh breeze. He hoped Molly would recover quickly after being shuttered in *Beatrice*'s hold for several days.

Will went back to the ship to get his things and bid Captain Dawkins and the other crew goodbye. Dawkins was in his cabin. Will tapped on the door.

Dawkins said, "I see ye're ready to go."

"Aye. Molly is in a field just off the wharf and is eating grass. She seems none the worse for wear."

"Well, Sonny, you're a natural sailor. Are ye sure ye don't want to stay on?"

Will smiled. "The first time you saw me you thought I was a fool."

Dawkins guffawed, "Aye, well, ye are that. But I could beat that out of ye, if ye stayed."

Will grinned. "Thank you for saving me from Tarleton's noose."

"Not a bit of it. Ye showed Mowbray a thing or two today. I've never seen anyone shoot like that."

"I'm not proud of killing another man."

Dawkins said, "Aye, none of us are. That is, if we're right in the head. There are some who relish killing. Watch out for them, especially if they are in command."

Dawkins reached into his lock box and withdrew $240 in continental currency. "This ain't worth the same as them Spanish dollars, but it'll spend."

Will said, "Thank you, Captain. You saved me and you also taught me a lot. I hope to see you again, someday."

"Aye, I hope to be alive when that someday gets here."

Will shook hands with several of his shipmates. Will picked up his possessions. He looked over the *Beatrice* one last time, pausing to look at the shattered yawl, the broken rail, and the remaining blood stain from Watkins' death.

Marking this grim reminder of the brevity of life, Will turned and walked resolutely down the gangplank. He needed a room for the night.

CHAPTER 4 – THE TAVERN

Will put his saddle on Molly, but didn't tighten the belly cinch beyond that necessary to prevent the saddle from slipping. He tied his saddle bags and bedroll behind the saddle. Molly would not be going far. He needed to go only to the best tavern in Sunbury.

Leading Molly up the street from the wharf, Will consulted a man who said the best tavern in Sunbury was on King's Square three blocks up from the wharf where *Beatrice* was moored. Will turned right toward the west on the street before King's Square. In the square stood a liberty pole, the grass around it now overgrown. It was clear that the grass had once been trampled down to dirt. Across the street from the King's Square and the liberty pole stood the Eagle Tavern.

Will smiled. The Eagle was the name of the tavern in his hometown of Halifax, North Carolina. Will and his father, Zechariah Yelverton, had occasionally eaten there. Last year, in an unexpected encounter, Will and Zech had lunched at the Eagle with Colonel Allen MacDonald and his wife, Lady Flora MacDonald. Allen was held prisoner in Halifax after Moore's Creek. The luncheon was ironic in that Allen and Lady Flora had been instrumental in nearly getting Will killed.

Flora was famous among Scots for helping Prince Charles Stuart, Bonny Prince Charlie, to escape from the British after the Battle of Culloden near Inverness, Scotland. For her treason against the king, Flora had been exiled to North

Carolina where she and Allen had sworn loyalty to King George as a precondition to receiving a huge land grant in Anson County. The irony continued when Colonel Allen MacDonald led a Loyalist Highlander Battalion during the Battle of Moore's Creek Bridge. Will had served as armorer to the Patriot North Carolina Militia at that battle and later met the captive MacDonalds while leading a wagon train of captured Loyalist arms on the road to Brunswick Town, North Carolina.

The next morning the MacDonalds had been taken north toward Halifax and incarceration, while the arms train set off south toward Brunswick Town. Almost immediately, Will's arms train had been attacked by Allen's former troops. Clearly, Allen had sent a message to his Loyalists which resulted in the ambush. In the fray, Will had killed at least one Loyalist Highlander.

Months later, Will had been astonished to see Allen and Lady Flora at the Eagle. Allen was dismissive of his treachery in siccing Loyalists on Will's armor train, calling such action merely the exigencies of war. In a spirit of Bonhomme, Will accepted this explanation from the paroled MacDonald. A pleasant luncheon followed, and in a final irony, Will discovered he bore no ill will toward Allen and Lady Flora. As Will tied Molly to a hitching post and entered the Eagle Tavern in Sunbury, Georgia, he wryly considered he would not see Allen and Flora MacDonald, or anyone else he knew for that matter, at this remote little seaport.

Will walked into a warm room where the proprietor of the Eagle, Mr. Abraham Williams, welcomed Will to the hostelry. Williams was a Congregationalist formerly of Dorchester, South Carolina. Will smelled the wonderful scent of food cooking and wood smoke from the fire. Tomorrow would be March 1st, and with nightfall the wind had shifted to the northeast. A nor'easter was coming in, blowing frigid air down from Canada. With nothing to slow the northeast wind, the cold slammed into the Georgia coast, giving lie to the belief that the South was sunny and warm. Sunny, yes. But biting cold.

"Good evening, Sir! Would you need a room?"

Will said, "Yes, and I need a stable and forage for my horse."

Williams said, "It will be my pleasure, Sir, to accommodate your needs. We also have victuals and spirits. I drink no spirits, but I also do not condemn those who partake of them."

Will smiled. "Thank you. I am quite hungry. Do you have a stable hand who can take care of my horse and bring my possessions to my room?"

"Indeed! It will be done. Our prices are reasonable. A shilling a day for the room, a shilling for your horse including forage and grooming, and a shilling for two meals."

Will said, "Very well. I am not sure how long I shall stay. Can you post a letter?"

"Indeed, Sir. We have frequent coaches and boats to Savannah where letters may move on to other destinations. If you wish a letter to go on the express schooner to Savannah it is a bit more, but worth the cost, I think."

Will said, "When is the next express boat?"

"Tomorrow, Sir."

"Very well, I shall write my letter tonight and have it to you before the boat leaves."

Williams asked, "Would you like supper, Sir? We have venison stew, eggs, and grits as well as greens from the garden. Cheese as well."

Will enthusiastically said, "Wonderful!" Rubbing his hands together, Will asked, "Which way to the dining room?"

Will finished his supper and leaned back in his chair. After more than a fortnight on the *Beatrice*, food cooked by someone competent in the kitchen was a wonderful pleasure. Will looked around.

The room had filled with a variety of people. Travelers like Will were few. But all the rooms in the Eagle were filled and Will reflected that he was fortunate to have a place to stay. The rooms were occupied by officers of the Georgia Militia, a few Continental Army Officers, and the shipmasters who were in the busy harbor with their ships.

Sunbury was a bustling town. Will struck up a brief conversation with a Mr. Andrew Darling. Mr. Darling explained to Will that there were some 800 residents and that the number of ships visiting the port last year had exceeded 70, while the much larger port of Savannah had seen only some 150 ships. There were five busy wharves, and Darling owned one of them. Although not every lot in the town plan had been built on, there were many homes. In his brief time in Sunbury, Will had noticed the houses were well constructed. Each was a substantial building of two stories with frame construction and clad in white painted cedar shingles. Will smiled at the thought of how English this American village looked.

Mr. Darling had mentioned that the Midway Meeting house was some 10 miles inland and that many of the residents of Sunbury were Congregationalists, descended from the Puritans who first settled Massachusetts. Darling proudly told Will that the owners of the rice plantations in the area had shipped several tons of rice to Boston these past two years. What with the liberty pole and rice shipments, it seemed the area around Sunbury was a haven for patriots.

Two men in deep conversation occupied a corner table. One of them had a long, thin face with hair chopped off at collar length. The cloth of his coat belied his status as a well-to-do man. Perhaps a planter. The other man had the bearing of a military man, his face a bit oval shaped with an aquiline nose. He wore his powdered hair in a long que. Will found them interesting because of their intensity.

The man with the powdered que rose and walked over to Will's table.

"Who are you, Sir, and why are you watching us?"

Will was surprised at this direct approach. "I, uh...I uh..."

"Well, spit it out, man!"

Will sputtered, "I'm just off a ship and am here with no acquaintances. I have come from Philadelphia."

The man said, "You have not answered my question, Sir. Also, since you admit to being from Philadelphia, I must consider that you are possibly a British spy."

Will blurted, "Oh, God! There I was accused of being a Patriot spy! Now I'm accused of being a British spy!"

"Well, Sir, which is it?"

"I am no British spy!"

"I am Colonel Samuel Elbert, Continental Army. And you, Sir, are?"

"I am William Yelverton, gunsmith. Of New Bern and Halifax, North Carolina."

"And how come you to be in Sunbury, Georgia."

Will said, "Sir, I'm not going to be interrogated by you or anyone else as to my liberty or presence anywhere!"

"Oh, I see. Well, perhaps I shall have you arrested and held until you decide otherwise."

Will nodded at the Brander pistol in his belt and said, "I am here in peace, but I will not hesitate to defend myself."

Elbert looked hard at Will, and Will returned his steady gaze. "What shall I do with you, you insolent young pup?"

"Rich commentary from a man not many years my senior. I suggest you ask me civilly about my business and we discuss."

Elbert paused to consider and then walked over to the other man with whom he had been eating. They conferred and Elbert walked back over to Will.

"May I invite you to join us for a glass of sack?"

Will picked up his saddlebag and said, "I would be delighted."

Will sat in a chair with Elbert on his right and the other man on his left. Elbert signaled to Mr. Williams and said, "Kindly bring us a bottle of sack and three glasses."

To Will, Elbert said, "May I present Dr. Lyman Hall, one of our illustrious citizens and a successful planter. Also, he has the honor of being one of Georgia's signers of the Declaration of Independence. Dr. Hall, this young man is ..."

"William – Will – Yelverton. Gunsmith." Will furnished.

"Ah, just so."

Will said to Lyman Hall, "It is a great honor to meet someone who risked all for our liberty."

Hall made a dismissive gesture, but a slight blush made clear he enjoyed the flattery from both Elbert and Will. "What brings you to Sunbury."

Will said, "Tis a long story, and not very exciting."

Elbert said, "Do tell. We don't get much excitement around here. Except, of course, for Indian attacks and the frequent rustling of our cattle by the British from East Florida."

Will said, "Very well."

"My father is Zechariah Yelverton of Halifax, North Carolina. He is a planter and owns Branchton Plantation along the Roanoke River, just below the rapids. I had the honor of completing a journeyman apprenticeship in gunsmithing with Mr. Bert Koontz of New Bern, North Carolina, my adopted hometown. Governor Caswell was then a colonel and commander of the New Bern militia and he hired me to serve as armorer to the New Bern Militia. I participated in the campaign to subdue the Loyalist Highlanders who were threatening to take back the governorship of North Carolina. I was present at the battle at Moore's Creek Bridge."

Elbert's eyes flicked at Will.

"Later, I accompanied the arms train delivering captured muskets, shot, and powder to Brunswick Town, where I effected repairs on those weapons damaged in the fight. We were ambushed by loyalist highlanders on the road. Fortunately, the military escort fought off the ambushers and we proceeded to Brunswick Town without further incident."

"I was then apprenticed to Mr. Alexander Kennedy of Bear Creek, North Carolina, where I became a master gunsmith. Once complete with the year of apprenticeship and having my mastery papers, I set out for Philadelphia with the intent to purchase sufficient gun parts to provision a gun shop either in North Georgia or Western North Carolina in the over mountain area called Tennessee."

"Governor Caswell was kind enough to provide me letters of introduction as well as to place funds in safe keeping so that I may call upon his fellow Free Masons for financial assistance and avoid carrying large sums of money."

Elbert and Hall exchanged glances.

"I arrived in Philadelphia in early September of last year and presented Governor Caswell's letter to General Washington asking for safe passage for me to visit Lancaster, Pennsylvania, where gunmakers abound. General Washington was happy to grant me safe passage but asked that I delay my visit to Lancaster as the British were intent upon taking Philadelphia just then. The general asked me to lend myself and my horse to his needs and serve as a courier until the coming battle was decided. I had the honor of serving General Washington as a courier during the battle at Brandywine Creek."

Elbert again glanced at Hall.

"Alas, once the battle was decided, many Americans lay dead and General Washington was in retreat to Chester. I was swept along with the tattered army as Washington tried to keep his army between Cornwallis and Philadelphia. At last, General Washington was able to release me, with a letter of safe passage, to go to Lancaster. At Lancaster, I learned that there are no gun parts to be had. They having all been requisitioned by the militias and simply not available."

"After my failure at Lancaster I had the poor judgement to return to Philadelphia and become trapped there when Cornwallis took the city. The people of Philadelphia suffered privations during the winter, gentlemen. I was fortunate in that Governor Caswell had provided me letters of introduction to many of the City's elite who were kind to me. I was able to eat and was also fortunate to have housing. This was no small luxury given the British had taken every spare room to be found."

"I had an unfortunate encounter with a man named Banastre Tarleton. Major Tarleton is a British firebrand who upon seeing me repairing a British officer's pistol decided I was a spy and accused me of same. Only through good fortune was I able to escape that encounter. That night I fled Philadelphia. I was aided in the flight by some of the city's leading citizens whom I'd rather not name. I was conducted across the Delaware into Jersey by a guide and given a map to the coast of New Jersey where I was advised to seek passage on a privateer."

"I was briefly captured by Tarleton and his troops in the New Jersey countryside. They threatened a brief trial in the morning followed by a hanging. I was fortunate to escape in the dark and further fortunate in that they neglected to impound my horse. Tarleton personally attempted to shoot me as I was leaving the camp in the dark. I took this pistol out of his hand and rode hard for the coast."

Elbert sat back in his chair and drank some of his sack. Dr. Hall grinned and bobbed his head.

"At the coast I encountered Captain Obadiah Dawkins of the *Beatrice* and he took me on his crew. We arrived here today, after a fight with the East Florida privateer *Rebecca*. En route we took two prizes, and I profited from them sufficiently to defray costs of returning to my home."

"My horse is in the stable at this hostelry and it is my intent to now make my way back to my native North Carolina and consider my future. There will be a delay while my horse recovers from her days in the hold of the *Beatrice*."

Hall said, "My God, what a story!"

Elbert said, "I want to believe you, Mr. Yelverton. Can you provide evidence of the veracity of your story?"

Will considered, "Would you like to see my letters from Governor Caswell?"

Elbert said, "Indeed, may we see those?"

"You can see the ones I still have. As you might imagine, General Washington kept his letter. I do have letters addressed to others."

"Very well."

Will reached into his saddlebag and unwrapped an oilskin packet which held several letters. He withdrew letters from Governor Caswell to Dr. Benjamin Franklin, Colonel John Sevier of Western North Carolina, and Tennessee, and one addressed to 'Brother Masons."

Elbert poured over each letter and held each to the light.

"Why do you still have the letter to Dr. Franklin?"

"Dr Franklin is in Paris. His daughter, Mrs. Sarah Brache, called Sally, now lives in his home, at least she did until the British confiscated it. She was kind to me but didn't keep the letter. She introduced me to several of the leading citizens. Mrs. Eliza Powel was also kind to me in inviting me to her home often."

Hall said, "Indeed, Mrs. Powel is a wonderful hostess and quite a formidable lady. I enjoyed many dinners in her pink dining room."

Will looked at Dr. Hall appraisingly and said, "Her dining room is green, Sir."

"Indeed, it is green. Only someone who has dined there would know that. Did you have the pleasure of meeting Miss Peggy Shippen? Miss Peggy Chew? Dr. Benjamin Rush?"

"Yes, sir. I was privileged to make both the young ladies' acquaintances. Alas, Dr. Rush was with the Army, and I did not make his acquaintance in the field. Perhaps that was fortunate in that those who met Dr. Rush may not have survived the encounter."

Hall said, "I do not envy Rush his medical practice in the field. The Peggy's are both lovely, and are I'll guess, about your age. Why did you not pursue them, Sir?"

Will laughed, "I enjoyed their company, but I fear I am not of the status required to turn either of those pretty heads."

Hall chuckled. "Indeed. I fear no man is truly a match for either of them."

Elbert looked hard at Will. "I know Dick Caswell. This is his signature. The letter to fellow masons cannot be ignored. I am the Grand Master Mason of Georgia, and I will honor Grand Master Caswell's request. Welcome to Georgia, Will Yelverton."

Will breathed a sigh of relief. "Thank you, Colonel Elbert, Dr. Hall. My father, Zech, is a mason."

Elbert said, "Is he now? Well, doubly welcome, young fellow. And now, there is a very good bottle of sack that demands our attention."

Elbert and Hall turned out to be excellent company, and the sack was first-rate.

Will was warm and felt his face flushed a bit. He smiled to himself at the slight numbness around his mouth and nose.

Elbert was in command of Continental forces in the State of Georgia. He confided that there was political pressure among leading Georgians for a third expedition to British East Florida. In particular, Governor Houstoun was insistent upon punishing the Floridians for the constant intrusions into Georgia rustling cattle and burning farmsteads. Elbert mentioned some 3000 head of cattle taken just recently by British raiders.

Will said, "A third expedition?"

"Indeed," Lyman Hall said. "There have been two attempts to punish the British and serve notice to Florida's Governor Tonyn that Georgians are not to be trifled with. Unfortunately, we have failed in both those attempts. I fear a third attempt will be no more successful."

Elbert said, "We have had many difficulties with our plans to invade and punish Florida. The second attempt failed when President Button Gwinnett and General Lachlan McIntosh disagreed over who would command. At that time, the governor of Georgia was called the president and our dear friend Mr. Gwinnett was quite outspoken and forceful. He and General McIntosh fought a duel over the matter. Both were wounded, but Mr. Gwinnett died. General McIntosh was sent north to join General Washington, else he might have been convicted of murder and hanged by President Gwinnett's people. We must avoid that kind of problem this time."

With that, Elbert and Hall rose to leave. Elbert said, "Welcome to Georgia, Will. I wish to discuss our plans with you.

Perhaps you will agree to serve as armorer to our coming expedition to Florida."

Will said, "I'm honored, Sir. I do intend to return to North Carolina soon."

"Well, consider what might be done to help our cause, and we will meet soon."

Elbert and Hall departed, leaving a slightly tipsy Will the remainder of the bottle of sack.

The room seemed a bit fuzzy to Will, but not exceedingly so. He watched the flames dance in the fireplace. His head was thick with the day's events, the discussion with Elbert and Dr. Hall, and of course the sack put cotton between his ears.

Still, Will wondered if it was a drunken fantasy when Martha Black walked into the room.

CHAPTER 5 – OF ALL THE TAVERNS...

Like many taverns Will had visited, the Eagle had a bar where a locking frame hung down from a hinge. After hours Mr. Williams could simply lower the hickory frame and lock it in place with a large padlock, securing his valuable stock of drink. The bar had several clay bottles on shelves. Rum, brandy, sack, local wild grape wine. There were a few glasses and mugs on shelves close to hand for the barman.

Will watched Martha Black saunter up to the bar like a man. She wore trousers tucked into flare-topped leather sea boots. Her white shirt was linen, its tails crossed over her ample, unfettered breasts and tucked into her trousers. The shirt left little to the imagination, barely hammocking her breasts. Her breasts moved with the rhythm of her step. Martha obviously ignored the custom of wearing stays like other women. Her black hair was loose, swept away from her face. Wild and wind-blown, its only adornment a small red ribbon more utilitarian than decorative. A pistol was jammed into the red sash around her waist. For Will, the only thing that made this woman the Martha he knew was the oval shape of her face and her flashing, dark eyes. That, and her purposeful walk as she crossed the room. Will remembered the lilt of her hips as she led him from the front door of the Black's mansion in New Bern to the veranda.

Martha was daughter to Charles Black of New Bern, North Carolina. Charles was the most successful businessman in that part of North Carolina. Part importer, part smuggler, Charles Black created a most respectable maritime business. Martha was a rich girl.

Martha had been Will's fantasy girl. Will, never a member of the well-to-do class of people in New Bern, had no hope of catching Martha's eye. Will watched her from a distance wondering what she was like. Yet, over the years from about age 12 to age 17, Martha often made sure their paths crossed. She was always pleasant to Will and made herself open to him. Once, she reassured Will that he was a gentleman not because of his birth or wealth, but because of his kindness. Will spirit had soared into the heavens over that gentle compliment.

Martha's older brother, Chuck, a terrible bully, had sensed the budding relationship and worked incessantly to cause Will no end of pain. Martha had circumvented Chuck's protectiveness and managed more than one assignation with Will. Will was both smitten and confused by Martha's openness to him.

After his apprenticeship with Kennedy, Will returned to New Bern to learn that Martha had been using him as a decoy to distract her father and brother while she plotted her escape from the smothering life of a rich girl. Martha ran off with one of Charles Black's sea captains, a man she had met when she was in her teens. For his part, Chuck had apologized for his mistreatment of Will.

And now, in a tavern in Sunbury, Georgia, Martha Black had walked back into Will Yelverton's life.

"Hello, Will."

"I thought you were gone for good."

"Seems we're both at the end of the world."

Will sat back in his chair. "Of all the taverns in all the backwater ports in all the world, you walk into this one. What brings you to the Port of Sunbury?"

"I could ask you the same question, Will."

"Aye. I'm here running from a hangman's noose in Philadelphia where I was falsely accused of being a spy. You?"

"I'm first mate of the Raven, the three masted schooner tied up at Spaulding's Wharf. The captain is my husband, Manoah Compton. My father disowned me and discharged Manoah. Of course, Manoah is a marked man where Charles Black is concerned, and there is no employment for someone so marked. The Raven is an independent ship bought with Manoah's earnings from privateering these past two years."

"What made you choose the life of a seafaring woman?"

Martha's laugh rumbled from deep in her being. "I didn't want to be someone's ornament. My father allowed me to spend a summer at sea when I was eleven. Manoah was the captain of the Seagull. He treated me like a member of his crew and allowed me to be a sailor. I quit wearing dresses and stays two days out of port and switched to trousers and a shirt. I learned to swear like a goddam sailor and how to handle a sailing vessel."

Martha continued, "Do you remember I told you I loved being on a ship, barefoot and climbing the rigging? Well, it's true. Not only do I love the sea, but I realized I loved Manoah."

Will said wryly, "When you freed yourself you also freed me in ways you do not know."

Martha said, "You speak of your girl Abby?"

Will glanced up sharply, "How do you know about Abby?"

Martha's face softened. "I saw Chuck last year. He was conciliatory and apologized to me. He should have. He and father mistreated me terribly. He mistreated you as well. He said he had also apologized to you. He said you had found someone, and her name is Abby."

"Yes, perhaps. I resisted Abby's gentle overtures for a year while I was in Bear Creek. I was faithful to you, though I was tempted. I planned to see you right away when I returned to New Bern and find out if you still wanted me. Of course, you sent Bet to me to tell me you wanted your locket back, answering my question."

Will peered across the room, as if trying to look into the future. "Who knows if Abby is waiting for me? I have written, but there has been no reply. That is not a surprise with the war.

53

I don't know if she has received my letters. I will write to her tonight. I owe letters to several people. My parents, the Koontz's, Governor Caswell. One promise I demanded from Chuck was that Bet not be punished for her part in your deception. She was merely your slave doing your bidding. I hope she was not mistreated."

Martha's eyes softened. "Bet was loyal to me, and no, she was not punished. At least she was not beaten. I fear she was sold to a family in Wilmington. I have searched for her in hopes of buying her and setting her free. I bear great shame for Bet."

"You should."

Martha's eyes were briefly hooded. Then she brightened. "Well, I came to buy a bottle to take back to the ship. What a pleasant surprise seeing you Will and knowing you are alive and well."

Will said, "I'm alive."

Turning to go, Martha smiled sadly. "Don't hate me, Will."

Will said, "Oh, to the contrary, Martha. I sincerely don't hate you. I've seen so much death, sadness, and loss these last months that I begrudge no one success, safety, and happiness. I wish you well. And I hope you find Bet. She deserves better than what she got."

Martha paused, "You deserve better than me, Will."

CHAPTER 6 - THE CONTRACT

First light filtered into his room, and Will awakened with a blistering headache. Too much sack. Will thought, "Ugh, God! I should know better."

The excess of sack from last night also made Will think of his time in Philadelphia. His mind wandered to the freezing days and snow and his brisk walks from the Tun Tavern to Frances Montravalle's lodgings. He also thought about the excesses Frances brought to him. He felt a heaviness in his loins. Martha intruded into his thoughts. The surprise of Martha's walking into the tavern downstairs still shocked him.

Will drifted some, wishing the headache would subside. Abby quietly insinuated herself into his thoughts. In Will's dream Abby stood quietly looking at him and smiling. She turned away and, in a moment, was nude, washing by the mill race just like he had witnessed her to do all those months ago. He drifted farther into a dream of Abby. She came to him, her nipples pink just like Frances'. He kissed her, and in the dream when he opened his eyes, Abby had become Frances. Will had a thundering erection. He committed the sin of Onan. It could not be helped. Later, he would wonder if it was Abby or Frances who had aroused him so. Or was it Martha?

In the afterglow, Will drifted a little. He knew he'd never see Frances again. That was all right. But Abby? Abby was important. Dear. Gentle. Maybe just a little naughty. Perfect. He longed to sit with Abby as they had beside a fire outside the

Kennedys' home. Warm in the fire glow despite a fall nip in the air. Would he ever have that again? He dozed.

Soon, Will could smell cooking fires from the Eagle's kitchen. He could smell himself, too. He realized that days aboard the *Beatrice* without washing in fresh water and soap had resulted in a certain animal ripeness that needed attention. The nor'easter blowing outside his window rattled the walls every now and again. The building was well built, but the howling wind penetrated even the tiniest crack, and frequent drafts of cold Canadian air dragged thousands of miles across endless sea eddied around Will's room. The chill in his room suggested a thorough wash would have to wait. Will pulled the thin covers up and thought about how he could get warm enough to get out of bed.

Will's empty stomach finally won the battle of warmth versus getting up and about. He climbed from under the covers and stumbled across the room to the pitcher and bowl on a washstand. He took the sliver of soap and plunged his hands into the chill water. Fortunately, it was not so cold to keep the soap from making suds when Will rubbed it vigorously. Working up a lather added a tiny bit of warmth to the soap and water, and Will managed to wash. The cold water in his arm pits and crotch made him jump around, but he was determined not to stink.

Clean but chilled, Will crawled back into the still warm bed in a vain attempt to warm back up. Frustrated, Will threw off the covers and pulled out his clean shirt and breeches. Clean stockings under his boots felt good against the chill.

It was not yet seven of the clock, yet Will felt late. He hurried downstairs to the dining room to take advantage of the fire. Today the fire was built up quite a bit. Georgians had thin blood from being in the heat most of the year. For them, today was akin to the Philadelphia blizzards Will had experienced just a few weeks ago.

Will ate fresh eggs and some delicious smoked bacon. A slave girl, perhaps 14 years old, fried the eggs expertly in butter on a pan called a spider over the coals in the hearth. The spider had three long legs that kept it standing over the coals. A glob of stiff grits with some butter rounded out the meal. Hot biscuits reminded him of Becky Koontz's cooking. Will gave the slave girl a penny and got a brilliant smile as a thank you.

As Will finished the eggs and bacon and put some butter on the last of his biscuit, a soldier in a blue uniform coat opened the tavern door letting in a blast of cold air. The soldier looked around the room and walked over to Will.

"Your name Yelverton?"

"Aye."

"Colonel Elbert requests your presence in his office at your earliest convenience."

"Is his office at the Fort?"

The soldier smirked, "Aye."

Will thought his question had been reasonable. He replied, "Please tell Colonel Elbert I will attend him as soon as I have checked on my horse."

The soldier nodded and stopped by the fire to warm his back side. Then he left, the door again admitting a blast of brittle, northern chill.

Deciding Elbert could wait after such a rude invitation, Will warmed his core sitting with coffee for half an hour by the fire. He perused a week-old issue of the Georgia Constitutional Gazette. A considerable argument was raging over treatment of Loyalists in Savannah. Several demanded they be dispossessed. Others insisted upon tar and feathering followed by the errant Loyalist being exiled.

Will allowed himself a small smile. Patriots had decried people in Philadelphia as Loyalists merely for being acquainted with a British officer. The Philadelphia elite like the Powels walked a tightrope maintaining their position and home while not declaring loyalty to the king.

After a pause by the fire to get his clothing warmed to almost scorching, Will threw on his heavy Pennsylvania coat and muffler and went to check on Molly.

The stable hand, a young negro slave who looked about 13 years old, said, "This a fine horse, Sir. She was kind of tired lookin' last night. She doin' better today. I groom her and got her some food last night. This morning she eat some hay."

"What is your name?" Will asked.

"Jim, Sir."

"Well, Jim, I will give you an extra tuppence a day if you take extra good care of her. Can you get her an apple or a carrot?"

Jim beamed. "Yes, sir. We got some carrots. And I'll get her plenty of hay and walk her around some as soon as it's warmed up. She don't need to be out in that cold wind today."

Will nodded, "She's been cooped up in the hold of a boat for over a fortnight, and I rode her hard before that. I really want to get her health back."

Jim said, "Yes, Sir. You can count on me."

"I knew I could, Jim." Will handed Jim a shilling. "That'll be down payment for the week. I'm not sure how long I'm going to be here, but that's yours."

Jim looked at the shilling like it was the crown jewels. "Yes, Sir. Thank you."

"Now, Jim. I was told I might find Colonel Elbert at the fort. Does that mean the fort with the dirt walls at the bend in the river?"

Jim nodded vigorously. "Yes, Sir. Onliest fort around here."

"Thought so. Thanks, Jim."

Will walked out of the stable and between buildings to the street in front of the Eagle. He turned to the East and immediately his eyes watered from the strong, steady wind from the northeast. Pulling his muffler up and ducking his head into the wind, Will's broad brimmed hat shielded most of his face. Even so, by the time he had walked the quarter mile to the single gate in the fort's wall, Will's face felt numb.

A sentry at the gate wearing a blue Continental uniform coat, moccasins, and deerskin breeches looked him over and said, "Colonel Elbert is in the officers' barracks, Sir. Tis yonder, across the parade." With that, the sentry quickly turned his back to the wind and stepped to keep the fort wall between him and the northeast wind. Will wondered if all the soldiers in Georgia were equally surly.

Head down into the wind again, Will hustled across the parade ground toward the brick building the sentry had pointed out. He did not pause to gauge his surroundings but thought the fort must occupy about an acre of land.

Yesterday, Will had seen the fort from the deck of the *Beatrice*. As they had stood into the harbor, the wind had been a light breeze and Will had looked over the fort. He had noted the fort had dirt walls with some wooden palisades, cut pine trees stood up vertically in the ground with points on their tops.

Now he looked at the fortification from a different angle, though the chill wind hurried his examination. Through watering eyes, Will got the impression of a large rectangle with

60

some kinks in the walls so that they were not perfectly straight. He knew these projections were called bastions. Will thought the bastions were to allow shooting down the length of the wall should someone try to breach the wall or scale it. He had a glimpse of several cannon mounted inside the dirt walls and an equally brief view of the Medway River just in front of the longest of the walls. Most of the cannon he saw were along that longest wall, although there were cannons on the end walls and near the single gate. His glance suggested maybe 20 cannons. Will thought the fort was well defended, and the bend in the Medway River just before the harbor was well covered by the fort's guns.

Will opened the door to the brick officer's barracks and stepped inside. A man wearing a blue coat and buff breeches of a Continental officer looked up from a paper and said, "Mr. Yelverton?"

"Yes."

The young officer stood and offered his hand. "I am Lieutenant Nathan Pearre, Third Battalion Adjutant, at your service." He pronounced it like the French, "Pierre."

"A pleasure to meet you, Lt Pearre. Colonel Elbert had asked to see me?"

"Indeed. He is in with Lt Colonel McIntosh, Commander of the Third Battalion. Please take a chair. I expect they will be finished very soon. We have some hot coffee on that hearth if you would like some."

Will said, "Thank you. I had no idea it would get so cold in Georgia."

Lt Pearre waived a hand at the northern walls of the room. "Two or three times a winter we get this cold blast. It causes problems, to be sure. Many people hereabout have no real warm clothing."

Will smiled. "I was in a similar situation in Philadelphia before Christmas. This used coat was very dear at the market, and I'm lucky to have been able to get it."

The door opened and Elbert stepped into the room. He was accompanied by a tall man with red hair and a serious expression.

"Ah, Will. Thank you for coming to visit with me. I see you have met Lt Pearre. May I present Lt Colonel John McIntosh commander of Sunbury's fort?"

Will offered his hand saying, "It is my pleasure to meet you, Sir."

McIntosh replied, "The pleasure is all mine. I understand you are quite a marksman."

Will glanced at Elbert.

Elbert chuckled, "I spoke with Captain Dawkins of the *Beatrice*. He told me of your astounding marksmanship in action with *Rebecca*. The story of how you took off Mowbray's hat made me laugh out loud, Sir."

Will smiled. "Actually, I missed."

McIntosh said, "You didn't miss with the lookout in the rigging. Perhaps taking off Mowbray's hat from 200 yards on a pitching ship in the middle of the ocean was more effective than hitting him. He doesn't know you missed. He'll be keeping his head down in the future, I'll own."

Lt Pearre laughed out loud. "My goodness, Sir. I did not know you had such ability."

Elbert said, "Mr. Yelverton is young, but it appears he's quite accomplished." To Will, "Please join us in the office for a chat."

Will, Elbert, and McIntosh went into McIntosh's office and closed the door.

"Let's sit in front of the fire," Elbert said. And the three men drew up chairs before the hearth where a fire was smoldering, making the room pleasantly warm despite the frigid wind blowing outside. Occasionally wind would make the smoke eddy back into the room, it's harsh odor a tolerable reminder that they were not freezing in the wind outside.

The office had a glass window, a luxury that Will enjoyed as he watched a small tree limb tumble across the parade. The limb was driven all the way to the far fort wall where it lodged.

Elbert said, "I won't beat around the bush. We need your gunsmithing skills. I have an army here with a variety of weapons, many in questionable states of repair. Are you willing to accept a contract to repair them?"

Will said, "I must go to North Carolina as my family have no idea about my status. But my horse is weak from being aboard ship for nearly two weeks. She needs to be exercised to get her strength back before I can travel. I am, therefore, available to you, Sir, for perhaps a fortnight. Would that be sufficient?"

McIntosh said, "We would like to have you here permanently, Sir, but two weeks' concentrated effort should put right most of our small arms."

Elbert concurred. "Yes. I wish we could convince you to join our military. As you know, I am commander of Georgia's Continental Army forces and Colonel McIntosh is Continental Army commander of this fort. We also have militia forces in the state. They are commanded by the Governor, Mr. John Houstoun. We would propose to Mr. Houstoun, that you also repair militia weapons."

Will nodded his ascent.

Elbert continued, "The British have used their Florida Rangers to rustle cattle south of the Altamaha River. They also foment unrest among the Indians – particularly the Creeks, who resent us. We never know when there will be a raid. Our blockhouse fort at Barrington on the Altamaha, now called Fort Howe, sits astride the King's Road that goes from Savannah to St Augustine. Fort Howe has been the main impediment to the

British coming north by land. This little fort here at Sunbury has been the impediment to British seaborne incursions."

"Governor Houstoun is insisting that we mount an expedition to punish the British in Florida. General Bob Howe is commander of all Continental Army forces in the Southern Department. He is our commanding officer. General Howe and Governor Houstoun are at odds regarding this proposed expedition. I am aligned with my commander in observing that we have had two failed expeditions to Florida. I believe a third expedition will likely be no more successful. Regardless, I will follow orders, and go forward with the expedition when so directed. I would be happy if you would accompany the expedition as armorer."

Will said, "I appreciate your confidence in me, Colonel Elbert. Let us begin with the two-week contract to repair weapons here."

"Very well, Will. That will give us time to convince you to join us more formally in a uniform. We can pay you in Spanish dollars at the rate of one piece of eight per weapon repaired. Is that acceptable? If so, can you start today?"

Will said, "That rate is acceptable. Is there accommodation here in the fort for me? I am expending significant funds at The Eagle. I also have Molly, my horse."

"Yes, I believe Lt Pearre can find you officer accommodations and provide a work area near the blacksmith shop. I'm sure we have room in our stables for your horse."

Will said, "Very well. I will move my personal effects and get set up today. My horse will stay at the Eagle's stables this week where I have a stable hand taking care of her. I'll bring her here next week."

Standing, McIntosh offered his hand. "I'll ask Lt Pearre to arrange your quarters and prepare a contract so you can be assured of your compensation. Welcome to our small company, Will."

CHAPTER 7 – LETTER TO ABBY

That afternoon Will took time to borrow a pen and foolscap from Lieutenant Jim Pearre and beg use of a desk for a few minutes to write a letter to Abby. He was embarrassed he had not taken time to do this sooner. He excused it by thinking about how he could easily have been at the end of a rope rather than sitting in a warm office in Sunbury, Georgia, writing a letter to the woman he loved.

Sunbury, Georgia

March 3, 1778

Dear Abby,

I have the honor of writing finally after many distractions. I am sorry I have not written, nor have I escaped the events that keep me from returning to North Carolina. I hope this finds you well and happy, along with the rest of the family. I miss everyone at Bear Creek. Most of all I miss you. I think of you often and hope I can get to North Carolina soon. I think of little else but you.

I hope you received my last letter, sent in haste, as I rushed to leave Philadelphia. As I mentioned in that letter, I was falsely accused of spying and thought it better to quickly depart Philadelphia before the British decided that I was truly a spy and hanged me. Some of the leading citizens of Philadelphia, who knew me to be not guilty, assisted me and provided a guide to get me out. The guide got me to New Jersey where I stayed overnight with some people who are patriots. They provided me a map to the Jersey shore, and I departed at dark the next evening.

I was captured that evening by the same British officer who threatened me in Philadelphia. Major Banastre Tarleton said that finding me in Jersey proved I was a spy. I was manacled in a tent and told there would be a trial in the morning followed by my hanging. I was so scared because I thought I would die without ever seeing you again. I was lucky to escape the manacles and get away. My escape was not without incident as Major Tarleton tried to shoot me. I took his pistol which I carry now as a good luck charm.

I was very lucky to get to the Jersey shore and find a privateer who was willing to take me and Molly out of Jersey. At that point I cared not where we went. A fortnight later and after a brief battle with a British privateer, we landed in Georgia. Where I now am.

I have been assured I will soon be allowed to leave Georgia and travel to North Carolina where I hope to see you and my parents. I know not when that travel will happen. I hope soon. There are others I need to see, but none as important as you.

Dearest Abby, you occupy my thoughts constantly. I hope you can write back to me. I am in Sunbury, Georgia, at the Fort, so a letter addressed to me in care of Colonel Elbert or Lieutenant Colonel John McIntosh at the fort should reach me. Please do write as I miss you terribly. You are never far from my mind.

As always, I remain,

Yours,

Will

CHAPTER 8 – FORT HOWE

Will moved his personal effects into his room in the Sunbury fort's officer barracks. He was provided an unheated room over Lt Colonel McIntosh's offices. The lack of heat was no matter because the fireplace that served the offices downstairs provided warmth to those rooms adjacent. Then, the nor'easter that had blown in blew out just as quickly. It was replaced with gloriously cool days and not a cloud to be seen. The sky was like a blue crystal.

Will inhaled deeply the distinctive smell of coastal Georgia. It was the smell of marsh and woods, salt water and rotting vegetation he had first detected as *Beatrice* stood into Sunbury. Will thought the smell was warm and welcoming. There was a hint of wood smoke in the air.

Others he spoke to were not as enamored of the Georgia coast. One soldier who was getting his musket repaired told Will of the many, many malaria deaths. The soldier's brother had sickened and died a rough death, sweating, and shaking until he had no strength left. No one knew where the disease came from, but it seemed to arise in the warmer, wetter months. Will thought perhaps he should get out of coastal Georgia before the weather warmed up. No matter, he was leaving for North Carolina when Molly was fit for the trip.

Will worked 12-hour days, during the daylight hours when he could see small parts without using a candle. The soldiers were detailed to bring him their muskets, fowling pieces, occasional rifles and, rarely, pistols. Will had devised a three-step process: assess the firearms and identify those which needed repair. Step three was to repair the easy-to-fix guns right away, and then work on the more difficult to repair when time permitted. A few weapons were totally unserviceable, and their only value was in being stripped for parts. Will's process pleased Elbert and McIntosh because the percentage of readiness was quickly increased.

A week later, Will collected Molly from The Eagle's stables. She was much improved, but not yet ready for a ride much less being taken on a long trip. Will patted her neck and gave her a carrot. Molly whickered softly and stamped her foot. Jim, the stable boy who had been caring for Molly, came in.

Will said, "Jim, she's doing much better."

Jim said, "Yes, Sir. I walk her in the morning and at dusk every day. She's been getting hay and there's plenty of grass over in King's Square. She's still tired and weak, but I think she's better."

Will said, "I'm going to take her to the stables at the fort, but I'll pay for you to come take care of her. Here's a shilling. I owed you tuppence, and you earned the rest for all the extra work. I'll pay you a shilling a week to come walk her and make sure she's getting stronger."

Jim grinned. His expression said the shilling was a fortune to him.

Will arranged with Williams at the tavern for Jim to visit the fort in the morning and in the evening to exercise Molly. He paid Williams two shillings for the week to cover the cost of Jim's work. Will did not mention that he was tipping Jim on the side. That was not Williams's business. In all, Will would save two shillings a day by stabling Molly at the fort. That made the cost for the week three shillings. Molly also would be close enough so he could visit her and take her out for a walk.

Elbert walked into the gunshop and said, "You have truly improved the weapons of the army, Will."

"Thank you, Colonel."

Elbert said, "Our troops at Fort Howe cannot abandon their post at Barrington to come here to have their weapons inspected. Can you travel out there? I would send you with an armed escort because the Indians as well as occasional British raiders might be about in that area. I would expect to pay a bit more because I would be asking you to go in harm's way. Would captain's pay of $20 per month suffice?"

Will said, "Certainly. I'll be happy to go. I would require a horse because Molly is not quite ready for a long ride."

Elbert said, "I'll get you a good horse. Lieutenant Fitzpatrick will escort you with six troopers. When can you leave?"

Will said, "I have a few weapons to repair, but they can wait. We can leave day after tomorrow. I'll need tomorrow to prepare. I'll need to take some parts and so on. I'll take a couple barrels as well. I think a pack horse can carry everything I need. If I run into some weapons that need more extensive repairs, I'll need to exchange them for a serviceable weapon and bring them back here. How many men are at Fort Howe?"

Elbert said, "There are 40 men plus three officers. I estimate there are some 50 weapons."

"Very well. I'll take five muskets to exchange, and sufficient parts to repair others."

At dawn two days later, March 9, 1778, Will mounted his loaner horse, Old Tom. Tom was a two-year-old bay gelding. He looked fast but didn't have the personality of Molly. Will had tied his bedroll behind Old Tom's saddle. His saddlebags contained his gunsmithing tools on one side and his personal effects including a clean shirt and stockings as well as some dried meat and a fire-starting kit on the other. Will's ancient, but effective, horse pistol rode in the leather bucket holster in front of Old Tom's saddle. Josie was in her case alongside Will's saddle. Next to her was Will's other hand-made rifle. This weapon was effective and accurate, but it was not the rifle that Josie was.

Will wore his homespun hunting shirt and breeches. His knee-high boots were supple leather, buttoned at the sides. Some of the buttons were cloth covered gold pieces, a secret stash of funds in case Will was in desperate need. Across his shoulders Will wore his shot pouch and powder horn. Uncle

Ewan's razor-sharp Scottish dirk hung at Will's right side. Tucked into Will's belt was the Brander pistol he had taken from Major Banastre Tarleton that frightening night in New Jersey when he escaped the hangman's noose. Slung diagonally across Will's back was his .69 caliber English Dragoon Carbine.

Lieutenant Fitzpatrick and the six troopers mounted their horses. The pack horse carried the extra muskets and barrels. They trotted out the gate with Fitzpatrick and Will in the lead. Two troopers rode two hundred yards ahead of the small formation, and two troopers rode some distance behind.

Fitzpatrick said, "My given name is Patrick. Call me Pat."

Will said, "Please call me Will."

"You're armed to the teeth, Will."

"Indeed. I was almost killed at Moore's Creek, then I was ambushed on the road to Brunswick Town, attacked by highwaymen near Bear Creek, North Carolina, and then accused of spying in Philadelphia. I was shot at by riflemen at Brandywine. I shot back when I had the chance."

"I should say so," Patrick said. "So, you are from North Carolina?"

"Aye. New Bern is my adopted hometown. My father is a planter in Halifax, Edgecombe County."

"Ah. I'm from Nansemond County in Virginia, just over the state line from North Carolina. We're neighbors. Many of our soldiers at Sunbury are from Virginia and North Carolina. You're in good company."

Will grinned. "I certainly am. How far is it to Fort Howe?"

Fitzpatrick squinted at the dull March sun. "It is some forty miles. We'll be riding most of the day. We'll ride out to the west to Midway Meeting House and then some distance further west where we'll pick up the King's Road south. We will stop to water the horses in a while, and I'll show you the map."

Fitzpatrick paused to wipe a drip from his nose. "Savannah burned last week. An express schooner arrived yesterday with that news. Governor Houstoun pushed a bill through the Assembly rebuking several notables who are Tories. Perhaps they burned the city in response. Many houses were reduced to cinders."

Will said, "I've not been to Savannah. Still, that makes me sad. I saw in the Gazette the arguments about Tories. That was two weeks old even then."

"Aye."

The little detachment trotted along making good time. Soon, Will saw a white clapboard church that had a steeple. Pat explained that it was the Midway Meeting House.

"Most of the people hereabouts moved from South Carolina. They're Congregationalists like the Puritans who settled Massachusetts. Some of these folks descend from those same Puritans."

Will asked, "But they serve sprits and beer in the Tavern."

"Indeed. But the Congregationalists are not abstemious. They have always had their beer and liquors."

Will said, "I had always heard they were against consuming alcohol."

The little troop trotted on West away from the Midway Meeting.

Will asked, "Seems we're going a long way West if we are to go south."

Pat said, "Yes. You will become familiar with this area soon. From the coast inland for several miles is riddled with swamps, rivers, creeks, and marshes. Good for rice culture, bad for travel."

Will soon saw some wide rice fields that had dikes and wooden sluice gates to control the flooding needed to grow the crop. In one of the fields Will saw a dozen Black slaves working the crop. He asked Pat, "I suppose slaves are a requirement for this crop?"

"Oh, there could be no rice crop without slaves. Georgia was not a slave colony until about 1750 when the trustees voted to allow slavery. There were no real large crops or plantations to speak of before then. When slavery was permitted, the rice growers came on in great numbers."

They were reaching the King's Highway, and Pat pointed northwest. "Yonder is Bull Town Swamp. The man who owns it is named Dr. LeConte. He moved here from New York and set up his plantation. Woodmanston, it's called. I hear he has a horticultural garden that is envy of many botanists. The plantation house was burned a couple years ago by Indians raiding across the Altamaha. His home is now a blockhouse. He could not have a plantation here without the slaves."

Will asked, "Where do they get slaves here?"

Fitzpatrick shrugged. "Sold at auction in Savannah and Charlestown. Some come in at Sunbury. They seek out and enslave Negroes from West Africa because they have a rich rice culture there. Those slaves are valued over others because they know how to raise rice."

Will said, "The Negro slaves taught the whites how to grow rice?"

"Yes. But the whites designed much of the structure you see. They designed the sluice gates, they're called trunks, that control the flooding of the fields. On the other hand, the Negroes from West Africa taught the white men how to push the seeds into the ground and cover them so they will not float away when the fields are flooded. Cover them too much and they won't sprout. Cover them too little and they float away."

Will looked at the Black men and women toiling in the rice field. They were knee-deep in water. The dikes on all sides seemed to hem them in. It was like a miniature prison camp.

Will said, "That looks most miserable. It must be terribly hot down in that field and the dikes block any wind."

Pat nodded. "I'm not sure white people could tolerate the heat. Plus, white people seem to get sick here and die from malaria. For some reason the Negroes don't get as sick."

Will rode on, lost in thought. His mind turned to Caesar and Jack, brothers who were former slaves his father had manumitted. They were living in Philadelphia, now. Will and Jack had been childhood playmates. They had hunted and fished together. While Jack had been technically Will's slave, Will never saw the relationship as master and slave. Caesar had saved Will's life once when Will's older brother, Benjamin, tried to drown him.

Will thought, "I owe Black people a lot. I could be proud that Daddy set them free, but it seems that freeing someone you originally enslaved is not really doing them a kindness. It's more akin to returning them to their formerly free state. Freedom is not something you should be given. I think, like Jefferson said, it's an inalienable right."

As he rode, Will tried to reconcile several thoughts. "I know Daddy said he was going to free his other slaves. Something about Mr. Jefferson's declaration and needing to live up to it. I hope he has freed them. But where will they go? I

78

know poor Bet was mistreated when she was sold after Martha ran off. That's not right, either."

Will said to Pat, "Tis confusing that we fight Britain for our freedom, but we chain Negroes and force them to work in a sweltering field."

Pat nodded and shrugged. "Tis beyond my ability to solve, I'm afraid."

Late in the evening the little troop rode up to Fort Howe, at Barrington on the Altamaha River.

Will looked across the river which he judged to be perhaps ½ mile wide. It was fast and brown like a murky cup of strong tea. The sandy bottom was visible and white. Will saw a couple holes where bass spawned. He smiled as he considered that the fishing here must be good. It reminded him of his youth, going fishing with Dicky Caswell and Sam and Noah, his best friends in New Bern.

He also thought about how he and Jack fished at Branchton before Benjamin tried to drown him and Mama and Daddy sent Will to live in New Bern with Aunt Patience and Uncle Ewan. The smell of rotting leaves and dead vegetation that floored the forest caused a shiver to run up his spine. It reminded him of the stink of the mud in his nostrils when Benjamin tried to drown him.

Fitzpatrick hailed the fort. "Ho! Fort Howe! Lieutenant Fitzpatrick with troopers from Sunbury."

"Advance and be recognized," came the reply.

The small group trotted forward a few yards.

"That'll be close enough. Dismount and walk your horses to the gate."

Will and the others dismounted and walked forward. There was a pinewood gate in a palisade made of dirt and pine logs. The palisade abutted a blockhouse fort that was built on a sandy bluff ten feet above the water of the Altamaha.

To the right of the fort was a ferry landing. It was lined up with the King's Highway, the road they had been traveling on all day. In the distance at the other side of the river, Will saw a ferry boat like the one he had ridden across the Delaware to escape Philadelphia. The memory made him shiver slightly. This was the Barrington Ferry.

The commander of the fort, a captain who's name Will did not catch, came out and welcomed the group. He said there were no real accommodations inside the blockhouse and invited the troop to pitch tents inside the palisade.

Fitzpatrick and his troops were offered some canvas tarpaulins which they rigged to make lean-tos against the back palisade wall. They rigged one as a tent fly where Will could work on the guns. A rough wooden plank on two sawhorses served as Will's workbench.

For the next two days, Will worked on the various muskets, a couple pistols, and one rifle that were the fort's weapons. Three were completely unserviceable and Will replaced them. He replaced one musket's barrel. Several had weak locks, and one needed a new stock. Will carefully checked every weapon. Assured he had done what needed to be done, he informed Lieutenant Fitzpatrick that his work was done, and they could leave the next morning.

The members of the troop enjoyed some stewed squirrel with a bowl of rice. Whoever cooked this repast used plenty of black pepper and some salt as well as making a thick brown gravy that was the perfect complement to the gamy flavor of the dry squirrel meat. Will smiled as it reminded him of his childhood at Aunt Pat's table. She and Uncle Ewan had taken him in and treated him like their own child. He missed them both, dead these last two years.

An hour before dawn Will and the others saddled their horses. Will put his saddlebags together and placed them on Old Tom. They were leaving at first light, so Will put his weapons on Old Tom except for the English Dragoon Carbine and the Brander pistol. They were ready to leave at first light.

The horses and equipment ready, Will and the troops sat down to rest before their trip. Quiet descended on the little encampment. Crickets buzzed in unison. Somewhere a night bird called. Will could hear the gurgle of the river running past the fort. Will dozed.

The woods were silent. Will awakened wondering what was odd. He listened, but all he heard was stillness and an occasional rustle of leaves in the trees. Then he realized the crickets were no longer singing. There was no noise at all. He sat up and looked around. The sky was lightening. It was those quiet minutes before the dawn. The embers from a small cooking fire pitched faint shadows against the blockhouse wall. He heard snoring coming from inside.

A sentry stood next to the palisade. The sentry was not looking at much of anything. He simply stood in place. Will realized the sentry was asleep.

Nudging Patrick Fitzpatrick, Will said, "Pat, wake up. Something's wrong."

"Huh, what?"

Will quietly said, "I think something's not right. It's dead quiet and that sentry is asleep."

Pat sat up and looked around. He said, "Seems alright to me."

As Pat stood and walked to the sentry, a bird suddenly flew from the trees nearby. Peering over the palisade wall, Patrick shouted, "Alarm! Alarm! Enemy at the gates!"

Will jumped to his feet and cocked the hammer on his English carbine.

The other troops scrambled awake and fumbled for their weapons.

Boom! A musket fired. The flash briefly blinded Will. When his eyes adjusted, Will saw an Indian standing at the top of the dirt wall. He was bare chested, his upper body and bald head painted blood red. The Indian had a tomahawk in one hand, musket in the other. The Indian pointed the musket one handed across the palisade at one of the troops next to Fitzpatrick. Will shot him with the carbine. The .69 caliber ball took the Indian just below the collarbone and knocked him backwards off the parapet.

Several more muskets rang out. A ball whizzed past Will's ear hitting a troop to Will's left. The trooper fell forward into the dirt and did not move. Will kicked the fire to get it to flare up, adding at least some illumination to the faint light. Dozens of men were climbing up the outside of the palisade and more were storming the gate.

The captain in charge of the fort shouted, "Everyone to arms." The loud bang of a musket cut him short, and he fell backwards, a large blood stain spreading on his chest.

Fitzpatrick gathered the Sunbury troops near the gate. "Everyone load! Prepare for volley fire."

Will quickly tore a cartridge paper with his teeth, primed the carbine and threw the cartridge down the bore. He banged the carbine butt on the ground to seat the charge. No time to ram it. He hoped it would work.

The enemy poured over the walls and British rangers got the gate open.

Fitzpatrick shouted, "We will aim and fire one volley and then retreat to the horses. This situation is lost, and we will have to retire. Wait for my command. Remember to aim low."

The enemy clustered near the gate. Fitzpatrick saw an opportunity and pointing at the gate with his sword shouted, "Aim...fire!"

The six muskets blazed out almost as one. Will's carbine thumped his shoulder hard. Several of the group of enemy intruders went down wounded. The enemy moved away from the gate, and Fitzpatrick shouted, "To horses!"

Will threw the empty carbine across his back and drew the Brander pistol. He ran with the group through the open gate. They rushed to their horses.

A British ranger ran at Will, teeth bared, a tomahawk raised to strike. Tarleton's pistol kicked hard as Will shot the ranger in the face. Stuffing the pistol in his belt, Will got a foot into one of Old Tom's stirrups as the others mounted. Swinging a leg over the saddle, Will hauled Old Tom's head around. A ranger grabbed at his right leg, and Will kicked the ranger hard in the shoulder. Putting his heels back, Will urged Old Tom to a gallop and he joined the troop as they rushed north on the King's Highway. Somewhere behind him Will heard a musket thump and a ball whizzed past to clip a limb off a pine.

About half a mile from Fort Howe and out of musket range, Fitzpatrick paused the troop. Will looked over his shoulder and could see a flame licking out of the upper floor of the blockhouse. Part of the palisade was on fire. Occasionally, a musket cracked. A hollow boom followed by a sheet of flame bursting out of the windows of the blockhouse suggested a keg of powder had gone up.

Lt Fitzpatrick said, "Nothing we can do now. The fort is lost. We ride. Trooooop...at the trot...For-ward!"

They trotted along in silence. No sense in hurrying, the nearest help was at Sunbury, a full day away. It would be a long ride.

CHAPTER 9 – INVASION PLANS

T he exhausted detachment arrived at the Fort in Sunbury. It was not that the ride was tiring. It was that the rude awakening by an attack, the near-death experience for Will and the troopers, and then the frantic departure, had taken a toll on their spirits. They had hardly stopped on the return trip, only pausing to let the horses drink and eat some grass on the roadside.

Lieutenant Pat Fitzpatrick had sent one of the troopers ahead to Sunbury to inform Colonel Elbert of the attack on Fort Howe. Pat confided that he was certain that Fort Howe had been reduced to ashes and the two small artillery pieces there were either stolen or rendered unusable. He also thought there had been losses of perhaps 20 men, including the fort's commander. Several others were missing, either captured or escaped into the woods.

"How do you think they sneaked up on us?" Will asked.

Pat replied, "the ferry was tied up on the north side of the river, so that was not the way. The river is too deep to ford and very swift. My only guess is that they swam the river. Probably started well upstream so that the current deposited them near Fort Howe. It was a total surprise."

Elbert strode out to meet the small group. "Happy to see you all alive, Lt Fitzpatrick. Mr. Yelverton, you seem to be able to find a fight."

Fitzpatrick said, "Thank you, Colonel. May I make my report, Sir?"

"Indeed, dismiss your men to their duties with their horses. Please take a few minutes to refresh, and then you and Mr. Yelverton may join me in Lt Colonel McIntosh's office."

"Yes, Sir." To Will, "Will a quarter hour be sufficient for you to be ready?"

Will said, "Yes."

Will and Pat Fitzpatrick sat in the small commander's office with Elbert and McIntosh.

Elbert said, "Again, I'm happy that you both survived the encounter with Lt Colonel Brown. Undoubtedly, that's who attacked you. Who else would have the cheek to pull off such an attack?"

Pat said, "I believe you are right, Sir. There were Indians in the group that attacked the fort, but it was mostly white men wearing green jackets. Many seemed soaking wet, leading me to believe they swam the river. That was a mad idea with the Altamaha's current and the brisk weather we've had of late."

"Aye. Tell me what happened. And I'd like also to hear any input you might have, Will."

Pat told the story of being awakened by Will and how he had seen a group of men rushing the fort in the half-light of the early dawn. He told of a couple musket shots early in the engagement before chaos descended on the fort. He explained how the detachment had been prepared to leave and thus been together in a group.

"We were fortunate, Sir, to fire an effective volley which cleared the gate area permitting our withdrawal. The situation in the fort was hopeless, and I judged we had no recourse but to mount and ride."

"Will, er, Mr. Yelverton, acquitted himself quite well, Sir. He shot an Indian who was scaling the rampart, brandishing a tomahawk, and aiming a musket. Later, he shot a Ranger in the face at point-blank range. I don't know if the first enemy died, but the second one almost certainly was dead before he hit the ground."

Elbert smiled. "Mr. Yelverton has a reputation as a dead-eye."

Will said, "It gives me no pleasure to shoot another man, but in both cases I had no choice. Best to be sure the enemy is not able to continue the fight."

Elbert looked at Will and nodded. "Do you have anything to add to Lt Fitzpatrick's account?"

"Sir, I believe Lt Fitzpatrick's account is complete and detailed. He comported himself as an officer should with calm leadership under fire, especially in this unexpected situation. He assessed the dire situation and recognized his responsibility to get his troops out of harm's way when the situation was hopeless. I'm convinced that we are alive today because Lt Fitzpatrick made the right decision to abandon the position. With exception of a couple sentries, at least one of whom was asleep, the entire Fort Howe contingent was caught inside the blockhouse. There was no value to anyone if we had remained."

Fitzpatrick blushed and looked down at his hands.

Elbert said, "I concur. Well done, Pat. Let me tell you both what I think is happening. First, I should have predicted the attack on Fort Howe. It is unfortunately common knowledge that we are planning a third invasion of East Florida. Of course, Fort Howe is an important base for us to gather our troops for any invasion of Florida. I suspect this was Governor Tonyn sending Brown and his raiders, plus his Indian friends, trying to get a jump on us."

Elbert continued, "Second, we have reports that a Loyalist named Schophol in South Carolina has gathered a contingent of some 300 men and is soon to march south to Florida to join the British forces there. Schophol was a leader of the Anti-Regulator movement in up-country South Carolina. Of course, the path to Florida is through Georgia, and the Scopholites, as they are called, will surely be coming through on their way south. This attack might have been to clear the way for the Scopholites."

Elbert concluded, "A third possibility is that this was a diversion for a seaborne attack on us here in Sunbury. I have scouts out on the rivers going all the way down to the St Mary's and St John's Rivers. I hope to hear something from those scouts soon. Regardless of all that, well done to both of you."

Pat said, "Stand you to a drink at The Eagle, Will?"

"Certainly. I will need a few minutes to put my gear away and check on Molly. I want to be sure Old Tom is well cared for. He's a good horse. Say, half past five here at the gate?"

Pat nodded. "I'll be here."

Will first went to check on Molly who was looking better all the time. Old Tom had done well for Will's needs on this trip, and he gave him a carrot. So that Molly would not be jealous, she got a carrot, too. Old Tom was not the horse that Molly was, but he was a solid mount.

Will put away his gear and washed the road dust off. He put on his clean shirt and took a bundle of soiled clothing with him. Mrs. Williams took in washing, especially for officers, and Will would drop off his clothes while he was at the Eagle.

On the way to the Eagle, Will noticed that both the *Beatrice* and Martha's schooner were gone. He smiled to himself. His seafaring days were over. At least, he thought so.

Pat and Will had a companionable drink and ate a robust dinner of mutton chops and greens. Mrs. Williams offered a salad she called sla'. It was quite good. The sla' was shredded crunchy cabbage and carrot mixed with some thinly sliced garden onion, a bit of green pepper, and diced apple all mixed with a dressing made of vinegar, oil, spicy mustard, black pepper, and honey.

It had turned off chilly yet again. The wind was again blowing hard. This time from the northwest.

Pat said, "It will blow around to the northeast again, so we'll have a couple of miserably cold days like a couple weeks ago. After that, I suspect all we'll see is heat and wet!"

Will asked, "I hear people sicken and die in the heat. Is malaria a problem here?"

"Oh, Aye. We see lots of death in the warmer months. The graveyard up the hill is quite full of dead soldiers. We note their names and try to record their deaths. There are no headstones. No funds for that, you see. The commanders write letters to the families, but it is not known if the families receive the letters. Tis sad, Will. Today's fight at Fort Howe was brutal and we lost men, but we lose many more to disease than to battle."

Will nodded. "These Scopholites that are coming. They're Loyalists of a different sort. Anti-regulators. Sorry bunch, the regulators, though. What do you think of the threat from the Scopholites?"

"I reckon they'll be west of here. They are from up-country in South Carolina, and their path to Florida is more

91

through the piedmont of Georgia. Up near the fall line. Indian country. Creeks who are friendly with the British. I think the British Indian agents are fomenting trouble that way."

Will wrinkled his brow. "Colonel Elbert mentioned seaborne trouble."

Pat said, "Aye. The British Navy and privateers from St Augustine are active out in the sea lanes in the Atlantic, as you personally experienced."

Will grinned at that. "Aye, Captain Mowbray was persistent, but unlucky."

Pat continued, "We have only limited Naval power in Georgia in the form of some sailing galleys. I believe there are four such ships – big boats, really. They're in Savannah. I believe South Carolina has a similar navy, if you can call it that. A few shallow draft galleys mounting some heavy bore cannon, typically in the bow, is about it. There are some Yankee privateers that are blue water sailors hereabout."

Will asked, "Is it possible the British would mount a seaborne attack on the fort here?"

Pat said, "They would have a rough go of that. There's not much chance of a man o'war or a transport getting past the fort's guns. They must make that south tack in the harbor entrance on the Medway, and that puts them right under main battery of our guns for an extended time. They could use ships to blockade us in here, I suppose. But tis costly to keep ships on station for a blockade."

Pat continued, "What worries me, and I think other officers at the fort, is the possibility of the British landing somewhere and then marching on the fort from landward. As you saw on our ride to Barrington and back, there are swamps and marshes and all manner of rivers and creeks. It's very boggy for an army. Until today, Fort Howe was a solid impediment to a land approach because the only useful land approach is to come up the King's Highway and cross the Altamaha at the ferry, following the roads we took to come here. Now that the fort is gone, that approach is much more likely."

Pat stared into the distance briefly, not really seeing. "The only other avenue would be to find some solid land where they could unload an army and come at us from some unexpected direction across the marsh."

Will said, "Thank you for that information. I'm not sure how long I will be here. I'm almost finished with the gun repairs for the troops. And I hope Molly is ready for a trip to North Carolina soon. I really must go back there and allay my family's fears of my death. I mean I have written to them since landing here, but who knows if they have received the letters."

"Aye. Tis hard to be away for a long time, and them not knowing of your fate."

Will tossed and turned that night, reliving the rude awakening of the morning. He rose, grumpy and tired, from a near-sleepless night. He washed perfunctorily, gasping at the chill water. Then, he stumbled down to the officer's mess where he had some gluey grits and an egg that was running with grease. He was sitting at his workbench when Elbert strode into the gunshop.

Will looked up and said, "You look troubled, Sir."

"Indeed, that is the word of the hour. General Howe will march with 400 Continentals to Fort Howe. The troops will arrive there in a very few days. End of the week, I think. Our other plans for marching on Florida continue apace. Georgia Militia under Governor Houstoun and General Screven will soon march to link up with our forces. I believe they will meet us at the Satilla River, between Fort Howe and the Saint Mary's River."

Elbert paused. "Did you notice the galleys tied up at the wharves?"

Will replied, "Galleys, Sir? No, I did not."

"Aye, the Georgia Navy arrived yesterday. Commodore Oliver Bowen brought the boats here to prepare for the march. They will support the invasion plan by transporting a battalion of troops to St Mary's."

Will said, "Sounds like quite an undertaking, Sir."

"Aye. I will get the crews of the galleys to bring their weapons for your examination."

"Very well, Sir. But I sense there is more to this conversation."

"Aye, Will. Perceptive for a youngster. The British Navy ship HMS *Galatea* and some smaller Florida ships have stationed themselves around St Simons Island. Reports are that *Galatea* cannot cross the bar and is in the open ocean, but *Rebecca* and *Hinchinbrook* have moved inside the St Simons Inlet and are patrolling. Other reports are that those two ships have also moved north of St Simons and are patrolling the Altamaha Sound. I think you can see the problem this presents."

"Aye, Sir. They stand to impede our Navy from moving troops south. They also threaten the troop encampment at Fort Howe. It seems to me that Fort Howe, though burned, is an important outpost. I also think the British Navy will play havoc with our position here if they are unimpeded."

"Again, perceptive. We have another problem in that, although the galleys were built at Savannah just last year, they have deteriorated quickly in the elements and repairs are needed. The crews are also not as well trained as we would like. I need the best people I can get for these galleys, Will."

Will asked, "Are you saying you want me to be on the galleys?"

"Will, you have proven yourself to be extremely resourceful. You also are an amazing shot with that rifle of yours. We will have to challenge the British to assure we can use the inland waterway, else our invasion will fail. You know Mowbray better than anyone here. I simply need your help."

Will said, "I cannot claim to know Captain Mowbray. I merely was onboard the *Beatrice* when Captain Dawkins put on a display of seamanship for Mowbray."

"Aye, well, Mowbray needs his hat shot off again."

Will grinned. "You, Sir, are a hard man to refuse."

Elbert said, "Good man! I am considering getting the galleys ready for action and making the crews robust. Then, we shall sail to challenge the Floridians!"

"I am still hoping to get back to North Carolina and then head for the frontier. I believe my future is either in North Georgia or Tennessee. There's a girl..."

Elbert grinned. "There we have the truth! There's always a girl, my young friend. I hope she's of the same mettle as you!"

"Indeed, Sir. She is."

Elbert said, "On another topic, are you at a place with your gunsmithing where you might take a few days and accompany me to Savannah? There are people I want you to meet. A young man who stands well with Dick Caswell and General Washington should be introduced to the leaders in Savannah."

"Yes sir, I can get away."

"Very well, we leave at daybreak. We'll take the express schooner and be there by noon."

CHAPTER 10 – SAVANNAH

Will rose before dawn and washed thoroughly. The night had been warmer and residual heat from the fireplace downstairs kept his room from being frigid.

He packed his best clothing and dressed in his second best for the trip. His blue coat and black tricorn hat were a little battered, but he thought perhaps someone in Savannah could attend to those for him. He had some white breeches and stockings. A pair of good black shoes with buckles rounded out his best wear. He thought ruefully that had he received more notice of this trip he would have taken his clothes to Mrs. Williams at The Eagle. Never mind...they would have to do.

He considered weapons and other aspects of his packing, ultimately deciding to take the Brander pistol and Uncle Ewan's dirk. He packed a small shot pouch with a dozen balls and a small horn of powder for the pistol. That, too, would have to do.

Before daybreak, Will ate eggs, toast, and a glob of glutinous grits. A piece of ham rounded out his food for the day. At least, he thought, it would hold him until Elbert informed him of their plans.

The fast express schooner stood out of Sunbury Harbor, crossed St Catherine's Sound, and turned north into the Bear

River that ran behind Ossabaw Island. Once in the Bear River, the schooner's captain packed on the sail and the thin-hulled boat felt like it was flying. The gray-green water of the Bear River curling back from the schooner's bow became more murky brown as the island passed.

Elbert said, "These inland rivers are our passage, and they are protected from the Atlantic. We can move quickly when the weather is good. Most people with any means hereabout have boats. Many have small sailboats; others have rowing vessels with slaves to row them. The government has a good many small scout boats mounting a swivel gun in the bow and crewed by an officer and several men. Slightly larger scout boats may have a small carriage gun in the bow, perhaps a three pounder. Those scout boats patrol the rivers and do coast guard duties."

Elbert continued, "In addition to travel, these many thousands of miles of marshes and rivers are a cornucopia of food. You, no doubt, have enjoyed the fish and oysters here."

Will smiled. "I particularly love fried shrimp. I had never eaten shrimp until I came here. In North Carolina many people think them bugs and would not eat them."

Passing Ossabaw, the schooner crossed out of the Bear River and edged the sound to turn west into what Elbert said was the Little Ogeechee River. Just two or so miles into the Little Ogeechee, the schooner tacked north into the Skidaway River. Once again, the skipper piled on the sail and the schooner shot forward at what Will thought was breakneck speed. He loved the whistling wind in his face and the dark smell of the marshes flashing by on either side of the schooner.

Elbert pointed out that the island on their starboard beam was called Wilmington Island. On their port beam was Skidaway Island. The smaller Isle of Hope soon was in view.

Colonel Elbert raised his arm and pointed to the south end of Isle of Hope. "That is Wormslow Plantation. Dr. Noble Jones built the plantation. Dr. Jones was among the colonists who arrived on the first boat to Savannah, the Ann. He passed from this life some three years ago. Now Wormslow is property of his son Dr. Noble Wymberly Jones. Dr. Jones is quite a patriot, and I hope you will meet him during our visit to Savannah."

The Skidaway River soon gave way to a large body of water. The schooner tacked west and Colonel Elbert said, "We are now in the Savannah River. Tis but a few miles and we shall be arriving at the City. I fear Savannah was badly damaged by fire this past month."

Will said, "Lieutenant Fitzpatrick told me of the reports that the fire was perhaps set by Tories."

"Aye, well, these days any calamity that befalls our fair State is blamed directly upon the Tories. Or the Whigs if you are a Tory! Still, one must wonder since our lawmakers seem intent upon dispossessing anyone with Loyalist sentiments. It is not hard to imagine a dispossessed Tory taking revenge with a match."

Soon, the schooner approached Savannah. Will saw wharves stretching a long way down the south bank of the river. The south bank was a high, sandy bluff, topped with some buildings. One, the largest, flew a striped flag that Will recognized as the same flag flown by the Continental Army at Brandywine. Will reckoned that to be a government building.

There were snags in the river to the north side. Will also saw some jagged poles sticking up that he recognized as masts of sunken ships. Will asked Elbert if there were many sunken ships.

Elbert replied, "No, not too many. We did sink several ships to prevent the British Navy from sailing straight into our harbor and bombarding the city. There is a small battery on the south side of the river that we passed a mile back. Savannah does not have a fort like Sunbury. I have tried to convince the elders to fortify Girardeau's Plantation back some distance and a perfect landing place for an invader. Alas, the elders do not listen to me."

Will was surprised when the schooner ran past the city and kept heading west.

Colonel Elbert said, "I can see you're a bit surprised we have not docked. We're going upriver a way to Rae's Hall, my wife's family home. My wife, Elizabeth, is daughter of Captain John Rae who was a businessman of great note and a man who worked with the Indians. He was fair to the Indians, and they got along. I was fortunate to work with Captain Rae and to serve as Indian agent. We will stay at Rae's Hall during our visit."

Will said nothing but was most impressed. Elbert was a man of considerable stature who had befriended him.

Soon a high bluff on the south side of the river came into view and the schooner tacked toward a dock built at a low point in the bluff. The schooner docked and Will and Elbert stepped ashore. Two porters brought their baggage and loaded it into a wagon that was kept in a shed. Soon, a Negro came from the high side of the bluff leading a dray horse which he quickly hitched to the wagon.

Will and Elbert climbed aboard and rode to the top of the bluff where Will saw a large home bounded on one side by the river and a broad belt of high trees and on the other side by flat, timeworn fields.

Elbert said, "The house is Rae's Hall. This is called Pipemaker's Bluff. The Indian Tomochichi built his small town here. He was great friends with General Oglethorpe, and we all benefited from getting to know each other, Indian and White man. Captain Rae gained this land from the Indians and paid fairly for it. Now we have rice growing down near that creek you see, as well as on the adjacent islands."

Will said, "Tis a wonderful piece of land with grand vistas, Sir."

"Aye. I married well," Elbert said without humor or irony. A simple statement of fact.

They entered the front hall of the home that had been constructed of locally cut pine and cypress, the wide boards sawn from huge, old growth trees. The floors were wide planks of heart pine, joined tightly and hand polished to a shine. The furniture was a mixture of English tables and chairs and some hand-hewn, locally made furniture of oak and pine. Fine English China and silver were on display in a China cabinet next to a beautiful table.

A small, dark haired woman with close-fitting curls and large, bright eyes rushed into the room.

She cried, "Sam!" and threw herself into Elbert's arms.

Unashamed, Elbert held her close for a long moment. Then he said, "My dear, may I present my young friend Mr. Will Yelverton of North Carolina."

She blushed and said, "Welcome to our home, Mr. Yelverton. You must think me quite inappropriate."

Will said, "Not at all. These are times where men might not return home. I have a young lady in North Carolina who has no idea if I'm alive or dead. I have written to her, but have not stayed in one place long enough to receive a reply these last months."

Elizabeth Rae Elbert smiled, "I like you already, Mr. Yelverton."

"Please call me Will."

Elizabeth looked from Elbert to Will and back. "How long will you be here?"

"Only a few days," Elbert replied. "I must discuss military matters with some of the Assembly as well as meet with Governor Houstoun. Then, it's back to Sunbury and perhaps south."

Elizabeth's hands flew to her mouth. "South? Oh, God. Not again!"

Elbert said, "I fear so. But let us not dwell on that."

Elizabeth said, "Will, please go with Efrem who will show you your room. We'll have dinner in the dining room in half an hour."

As he turned to follow the liveried Negro named Ephrem, Will said, "Thank you, ma'am."

"Please call me Liz."

A delicious dinner, the midday meal, included some lightly fried, fresh caught fish, grits with fresh butter, greens, field peas, and some fresh beer that Elbert said came from a local brewery. Will marveled that fried fish and grits was so good. Perhaps it was because the grits were made with some cream and fresh butter and were not a tasteless glob like the dish he'd had at Sunbury. The greens and peas had a hint of dark flavor that Will tracked to bacon or smoky hog jowl. Hot pepper vinegar added a spark to the peas and greens. Will had missed this kind of food.

Colonel Elbert kissed Elizabeth and said, "We must go to town. I have matters I must discuss with the governor."

Elizabeth made a snorting sound.

Elbert smiled indulgently, "Now, now. It's the business of our freedom, my dear."

She said, "I'm not upset about the business of our freedom. It's that Houstoun is a politician and would sacrifice you and everyone else over his ambition!"

Elbert smiled. "Yes, dear. But we don't get to choose our bedfellows in a war."

"Harrumph! Well, y'all go on." She smiled, "Take this young man and expose him to the nastiness of political life."

Elbert said airily, "We shall change and, bedecked in our finery, attend our colleagues in the city."

Colonel Elbert and Will rocked along in a beautifully made carriage. The leather sides of the carriage were smooth and polished to a high gloss. The two-horse team was matched and beautiful, complementing the carriage. They pranced, headstrong and anxious to get along down the road.

The two men were dressed in anticipation of meeting the leaders of the State of Georgia. Will wore his blue coat and best shirt and breeches. One of Elbert's servants had blocked Will's somewhat battered hat, restoring its shape somewhat. Several weeks in a saddle bag had rendered it disreputable. Now it looked much better though Will thought it still a bit lumpy.

Elbert wore the uniform of a general of the militia. He explained that he held a dual commission in both the Continental Army and the Georgia Militia. He wore the militia uniform when meeting with senior Georgia officials. Although Elbert was not a large man like his predecessor, Lachlan McIntosh, his uniform was resplendent with braid.

They were rolling along the tree-canopied road that ran north-west along the Savannah River from Savannah to Augusta. Will smelled jasmine in the air, a pleasant scent to go with the quiet, country setting. Will looked at the Savannah River water that was reddish colored, unlike the gray-green water of the Medway or the tea-brown of the Altamaha.

Will asked, "Why is this river copper colored when the others are more green or brown?"

Elbert replied, "The soil of North Georgia is red clay. The water flows from up that way and is impregnated with that thick, sticky red clay."

"Tis truly unique in my experience."

Elbert said, "Aye, that red clay won't come out of your clothes. If you ever dig in it, you'll quickly learn that it's heavy and difficult to work. Astonishes me that things will grow in it. But tis rich with iron and when baked makes first-quality bricks for building."

Elbert changed the subject. "Governor Houstoun has raised the ire of the Tories in Georgia. He's recently elected to replace Governor Treutlen and he pressed for a series of acts from the Assembly punishing the Tories. Many have been attained for high treason and their lands and property taken. That is what is meant by a Bill of Attainder."

Will asked, "Were the Tories guilty of treason?"

"Tis hard to say truly. Lt Colonel Brown, who tried to kill you at Fort Howe, fights for the King. He is a South Carolinian. In a legal sense, how can he be treasonous to Georgia? On the other hand, the McGirth brothers are Georgians, but their activities are more akin to larceny than military necessity. They raid homes and plantations and rustle cattle, and I'm not convinced they do that truly in the name of the King. Nonetheless, Brown and the McGirth's as well as the former Royal Governor James Wright and others are all now lawfully dispossessed and branded traitors. The fire that swept through Savannah quickly followed the passage of those laws. I'm sure you see the possible connection."

"Aye, seems the fires were not caused by lightning."

"Indeed."

The carriage rolled along past a spot called Spring Hill on the outskirts of the city and on into the core of Savannah. Will saw several burned buildings and the tang of wood smoke was heavy in places. The road became a boulevard called Broughton Street. Trees that had been growing over the road gave way to more manicured plantings on the sides of the street. A stone sidewalk was a luxury Will had only seen in Philadelphia. The carriage slowed to a walk before stopping at the corner of Broughton and Whitacre Streets.

Will looked up at a sign which said, "Tondee's Tavern."

Elbert alighted with great bouncing energy and Will followed closely.

Elbert said, "This tavern is where the Sons of Liberty used to meet, Will. Now, many of the key lawmakers of our fair state meet here rather than hang about the stuffy state house. The food is good and the company better. Since many dwellings and other buildings were burned, we're lucky to have Tondee's."

They entered, and Will got the impression of a substantial room with dark paneling and the odor of leather and polished furniture. A hint of beer, spirits and Virginia tobacco smoke added to the smell. It was a place where men gathered.

A plump woman in an apron and mop cap shrieked, "Sam Elbert! Welcome!" Bustling over she said, "Who's your young friend?"

"This is Mr. Will Yelverton of North Carolina, Lucy. Will, I have the honor of presenting Mrs. Lucy Tondee. She runs this wonderful little venue and has done since her husband, Peter, went to his greater reward three years ago."

Lucy Tondee looked Will over and said, "You'll do. It is a pleasure to welcome you to our humble establishment. And you, Sam, know very well that I ran this place long before Peter passed on."

"Indeed, I do know that Lucy," Sam grinned. "Have you seen the Gov?"

"He's holding court in the back! I told him he'd be better with a fire brigade. He did not take kindly to that, but where else will his highness sit upon his throne but in the Long Room at Tondee's?"

Will followed Brigadier General Samuel Elbert, Georgia Militia, resplendent in his braid, to the back room where a long table was surrounded by clusters of men in fine clothing. Each cluster seemed intent upon some subject of great import. Will heard strident voices declaiming "Tories," and "Bloody British," and 'damn fire,' and several other epithets, as well as voices urging calm. Several men puffed on long white clay pipes, creating a fog of tobacco smoke in the already close room.

Toward the back of the room a man with a white powdered wig wearing a brocaded coat with a wide collar was sitting in an armchair with three other gentlemen sitting in straight back chairs flanking him. He looked up, and seeing Elbert said, "Sam! Back from the hinterland of Sunbury, I see!"

Elbert chuckled. "Tis a fine small town with much to recommend it, Your Excellency."

John Houstoun, Governor of the State of Georgia looked past Elbert and examined Will. He rose from his seat. "Who is this young gentleman?"

Elbert said, "Governor Houstoun, may I present Mr. William Yelverton of North Carolina. He is a friend of Dick Caswell, among other notables."

Houstoun stepped forward, thrust out his hand and said, "Welcome to Georgia, Mr. Yelverton."

Will shook his hand and said, "A great honor to meet you, Your Excellency."

"Tell me, how is Dick Caswell?"

"He was quite well when last I saw him, Sir. I regret I have not seen Governor Caswell for several months. My travels took me from North Carolina to Philadelphia where I was unfortunately detained by the Battle at Brandywine Creek and then the British occupation. I narrowly escaped the hangman's noose and came to Georgia on a New Jersey privateer."

"Did you, by God?! I must hear the full story one day. If I may be so bold as to ask, how old are you, Sir."

"Your Excellency, I will be 20 this summer."

Elbert put in, "Will is a master gunsmith and a fighter when he must be. He is not officially a military man but acquitted himself well during the unfortunate events at Fort Howe last week."

Houstoun looked hard at Will. "How came you to be at Fort Howe when that miserable rat Brown attacked?"

"Sir, I was there seeing to the garrison's muskets and other firearms."

"Not yet 20 and a master gunsmith. A man who has seen war and a fighter, to boot. Won't someone get this man a drink?"

The other three men stood and stepped forward.

Elbert said, "Will, these gentlemen are the leaders of our State. I have the honor to present, Major Joseph Habersham, Mr. John Milledge, and Mr. Edward Telfair."

Will made a small bow and said, "The honor is mine, gentlemen."

Habersham, a tall man with a hawk nose, appeared to be just a few years Will's senior. He offered his hand and said, "Will, is it? Call me Joe."

"Joe, I am most honored."

"We are glad to have you among us."

Edward Telfair, a laugh in his Scottish brogue said, "Dinna hog him all t' yersel' Joe."

Telfair was the same height as Will, making him taller than most. Will judged him about the same age as Will's father, Zech. He had dark hair in a que. Penetrating dark eyes sat over a notable bend in his nose.

Telfair asked, "Yer from Carolina, are ye?"

"Yes, Sir. My family owns a plantation in Edgecombe County, but I have made my home in New Bern while apprenticed as a gunsmith."

"Aye. Yer father would be Zechariah Yelverton, then."

"Indeed, Sir. My father is Zechariah. You know him?"

"Aye. Fine man he is, too. I ha' the pleasure of his acquaintance when I bide in Halifax a few years ago in tha' days before I came to this fair city."

Will made a slight bow, "I shall tell him of our pleasant meeting next time I am home."

"Aye, do tha', and tell him I remember him fondly."

Elbert put in, "Mr. Telfair has recently been elected Georgia representative to the Continental Congress. I hope the British quit Philadelphia soon so that the Congress may meet again in that city."

Will replied, "Philadelphia has suffered many privations with the coming of the British. People there are starving. I was fortunate to know some of the more well-placed citizens and was able to eat often at their tables. I also was fortunate to have a room at the Tun Tavern, else I'd have been sleeping in a doorway as many are doing. The British Army has denuded the countryside of every last food item. Sadly, so has our army."

"Aye," Telfair said. "War is a terrible business. We have been lucky in these past months not to be invaded. I fear that may change."

Elbert said, "A good reason for an expedition to Florida is to put them on their heels."

There were nods all around as John Milledge reached out his hand and said, "Welcome to Savannah, Will, please call me John."

"Thank you, John." Will said shaking Milledge's hand with a slight bow. "It seems we are the youngest people here."

"Aye. You and I are of the same age or nearly so. I've had to put up all alone with these old wheezers for many months."

Telfair snorted. "Dinna make me tan yer backside, ye wee brat!" Laughter all round made clear the bond of friendship among the group regardless of age.

Elbert said, "Will, these gentlemen took the Royal Governor prisoner and, ahem, rescued some 600 pounds of powder from the magazine in 1775. Twas quite a feat of fearless determination."

Habersham cracked a smile, "Or foolhardiness."

Elbert introduced Will to several other notables and finally stepped up to an older gentleman. The man, perhaps 55 years old with gray hair worn fashionably with curls over the ears. He had a prominent nose and penetrating eyes. A carefully knotted white cravat made his neck seem long. He wore a simple, but expensive, black frock coat. He was elegant but eschewed a powdered wig. Others seemed to defer to this man.

Elbert said, "Good evening, Doctor Jones."

"Sam, tis good to see you. You look well."

"Thank you, Doctor. I'll take that as a positive diagnosis."

"Ha, I wish all my diagnoses were that easy. And who is this?"

"Doctor Jones, it is my honor to present Mr. William Yelverton of North Carolina."

Will made a slight bow and Doctor Jones inclined his head. "The honor is mine, Mr. Yelverton."

"Good evening, Sir. Today I had the pleasure of seeing Wormslow from the express schooner. It looks a fine plantation, Sir."

"Kind of you to say. I heard you are a master gunsmith. Are you helping Colonel Elbert?"

"Yes, Sir. I am endeavoring to put the army's firearms in good condition."

"Wonderful. You must come visit Wormslow. I believe you would find several of my children to be similar age as yourself. They would certainly welcome a contemporary to visit."

"I should be honored, Sir."

In the carriage on the way back to Rae House, Elbert said, "A successful debut for you in Savannah society, Will. I also managed some required discussions with the Governor as well as some of the militia commanders. While I still have misgivings about unity of command, it appears the expedition to Florida is on. Moreover, I have approval to launch a challenge to the British Navy in the rivers near Saint Simons. That should provide some entertainment."

Will nodded as looked out at the clear sky and the brilliant display of stars against the inky blackness. He thought, "I wonder if the dead will find it amusing?"

CHAPTER 11 – THE FLEET

T
he schooner stood into Sunbury late in the day. The sun was low against the tree line in the West. Will stood in the bow, delighting in the breeze, and drawing in the now familiar odor of the marsh and rivers.

The last five days in Savannah had been quite a whirl. Elizabeth Elbert managed two delightful dinners, and Rae's Hall was very comfortable in the late winter of 1778. Georgia's winter was most other places' spring and Will delighted in sleeping in a wonderful bed with cool breezes drifting through his bedroom. Meanwhile, Elbert and Will had been on a rapid-fire schedule of visits among militia commanders, Governor Houstoun, Continental Army commanders and a representative from the South Carolina Militia.

The plan for the expedition to Florida was complete. Elbert thought invasion a poor idea, but said, "As a military man, I obey orders."

Candidly, Elbert told Will of his misgivings about the conflicting views of his commander, General Robert Howe, Governor John Houstoun, and the South Carolina Militia that somehow had been inserted into the entire plan.

After one of the visits with Houstoun, Sam Elbert said, "He is completely inexperienced as a commander but insists upon directing the Georgia Militia independently of General Howe's orders. That's a sure-fire recipe for a beating."

Will had cemented budding friendships with Joe Habersham and John Milledge. Will enjoyed his association with these educated and capable men. He thought of them in the same way he thought of Dicky Caswell, his best friend from youth. Dicky, son of Governor Richard Caswell of North Carolina, was from a wealthy family, but was not pretentious. The same could be said of Habersham and Milledge. The two of them took Will on a tour of the other taverns in Savannah, at least those not burned in the recent fire. Will reflected that getting tipsy with fellows near his same age was good fun and important to building friendships. He liked both Joe and John very much.

Will also made sure to be friendly and attentive to Edward Telfair. Telfair's acquaintance with Zech Yelverton was surprising and important to Will. Although they were separated by several hundred miles, Telfair made him feel connected to his father in an adult way that he had never felt before.

The week in Savannah was a revelation to Will about how senior leaders thought and behaved. It was flattering to be included in the rarified air of the leadership of the State. Now they were returning to Sunbury and Elbert was rubbing his palms at the prospect of driving the small British fleet out of Georgia's rivers.

Elbert commented on the galleys tied up at the wharves. "They look good. It appears the shipwrights have been working on them, getting them ready for action."

To Will, Elbert said, "Will you help me with getting the galley crews ready to go into action?"

Will said, "I am not a sailor, Sir."

"I know that. Neither am I. But we both spent time on the water in our lives. Can't be helped when you live near the coast as we both have. More important, I know about how the enemy thinks, and I think you do too. Ollie Bowen knows how to manage a boat, and each of the galleys has a captain. So, it's not exactly a case of you and me trying to tell them how to sail a boat. It's more about getting things organized. You are quite an organized young man. I've seen that for myself. Joe Habersham and his brother James will join us here, and I plan to lean on them, too."

Will liked Elbert very much. He also was excited at the prospect of working with Joe Habersham. Without thinking about his desire to head north to Carolina, Will said, "I will help you in any way I can."

"Good! We start tomorrow."

The schooner tied up at Darling's wharf in Sunbury at half-past four on March 20th. Will and Colonel Samuel Elbert disembarked and walked the quarter mile to the fort. A porter would bring their baggage later.

Will went immediately to check on Molly and Old Tom. Both horses were fine, and happy to see Will. Molly nodded her head vigorously and whickered. She greedily accepted a carrot and stamped her foot. Will thought she looked much better and seemed more energetic. She nuzzled Will's hand and snuffled him. Old Tom whinnied softly. He was excited to have attention and ate his carrot with gusto. Old Tom blew softly and nodded. Will said to both horses, "We'll go for a ride soon."

He checked in with Private Charles Cuthbert who had been detailed to help with the gunsmithing. All was well and the couple dozen muskets needing cleaning and oiling had been done. Cuthbert had been learning, and Will enjoyed being a teacher. After three weeks of working with Will, Cuthbert was proficient at taking apart a musket, diagnosing needed repairs, replacing the lock springs, and installing new barrels. The private had learned which repairs needed Will's attention and kept those guns aside. As a result, Will had few weapons demanding his attention, and he could focus on the galleys.

The next morning, Will accompanied Elbert to the wharves. Three galleys were moored there, bobbing gently with the light swell that flowed from St Catherine's Sound. Will looked at the boats.

Elbert said, "These boats were built in Savannah by shipwrights from Philadelphia. They were christened in honor of General *Washington*, General Lee, and President *Bulloch* of Georgia. *Washington*, *Lee*, and *Bulloch* will form our little flotilla. The fourth boat, the *Congress*, will remain in the Savannah River to protect the approaches to Savannah.

Will observed that the three galleys were of the same general form. Each was heavily built with an almost flat bottom around a keel of Georgia oak. The longest galley, *Washington*, was about 80 feet long, while the *Bulloch*, was just less than 50 feet. *Lee* was some 65 feet. They each had masts and lateen sails.

Will asked Elbert, "I'm a little confused, Sir. They're galleys so they are row-vessels, but they all have sails. Are they more sailing ships that can be rowed, or are they row-boats that can be sailed?"

Elbert chuckled. "Ha, well, they're both. Of course, tis better to sail because the work of rowing is exhausting. But, unlike a sailing vessel, they're not constrained by wind."

Elbert continued, "These are not safe in open ocean, Will. They're good in the inland passage because they don't draw much water and are stable gun platforms so long as the water is reasonably calm. Heavy seas and even choppy open water are not safe for these boats. St Catherine's Sound just out there would be dangerous with a heavy swell running."

Will asked, "Why do they have a bow but then the stern also appears to be pointed?"

Elbert smiled. "They're double-ended. Kind of a secret weapon. You can back the oars -- they're called sweeps – and the boat will go backward as well as forward. Very maneuverable, especially in some confined water. To answer your question about sail versus rowing, tis better to sail because the work of rowing is exhausting. The sweeps are about 20 feet long and double-banked. That means it takes two men per sweep to row the craft. But, unlike a sailing vessel, they're not constrained by wind, so the boat can make headway even in light or contrary winds. Even under sail, these boats are slow. They will never fly like the express schooner. What they lack in speed, they make up for in maneuverability, especially in shallow water with light winds, they can hold their own with a sailing vessel."

Will looked down the length of *Washington*. Her sweeps were shipped and bracketed inside the rails. The boat's guns were impressive. In the bow were two 18-pound carriage mounted cannon, one on either side of the bowsprit. Just aft of the two 18-pounders on each side 12-pounder was mounted on a carriage mount which could be swiveled to fire forward. *Washington* was the only galley with what might be called a broadside consisting of a 9-pound gun followed by three six pounders per side. In between the gunports were openings for sweeps, making some twenty sweeps per side for the galley.

Will realized this was far heavier ordnance than that carried by small blue water sailing vessels such as brigs, brigantines, and sloops. Swivel guns, mounted on the rails and loaded with grapeshot, were to deter boarding parties.

Lee was smaller than *Washington* but still carried powerful armament. She mounted one 18-pounder and one 12-pounder in the bow. The other armament consisted of two 9-pounders and two 6-pound guns as broadside mountings, with swivel guns mounted on the rails like *Washington*. *Lee* carried fourteen sweeps per side.

Bulloch was even smaller at only about 50 feet. She mounted one 12-pounder, two 9-pounder and two 6-pound guns along with the usual rail-mounted swivel guns to repel boarders. The smaller *Bulloch* mounted ten sweeps per side.

Although *Lee* and *Bulloch* were smaller and bore lighter armament than *Washington*, the three galleys were much more heavily armed than their adversaries.

Seeing Elbert on the wharf, Commodore Bowen and the galley captains all came ashore and gathered to greet the Colonel. Salutes and handshakes all around preceded Elbert saying, "May I present Mr. Yelverton of North Carolina. He is armorer to the Army and will accompany us on our coming adventure in Florida."

Will shook hands with Bowen and then each of the commanders. They were, Captain John Hardy, *Washington*; Captain John Braddock, *Lee*; and Captain Archibald Hatcher, *Bulloch*.

A slim, red-headed man with the sun-reddened skin of one who spends his time on the water walked from a flatboat moored behind *Lee*. He paused, waiting for Elbert to acknowledge him.

Elbert said, "Good morning, Sir. You are?"

"Good morning, Colonel Elbert. I am James Cantey. I am master of the flatboat you see moored just there. Governor Houstoun asked to come join this group and mount a pair of guns on the flatboat in support of your planned operations."

"Splendid! We shall have to consider how to use your guns to advantage. Welcome to you, Sir."

Elbert looked to the group and said, "As we have discussed, our fleet here will convey troops to North Florida to rendezvous with the rest of the Army. The latest scouting report has the Governor in Saint Augustine sending Royal Navy ships into the rivers around Saint Simons. Of course, our troop convoy into Florida will be impeded by that kind of defense."

Commodore Oliver Bowen, a transplanted Rhode Islander, said, "We must plan on how we will remove the British and then carry out our orders. I believe we must at least practice some ship-to-ship combat to be ready should the Royal Navy attempt to engage us."

Elbert said, "Capital idea, Commodore. I also propose for Mr. Yelverton to work with some selected riflemen to make the British crews miserable from range. Will has proved considerable marksmanship with a rifle from the deck of a heaving ship. I believe he will serve ably in that capacity."

Bowen looked hard at Will. "Are you the man who shot Captain Mowbray's hat off?"

Will said, "An unfortunate miss, Sir."

"Ha! By God! You'll do!"

Bowen, his Rhode Island accent evident, said to Elbert, "We will be practicing in the river and the sound for the next week. I have proposed the Governor pay for the use of the brig moored as Spaulding's dock there as an adversary."

Elbert said, "Next week I will go to Fort Howe and then meet this fleet at Darien in a fortnight after that. Therefore, three weeks from today we should be rendezvousing and embarking. Is that satisfactory?"

The Navy men all agreed.

Bowen and his captains turned to go to their galleys, and Will and Elbert walked back to the fort.

"This expedition is too complicated and has limited chance of success," Elbert said.

"What shall we do?" Will asked.

Elbert said, "Endeavor to overcome self-inflicted errors and seek to capitalize on our strengths."

CHAPTER 12 – DARIEN

Elbert said to Will, "I am pleased you will join us in this expedition."

Will asked, "What can I do?"

"I have a select group of riflemen who I want you to train to shoot from a moving boat so we might reduce the effectiveness of the British Marines who will undoubtedly be on the decks of the enemy ships as well as in their rigging. They'll be shooting down at us if you can't make them keep their heads down. Can you do that?"

"I shall try. Who is in charge of the riflemen?"

"Captain George Melvin. He is a good man and aggressive in a fight. He is in the 4th Battalion. Johnny Habersham, Joe's brother, is Brigade Major. Check with him to find out where they are camped."

"Very well. I'll get busy."

John – Johnny to his friends – Habersham, an ascetic-looking man with a slim nose, thin brown hair, and dark eyes, was a busy man. As Brigade Major he was essentially second in command of the troops and served as military secretary to General Howe. Will found this confusing, but Elbert had explained that though often junior in actual rank, capable officers were selected for a higher position such as Brigade Major which took advantage of their abilities long before they would have been promoted in regular succession. Joe

Habersham's youngest brother, John was only about 24 years old as he sat at a portable field desk carefully keeping count of the troops, copying orders, and managing correspondence. As a budding merchant in his father's business, he was well equipped for that task.

Will walked over to Habersham's desk which was set up under a tent fly in the parade ground area of the fort and waited until Johnny had finished with a paper.

Johnny Habersham looked up and said, "Good morning, Will. I see you are well, this fine day."

Will said, "I am. I see you're busy, so I'll not tarry. Colonel Elbert wishes me to work with Captain Melvin to develop skill in his riflemen who are to act as marines onboard our galleys. Colonel Elbert places confidence in my ability to shoot despite my own misgivings about it. He told me you would be able to tell me where Captain Melvin is camped."

Habersham snorted softly. "I think Elbert an excellent judge of your strengths, Will. Melvin and his small contingent are just down the bluff to the east of the outer wall of the fort."

"Thank you, Johnny. By the way, congratulations on your full majority in addition to your being Brigade Major."

Johnny Habersham laughed and muttered, "Thank you. I must say it sounds more glorious than it is." He reached for the next piece of correspondence as Will turned to go find George Melvin.

Will walked to where Melvin and his men were encamped. He carried Josie and his other rifle. Will was not sure he wanted to take Josie on another boat ride in the salt environment. He would try his older, .45 caliber rifle.

Melvin had selected a flat spot atop the bluff overlooking the Medway for his camp. There was no chance of being flooded out in a downpour. Since it was getting to be the season for heavy spring rains having a camp above the flood plain was important.

"Good morning, Sir. I am Will Yelverton. Are you Captain Melvin?"

"Aye. Welcome to you, Sir. Colonel Elbert tells me you are to teach us to shoot."

"No, I'm sure you and your men are excellent riflemen, else you would not be serving as marines for this expedition."

"Aye. But then, what then are you here for?"

"I thought perhaps we could all practice together, maybe shooting at a floating log to become comfortable with a moving target."

"Aye. Tis a good plan."

"I can also examine the men's weapons and smooth out any problems like lock timing."

"Another good idea."

Will said, "Shall we start tomorrow? I don't want to interfere with your command."

That evening, squalls rolled in, and heavy rain poured intermittently for hours. The wind whipped across the Medway, kicking up spray and large waves that broke against the wharves at Sunbury. The cold wind added to the misery.

The morning dawned with calm winds and receding clouds. The air was chill, but dry.

Good to his word, Will avoided interfering with George Melvin's unit. He and the men, there were 24, spent two hours the next morning, April 6th, going over the weapons. Will checked each one, tested the lock timing, and noting any problems like bends in barrels or other damage.

Will said to Melvin, "Your men have good rifles. They are in good shape. I did adjust the lock timing on a few and replaced the main lock spring on a couple. But these are minor concerns that have now been remedied. We can do some target practice this afternoon, if that is acceptable."

"Please do. Colonel Elbert has passed along through Major Habersham that we will embark on the galleys and depart in two days for Fort Howe. We are to escort a flat boat with provisions and provide a backup for river crossing for the army.

I am not looking forward to being on one of those tubs in a squall, I must say."

Will grinned, "They don't look really seaworthy, do they?"

Will worked with Melvin's troops for two hours in the afternoon. They threw a green tree limb in the river and waited for it to float out to the middle where the current made it bob and move erratically as it drifted slowly away. The recent storms made for more unsettled water in the river, adding a measure of realism to the shooting.

They took turns shooting at branches on the limb until it was well out of range. They determined that about 200 yards was the maximum range to be effective. Even when they missed the small limb that was the target, the splash in the water was close enough to make the shot effective against enemy troops.

Will asked Johnny Habersham for a small boat which they tied up next to the shore. Each man loaded his rifle, climbed aboard the small boat, and took a shot at a floating limb. This added the motion of a boat under their feet to the motion of the target. Each man got in several shots and their accuracy improved quickly.

Two more days of this practice along with Melvin's training of the troops in light infantry tactics had the troops ready for a fight. Melvin had the men running through the woods using natural cover and firing from a variety of positions. Light infantry tactics were used by riflemen in both the

American and British Armies, so this was critical training for Melvin's troops. Boarding the enemy ship was simulated by stacking several logs waist-high and the men rushing the logs as though they were the rail of a ship. They stacked the logs higher than the average ship rail because the galleys sat lower in the water than would a sailing ship. Privately, Will thought boarding an enemy ship would be extremely difficult under conditions where the two craft were bobbing in a swell and the ship's company were shooting back. Worse, being stabbed at with a cutlass or bayonet would make boarding a very dangerous proposition. Will was more optimistic about the possibility of shooting from a distance.

Will said to Melvin, "I think your troops are excellent shots, and I look forward to seeing you at Fort Howe. We leave today. I understand you are embarking on the galleys tomorrow."

"Aye. I hope to be at Fort Howe tomorrow night, next day at the latest."

Elbert sat his horse comfortably, despite the heat of the April day. He was leading the small detachment of men and horses from Sunbury to the ruins of Fort Howe. At Fort Howe there were some 400 Continentals encamped, staging for the third expedition to invade British East Florida. Will Yelverton rode Old Tom, his loaner bay gelding, by Elbert's side. On Elbert's other side, Major Joe Habersham rode on his white stallion, Mack. Brigade Major Johnny Habersham rode just to Joe's left.

Will had ridden Old Tom because he did not want to work Molly hard on a lengthy trip. He had taken Molly out for a few rides, and she was on the mend. Will thought she would soon be up to longer trips. Perhaps he could negotiate to buy Old Tom and they all would go to Carolina together? For now, Old Tom was Will's mount, and he was a good one.

Elbert said to Will, "Did Joe tell you about his exploits in '75 taking the King's powder?"

Will said, "Joe has been reticent about his exploits. I have plied him with sack and rum, but he has remained tight lipped."

Joe snorted. "You have not found sufficient sack to ply me, Carolina whippersnapper."

Johnny Habersham laughed. "I can attest that Joe can hold his liquor. Drinks me under the table at every chance."

Joe said, "No mercy for you whippersnappers. Tis important you learn from an experienced, older gentleman, such as myself."

Will snickered. He liked the Habershams.

Elbert said, "Since Joseph is being reticent about his exploits, I shall embarrass him with the story. 'Twas July of 1775 and beastly hot. Joe commanded the schooner Rebellion along with Ollie Bowen when the British tried to run our little blockade of the Savannah River. Ollie maneuvered the Rebellion with great skill, and Joe threatened to blow the

British ship out of the water. Their commander, Captain Maitland, surrendered. It was a wise choice. Rebellion mounted ten carriage guns as well as a goodly number of swivels. Took quite a cargo."

Will asked, "What was the cargo?"

Elbert smirked, "Twas some 14000 pounds of His Majesty's gunpowder intended for Indian trade as well as to shore up the British Army in Georgia. Some was kept for Georgia, some sent to South Carolina, and a goodly portion was sent to Boston. Sadly, the British never had a chance to use the powder, unless of course you count the rounds fired at them at Bunker Hill as using it."

Will looked at Habersham, "You are definitely buying the drinks at our next evening of fun and jest!"

Joe Habersham smiled his customary tight-lipped smile, but his eyes twinkled. "Shouldn't cost me much. You'll be in your cups after two or three rounds. I thought you Carolina boys were able to hold your liquor."

Will grinned. "I shall endeavor to give you a contest, Sir."

Elbert said, "Make him also buy a round over his arrest of James Wright. Sir James was the Royal Governor and Joe strode past the sentry at the Government House, walked into the Council Chamber, slapped a hand on Sir James' shoulder, and said he was under arrest. The council rushed out leaving Sir James to his fate. No one knew that there was no real force of men backing up Joe, just a couple fellows with muskets. Sir James could have simply had Joe arrested. Amazing audacity!"

Will said, "That's multiple rounds of best brandy, Joe."

Will smelled the burned timbers and dead bodies before the group trotted into Fort Howe. The dead soldiers had been interred but burned bodies and charred wooden timbers created a cloying stench that seemed to cling to the air. Elbert commented that only a few Americans had been killed in the dawn attack, but the unfortunate burning of the fort had created a scorched spot on the bluff overlooking the Altamaha.

Some 400 troops were encamped in the field behind the destroyed fort and along the road to Barrington Ferry. The commander reported to Elbert that several false warnings of attack had caused considerable distress among the troops. Worse, many men were sick with a variety of fevers. Several had died and their freshly interred corpses added to the feral odor of death that hung over the bluff.

Elbert confided to Will, "I fear this situation will continue to get worse. We must move soon toward Florida; else the army will be incapable of moving at all. We're marching to Darien day after tomorrow to join the galley fleet and push the British out of the river. It's either that or give this up and go home."

An hour later, a rider cantered into the camp at Fort Howe. Will was standing with Elbert when he read the message handed over from General Howe.

Elbert said, "I thought this might happen. The British have moved *Hinchinbrook* and *Rebecca* to anchor at the dividings above Fort Frederica. That puts the brigantine and the sloop squarely athwart the river, blocking our way."

Will asked, "What is the dividings?"

"Saint Simons is a barrier island, like Ossabaw and Saint Catherine's. The dividings is the place in the river behind the island where the tide comes together from each end of the island. Each day, twice a day, the tide rises and falls. The ocean tide rushes into the river behind each of the barrier islands and at some point, called the dividings, the tide from one direction meets the tide from the other direction. The river will be quite shallow there and when the tide turns vessels can be put aground in no time at all."

Will nodded his understanding. As a boy he had been with Uncle Ewan fishing when the tide changed in the river at New Bern, causing a surprising rush of water.

Elbert said, "I must talk to Johnny Habersham and order the troops to march for Darien tomorrow.

They left early the following morning, April 14th. Elbert's command included the Habershams, three captains, some 24 sergeants, and assorted drummers, fifers, and the army's armorer, Will Yelverton. There were three hundred and fifty soldiers, and a detachment of artillery with two field pieces. Each soldier carried fifty rounds of ammunition. They had each been issued food for six days and a blanket.

The officers and Will rode their horses while the sergeants managed the march order and kept the formations. Elbert ordered that the soldiers use route march order, which was more relaxed and open ranks. This approach was less fatiguing for the approximately 25-mile march to Darien. Elbert consulted with Johnny Habersham and agreed on a route away from the river to take advantage of high ground and an existing, though narrow, road. They would trend away from the Altamaha and then skirt down Cathead Creek before arriving in the small, military settlement of Darien.

Elbert explained to Will, "This area is well watered, making for excellent rice culture but poor travel for an army. We don't have the boats to transport this number of troops down the river anyway, so we walk on the high ground. Still, I can't rush this march for fear of exhausting the men. Too much sickness has already depleted our units."

Elbert continued, "Darien was once an outpost, and there's still a block house there. It used to be called Fort King George. Darien was settled by Scots Highlanders, and most of the inhabitants are descended from that warlike group. Darien started life called New Inverness. You've met John McIntosh. His people were among the first at Darien."

Will asked, "Is it a good harbor?"

"Aye, the harbor there and the wharves are excellent. We should be able to load the troops with little difficulty. From there to the Frederica River and its dividings is only a couple hours of sailing. I'm surprised the British ships have not approached Darien. The old fort is not well armed. Certainly not like the fort at Sunbury."

Will listened carefully, but he knew Elbert was talking mostly to clear his mind and articulate his planning. The conversation was more for Colonel Sam Elbert than it was for Will's edification. Still, Will learned a lot.

That night Will smiled as he climbed into his bedroll that had served him so well since the days of Moore's Creek Bridge, his trek to Philadelphia, and his desperate flight across New Jersey. He was also happy to have the shelter of the oil cloth to keep the damp ground away as he slept. The bedroll had also served him well on a trip to market with the Kennedys. The two nights he slept in it at the Lowden's Tavern in Carthage, North Carolina were memorable. The bedroll still held Abby's scent and Will drifted off, remembering the feel of her body against his and smell of her hair as she cuddled close, her head on his shoulder.

Two days later the 400 men force arrived at the high bluff in Darien. Joe Habersham explained that General Oglethorpe, the founder of Georgia, had laid out Savannah, Sunbury, Darien, and the budding town of Brunswick to the south on a plan with streets punctuated by squares. The troops were encamped on Oglethorpe Square, which was only a quarter mile from the wharves.

Two of the galleys were tied up at the wharves with the third, the *Bulloch*, standing guard at the mouth of the Darien River, just back from Doboy Sound and across from the northern end of Saint Simons Island.

Two miles further south at the dividings in the Frederica River, amidst the golden marshes, lurked the British.

CHAPTER 13 – FREDERICA

A nor'easter blew in the day Elbert's 400 men arrived in Darien. The frigid wind blew strong across the ocean and slammed into Coastal Georgia driving everyone indoors. That is, everyone who could get indoors.

Will said to one of the lieutenants, "I thought March was the end of cold weather hereabouts."

The officer shrugged and said, "I don't know. I am from Virginia, and this is my first season here. Few of our number are native Georgians. The colony has so few men, it being newer than the others, that they recruited the Georgia battalions from the Carolinas and Virginia."

Will nodded. "I'm from North Carolina. Our weather is warmer than most states, but we usually have cold into April. In Carolina, this chill would be no surprise. The men are suffering, and there's not much we can do."

"Aye. They camped on Oglethorpe Square but a good many have taken to the warehouses by the wharves or are huddled in the lee of the few buildings in this little town. At least each man has a blanket, not that a blanket does much good."

Will said, "It's the wind, more than the cold, I think."

Elbert and his officers were lodged in the homes of the more well-to-do citizens. Will threw his bedroll on one of the bunks in a junior officers' cabin on the *Washington*. There were not many such cabins under the quarterdeck, but Captain

Hardy assigned one to Will anyway. The cabin was tiny, and the galley wallowed and bobbed in the wind suddenly jerking against its mooring to add to the nauseating motion. A natural on the water who never got seasick, Will was comfortable out of the wind and rain. Will was careful to keep his powder dry, and hoped the men were doing the same. Will's horse was not a worry. Old Tom was stabled in Darien along with the officers' horses.

Captain George Melvin's 24 riflemen had sheltered on *Washington* along with the complement of Negro slaves who were rented to crew the oars. Fortunately for all those aboard *Washington*, there was sufficient space below decks to get out of the weather. The boat's wallowing while tied up at the wharf made some men sick, but at least there was shelter from the cold wind and spitting rain.

Morning, April 18th, dawned clear and bright. The nor'easter was gone, the wind and water were calm. Will had learned that nor'easters blew in quickly and, just as quickly, disappeared. Without the wind to deal with, the galleys were quickly ready for boarding.

The flat boat under Mr. James Cantey had been towed in by *Washington* two days ago. This was fortunate because the flat boat was not seaworthy in a blow like yesterday's nor'easter. Capt. George Young commanded the artillerymen and the two field pieces mounted on the flatboat.

By one o'clock in the afternoon, the galleys were loaded with the troops, provisions were on board, and the galleys cast off into the ebbing tide. It was a good idea to sail with the ebbing tide because the rush of water would carry the boats by natural action rather than having to expend the Negro rowers' energy. Better to save their strength against the need for maneuvering should a fight develop.

Will stood on the quarterdeck, discretely out of the way of Captain Hardy and the crew. Elbert stood closer to Hardy, quietly observing but not interfering with the business of commanding the ship.

The galley captains' seamanship and knowledge of local waters came to the fore. Captain Hardy in *Washington*, Captain Braddock in *Lee*, and Captain Hatcher in *Bulloch* were experts at their duties. Will watched as the three galleys, led by *Washington*, expertly conducted their tiny brown-water navy safely across the somewhat choppy Altamaha Sound, and to the approach to the Inland Passage. Will privately considered that the galley captains knew these waters, but the British probably did not. He thought that this was a major advantage in the coming fight.

Once past Broughton Island to the north of the Altamaha Sound, the little flotilla swung south and entered the Frederica River at its convergence with MacKay River. Once they made the turn into the Frederica River, the galleys encountered light southwest breezes, shifting to south-southwest, then south and east; by late afternoon the weather was calm, and the winds had dropped. Hardy ordered the sweeps deployed and soon the small craft were making headway against the light breeze.

Elbert stepped closer and commented to Will, "The creeks and tidal rivers hereabouts are confusing to those who have not navigated them before. Treacherous shoals lurk in places where tidal action deposits silt and mud. Oyster beds were to be avoided because they will cut the hull of a boat like a thousand razors, yet these same beds are covered at high water, making their location pure guesswork to the uninformed. These factors are to our advantage."

Will said, "I was thinking the same thing, Sir. We're fortunate the wind has died down."

Elbert replied, "Aye, Will. I'm a fair-weather sailor, and t'would have been miserable to be here with the nor'easter of the past couple days."

Elbert said, "I am well satisfied with our progress. Sunset is at near seven of the clock tonight, and twilight will prolong the day for another half-hour. I intend to land some infantry and the artillery from the flat boat on the high ground at St Simons and have them march to old Frederica Town and the remnant of the fort there. Having a garrison with artillery on land, with marsh the other side of the river, means we will command this reach of the Frederica River."

Elbert said, "I'm putting the troops ashore at Pikes Bluff, a mile and a half above Old Fort Frederica. There's a trace of a road from there so the soldiers won't slog through mud and marsh. More important, they can roll the guns unimpeded and no muddy marsh. I want them to invest the old fort by nightfall."

Will asked, "What happened to the old fort here?"

Elbert said, "Twas the second most important city and fortification in Georgia until we beat the Spanish in 1742. The War of Jenkins' Ear went on for a while, but the last major engagement was when the Spanish came north in 1742. They landed on the south end of Saint Simons and marched north on the fort. General Oglethorpe and his men met them at a place near a marsh and beat them soundly. It is said the marsh ran red with Spanish blood, thus the name of the battle is Bloody Marsh."

"The Spanish withdrew to Florida and, after other battles in the Caribbean, gave up the fight. That ended the war and Spanish incursions into Georgia. Once it was determined that the Spanish had given up raiding into this area there was no need for Frederica, and it slowly withered. A fire finished the little town just a few years ago. Part of the old fort still stands, but much of the outer parts have fallen into the river. It is still somewhat usable as a defensive location, and I intend to use it."

About four in the afternoon, *Washington* nudged up to Pike's Bluff on St Simons Island. *Washington's* crew threw lines around sturdy oaks up the hill and drew the bow up close, holding it steady while Lieutenant Colonel Robert Rae led the division of riflemen from *Washington* down gangplanks to take up positions in the woods to cover those disembarking from the boats. Major Roberts followed with the second division of riflemen and troops from the *Bulloch*. Captain Young landed with his artillery.

Will stood at the rail of *Washington* alongside Elbert and Captain Melvin whose orders were to remain onboard with his 24 riflemen. They watched Rae and Roberts organize the one hundred men and march off down the path, directly toward Fort Frederica. Will noticed that riflemen trotted out in front of the main body of troops, clearly probing in case the British had placed an ambush on the island. The two artillery pieces trundled along behind the main body of Rae and Roberts' troops.

Satisfied that the ground forces were sufficiently off on their mission to secure Fort Frederica and thus threaten the British flank, Elbert nodded to Captain Hardy. Hardy immediately ordered *Washington* to be cast off and move out into Frederica River. *Bulloch* followed suit.

Soon, *Washington* and *Bulloch* joined *Lee* in anchoring mid-stream across from Frederica. In the distance, perhaps a half-mile, Will could see two ships. A glance through Hardy's spyglass confirmed one was *Rebecca*. What's more, Will could also see Captain Mowbray prowling the deck. As Will looked at Mowbray through the glass, Mowbray raised his own spyglass and ran it over first *Bulloch* and then *Washington*. When he got to Will, he paused. Lowering his glass, he swept off his hat and made an exaggerated, mocking bow.

Elbert said, "Now what was that about?"

Will smiled, "I shot his hat off from the deck of *Beatrice* last month."

Next to Will, George Melvin said, "Did you, by God?!"

"Yes, and I suspect he'd like to have a chance to get back his honor."

Elbert smirked, "We shall endeavor to give him that opportunity, gentlemen. But it 'twill be on the morrow. Tis too late for us to engage in combat today. First thing tomorrow morning we shall see what can be done about running His Majesty's ships back to Florida. And giving Captain Mowbray the opportunity to join his hat with a hole in himself. For now, we shall content ourselves with sending a greeting for the evening."

Turning to Captain Hardy, Elbert said, "Let's give them a few rounds to alert them a bit."

Hardy said, "Very well, Colonel."

The three galleys were all anchored bow toward *Rebecca* and her companion Brig which Will soon learned was a captured South Carolina privateer renamed *Hinchinbrook*. Hardy communicated with *Bulloch* and *Lee* that each galley would fire two rounds from their main batteries to annoy the British and serve notice that Georgia had come to fight.

"Number one gun, Fire!" shouted the master gunner. *Washington's* 18-pounder blazed out and the entire galley

144

jerked from stem to stern with the astonishing recoil. It was the largest gun Will had ever encountered, and the pure power it projected thumped in his chest as though he had been hit by a giant fist. The huge ball splashed a whopping waterspout to the right of *Hinchinbrook*, the spray making a rainbow across the sky, the setting sun briefly painting the ship with a prism of color.

"Number two gun, Fire!" and *Washington's* 12-pound second bow gun thumped. Had the 18-pounder not just gone off, Will would have been more impressed. The 12-pounder blazed out a ball that kicked up a thirty-foot geyser of spray a few yards left of *Rebecca*. The main batteries of *Bulloch* and *Lee* followed suit, missing the enemy ships, but serving notice that the galleys carried terrific firepower and the Georgians were not afraid to use it.

As Will, Elbert, and Melvin watched, *Hinchinbrook* slipped her anchor and floated slightly toward the galleys, swinging to present her broadside to the galleys and dropping fore and aft anchors to remain athwart the river.

Hardy chuckled, "A guardian! They mount no larger than 6-pound guns that certainly can reach us but would do no damage. Tis like a feisty little dog yapping and baring its little teeth at a hound."

Elbert said, "I worry about the British ship of the line is that we have been told is present in these waters. If that ship were able to come into these waters, that would be a bigger cause for concern, I think."

Hardy said, "Aye. Those two in front of us are not to be dismissed. They have puny little four-pound guns, but should they get in close and be able to open fire on us, they could do damage. We must be on our guard that a shift in the wind does not favor *Rebecca* and *Hinchinbrook* slipping anchor and rapidly bearing down upon us. Being boarded by a couple companies of Royal Marines could be disastrous. We must be ready to instantly respond should the wind shift unexpectedly."

Hardy continued, "I'm told the ship you mention is *HMS Galatea* and she is anchored in St Simons Sound. She mounts some twenty 9-pound carriage guns. I'll wager we can see her masts from here if we look hard enough. I'll also wager her captain is not fool enough to attempt to sail into this river. Shoals and eddies being what they are, he'd be aground in a trice."

Elbert said, "Aye, then I want to send a scouting party from the shore party to the south end of the island to see if *Galatea* is there. Also, is she alone?"

As they were talking a boat pulled alongside *Washington* with a small group of captured British Marines and two seamen belonging to *Hinchinbrook*.

Elbert said, "Take them below and don't let them talk among themselves. We shall question them shortly. Have the boat take this message to Lt Colonel Rae to reconnoiter the south end of the island with special attention to British vessels in the sound."

Elbert handed Hardy a written note to that effect, and Hardy passed it along to the sergeant in charge of the boat.

Later, Elbert said, "The prisoners were at Fort Frederica, manning a lookout. The interrogation was fruitful. They confirmed that the brigantine in the river yonder is, indeed, *Hinchinbrook*. Of course, *Rebecca* we've already recognized. *Hinchinbrook* is the captured South Carolina ship, Defence, and has a crew of perhaps 40, and *Rebecca* has a similar crew with a company of Royal Marines embarked, as well. Both boats carry 4-pounders, and not many at that – eight to ten a side on *Hinchinbrook*, four a side on *Rebecca*. Still, respectable should we board them, or if they should get inside our defenses and effect a broadside. I also emphasize their swivel guns as being murderous to a boarding party."

"There is a small brig that we haven't seen. Doubtless she is upriver from the dividings and masked from view by the marsh. The prisoners all separately stated this vessel is called a watering brig and mounts only two small guns, a 3-pounder and a 2-pounder. She is not a threat but would be a nice prize should we be able to capture her. One man said she is called *Hope*, and was a prize captured by Captain Fanshawe of HMS Carysfort, a ship of the line. *Hope* was taken with her crew and passengers to Saint Augustine. The man said the passengers were Frenchmen who were volunteers to fight for our cause, but they are now interned in Fort Saint Marks, the old Spanish Castillo.

That is unconfirmed by the others, but it surely has the ring of truth."

Elbert looked around the table and said, "Now, gentlemen, to our plans for the morrow."

Around eight of the clock, a lookout called out to the Officer of the Watch, "Enemy ships have weighed anchor, Sir."

The Officer of the Watch quickly informed Captain Hardy and Colonel Elbert who hurried on deck.

The Officer of the Watch said, "Sir, they appear to be moving off. I can see their wakes in the moonlight."

Hardy looked through his spyglass but could see nothing more than the wakes and a glimmer of movement, "Aye. I'll own they're moving to a more advantageous position and readying for action. They know we're coming for them."

Elbert nodded. "As discussed, gentlemen. First light we shall engage."

CHAPTER 14 – THE RIVER

Will Yelverton clamped his tricorn had on and adjusted it to the side so he could shoot without the hat getting in the way. He walked out his cabin door. He wore his hunting shirt, breeches, and tall boots. Slung over his shoulders were his powder horn and shot pouch. Uncle Ewan's dagger, honed to a scalpel-like edge, hung from his belt. The Brander pistol was loaded and shoved into the belt, close to hand if needed. The English Dragoon Carbine was strapped across his back.

In his hand Will held the .45 caliber rifle he had made during his final apprentice year with Mr. Bert Koontz. Although this was not the beautiful weapon that was Josie, this was a moist, salty environment and Will was loath to expose Josie to more sea spray. Poor Josie had already required intensive cleaning and oiling to remedy the salt exposure on *Beatrice*. While the .45 was not Josie, it was still a deadly accurate rifle. Will could drive a nail at 200 yards with the .45. Josie remained in Will's cabin, carefully encased in the soft deer hide scabbard that Abby had made.

Will climbed up onto *Washington's* quarter deck and stood next to the rail. It was still dark, but a hint of light shown in the east. Soon there would be battle. Will was not afraid. He hated the thought of killing and wished this entire situation were not so. "But," he ruefully thought, "wish in one hand and spit in the other and see which one gets wet."

Colonel Sam Elbert joined Will at the rail. "We're in it now, Will."

"Aye. We are that."

"We're going at 'em first thing. I want them on their heels trying to respond to our sally rather than giving them the initiative. They're still sitting just beyond the bend they backed up to last night. Rae's men have been watching them all night and they have not moved. We were fortunate to have clear skies, so the stars and a glimmer of moonlight made the ships visible. Rae reports that there were some comings and goings of small boats."

Will looked at Elbert inquiringly.

"Aye. Rae believes they've added some Marines and perhaps some sailors to the ships' complements. I rather suspect that means they expect to board us. If I were commanding those ships, I'd come at us full bore at the earliest opportunity. The idea would be to deny us more than one or perhaps two shots with our bow guns before they would be alongside and boarding us for a bloody hand-to-hand fight. Well, they're not going to get that chance."

In the background Will could see Hardy pacing back and forth giving brief orders. Some of the crew were weighing the anchors, first the stern anchor, then the bow. The other two galleys were engaged similarly. Will heard Hardy say, "Run out the sweeps. At my command, we shall begin rowing. When we clear the point, we shall quickly align all three galleys bow on to the British. Immediately our anchors are set, we shall commence firing."

As Will watched, the other galleys were made ready and Hardy called out, "Full speed ahead!"

The Negroes on the sweeps began to pull. Two men per sweep, one standing along the keel on an elevated platform, the other sitting on a bench just below, pulled, swept, pulled, and swept. *Washington, Bulloch,* and *Lee* shot forward!

Pull, sweep, pull, sweep, pull... The galley's quickly cleared the point of land revealing the British ships which still sat at anchor. Hardy commanded turns so that *Lee* turned short, *Bulloch* wider, and *Washington* wider still to make the turn and end up in line-abreast formation, their heaviest bow ordinance pointed at the British.

Hardy shouted at the top of his lungs, "FIRE!" All three galleys fired in rapid succession. Five heavy cannon balls flew at the British ships and the galleys' crews quickly began reloading.

Panic ensued on *Hinchinbrook* and *Rebecca*. Sailors ran around the decks frantically. *Hinchinbrook* was still sitting broadside in the river. It's puny 4-pound guns banged out, but the balls dropped into the water well short of the Americans.

Will saw a sail on *Rebecca* start to unfurl but it flapped listlessly. There was no wind! The galleys' lateen sails remained furled tightly and Hardy relied upon the sweeps. Will looked to Elbert who had a tight-lipped half-smile.

Will watched Hardy and the other two galleys as the sweeps kept churning. Hardy paused waiting for the right moment. Then he shouted, "Ship oars! Drop anchor!"

The galleys snubbed up tightly on the bow anchor chains and started to swing with the momentum. But Hardy and the other captains quickly gave orders to back the sweeps as necessary to stabilize the boats and then ordered the stern anchors dropped to steady their positions.

"Fire!" shouted *Washington's* Master Gunner and the entire galley bucked hard under the double reports of the 18- and 12-pounders. Almost simultaneously, the 12-s and 9-s of *Lee* and *Bulloch* slammed, jets of red-orange flame shooting out toward the British ships.

Hinchinbrook's main mast snapped and dangled. *Rebecca's* sails, still hanging limp, suddenly were holed. Splinters flew from the rails, decks, and a piece of bowsprit dangled from *Hinchinbrook*.

Elbert handed Will his spyglass. Will could see various rigging on both British ships dangling uselessly. Sailors ran up and down in the undamaged rigging attempting to get some sails to catch wind. There was no wind to be had, and the two ships were becalmed and forced to endure the cannonade.

Will could see smoke popping from the shore opposite the British ships. Between cannon shots, the crackle of small arms could be heard. A sailor in the tops of *Rebecca* collapsed, and fell, his lifeless body splashing into the river.

Will heard Hardy order a change from solid shot to canister. The onslaught of cannister shot raking across the decks of the British ships created carnage and chaos among the crews. Canister rounds also shredded the canvas sails into ribbons. Will considered that neither ship would be doing much sailing with the rigging and sails in such shape.

Will saw a longboat lowered over *Hinchinbrook*'s side where a direct hit from a 12-pounder splintered it into matchwood. Another boat from *Rebecca* appeared at the bow of *Hinchinbrook* which cut its anchor cables and started to swing to align with the river. The small boat took up a cable from *Hinchinbrook* and started rowing to tow the larger ship away from the pounding fire of the galleys. *Rebecca* cut its anchor cables as well and swung in line with *Hinchinbrook*. Another small boat picked up a cable from *Rebecca* and began an attempted tow of that ship, too.

"They are running! But, where to?" Will wondered aloud.

Elbert said, "I think they're seeking a tactical advantage in the form of getting behind a bend in the river out of our fire, and then pulling up short, forcing us to come in closer if we want to engage. I think they are also looking to lure us into deeper water and perhaps into the sound beyond to get *Galatea* into this fight. Her 9-pounders would be a match for us and the larger water would advantage them over us because they're more deep water craft."

Will said, "I see a leadsman swinging and throwing the lead. They're cautious about the depth."

Hardy overheard this and said, "Aye. And they'll be surprised if they throw that lead into a scour hole."

Will looked at Elbert for an explanation. "The tide in these back rivers moves with great speed in certain places. For example, when it makes a turn the water speeds up and scours out a deep hole but piles up a shoal on the other side. Throwing a lead into one of those may show several fathoms of water under the ship, when actually there is quite a shallow sandbar just ahead. It is not uncommon for an inexperienced captain to be tricked into running aground."

Will said, "We'll pound them into splinters if they run aground!"

"Aye," Elbert grinned. "T'would be a shame."

Hardy said to no one in particular, "They're desperate for a change in the tide which won't be forthcoming for another three hours. The tide is on the ebb and is not in their favor. Were the tide on the rise, they'd be running with it and perhaps they'd avoid a shoal. They'll soon run aground, I'll own."

The British ships continued running down stream, and the galleys rowed just inside the range of the 9-pound guns.

This placed the galleys in position to fire continuously with their main guns while the British ships' 4-pounders were utterly useless.

Elbert's teeth were bared in a satisfied grimace. The cannonade continued slamming away, thumping Will in the chest with every round. Will's head began to hurt, and his teeth felt on edge. His muscles were taut with strain.

Rebecca suddenly stopped, dead in the water. *Hinchinbrook* followed suit almost instantly as she ran aground, head and stern aligned with the river. The small brig, *Hope*, slewed to a halt just to port of *Hinchinbrook*.

The *Hope's* crew threw a boat overboard not waiting to lower it. Several men quickly debarked the brig and began hauling on oars on the small boat.

Hardy said, "This place is called Raccoon Gut. I thought they might have trouble getting past this shoal. There's quite a scour hole on the east side where the gut comes in. They're hauling the anchor to try to kedge the brig off that sandbar. 'Twon't work, but we shant simply murder 'em for tryin'. Cease fire! Cease fire!"

The three galleys dropped anchor, steadied, and held fire while the *Hope's* crew attempted to get their little craft off the sandbar.

Hardy said, "They'll find the bottom here is soft, slimy, clay that sucks and holds. That ship is stuck fast, and those

155

crewmen will soon be up to their waists in that muck and worrying about getting back in their boat before the tide turns and drowns them."

Will thought perhaps a quarter hour passed before the men in the small boat gave up on attempting to pull the ships off the bar by pulling against the anchor that they had carried out and wedged in the stream. The men pulled their muddy fellow crewman aboard the small boat and rowed back to the *Hope*. They could soon be seen scurrying around the small brig which was heeled over quite hard. *Hinchinbrook*'s crew appeared to be attempting to wench a couple of their guns onto the quarterdeck to train them downriver at the galleys.

Hardy snorted. "Damn fools. Abandon ship! I'm going to blow you to kingdom come! Weigh anchor. Oarsmen, full speed ahead! Master gunner! Open fire!"

The galleys began anew with their rapid, bass-drum pounding of shot and cannister. The sweeps rose and fell at a rapid pace and the galleys began to close the distance. Melvin's men lined the rails behind *Washington's* sweating gunners, ready to shoot at the Royal Marines on *Hinchinbrook* and *Rebecca*.

As the galleys closed within 100 yards, a few puffs of smoke started popping out from the British ships. A musket ball whizzed past Elbert and Will, spraying small splinters as it smacked into the quarterdeck rail. A Royal Marine could be seen standing in full view, ramming a new cartridge down his musket. Elbert turned to Will and raised an eyebrow.

Will checked the prime on his .45 rifle and set the trigger. He cocked the rifle and leaned against the rail to steady himself. The Royal Marine finished loading and cocked his musket, he swung it up to aim at *Washington* when Will's .45 caliber ball hit him high in the chest, flinging him backward.

Elbert said, "I believed you when you said you shot Mowbray's hat off, but this proves it."

"Aye, but I'm not proud of it."

"Of course, you're not. But this is not a game, and they would have rejoiced had that ball hit any one of us."

As Elbert said that, Will looked across the narrow distance to *Hinchinbrook* and saw boats pulling away, loaded to the gunwales with men. He said, 'Look there! They are abandoning the fight and rowing away."

Elbert said, "By God, Sir. They've given up the fight."

Hardy shouted, "Cease fire! Cease fire!"

The silence that descended was only punctuated by the slap of oars, both those from the galleys and the small craft quickly rowing away from the disabled ships. It was just 10 of the clock and the sun had quite a way to go to reach it's mid-day zenith. The battle had taken some four and a half hours.

Although he had not done much physical activity, Will felt exhausted.

Elbert was exultant. "We must quickly board the ships and secure them."

Hardy said, "Aye, I believe we have sufficient crew and other men to sail them, but yonder brigantine will require a great deal of work to be seaworthy. The sloop is perhaps usable with some small repair."

Elbert said, "I want to go aboard and assess the ability to use them to pursue *Galatea* if she is still in the roads between Saint Simons and Jekyll."

Hardy said, "I will order a boarding party to go aboard and secure the three ships. I am concerned that there may be some enemy crew remaining aboard and they might put up a fight."

Hardy proved right on all counts. There were enemy crew still on board the ships and they had to be removed. *Hinchinbrook* was severely damaged and would require time in Sunbury or Savannah to be made useful to the Patriot cause. *Rebecca* was less damaged and once the tide floated her, and her sails were repaired, she was ready for use.

Elbert called a council of war among his commanders and the ships' captains. Will sat in the corner listening to the discussion.

Elbert said, "Gentlemen, I would propose we take *Rebecca*, arm her with some of our heavier ordnance, and challenge *Galatea*. If *Galatea* still sits in the sound near Jekyll, I believe we can take her."

Hardy said, "Do you propose to involve the galleys in that open water?"

"Aye, I believe we can force *Galatea* to fight in the shallow water up near the islands and pull in the galleys to good effect."

The other galley captains said in unison, "I doubt that will work. *Galatea* can disengage at will and simply stand out to sea if the fight goes against her. On the other hand, once we are committed, we cannot disengage so easily, especially if the water in the sound is kicking any kind of swell."

Elbert said, "Rae has passed us a message just the last hour that *Galatea* is still moored against the north end of Jekyll."

John Braddock, Captain of *Lee*, said, "Sir, we cannot hope to take the galleys across the Saint Simons Sound with crews of rented Negro rowers who are not experienced beyond simply pulling on the sweeps. Our other crew are more soldiers than sailors. We are outgunned by *Galatea* except when we face her bow-on. *Hinchinbrook* is battered to pieces. Even if we could quickly repair her, she's no match for *Galatea*."

Hardy put in, "I believe we had only provisions for the men for six days and that was five days ago. Feeding and water will quickly become critical, I fear."

Elbert replied, "I concur. That is why we must put *Hinchinbrook* into action and act today."

Hardy said, "I believe we must assess *Hinchinbrook* thoroughly before committing to a course of action challenging a British ship of the line."

Nods around the table closed the discussion for the moment.

That afternoon and the next day the experienced Navy men examined the damage to *Hinchinbrook* and *Rebecca*. The damage to *Hinchinbrook* was extensive. She would not be usable for a fight any time soon.

There were provisions on both ships that fed the crews and soldiers of the Galleys for a few days. This permitted the Georgia Navy to remain on station for three more days as they considered attacking *Galatea*.

There were papers and other useful items left behind on both ships. Elbert poured over these with great interest.

He also continued to press for ideas about how to take on *Galatea*.

Will spent a couple pleasant days hunting on Saint Simons Island. There were some deer and some turkeys. Will took a couple of each which were sent out to *Washington*. He was happy to be on dry land.

On April 23rd, Will returned to *Washington* and went to his tiny cabin shared with George Melvin.

Melvin said, "Welcome back from your trip to shoot. Haven't seen you since the battle. I saw you shoot that Marine. Damn, Sir! You're young but a crack shot!"

Will nodded. "It gives me no pleasure to shoot another man. But, as Colonel Elbert said, it's a fight and they'd happily kill any one of us without a second thought."

"Aye, tis true."

A tap on the door interrupted the conversation. It was Elbert. Will and Melvin stood.

Elbert said, "We're withdrawing back to Darien. *Galatea* abandoned many of the escaped crews to their own devices rowing those small boats back to Florida. Rae reports *Galatea* stood out to sea an hour past, so our opportunity is gone. I have ordered crews aboard the captured British ships, and they will sail them to Sunbury for repair and refitting so we may use them."

Elbert continued, "It was a great victory, Gentlemen. Everyone is to be commended. I wrote as much to General Howe after our victory. Once in Darien we shall begin preparations to march on Florida. We have the advantage here."

Will and Melvin both said, "Congratulations, Sir."

Will, suddenly drained of energy, flopped on his tiny bunk.

CHAPTER 15 – HOMEWARD

The *Washington* rowed up to the wharf in Darien, Georgia. It was Tuesday, April 20, 1778. Will Yelverton, his personal gear packed, was ready to disembark.

Colonel Elbert tapped on the door to the small cabin that Will shared with Captain George Melvin. Will looked up and grinned. Although Elbert was not especially tall, he had to stoop to keep from banging his head on the door.

Captain Melvin stood and said, "I'll just go check on my men so you gentlemen can have privacy."

Elbert said, "Thank you, Captain Melvin."

When Melvin had gone, Elbert said, "I won't try to change your mind about leaving."

Will said, "I must go to North Carolina. The last time I was gone for a length of time, some of my family had died and there were other events that needed my attention. I have not seen my family now for nine months. Who knows what the war has done with them? I have had no replies to my letters."

Elbert nodded, "There's the matter of your young lady, I think. I know that I am fortunate that I can serve our cause near my home and be able to attend to business when needs must. I assure you that were I separated from Elizabeth for a long period with no communication I would be most deeply concerned for her welfare."

Will nodded. "Aye. It's been nearly a year. For all I know, she may have sickened and died. My imagination has run rampant about such a terrible prospect."

Elbert nodded. "Aye. I do understand. I have signed a letter to Lt Colonel McIntosh directing that you be paid for your monthly service in the form of a receipt that says you now own Old Tom, the horse. There will also be coin to pay for the weapon repairs. That's 300 pieces of eight, or $37.50 in Spanish Dollars. That is what you asked for, correct?"

"Aye. Molly is doing well, and I hope she's able to travel soon. But for now, I shall leave her at Sunbury. I hope I can leave her stabled at the fort. I do have a young fellow from the tavern stable who is exercising her every day."

"Of course, Molly will be kept at the stable and well cared for by our troops as well. That's in my letter to McIntosh. If keeping Molly is what it takes to get you back here from Carolina, then so be it." Elbert grinned at his own cleverness.

Will said, "Thank you, sir. And I shall return. I wish to see North Georgia. I still hear that Wilkes County and west of there has good land for granting once the war is over. Perhaps you would support me in a quest for a land grant?"

"Indeed, that would be my honor. You have already fought for Georgia and the nation as a civilian volunteer. Are you sure I cannot entice you to the uniform? I would guarantee you a majority immediately."

"Perhaps, one day, Colonel. And that is most generous and well more than I would deserve."

"Nonsense. Your service as a courier for General Washington would make you a major on his staff as a minimum. Do consider my offer, Will. It is most sincere. You would make a fine field officer."

"Of course, I will consider your offer, Colonel. My appreciation for that is heartfelt."

They felt the *Washington* bump against the dock and then settle.

Elbert smiled, "Well, you'll be off. There is a detachment of riders leaving for Sunbury this morning. I suggest you travel with them, Lt Colonel Brown and McGirth's raiders are frequently abroad in this part of Georgia. Brown is bad enough, but McGirth is terrible in his wanton theft and destructive raiding. When you travel north toward Carolina, I also recommend you find a group of Patriots to travel with. There are Tories and other opportunists who are no more than highwaymen."

"Aye. Thank you, Colonel."

Elbert stuck out his hand, "I hope to see you soon, Will. Go with God."

Will grinned, shook Elbert's hand, and said, "I will return before summer's end."

Old Tom trotted up to the gate at the fort in Sunbury. The sentry said, "Who are you, Sir?"

"I am William Yelverton. I come from Darien to collect my personal effects and move along. May I see Lieutenant Colonel McIntosh?"

"Is he expecting you, Sir?"

"Well, considering I have just come from the Galley *Washington*, I'd say no."

"Please wait."

The sentry turned to another private and said, "Please ask Colonel McIntosh if he will see a Mr...."

"Yelverton." Will said.

The other private walked off toward the officers' barracks and McIntosh's office.

Will dismounted from Old Tom and led the horse to drink at a nearby trough. Old Tom drank greedily and then jerked his head toward a patch of grass. The smell of spring was in the air. Will noticed some scents of jasmine. Yellow pine pollen was everywhere. Splashes of wild azaleas and rhododendron painted the woods. A dogwood tree bloomed white among the scrubby oaks and pines near the fort.

As he led Old Tom to the grassy spot, Will said, "I guess you're hungry, boy?"

Will looped Old Tom's reins around a sapling and patted his neck. "We're going on quite a trip, boy." Old Tom pawed the ground and snorted. The pine pollen was making him sneeze.

Shortly, the private returned and conferred with the sentry. Their attitudes changed noticeably.

"Sir, the colonel will see you right away. I understand you know the way?"

"Yes, thank you," Will said as he ambled off toward the colonel's office.

The next morning, Will and Old Tom joined a troop of Georgia Militia that was trotting off toward Savannah. The timing was perfect as Will heeded Elbert's warning that McGirth and other highwaymen, called banditti, were about. Elbert had told Will to be comfortable in staying at Rae's Hall and provided him a letter to Elizabeth asking that she offer hospitality.

Late that day, after traveling with the troop and eating dust the whole way, Will arrived at Rae's Hall, west of Savannah. Because of the fire last month, there were no accommodations in Savannah for man nor horse. Will was glad of a roof and a bed.

Elizabeth was delighted to see him, and she had her servants clean his clothes. Elbert's stable hands groomed Old

Tom and stabled him for the few days Will would be staying. Will enjoyed a thorough wash with warm water. He had not been clean in over a month.

Elizabeth said, "Your timing is perfect, Will. I have asked some of the better citizens of our area to come to a small gathering tomorrow night. It was already planned, but now we have a wonderful opportunity for you to tell us about the wonderful victory in the river at Frederica!"

Will smiled, "I will enjoy meeting your friends, ma'am. The victory was your husband's, and I hope the telling makes that clear to all."

"I am only a few years your senior, so no more 'ma'am' ... do call me Liz. Ma'am makes me feel old. Hearing the story will be so exciting, and I'm sure you will miss no detail no matter how small it might be."

That evening, Will collapsed into the bed. He was not yet 20 years old, but the last weeks had been physically and emotionally demanding. He had killed yet another man. Unlike the Highlander at Moore's Creek Bridge, whose face was emblazoned in Will's brain, the Royal Marine who died on the fantail of *Hinchinbrook* was faceless. He was merely a Redcoat with a dark hat and a musket pointed at Will and Elbert. The Redcoat was dead, and Will did not care.

He slept soundly.

The next evening Liz threw a pleasant little party that included some of the people Will met on his earlier trip to Savannah and others who were new to him.

Will wore his best clothes. Liz Elbert's servants had cleaned them and made them as presentable as possible after their many months of being carried many miles in saddlebags. Still, his blue coat and dress shoes with silver buckles were presentable, if worn. He had a clean white shirt and a fresh white stock. Will supposed that his clothing had been acceptable in Philadelphia and would be similarly accepted here.

Will was pleased to see Dr. Noble Wymberly Jones who said, "I see you're back from the wars, Mr. Yelverton."

Will said, "Dr. Jones, please do call me Will. And yes, I have taken my leave from Colonel Elbert for a brief time to travel to my home in North Carolina."

Jones said, "Have you met my brother, Inigo? We tease him that he's named for the famous architect!"

Will utterly missed the small joke about Inigo Jones. He said, "It is my honor to meet you, Mr. Jones. Are you an architect too?"

Guffaws all around and a back slap for Will. "Very good, Sir! Ha, my brother the architect!"

Inigo Jones said, "Pay them no mind, Mr. Yelverton. They are amused by their own joke. And no, I am not an architect, though I am most honored to share a name with the famous designer of The Queen's House at Greenwich. Of course, tis not politic to be proud of things English these days."

Will affected to understand this jest and smiled knowingly.

Dr. Jones said, "Have you met my daughter, Charlotte?"

Will turned to meet a spectacularly beautiful young woman. Her flashing dark eyes were captivating. They looked out from an oval face crowned with auburn hair that escaped the edges of her linen cap. She had fine features and delicate ears that were adorned with tiny pearl drop earrings. Her skin was smooth and unlined. Will saw she was about his age.

Charlotte Jones wore a rose brocade dress over a white petticoat. It was relaxed and hung in pleats from her shoulders. Because this was an informal gathering, she wore no hoops under her dress, and the garment flowed with her movements. Will noticed all this because her movements were graceful and alluring.

Will bowed formally and said, "It is my honor to make your acquaintance, Miss Charlotte."

Charlotte said, "Tis a high honor for me, Sir, as I understand you have fought valiantly with our forces."

Will smiled and made a dismissive gesture. "Miss Charlotte, I was merely pulled into military fights that I could not avoid."

"I don't believe that. I hear you are quite brave. I also know you are quite the chameleon. On the one hand, I hear you are a gunsmith, adept with your hands, and on the other you are also associated with the highest society in Philadelphia. Which is it?" She teased.

Will teased back, "You mock me, ma'am."

"Nay, I do not mock you, Sir. I merely point out that you are unique and intriguing. I should like to know you better, Sir, so that I may judge for myself."

"I leave for North Carolina this week. Perhaps upon my return?"

"Perhaps, but I may not be available upon your return. If you wish me to know you it may be politic to move with alacrity, Sir."

Will smiled. "I shall consider that. It will speed my journey."

Just then Governor Houstoun stepped up and said, "I must steal Mr. Yelverton to tell me of the strategic situation down south."

Will said, "Miss Charlotte, I shall think upon your challenge."

Charlotte said, "Tis not a challenge, Sir. But if you think you should take up an invisible gauntlet, who am I to argue?" She tapped her fan against her right cheek as she walked away.

Houstoun dragged Will off into a corner and said, "God's teeth, man! She's but a young woman, and there are thousands of those. The war's the thing! Now tell me about the fight in the river. Did Elbert acquit himself well? I leave soon to take the Militia to join him in the conquest of Florida."

Later, Will managed to extract himself from Houstoun's grasp and circulate among the others.

James Jackson stepped up and said with a decided English accent, "Honored to meet you, Sir."

Will replied to Jackson, "Sir, the honor is all mine."

Dr. Jones interceded and said, "Mr. Jackson is one of our most leading citizens. He is a lawyer and quite a revolutionary."

Jackson said, "Would that I had been ordered to join the expedition. My unit has been directed to maintain defense of Savannah."

Will said, "We had good fortune at Frederica. There was no wind. All advantage was to the galleys since the British ships could not maneuver. Colonel Elbert was concerned that the *Galatea* might slip out of her moorings in Saint Simons Sound and move north with other ships to menace Savannah."

"Really?"

"Aye. He ordered the galley *Congress* to remain in the mouth of the Savannah to guard against an intrusion. Your units being here is of great importance, I would think. *Galatea* has stood out of Saint Simons roads and is at sea. She could

172

easily threaten Savannah. The city is fortunate to have you here, Sir."

Jackson smiled a tight smile. "Kind of you to say, Sir."

The next morning, Will came downstairs refreshed from another good night's sleep. He was storing up some rest knowing that much of his sleep in the coming days would be in his bedroll huddled against the chill of the night as he traveled north.

Will relished the smell of fresh bread baked in the Elberts' kitchen. It wafted through Rae's Hall and permeated the rooms, even up to Will's second floor room. That smell awakened him this morning and he came down hoping for some fresh cold butter and a piece of that wonderful smelling bread.

He came into the dining room and said good morning to Liz Elbert.

Liz said, "You, Sir, have made quite an impression upon our gentry in Savannah. Dr. Noble Wymberly Jones thinks highly of you. Inigo thinks you a great jokester. James Jackson, who is a firebrand, and a duelist, counts you a friend. Well done, there."

"I merely chatted with them. I admit I did not understand the joke about Mr. Inigo Jones but decided keeping my mouth shut and being thought a fool was better than opening it and proving the point."

Liz threw her head back and laughed. It was a deep, contralto sound that was at once open and unabashed and at the same time alluring. Will realized he liked this woman very much and felt she was as good a friend as her husband.

"I know you are educated and can read and write, Will. Many cannot. We have an extensive library here. When you have time, you may wish to peruse the Colonel's books and thus extend your learning."

"I would be very pleased to use the library, Liz."

Liz looked at him with a frank gaze. "Charlotte Jones is smitten."

"I beg your pardon?"

"You know very well she was flirting with you shamelessly."

"I am not experienced with the fair sex," Will admitted.

"I think you are far more experienced than you want to let on."

Will grinned. "I wish that were true."

"No, you don't. Then you would not be the kind, gentle man you are."

"A woman told me once that I was a gentleman not because of birth but because I am kind. I believed her, but she ill-used me."

"Martha?"

Will's eyes widened, "Yes, but how did you know."

"Sam told me you saw her in Sunbury. I hear she was a surprise in her pirate garb."

"Uh...well..."

"We women are more than a dress and pretty perfume, Will."

"I know that."

"I'll wager – do not be embarrassed – I'll wager some socialite in Philadelphia took you to her bed."

Will blushed scarlet. He looked around the room as if to escape. "I...well, uh...I..."

"Ha! I'm right. You can tell me. An older woman showed you a life beyond those limits you had lived within, I think."

"Uh, I mean, well...yes. Her name was Frances Montravalle. She was underappreciated wife of a British Army captain. The captain did not attend to her as he should, yet he dallied with other women all the time. She lured me in with food. I was hungry and trapped in Philadelphia after the British occupation. There was no escape from that city, and though I had money there was no food to buy. The well-to-do smuggled in food, and I am embarrassed to say I ate at their tables. Mrs. Montravalle invited me to tea, and it turned into quite a bit more than that."

"Hum, did it now?" Liz grinned, "Your secret is safe with me, Will. Now, let me tell you about women. We like physical pleasure as much as men, Will."

Will blushed scarlet, "Uh, Mrs. Montravalle demonstrated as much."

Liz smirked. "Indeed? Ha! Of course, she did! Now, we must discuss how you will woo Miss Jones."

"Liz, I must tell you that there is someone in North Carolina who occupies my heart.

"Ah?"

"Yes. Her name is Abby. She is a simple country girl who is right for me."

"Perhaps. Are you going to her now?"

"Aye. I hope she is still waiting for me. I have written to her but have had no reply. My trip to North Carolina is both to see family and to see Abby."

"Have you bedded her?"

"We have slept together, but no congress has occurred. She made clear she is willing, but I care for her and her family and would not betray them all. I would marry her first."

"God, but you are a good man, Will. You must go to North Carolina and seek her out. But know that Charlotte Jones is quite smitten and awaits you in Savannah."

176

"Aye. I am most flattered. And I will return. Molly is here."

"God! You have a bevy of women!"

Will grinned. "No, Molly is my horse."

Liz guffawed and threw a roll at him.

Will was in Elbert's library looking at the wonderful collection of books, maps, and other documents. He was bewitched with the opportunities presented by all this knowledge. He selected a Roman history book by a man named Gibbon. It was recently published, and the idea intrigued him that Rome, a great empire, could fall.

Going in search of Liz Elbert, Will hoped to borrow the book to read on his journey.

"Of course, you may borrow that book, Will. History is so fascinating. The Romans were very naughty, too."

As they were talking, Liz spotted a rider trotting up the drive to the front of the house. "I must see what this is."

They walked out front to greet the rider who handed Liz a sealed letter from Elbert.

Liz said, "Thank you, may I offer you refreshment? Does your horse need feed and water?"

"Thank you, Ma'am. I shall go 'round the back."

"Very well. Do let me know if you require anything. Will you wait for a reply?"

"Aye. I should be happy to await your reply to the Colonel."

Liz broke the seal and read quickly.

"Ah, thank God! I was worried this would be bad news."

Will raised an eyebrow.

Liz said, "Tis not bad news, but Sam is letting me know they will be stepping off for Florida shortly. The army has been encamped at Fort Howe and has moved south to the Satilla River. Fort McIntosh was at the Satilla before Brown or McGirth, one or the other, burned it and ran off the poor garrison. I think several were killed in that raid last year."

Liz looked around the entrance hall for a moment. "Sam says they await the arrival of Governor Houstoun to take charge of the Georgia Militia. He also said that General Howe has arrived and units from South Carolina are there. Several hundred men are now encamped. There is sickness, and men are dying without firing a shot."

Will said, "Aye, there were many sick at Fort Howe before we went to Darien and Frederica."

Liz nodded, "Worse, Sam says there are constant squabbles over command, and Houstoun's impending arrival will only make matters worse. I'm sure you noticed that John Houstoun is irascible, demanding, and certain of his views,

178

regardless of their accuracy. He styles himself a military man, but he has no real experience. Of course, that is galling to deal with even in the best of circumstances. Sam says he fears this expedition will meet the same fate as the previous two attempts."

Will replied, "Yes. Colonel Elbert said the first two expeditions were disasters."

Liz smirked, "Yes, they were. Sam asks after you. I think he sees you as the younger brother he didn't have. You know he was orphaned at 14? No? Yes. Very sad. I shall quickly pen a reply. Do you wish me to tell him anything?"

Will smiled. "Please tell him his wife has treated me with wonderful hospitality, and I appreciate that. I shall be leaving on the morrow, and I wish him great success and best luck with victory over the enemy. I insist he be cautious of his own person and not be killed. I will return before the fall and will bring back his book by Mr. Gibbon."

Liz said, "Very well. I shall also tell him I am scheming to see you attached to Miss Charlotte Jones."

CHAPTER 16 – THE ROAD TO CHARLESTOWN

The stable hand brought Old Tom to the tree lined, gravel driveway in front of Rae's Hall. Old Tom was already saddled for the trip. The stable hand took Will's saddlebags and bedroll and strapped them in place behind the saddle. Will carefully strapped his two rifles into place. He took extra care with Josie, pausing to run his hand over the soft deer hide scabbard that Abby had made. He dropped the ancient horse pistol into the holster bucket in front of the saddle. Will had carefully loaded the horse pistol with buck and ball. It had saved his life before.

The spring day was warm, and the sun made it hot. Will stood in the shade of the house. He had donned his well-worn hunting shirt. Where the shirt was once a light tan color, it was now near white with sun exposure and washing. His hunting breeches were clean, but mended and splotched with stains from a variety of activities over the past year. His boots were similarly worn, but serviceable. Though his clothing was worn and somewhat battered, Will still cut a dashing figure with the English Dragoon Carbine slung across his back and his Uncle Ewan's dirk dangling from his belt. Tarleton's Brander Pistol tucked in the belt completed the look.

Liz stepped out the door and stopped dead still. She said, "Mercy! I know what got Miss Charlotte's attention! Heavens!" She fanned herself. "Do you have the letter to Francis and Sarah

Yonge at Yonge's Island? They will be happy to offer you accommodation."

"Aye. And thank you for that. I also have Colonel Elbert's letter of introduction he wrote for me before I left Darien."

"Never mind. Sam and I count you as family, Will. I'm sure the Yonge's will welcome you, as well."

"Thank you, Liz. And thank you for a pleasant stay these last few days. It was a wonderful respite from all the travel and strife of the past months."

"You will, of course, come back?"

"Yes, Ma'am, I shall."

"I told you not to call me ma'am!"

Will grinned as he mounted Old Tom. "I shall give the Yonge's your regards and return in early fall."

Liz called, "Goodbye, Will," as Old Tom cantered down the drive heading toward the river.

Will and Old Tom trotted along the road beside the copper-colored Savannah River. He was headed toward the main road that led to South Carolina. There was a ferry at a spot called Rochester, so he would not have to ford the river.

As he approached the Ferry dock, a troop of South Carolina Militia was waiting to board.

Will trotted up to the lieutenant in charge and said, "I am traveling to Yonge's Island. Would you happen to be going that way?"

"Aye. Close thereto. You are?"

"My name is William Yelverton. I am a gunsmith and have lately completed a contract with the Continental Army at the fort at Sunbury. I am returning to North Carolina and would appreciate the opportunity to ride with your troop."

"How do I know you are not a British spy?"

"Perhaps this letter of introduction from Colonel Samuel Elbert would help with my bona fides?"

The lieutenant reached out his hand for the letter and Will watched as the lieutenant read. The lieutenant's lips moved as he read, and it was obvious that reading was a task for this young man. Elbert's signature attached at the bottom was perhaps more persuasive than the actual words.

The officer looked up and handed the paper back to Will. "Please join us, Sir. I request you ride alongside our other fellow traveler yonder. We go to Purysburg, on our way to Charlestown."

Will looked toward the end of the small column to see a somewhat nondescript continental officer. A middle-aged lieutenant colonel who was of intermediate height and grizzled, somewhat ragged brown hair. His uniform was well tailored and suggested a wealthy family.

Will thanked the lieutenant, whose name was Burlis, and turned Old Tom's head to walk back to the lieutenant colonel.

"Good morning, Sir. I am William Yelverton. It appears we are to be traveling companions."

"Indeed? Did the young'un leading this caper check your papers?"

"Aye. I have a letter from Colonel Elbert."

"May I?"

"Of course."

The lieutenant colonel examined the letter and paid attention to Elbert's signature. "Good enough for Sam Elbert, good enough for me. My name is Frank Marion."

Will said, "It is my honor to travel with you, Sir."

"Why are you not wearing a uniform?"

"'Tis a long story, Sir."

"'Tis a long ride."

The small detachment led by Lt Burlis dismounted and walked their horses aboard the Rochester Ferry. Will noticed that Lieutenant Colonel Marion's legs were somewhat short and appeared deformed. He walked with an odd gait, but nonetheless was vigorous and not slowed by his affliction.

Will watched the river. The current split into swift V's at each snag. A small branch floated past at a rapid pace, the few leaves still clinging to it waiving with the breeze.

Fortunately, the Ferryman was skilled, and his cable was obviously strong. The boat moved quickly across the two-hundred yards from one shore to the other. The detachment paid no fare, but Will and Marion each paid a shilling. Will thought this exorbitant, but it was preferable to fording the treacherous water.

As they departed the ferry landing the horses hooves kicked up fine dust. The surface was better than many of the roads Will had experienced on the coast of Georgia. Although there were plenty of swamps, the road was laid out on the sandy soil that was higher than surrounding wetlands. The route was circuitous, but the horses did not bog in mud.

Marion said, "This land is imminently defensible if you know how to navigate the swamps. The British tried to take Charlestown two years ago and failed. Had they succeeded, they would have found themselves bottled up by the rivers, swamps, and streams."

Will said, "Aye. I was at Moore's Creek Bridge and we heard of the fight at Sullivan's Island after the British abandoned their efforts in North Carolina. Were you there?"

"Aye, I had the honor of commanding a company at Sullivan's Island. I served under General Moultrie. We suffered a hellish bombardment, but the British could not make a dent in the palmetto logs of the fort."

Marion eyed Will sidelong, "Impressive that you were at Moore's Creek. Your youth belies your experience. I am most interested in your analysis of the fighting around Philadelphia. You were saying that Washington did what he could to keep the British out of that city?"

Will said, "Aye. But after the beating we took at Brandywine he constantly strove to place his forces between the British and Philadelphia. In the end, he was faced with the choice of protecting the army's materials and other supplies at Reading or defending the capital. The supplies were more critical, so he put the army there. Lord Howe disengaged and took Philadelphia. After being flanked at Moore's Creek and again at Brandywine, I fear our armies are vulnerable to British experience and training. Fighting them head-on may not be our best option."

Marion looked thoughtful, "How did you come to be caught up in Philadelphia?"

Will said, "I had business in Pennsylvania hoping to purchase parts for my gunshop and made the mistake of returning to Philadelphia after my visit to Lancaster and other gun making areas of Pennsylvania turned up nothing. I was considering how to safely leave the city when the Redcoats came marching along Market Street. That put an end to my escape plans for several months."

Will continued with his story of how he had been accused of spying and escaped across New Jersey. The sea battle with *Rebecca* fascinated Marion.

"Shot his hat off, did you? By God! That is a knee-slapper if I've ever heard one!"

Will cut his eyes, "Aye, truth to be told, I missed. I was trying to kill the bastard. He was intent upon taking *Beatrice* as a prize and that would impede my plans."

Marion said, "The war has impeded many a plan, young fella'."

About 15 miles after crossing the Savannah, the small detachment arrived at the American camp at Purysburg. Several hundred troops were camped at the small crossroads. One or two plantation houses were in the area, but not many other settlers were in the area. Will saw Negroes working in the fields, the brutal May sun making their skin wet with sweat. Many wore battered straw hats. Their clothing more rags than recognizable as shirts and breeches. Most had no shoes. They worked with hoes or rakes to weed the crops that Will saw were cotton.

As they passed the fields and saw the sorry state of the Negroes, Will thought that his family and the Koontz's owned Negroes, but did not neglect them in this way. He thought again about how his father, Zech, had said he would free his slaves. Will wondered if that had happened. Will realized how much he abhorred slavery.

Purysburg proved a brief stop for the travelers. Lieutenant Burlis reported to the commander while the troops, Lt Colonel Marion and Will watered their horses and ate some of the meat and watery grits at the mess tent.

New orders in hand, Lieutenant Burlis walked over to Marion and Will. "We're heading on to Charlestown. I'm ordered to go there by tomorrow. I believe the troops will be part of the defenses of the city.

Marion nodded. "Probably a good idea to reinforce Charlestown. We have been getting hints that the British are dithering about their next move. Who knows? It might be to come south."

"Aye, sir. If you and Mr. Yelverton care to continue with us, please mount up."

Some hours later, the small detachment paused at one of the many creeks cutting their path. Purysburg was behind them, so Will considered they had traveled some 20 miles since the ferry. The horses drank and drank, so did the troopers. The day had a kind of sun-lit brilliance that hurt the eyes.

The group forded the creek and went on. Will noticed that there were subtle changes in the vegetation and the soil. He spotted some rice fields off in the distance when there was a break in the foliage.

Marion said, "We're passing by Beaufort and Port Royal. There were Spaniards there over two hundred years ago. When the British moved in, they were forced out. Beaufort is quite pretty, but malarial. I wouldn't live there in the summer. Most people with means move upland in the summer to avoid the bad air in the swamps." They trotted on.

Will said, "Do you think we'll make Yonge's Island by tonight?"

Marion said, "Nay. I believe we will be forced to camp on the road tonight. I believe we will stop at Pocatalico. Tis a small Indian village near a creek of the same name. There is a bridge there, so it will be a good place to camp and then move on in the morning."

True to Marion's prediction, the small horse troop crossed the bridge at Pocatalico. Again, the troops were free but Will and Marion each paid a fare of ten cents per man and five cents per horse. The troop soon found a sheltered field to pitch a camp. Will was happy he had his bedroll with its oil cloth to keep the damp away.

Will took Josie and walked out into the woods. He walked quietly for about 100 yards and leaned against a tree. His sharp eyes ran along the ground where he saw a great many cloven pointed deer tracks heading toward a quiet spot in the Pocatalico Creek. Will waited as the sun slowly dipped toward the horizon.

Just at dusk, a six-point buck stepped out of the brush and stood, twitching its ears, testing the wind with its nose. The buck pawed the ground and looked in all directions. Satisfied that it was safe, the buck stepped another couple paces into the small clearing and turned toward the water. Its tail swished back and forth.

WizCraaaak! Josie dropped the buck in its tracks. The deer never knew what happened.

Will quickly cut the deer's throat to bleed it out and whipping Uncle Ewan's dirk down the deer's carcass opening the abdomen and dropping the guts where the deer fell. Will cautiously removed the offal, avoiding puncturing the bladder or bowels. He quickly cut the head from the animal. The remaining carcass was now easy to pick up. Southern deer were not large and after dressing out this one weighed well less than 100 pounds.

Will walked back into the camp area with the deer carcass.

"Ho!" shouted two of the troopers. "Sir, you have earned your keep!"

One of the troopers came rushing over and took the carcass. He said, "I'll skin it out, young Sir. We shall have steaks this night!"

While the troopers were skinning out the deer and portioning the meat into steaks, Will helped gather wood and build a fire. The detachment was lucky to find dry wood that would burn. Although it had been hot during the day, the evening chilled quickly, and a roaring fire provided both light and warmth. Will rejoiced that there was no rain.

The venison was exquisite. Will's quiet stalking at the water hole and not alarming the deer before it was suddenly dead meant there was no musk in the meat. It was not tough because the muscles were not tense when the animal had departed this life.

Marion said, "You are quite resourceful, Will. I want you to consider joining my regiment, the 2nd South Carolina."

Will replied, "Thank you, Colonel Marion. Colonel Elbert has offered me a majority should I join his units, but I am hesitant. My future lies on the frontier, and there are things in my life that I must attend to before I would commit to joining the Continental Army."

Marion replied, "I understand that situation. My plantation at Pond Bluff worries me when I am gone. Not only do I worry that some banditti might come and burn it but also the Negroes may leave or be enticed to violence. I treat my Negroes well. Certainly, they are better off than most. Definitely better than those poor souls we saw working that field today. But still, they are enslaved and that must rankle."

"Aye. I understand. I inherited a fine farm near New Bern. I also stand to inherit another farm and gunshop, in New Bern as well. My parents own quite a fine plantation in Halifax, North Carolina along the Roanoke River. I have but one brother, and I know not how fair my parents. My parents age, of course. My brother is feckless and dangerous. As you can imagine, there are risks I must consider."

Marion was dozing. He said, "You have much to ponder for one so young. My offer stands."

Will slept soundly despite some annoying mosquitos and a heavy dew that spattered among the trees. At first light the troop ate more venison with some of the troopers packing away roasts in their saddle bags. One trooper had procured sufficient eggs from a settler, and these were scrambled in a pan to go with the venison steaks roasted over the fire. The troop mounted at full light and set off. One of the troopers had a haunch of venison hanging from his saddle. It flounced on the sweaty horse, and Will was glad he would not be eating that meat.

Marion said, "We shall be at Yonge's by perhaps 4 pm. Just in time to enjoy a rest on Mr. Yonge's piazza."

"What is a piazza, Sir?"

"It is what we South Carolinians call a long porch. They are usually oriented to take advantage of evening breezes. Quite pleasant."

They trotted along amiably chatting about the weather and the possible hunting and fishing in the rivers, swamps, and woods along the roadside.

At eleven the troop crossed the Dawhan River which required fording at a low spot. Old Tom did well fording the stream, as did Colonel Marion's horse, Ball. But the passage was not without some drama as one of the troops was swept downstream for a quarter mile before he could get out of the water. The lieutenant captured the trooper's horse and cantered to get the unfortunate trooper.

Back on the road, the troop paused at noon at the small intersection of two roads at a place called Carnes. They built a fire and roasted more venison. One of the troopers had been detailed to carry bread and the group ate roast meat with a piece of bread and drank water.

Will made sure Old Tom had plenty of water and that he was staked in the shade where he had his own patch of grass. Old Tom pawed the ground and tossed his head.

Will patted his neck and said, "We're almost there for the day, old boy."

The noon day meal done, and the horses rested and watered, the troop remounted and trotted on. Soon, at perhaps two of the clock, Lt Colonel Marion said, "this is the road onto Yonge's Island and the Yonge's plantation lies upon it."

He and Will trotted up to Lieutenant Burlis.

Marion said, "Lieutenant, I sincerely appreciate the escort to here and wish to thank you for the pleasant trip."

Burlis replied, "It was my pleasure, Sir."

Will said, "I echo Colonel Marion's appreciation."

Burlis said, "That venison was a wonderful treat last evening and this morning. I thank you for joining us."

To Marion, Burlis snapped a salute and said, "Sir, I wish you safety and success in our present conflict."

Marion returned the courtesy of the salute and turned to head down the road to Yonge's Island. Will trotted alongside him.

CHAPTER 17 - YONGE'S ISLAND PLANTATION

Marion said, "That young man may survive this conflict. He has a good head. Saving that trooper's horse and getting him back to the troop was well done."

As they trotted along the tree-lined road Will asked, "Do you know the Yonges?"

"Aye. But I have not seen Francis Yonge nor his wife Sarah in many months. It will be good to see them. They have a comely daughter of about your age. This should prove a pleasant evening."

Marion said that Yonge's Island lies thirty miles south of Charlestown. He explained that the Yonges owned the plantation at Yonge's Island, a plantation across the Wadmalaw River, two other near-by plantations, and at least one townhouse in Charlestown. They entered a long drive hedged with a profusion of Cherokee rose. At about 4 pm, Lieutenant Colonel Francis Marion and Will walked their tired horses into the yard of the Yonge's plantation. A liveried young Negro man quickly came out to take their horses.

In the near distance Will could see the creek and causeway that separated the island from the mainland. The two-story house was built of reddish gray brick with a large center hall. The front of the house was imposing. Two windows on either side flanked the main door which was served by a landing at the top of a sweeping, semi-circular staircase rising from either side. A second-floor balcony capped the main door. Second floor windows mirrored the first floor, creating a perfect Georgian-style façade. Stretching back from the façade, the rest of the house was several rooms deep. Several chimneys indicated the house would be warm in winter. They also indicated wealth; being able to burn that much kindling was expensive. Out buildings suggested an office and library as well as dedicated workspaces and a large kitchen. Just visible to a practiced eye was a row of slave cabins stretching behind the main home. The Yonges were clearly among the most well-off of South Carolina's planters.

The Yonge's butler, a distinguished, gray-haired Negro dressed in a brocaded waistcoat, buff-colored breeches, and shoes with silver buckles, opened the front door.

"Colonel Marion! Mr. and Mrs. Yonge are here and will be most pleased to see you and your young companion. Welcome, Gentlemen." With a courtly bow, the butler beckoned Marion and Will to enter the house.

Francis Marion said, "Thank you, Earl. It is a great pleasure to see you again. I'm glad you are in good health."

"Thank you, Sir. May I say you are looking well and quite impressive in that uniform."

Marion said, "Thank you. My young companion is Mr. William Yelverton of North Carolina."

195

"Welcome to you, Sir."

Will said, "Thank you, Earl. It is my pleasure to be here."

Earl turned to go into the house. "I shall announce you both."

"Frank Marion!" shouted Francis Yonge. "As I live and breathe, I thought you had been abducted by the British and secreted on a prison ship in New York."

"Ha, Francis. Nay, I have not seen the insides of those terrible vessels, Sir. Sarah! I am so happy to see you well."

Mrs. Sarah Yonge simpered prettily and fanned herself with a beautiful, pink silk fan. "Colonel Marion, I am most delighted to see you here and safe, Sir."

Marion said, "May I present my traveling companion, Mr. William Yelverton of New Bern, and other locales, North Carolina."

"Welcome, Sir!" boomed Francis Yonge.

Mrs. Yonge smiled and said, "You are most welcome, Sir."

Will replied, "Thank you both kindly for your hospitality."

Francis Yonge boomed, "Nonsense! Come in, come in. We'll have some tea." Lowering his voice in mock-conspiracy,

"Please do not tell our patriot friends that we indulge. What brings you our way?"

Marion said, "I had a brief visit to Savannah and on my way back needed to check with business interests in Charlestown. I thought a visit to you would be perfect since we have not seen one another in several months."

To Will, "And you, Sir?"

"I am on my way to my home in North Carolina. I spent some time with the Elberts of Savannah. Mrs. Liz Elbert insisted that I visit your home and while here she asked that I deliver this letter."

Accepting the letter, Sarah Yonge said, "Oh, how kind of you to courier a letter from Liz! As with the colonel, we have not seen the Elberts in months. This war..."

"Has been terrible for us all," finished Francis Yonge. "No matter, let us sit upon the piazza and take some cool air with our tea. Or perhaps Frank you'd like a tot of something stronger?"

Marion replied, "You know I don't drink, Sir. Tea will be lovely, and I shan't tell on you for having it."

Francis said, "Well, I shall have your share of the rum, then." He called out, "Earl, would you have Lou bring us tea and a tray with rum, brandy, wine, and cups? If we have benne wafers, they would be welcome, too."

Earl replied from the other room, "Yes, Mr. Francis. Right away."

A young black girl wearing a calico dress and bare feet soon came through the door with a tea cart. On the cart was a pot of hot tea, teacups, a bowl of sugar, and a small tray with a bottle of rum, a bottle of brandy, and carafe of red wine. There was a salver with small brown sesame cookies.

Sarah said, "Thank you, Lou. We'll serve ourselves. You may go."

Lou curtsied and quickly left.

Sarah said, "We have been fortunate in that our Caribbean connections continue to provide some small pleasures like rum from St Croix and sugar to go with it."

Passing the salver, she said, "The benne wafers require brown molasses sugar, and we would be bereft without it. Please have some."

Will tasted a benne wafer and was transported. Delicious, sweet, slightly salty, and an unidentifiable taste made them spectacular. "These are very good. If I may ask, what are benne wafers?"

Sarah Yonge said, "Benne is a word we use for sesame seeds. That is the secret flavor in these tiny cookies. We get sesame seeds from sea captains who trade all around the world. Benne wafers are very much a low country South Carolina delicacy."

Will smiled, "They are wonderful. Thank you so much for introducing me to these special tiny biscuits."

Sarah asked, "How came you to know the Elberts, Mr. Yelverton?"

Will replied, "Please call me Will. Tis a long story, but it started when I threatened Colonel Elbert with a pistol in the Eagle Tavern in Sunbury."

Francis Yonge sputtered, "Did you, Sir!?"

Will replied, "Indeed. I had just arrived on a New Jersey privateer and Colonel Elbert challenged me as a possible British spy. Having run from New Jersey after being accused as a Patriot spy, I was not minded to be so accused."

"What happened?"

"I provided Colonel Elbert with my letters of introduction from Governor Caswell, and we decided to share a bottle of sack with Dr. Lyman Hall who is a planter near Sunbury."

"I know Dr. Hall. Fine man." Francis Yonge said. "How come you to know Governor Caswell?"

"His son, Dicky, is my closest friend. Although I am not of their social class, Dicky and I attended New Bern School together, and we got into mischief when we could."

Colonel Marion said, "Will is young, but I ferreted out his story. He has fought at Moore's Creek Bridge, couriered for

Washington at Brandywine, dined with the gentry in Philadelphia, privateered, and just lately fought alongside Elbert at a naval fight in the river in South Georgia. He shot the hat off John Mowbray from a heaving ship in the Atlantic."

Francis exclaimed, "Shot the hat off that bastard Mowbray? Well done, Sir!"

Sarah said, "Francis! Language, Sir."

Francis looked owl eyed. "But, my dear, Mowbray must be of questionable parentage with his privations up and down the coast."

Will said, "He won't be privateering for a while, Sir. We took his ship at Frederica. *Rebecca* will soon be a patriot ship."

"Well done! By God, that's the best news I've heard in days, Sir. Ah, here's Eliza and Mary."

Will turned to see two pretty, well-dressed young women who were almost his same age. The men all rose from their seats and bowed in greeting.

One of the young women had Sarah Yonge's coloring. Dark hair and fair skin. She said, "Colonel Marion! Why, you're looking quite dashing in that uniform."

She looked at Will with clear speculation. "And who is this gentleman?"

Francis said, "Mr. Yelverton, may I present my daughter Eliza Wilkinson and her good friend, Miss Mary Proctor."

Turning to the ladies Yonge said, "Ladies, this is Mr. William Yelverton of North Carolina."

Will said, "It is a pleasure to meet both of you lovely ladies."

Eliza said, "Why are you not in uniform, Sir?"

Will said, "I...uh..."

Marion interjected, "Mr. Yelverton has acquitted himself well in fighting for our cause Miss Eliza."

"Hrummph...I hold no respect for a young man not in uniform."

Francis said, "Eliza, you will not embarrass our guest with uninformed judgements! Not all who serve wear the uniform."

Will said, "Tis fair to ask. I was apprenticed in North Carolina to become a master gunsmith. North Carolina law holds that an apprentice may not join the militia – we call it militia jury duty – until his apprenticeship ends. Nevertheless, I volunteered to accompany the militia to Moore's Creek Bridge as their contract armorer. After that fight, I returned to my apprenticeship. Upon completion of my apprenticeship, I found the militia had been largely released to their homes, the threat from the British having greatly reduced. It was then that I traveled to Pennsylvania in search of an inventory of gun parts so that I might open a gunshop in Tennessee or North Georgia. That is how I fell into being a courier for General Washington."

Eliza said, "So, if I understand it correctly, you have been pursuing your own goals and only incidentally have served our cause."

Will smiled, "It appears that way, does it not?"

Eliza said, "Harrumph! Come Mary." She tapped her left cheek with her fan, spun and marched out of the room, head high, back straight.

Mary Proctor looked confused, gave a rueful smile, and left the room behind Eliza.

Francis Yonge stammered, "I, uh, I'm deeply sorry for Eliza's affront to you Will. I hope you are not offended."

"Not at all, Sir. Emotions run high with our current fight. And truth to be told, I have been offered a majority in the Continental Army. I have deferred that decision until I can learn the status of my properties and other interests in North Carolina. Miss Eliza is not wrong when she assumes I am pursuing my own goals over those of our new nation."

"Sir, we all have goals and business. Tis not possible to divorce our cause from our business. You are blameless, especially considering you have been engaged in combat more than many of our monied young friends who strut about in uniform squiring young ladies about town."

Will and Francis Marion climbed the stairs to their rooms.

Marion said, "Don't be injured by Miss Eliza. She is hotheaded about the war, and she is also a very young widow. She was married for only six months before her husband died. Then, her baby died shortly after it was born. Suddenly, she had no husband and no baby. She moved back here to be with her mama and daddy."

Will said, "It must be hard to be suddenly alone after having many plans. Was her husband killed in the war?"

"No, he simply sickened and died. It was fast and inexplicable. The doctors said they had no idea what the flux was that took him."

◇◇◇

Will washed in his room, happy to get the road dust off. He donned his best clothes. He was even more self-conscious of their shabby condition. He resolved to visit Charlestown on his trip north and buy some decent clothing. Perhaps Colonel Marion would know a tailor.

A gong rang, which Will took to mean supper was served. He went downstairs and waited in the entrance hall at the foot of the stairs.

Eliza and Mary swept down the stairs. Eliza looked Will up and down and said, "Oh, you're still here?"

Will smiled and bowed slightly. As she passed, Mary gave him a small smile. She mouthed "I'm sorry." They went into the dining room and supper.

The dinner was an excellent venison stew and garden vegetables cooked with a piece of smoked pork. Late season cabbage and early turnips were also on the table. Fried okra, one of Will's favorites, rounded out the meal.

Sarah Yonge said, "We are having to make do with our own produce. The war has commanded a great deal of what the farmers make."

Francis Yonge asked, "Will, when you were in Philadelphia, did they suffer for victuals?"

"Indeed, Sir. The two armies were foraging the countryside in all directions. Patriot farmers would rarely cross into Philadelphia to bring produce because it might be confiscated. Many people were reduced to eating what they might have laid by in their root cellars."

Eliza said, "You don't appear to have missed any meals, Mr. Yelverton."

"I missed my share but was fortunate to have friends among the city leaders who seemed to have a supply of foodstuffs. They were kind to invite me to their tables often."

"Humph...seems you depend a great deal upon others, Sir."

"That is true."

"Eliza! You must apologize for being so impolite to Will. He is a guest in our home."

"I will not!"

"Then you may leave us."

Will said, "Please, don't have family strife over me. Perhaps I should depart and restore the peace in your lovely home?"

Francis Yonge said, "Nonsense!" Turning to Eliza, "You falsely accuse Will of acting in his own self-interest, yet you troll the parties of anyone in Charlestown where an eligible bachelor might appear. Your only criterion being that such a bachelor must wear a uniform. That sounds quite like self-interest to me."

Eliza welled up, and tears started. "I'll be going to my room. Mary?"

She rose from the table, and the men all rose as well. Eliza swept out of the room and flounced noisily up the stairs.

Mary Proctor remained in her seat. "I'm hungry, and I think Mr. Yelverton is a most interesting person."

The room burst with laughter, and the strain was relieved. Upstairs a door slammed.

Will considered that not everyone would be his friend. After a life of Chuck Black and Isiah Koontz bullying him and Martha Black's deceit, the carping comments of a bereaved young woman would not hurt him. Still, he felt sad that his hosts were embarrassed by his presence.

During the rest of the dinner Will studied Miss Mary Proctor. He observed that she had light brown curls and wore no cap, this being an evening at home. Her dress was well made, and the cloth was nice but clearly had not come from England. It was a rose-pink color with a light gray pinstripe over a cream-colored petticoat. Again, because she was at home, she wore a relaxed dress. He had learned this type of dress was called a night gown. Her ample bodice was modestly covered with the same cream-colored material as the petticoat. The skin of her throat was flawless. Most of all, Will liked her eyes. Aside from being beautifully shaped and flashing with mirth and dark depths, they were kind. Mary Proctor had naturally pink cheeks and creamy skin. Her smile was quick and full of mirth with no artifice. Will decided Miss Mary Proctor was everything Mrs. Eliza Yonge Wilkinson was not.

After dinner the men went to the piazza and smoked clay pipes. Marion abstained, but Francis and Will enjoyed a small tot of brandy.

Lieutenant Colonel Marion said, "I hope Eliza will soon find someone. She seems sad and alone, Francis."

Yonge said, "She had such hopes and then with an unimaginable swiftness they were all dashed. Now the war has taken so many of our eligible young men to military duties and

206

she is left in an untenable situation where want and fulfillment are at odds."

Will was quiet.

"What think you, Will?"

"Sir, I don't have an opinion of Miss Eliza. Her situation will doubtless be shared by a great many young women as this war continues. I have a young lady who has made clear her interest. My fear is she will be left in Eliza's predicament should I accept her overtures. On the other hand, life must go on."

Will paused. Then said, "As to Miss Eliza's opinion of me, I can do nothing to change it. I am no coward, but I do make no bones that my future is on the frontier and the war is not foremost in my thinking."

Marion said, "Well said, Will. Francis and I both have plantations that are being crushed by the embargoes and the dislocation of everything. I must balance commerce and duty to be both a planter and a war fighter. And if you intend to make a life on the frontier, you're no coward.

CHAPTER 18 – FRANCE

ill opened his eyes. The sun was just cracking the horizon. The landscape visible from his prone position was suffused with an admixture of gray shadows and sunlit edges. It was so quiet that Will heard wind soughing in the trees from across the water.

Will stumbled across the room, fearing that he had overslept. He hastily dressed in his clean shirt and breeches which the servants had washed for him yesterday. He put on his hunting boots. Will ran a comb through his sandy blond hair and tied it back with a ribbon. He looked in the mirror and hoped his appearance was acceptable to his gentrified hosts.

Taking a deep breath, Will opened the door and stepped into the hall. He breathed a sigh of relief. He was alone. He silently walked down the stairs and stepped out onto the piazza to take a deep breath of the May morning.

Sarah Yonge was sitting on a settee drinking a cup of tea.

"Good morning, Will."

"Good morning, Mrs. Yonge."

"I trust you slept well."

Will said, "I slept so soundly. It is so quiet here, and the smell of the sea is like a sleeping tonic."

"Indeed. I have always loved this place. I must apologize for Eliza. She is terribly empty after her husband's death and the loss of her baby. But it is no excuse for her to suggest you are not a patriot. Worse, she suggested you are a coward, which I know to be false."

Will said, "Oh, I've been plenty scared, Mrs. Yonge."

"A fool is not scared, Will. A coward runs away and dies a thousand deaths. I am certain you have never run."

"Well, I did avoid a Tory cavalry patrol that was stealing my armory wagon. But I tell myself that it was more important to warn Governor Caswell, then a colonel in command of the New Bern Militia, than to attempt to foil the capture of gun parts and some beeves that were on their way to the militia at Moore's Creek."

"That was not running nor was it cowardice. It was a sound decision to avoid being captured and taking a warning to our forces. Was it dangerous to ride to Colonel Caswell?"

"Aye. There were Tories all around."

"And when you got to the Colonel was your information deemed important?"

"Uh, I suppose so. The Colonel had not known the Highlanders were on that side of the creek. So, he moved the camp across the creek and dismantled the bridge. That resulted in a complete disaster for the Highlanders."

"And did you cut and run, or did you fight?"

Will said, "Oh, I was so exhausted that I slept in place with my friends who were in the militia and in the morning, we defended a shallow crossing. I have bad dreams about killing a Highlander who rose out of the creek and was about to kill my friend. I see that man's face over and over."

Sarah smiled. "This is very simple to me, Will. You are a brave man who has done more for his country than most of the fops running around Charlestown preening in their blue coats and acting as though they can actually use the little hanger sword they wear. They are play acting at being an officer of the militia, or worse, the Continental Army. Better that you are true to your own plans for your future. Do not be put off by Eliza."

Sarah continued. "Now, please don't be embarrassed, Will, but Liz Elbert told me in her letter that you need a woman. I agree. By the way, she and Sam are most taken with you, and they say Savannah society is, too. You have also proved yourself a brave man. Liz says you have a bright future in Georgia should you want one."

Will looked out across the garden next to the piazza. He tried to think of what to say.

Sarah said, "Cat got your tongue? That's fine. I am your ally, Will. Francis thinks you are quite a man. Colonel Marion told us in confidence that he's met few young men who are impressive like you are. You have friends here. Ignore Eliza. Be kind to Mary. She is taken with you."

Will nodded and looked out toward the fields.

Sarah said, "Now, I suspect you are ravenous. You will find quite a fine array of eggs, bacon, grits, and other food in the dining room. Our grits are not watery because Francis insists they be made with milk or cream. One to one cream to grits and then water three times the amount of grits. We also don't spare the salt and pepper. Our cooks work those grits for a couple hours, adding water, sometimes chicken stock if we have it, so that they're smooth and not gluey. Also, I noticed you like fried okra. We don't usually eat that for breakfast, but I asked them to prepare some today."

"Thank you, Mrs. Yonge."

"Sarah, Will. Call me Sarah."

Will said, "Thank you, Miss Sarah. For being my friend and for your wonderful hospitality."

Will surprised himself by eating eggs, bacon, grits, two helpings of fried okra, a small venison steak that had been grilled to perfection, and a slice of toast made of wonderful yeast bread that reminded him of Becky Koontz's kitchen. Having eaten similar yeast bread at the Elbert's, Will mused that perhaps all well-to-do planters' kitchens had such bread.

True to her word, the grits were absolutely the best he had ever eaten. They were coarser grind than he was used to, but they were smooth, slightly salty, and had a wonderful creamy taste. He filed away in his mind the three water, one cream, one grits measure.

Will was resting in his chair at the table, sipping a cup of warm cider, when Colonel Marion walked in.

"You, Sir, are an early riser!"

Will grinned. "No, I did sleep heavily, but I simply could not sleep any longer. I'm so used to sleeping in uncomfortable circumstances that the bed was too good for me."

"I can tarry today but must move on tomorrow. Will you join me?"

"Aye. I must be getting along as well. I wonder if you would be kind enough to introduce me to a tailor in Charlestown? My clothing has become shabby after the many months of being dragged around on a horse."

"Of course. We shall visit Mr. James Wakefield, tomorrow. He is tailor to most gentlemen in this area. That is, if his establishment has survived the fire earlier this year."

Francis Yonge walked in. "God! I should watch out for how much brandy I drink!"

Marion chuckled, "Now you know why I do not imbibe, Sir. I recommend several eggs and some coffee."

Yonge rolled his eyes and got a plate. "How are you this morning, Will."

"Sir, I am doing quite well. I thank you for your hospitality."

"Nonsense. Call me Francis. Sarah read me parts of Liz Elbert's letter. Liz and Sam Elbert are quite large fans of yours, and Liz attested to your heroism. I apologize again for Eliza. She displayed her ignorance last night."

Will made a dismissive gesture. "Mr. Francis, I'm sincerely grateful for friends like Liz, Sam, you, and Miss Sarah. Thank you for your kindness."

Eliza and Mary came into the room.

Eliza pointedly ignored Will. "Good morning, Daddy. Good morning, Colonel Marion!"

Mary smiled at everyone, and when everyone was otherwise occupied, winked at Will. She said, "I'm thinking about going for a ride this afternoon. Mr. Yelverton, would you accompany me? I would be glad of the protection."

Eliza spun around wide eyed. "You need better protection than this coward!"

Mary said, "Eliza, we have been friends since childhood. I love you. I will not countenance you abusing Mr. Yelverton."

Eliza gaped at Mary. "You cannot be serious! I insist you take my side!"

"Sweetie, you don't have a side here. Talk with your mother about the report from Colonel and Mrs. Elbert of Georgia. Their good opinion of Mr. Yelverton is sufficient for me."

Eliza huffed and stormed out of the room.

"Well said," Francis Yonge commented. "If she keeps flouncing away from meals she will waste away from hunger."

Mary sat down with a substantial plate of food. "I'm quite famished this morning!"

In the distance, a door slammed.

At mid-morning, Francis Yonge said, "Will, I would be happy to show you some of the plantation, if you would like to join me."

"I would be delighted, Sir."

They set off at a walk, looking at a variety of gardens where Yonge was testing different varieties of plants. He was particularly proud of a tomato varietal that blushed red and purple. He was also pleased with a variety of Indian corn which he said had fuller kernels and was so sweet it could be eaten raw.

They wandered down to two rice fields where Negroes were bogging in knee-deep water tending rice shoots that were visible above the water.

Yonge said, "Were it not for rice, I fear we would be bankrupt, and people of South Carolina would be starving. Currency is now quickly inflating, and goods are in short supply. Colonel Marion said you want to buy a suit of clothes in town. I wish you good luck in finding something at a price that is not high as the heavens."

Will replied, "Aye, Sir. My one suit of good clothing has become shabby from being dragged around in my saddlebags as well as from many wearings. I feel quite a vagabond."

"You look just fine, my young friend. No one these days has stylish clothing made with European cloth. Well, almost no one. There are a few, but I think those may be smugglers or aligned with smugglers."

"Aye, I know a couple people who are smugglers and privateers, whichever is most convenient at the moment."

Yonge chuckled. "Yes, there are plenty of those."

They arrived back at the house in time for a light meal that Sarah called luncheon. Fresh bread and small pieces of meat and some salad made from lettuces grown in Francis' garden. The strange red and purple tomatoes were sliced, and Will found them delicious, despite their odd appearance.

Mary walked in wearing a lightweight frock made of gingham that was clearly designed for sport. She had a lovely bonnet in her hand She asked, "Are you ready for our ride?"

Will smiled widely and said, "Yes. Miss Mary, you know the good riding trails, so I am in your hands."

They walked down to the stable where the hands had already saddled their horses and brought them out into the little exercise yard.

Will had brought along his brander pistol tucked into his belt as well as the English Dragoon Carbine which he put in a scabbard beside his saddle. Uncle Ewan's dirk hung from his belt.

Mary said, "You look quite warlike!"

"Tis a good idea to be armed these days. Banditti are around, though I think they may not be bold enough to come to this plantation."

They mounted, Mary sitting side-saddle, and trotted out of the stable yard.

They rode at a walk down to the river and then along a path Mary knew that ran close to the water. The area was quite deserted. It was cooler near the water, with a fresh breeze that floated off the water and pushed away the mosquitos and other biting insects.

Mary told Will of her childhood, growing up on Wadmalaw Island. She pointed out the island across the river. "My parents own a large plantation there that abuts the Yonge's holding. We are not of the same wealthy class, but my parents worked hard. I have been well treated. Unlike many of my girlfriends, I was educated by a tutor. 'Tis a blessing to read and write. I can cypher, too."

Will said, "We have similar backgrounds. My parents are small planters in North Carolina. I was fortunate to be sent to live with my aunt and uncle in New Bern where they have a public school. I hated school, but I learned to read and write as well as to do arithmetic. 'Make the little "a" just so.' If you didn't

Mr. Tomlinson would whack you with his hickory stick. He walked the room tapping that stick on the floor."

Mary chuckled, "One must make one's letters with precision." She pointed. "Up ahead is a meadow that is beautiful. It will be even more beautiful if we dismount and tarry a while."

They walked their horses into a lovely meadow bordered with woods and a hedge of wild roses. Mary led them to a spot near the middle of the meadow and dismounted. The spot she had chosen was cool and pleasant in the shade of a giant live oak. She tied her horse to a small bush, and Will did the same. He finished tying the horse and turned around to see Mary sitting on a blanket. She met his eyes.

"Are you going to stand there rooted to the spot or are you going to join me?"

"I worry this is not safe."

"Nothing is safe these days. But being in the middle of this field with horses immediately to hand and you with that frog-gig and two guns makes us as safe as we can hope to be. Now come here, please."

Will took the carbine from its scabbard and laid it down next to their blanket. He put his pistol and Uncle Ewan's dirk next to it. He flopped on the blanket next to Mary.

"We will not fall in love, Will. There are too many impediments. I could love you, but this war, your home in North

Carolina, your woman in North Carolina (shush, I know about her), and my obligations with my own position here are perhaps too much. But we can take this time with each other. I know you leave tomorrow."

Will nodded. "I know things would be difficult for us. But perhaps we will meet again. Would that be bad?"

"It would be wonderful but contriving to meet may be difficult. Perhaps you might come to our plantation at Wadmalaw, but my parents would immediately assume you are courting me. Would you be courting me? No? Then, you may write to me. Would that be acceptable?"

"Yes."

Mary leaned forward and turned her face to his. Will kissed her and she kissed him back. He had been so alone for so long that his heart felt it would burst from this human contact.

Will held her close and they kissed. He ran his fingers down the side of her face. She turned her head and kissed his palm. No one had ever done that before. Not even Frances Montravalle. Will had a bursting erection and his heart hammered.

Mary said, "You are a good man, Will. I can tell you have a good heart."

Will said, "I fear the war and the killing, and the constant danger will make me unfeeling and cold. At the fight at Frederica River, I shot a man and didn't even think about it."

Mary said, "Shush...I know you have a good heart. I know you are a good man."

She kissed him and he kissed her back.

They trotted into the stable yard about an hour later. Will had picked the few strands of grass from Mary's hair and she had shaken out her calico dress. They looked the very example of probity.

Will patted Old Tom on the neck and gave him an apple. Old Tom whickered and tossed his head.

Will said to the stable hand, "I leave with Colonel Marion tomorrow. Will you curry my horse tonight and be sure he is well watered and fed?"

"Yes, sir."

Will handed the stable hand a shilling. "Please also take care of the Colonel's horse as well. We leave together."

"Yes, sir. And thank you sir."

Will walked toward the house lost in thought.

On the way back Mary had said, "You know that Eliza is smitten with you, don't you?"

"What?!"

"Oh, yes. She saw you and her knees went weak. I saw it. But she has committed herself to marrying a military man, and she is frustrated that you are not one."

"But she has made clear she detests me."

"'The lady doth protest too much, methinks.'"

"Huh?"

"You know, silly. Shakespeare."

"Ah, yes."

But he did not know.

Supper was not as strained as prior gatherings at Yonge's Plantation. Eliza was on better behavior.

The food was good and plentiful. Will ate heartily.

Mary chatted brightly with everyone while Eliza seemed thoughtful and not as vocal as before.

After supper, the men went to smoke and have brandy on the piazza while the women went to a sitting room where they chatted and did some small embroidery that they found pleasing.

As the men settled into their chairs in the waning light of the sunset, they heard hoofbeats coming rapidly up the drive.

All three men hurried to the door to see who was coming. Will thought he might need to run upstairs to get his weapons. Was this a banditti?

A rider reigned in scattering gravel as the horse struggled to stop from a full run.

The rider shouted, "The French have signed an alliance with America! The British declared war on the French in March! The Frenchies are in the war, Sir!"

Marion cried, "By God, Sir! This is momentous news! We shall certainly be free now!"

The rider shouted, "Aye. The news arrived in Charlestown by fast packet ship today. Couriers have been riding among the plantation owners spreading the news."

The rider turned his horse's head and started to trot toward the drive.

Yonge shouted, "Do you wish refreshment, Sir? Your horse?"

"Nay. I shall refresh at the next stop." Spurring his horse, he cried, "Liberty forever!"

Yonge went to tell the women of the momentous news. Will and Marion returned to their seats and clay pipes.

Will asked, "What will happen do you think?"

Marion said, "I think there will be naval engagements right away. Perhaps followed by French forces on land here. We must be aware that England will respond right away with something. I wonder if they won't again try to move against the south?"

Francis Yonge returned to his seat, "I'm not a military man, so I have limited ability to comment. I fear you may be right about a new offensive here in the south."

Will said, "Georgia is engaged in an invasion of British East Florida. Colonel Elbert is doubtful of success. He told me that General Howe cannot consolidate the command because South Carolina militia will not accept orders from the Continental Army. Worse, Governor Houstoun of Georgia insists upon commanding the Georgia Militia himself. I have had the honor of meeting Governor Houstoun and he is headstrong. Elbert fears they will bicker and lose momentum."

Marion said, "Failing at the invasion of Florida would create an open door to our south. Since its founding Georgia has existed as a buffer against Florida, first the Spanish and now the British."

The men discussed other news. The British were still in Philadelphia, but the weather had shifted into spring, and they speculated about when the armies would clash again.

Will said, "There was to be a grand celebration in Philadelphia of Lord Howe's departure. They called it the Meschianza, which I understand is Italian for 'big party.' A Major Andre' was planning it. He hired me to repair a broken French dueling pistol, and while at his lodgings – in Benjamin Franklin's house, by the way – I was accused of spying by a man named Major Banastre Tarleton. That's when I ran."

Marion swore, "God's teeth! But the British are an uncontrolled rabble. We starve, the people of Philadelphia starve, and they throw an extravagant party. Their officers instigate false charges and hang our people indiscriminately. Washington can do little because the British outnumber us and have all the resources needed to maneuver. Thank God the French are in this now!"

Francis said, "Aye, would that we could solve the war tonight. But tis late, and I am old. I shall retire."

Marion said, "We have a ride before us tomorrow, so I will retire as well."

Will rose and said good night and went to his room. He took off his clothes, washed, and flopped on the bed.

Mary had kissed him. France had entered the war. And, inexplicably, Eliza was smitten with him.

And who, or what, was Shakespeare?

CHAPTER 19 – CHARLESTOWN

Will sat on his bed and glanced over his personal effects. He had mostly arranged them to pack and leave early. It was some thirty miles into Charlestown. Will did not relish another day in the saddle, but each tiring day moved him closer to North Carolina and home.

Will thought about his afternoon dallying with Mary in the meadow. He lay back in the soft bed and allowed the day's events to play through his mind. He became burstingly erect. He closed his eyes, and the women came to visit in his mind. Frances, Mary, Charlotte Jones, Abby.

Images played in his mind, and his breath grew hoarse. Soon he could no longer resist the sin of Onan.

The morning dawned bright and clear. Will awakened and stretched and noticed his loins ached. It was a pleasant ache. Toward the culmination of last night's tussle with Onan, Abby had loomed large in his mind. He remembered her scent and the warmth of her closeness in his bed. Onan had emptied his loins and reduced his burning ardor.

He felt a little sad.

Was he sad because he was leaving Mary? Sad because he was emotionally committed to Abby, but had dallied with Mary? Was he still a moral man? Had he ever had morals?

Will knew he was sad because he had learned of his own ignorance. The book about Rome had both opened his eyes and shamed him with his lack of knowledge. He was resolved to read and learn. This thing called Shakespeare was atop his list of things to inquire about. Will reflected that he would have time to consider these questions during his ride.

He rose and washed. He looked at himself in the mirror. Having a mirror was a wonderful luxury.

Will looked to see if he had become the Devil.

After a wonderful breakfast of eggs, fried fish, and those wonderful, creamy grits, Will and Colonel Marion came out to the front and found their personal gear had been strapped in place on their horses. All that remined for Will to do was to put his horse pistol in Old Tom's holster and put his rifles in their scabbards.

Will wore his customary hunting shirt over a linen shirt. He had on his breeches, scarred with patches and repairs. His belt held Uncle Ewan's dirk and Tarleton's Brander pistol. Along with his powder horn and shot pouch, the English Dragoon Carbine was slung across his shoulders.

They were ready to leave for Charlestown.

The Yonges came out to bid them farewell. Mary came too. She was lovely in a kerchief and light blue summer dress that fell from her shoulders to her ankles. Will's heart twisted. Had he fallen in love with this fine young woman?

Eliza stepped out the door. She was more dressed up than Mary. She surprised everyone by walking straight up to Will and saying, "Mama told me of your exploits. I owe you an apology. You are most certainly not a coward. I wish very much you would wear the uniform and be formally a member of our army, but I understand your plans. I wish you success, and I hope you will forgive me for being so rude."

"No apology is necessary, Miss Eliza. You are entitled to your opinion."

"Not when it is wrong. Farewell and bon chance. And now I shall return to the house before my embarrassment at being a fool makes me bawl." She swept away and quickly up the stairs and inside.

Francis and Sarah smiled. "I'm so glad she came to her senses," Sarah said.

Francis said, "I'm not one for long goodbyes. I wish success and victory to both of you. Please do keep in touch. Our door is always open."

Mary said to Francis Marion, "Please continue to defend us, Sir. I believe you will be a great hero for us all."

Marion blushed and said, "Thank you. I shall endeavor to keep the British at bay."

Mary turned to Will. "Thank you for escorting me yesterday. It was an absolutely wonderful afternoon. She took his hand and boldly kissed his cheek before turning and quickly following Eliza back into the house."

Sarah smiled at Will. She quietly said, "I can help with that, if you wish. Do come back, Will."

Will smiled back and mounted Old Tom.

Marion said, "Come on, Son. We have thirty miles to go and 'twill be hot as the day goes on."

Will said, "Goodbye Miss Sarah, and thank you for the hospitality. I hope to see you all again."

He turned Old Tom's head and followed Marion who was already trotting down the drive. Before he reached Colonel Marion, Will pocketed the small square of paper Mary had discretely handed him. He knew without looking that it was an address where he could send a letter.

Will felt good she had kept her word, but it also caused him concern. Mary burned hot in his brain. But what of Abby? In the back of his mind was also Charlotte Jones in Savannah. And Eliza? Perhaps it was true that Eliza actually liked him and had hidden it behind scorn.

He smiled. Several remarkable women were noticing him. He remembered a phrase Miss Becky Koontz often said, "When it rains, it pours." Now he knew what that meant.

Will and Lieutenant Colonel Francis Marion trotted along the road toward Charlestown. The horses' hooves kicked up little tornadoes of dust along the well-traveled path. Insects sang in the grass. A hawk circled lazily looking for prey. There was little wind, and the sweat popped, bathing Will's face and trickling down his backbone.

Marion said, "I have considered the British coming up from Florida. It seems a certainty. Especially if General Howe cannot suppress them with this invasion. I understand Tom Brown raids constantly in Georgia. He is a South Carolinian, you know. From up around 96 area. That's across the Savannah River from Augusta. There are other banditti around making life miserable, especially in the back country. That dog McGirth is also a South Carolinian, I'm sad to say. He's even worse with his army of low-lifes who would steal from their own mother."

Marion continued, "If the British are allowed to move about freely in Georgia, they will be emboldened to take Savannah. Charlestown will follow suit and 'twill be a difficult time dislodging the British."

Will said, "Let us hope General Howe is successful, then."

"Aye, hope is one thing. Action is another. It has been a problem for patriot forces from the beginning as to who will command and who will follow. I fear hope will not remedy poor leadership. If we lose Charlestown, then our army will be difficult to manage. I have plans to go to the swamps and strike at the British like a thousand deer fly bites. I'd welcome your assistance, Will."

They were silent for a while. The day buzzed with insects, and a light breeze finally sprang up, drying the sweat and providing a slight cooling feeling. Somewhere a bird sang a symphony of trills and tweets.

Will asked, "Colonel, do you know of Shakespeare?"

"A little. Why do you ask?"

"I am uneducated and sometimes feel a fool in genteel company."

"I'm not so educated myself. You are certainly not a fool, and education can be had from books, Sir. Being educated is not a matter of class, though well-to-do people often can afford a tutor or school for their children. The well-off also have books. Those not so privileged must get the education for themselves."

"Indeed, but where shall I find books? I have borrowed a most enlightening book about the Roman Empire from Colonel Elbert. But is Shakespeare in a book?"

"Oh, aye," Marion smiled. "Shakespeare is in a book. We shall try to find it in Charlestown. I know a bookseller."

"And what is it about?"

"Shakespeare is a playwright, my boy. He wrote plays some two-hundred years ago. There are books that hold his collected works. Although his plays were written a long time ago, they still have meaning. His sonnets – a kind of poem – are also captivating."

"I have never been to a play. The British put on plays in Philadelphia, but I thought it silly."

Marion said, "Not really my cup of tea, either. Plays are rare these days. But they can be quite entertaining. They tell stories about the lives of others. A well-done play can put you in the mind of the person on the stage. We shall find a book of Shakespeare."

Soon, the heavy woods of Yonge's Island and its surroundings gave way to marshes similar to the ones in Georgia. More brown, less lush, and not as large. The breeze picked up once they cleared the woods. Will noticed that there was an exchange of miseries and pleasures when they exited the forest. Less shade, more breeze. The day was still miserably hot, and the sweat trickled. The tide was out, and oyster beds were visible in the creeks. There was a strong odor of oysters, mud, and dry marsh grass. A heron walked stalkily in the shallows, it's needle-pointed beak poised to skewer an unwary fish. A flight of five pelicans silently glided by, each bird exactly in position slightly behind and to the side of the lead bird.

Will dozed slightly in the heat.

Trotting into Charlestown, Will was saddened to see many structures burned, and the cloying, heavy smell of wood smoke stuck in the back of his throat. Marion explained that there had been a terrible fire in January. Some people believed the fire was not accidental. Will wryly thought this similar to Savannah's 'accidental' fire. The timing was a little too coincidental for Will's taste.

The travelers were lucky to find rooms in McCrady's Tavern on Bay Street. It was fortunate that McCrady's still stood. Perhaps the building survived because it was brick and many others that burned were timber. Now the frame buildings were charred sticks, while McCrady's remained a robust building.

Edward McCrady himself greeted Marion and Will. "Good day, gentlemen. Colonel Marion! Welcome to my fine establishment. And you, young Sir. Welcome as well. I shall have your horses stabled and curried. Your baggage will be delivered to your rooms. Will you want to dine tonight? Yes? Very well. Supper is at 6 of the clock. Tonight, we have beef stew and fresh caught snapper fish that is very good."

Marion and Ed McCrady chatted amiably. McCrady was a militia captain in Charlestown and had ridden with Marion in past days when there was Indian trouble. They were comrades. They speculated about France's entry into the war and shared a hope that the French would help win freedom for the States.

Marion said, "Let us see if my tailor, Mr. James Wakefield, has any clothing that will suffice for you. In the past he has been able to procure Irish shirting, sheeting linen, muslin, and cambric. Perhaps his establishment survived the fire, and he has materials."

They walked three blocks past burned buildings and empty lots and turned inland to find Wakefield's establishment had been spared in the fire. Mr. Wakefield was thrilled to see Colonel Marion. Will smiled when he realized that most people knew Francis Marion.

A small man, Wakefield reminded Will of a bird. Wakefield fluttered around Will with a tape measure and pencil, jotting down measurements and humming a tune.

Wakefield said, "We do not have much in the way of European cloth, I'm sad to say. But, locally made fabric is useful and can make a good substitute. It is not as fine to the hand, but it is the best we can find. With the war, many are wearing black and not as much in the way of ruffles and buckles."

Will said, "I'm not much for ruffles anyway. Black will do nicely. My old blue suit is shabby. But I am traveling to North Carolina. When can a suit with a spare pair of breeches be ready?"

"When do you leave?"

"I hope to depart the day after tomorrow."

"I shall have the entire suit and breeches complete for you by noon that day, Sir."

"Very well. Do you also have hunting breeches such as the ones I am wearing? I would like to have two of those if you do. I need three linen shirts, as well as a dress shirt to wear with the formal suit. Also, my stockings are in terrible condition."

"I shall have everything for you, Sir."

"Very well. And the bill?"

"Ah, well things are not as fairly priced these days. The total bill for all this will be £10. Unfairly high, I know, but goods are near impossible to get."

Will said, "Ten pounds is acceptable for all this. Tis not like I buy new clothing every day."

Marion asked, "Mr. Wakefield, do you know if Mr. Robert Wells' bookstore survived the fire?"

"Aye. We're fortunate that his store was not burned. Had it caught fire there would have been much destruction since the store is packed with paper, print, books, and the like."

"Thank you, we shall visit Mr. Wells."

"Do give him my regards, Sir. And Mr. Yelverton, I shall see you in two days."

At dinner Will asked Marion, "Do you suppose I can get a ship from here to New Bern? The prospect of riding 250 miles is not pleasant. I don't like the idea of sleeping in the woods for several nights, either."

"Let's visit the wharves. I know the harbor master."

The harbor master said there was a schooner leaving in three days for New Bern. He was not sure if the schooner would take Old Tom.

Will and Francis Marion walked down to the dock where the schooner was moored.

"Ho, the ship!" Will called.

"Who calls?"

Will called, "I seek passage to New Bern."

The master of the ship called, "Come aboard and talk."

The next morning, Will sat in the dining room of McCrady's eating porridge and a slice of sausage. He had tossed and turned the night before, his head filled with images of Mary Proctor, Abby handing him the scabbard for Josie, his rifle, Martha in a pirate costume her breasts swaying uninhibited under her linen shirt, and auburn-haired Charlotte Jones dressed in finery and mocking him.

Lieutenant Colonel Francis Marion walked in on his damaged legs and plopped into the chair opposite Will. "Today

I have business with some shippers for my crops. But we shall make time to visit Mr. Robert Wells, bookseller."

Will smiled. "You are too kind to me, Colonel."

"Nonsense. I want you to regard me in a positive light so that one day you might join me in fighting these accursed British."

"Perhaps I will, Sir."

They walked out the front of McCrady's and turned south on Bay Street. Walking along, Will noticed it was already quite warm. The day would be hot, a good day to do little but sit on a Charlestown piazza drinking cool water and perhaps reading a book. Reading was his new pastime. Will smiled. He had never had a pastime.

They crossed Broad Street and Will noticed the homes became even more opulent. There was money in Charlestown. Many homes had long piazza's enclosed in walled gardens, the house stretching back the depth of the lot, but narrow on the street end.

They turned right and walked west on Tradd Street three more blocks to Meeting. There, they found the bookseller Mr. Wakefield had accurately said survived the fire.

"Good mornin' Gentlemen," said a small, grizzled man with a Scots accent. His waistcoat was grubby where he had rubbed ink-stained hands. "Wha' brings ye to ma' wee establishment this fine day? Is that Colonel Marion, Sir? Yer mos' welcome in ma' wee store."

Marion said, "Hello, Mr. Wells. I bring a new client for you. Mr. Yelverton of North Carolina seeks a volume of the works of Shakespeare."

"Aye! Do ye' now? D'ye no' want to read a real poet like Rabbie Burns? I have a small pamphlet o' his works. He's a budding Scots poet who makes Will Shakespeare seem a mere scribbler. This wee pamphlet is among the first of young Rabbie's writin'. I'm certain you'll like it."

Marion laughed. "Ah, Mr. Wells. You're a true Scotsman through and through. Perhaps you could interest us both in Mr. Burns poetry, but only if we may first see the works of the Bard."

Wells shook his head and muttered, "Aye, well, come this way, if ya' must."

Wells led Marion and Will down a corridor formed by floor-to-ceiling bookshelves of dark wood filled with a profusion of books. Will noticed a musty, old paper smell. It was fortunate that this place had not fallen victim to the fire. A spark would turn the entire building into a roaring inferno, and all this wonderment of words and ideas would be ash.

"Here we are, Gentlemen. I ha' several books of Shakespeare. But the best ones are either the one by Pope in three volumes or the one by Theobald in seven volumes. Are ye travelin', Sir?"

Will said, "Aye. These days my life is on the road."

"Then I recommend the Pope. Three books being more manageable than seven."

Will said, "Then I shall accept your recommendation, Sir. And I shall accept your recommendation of the poetry of Mr. Burns. I am hungry for learning, Sir."

"I like ye, young man. Yer discernin', and ye'll not be disappointed in either of the books."

That afternoon while Lieutenant Colonel Marion was off handling his business interests, Will sat on the porch at McCrady's and leafed through his new books. The first books he had ever owned. Books inadvertently recommended to him by Mary Proctor. He searched for the phrase she had said about the lady protesting too much.

He finally found the words and discovered they were in a play called, "Hamlet." He read the play. His reading was slow, and he worked hard to understand. It seemed to be in pieces called Acts. Soon, he found he could see the people in his mind. He learned Hamlet was a story about a royal family. It was a tale of betrayal and murder. He wondered if King George's family was a group of similar plotters and murderers?

Now he understood what Mary meant when she said Eliza protested too much. It seemed that denying a thing so strongly most likely meant it was true. Later, he pondered what Hamlet meant when he said, "To be or not to be…" Will thought maybe Hamlet was thinking about suicide, but he was not sure. Was Hamlet's life so bad he wanted to end it himself? It seemed to Will that life was too short already.

Will thought about all the hard times. He had been taken from his family at age six. Lived with his Aunt Pat and Uncle Ewan, who he knew loved him. Yet, they sent him to live with the Koontz's as Mr. Bert's apprentice. He had known hurt and heartache. His brother, Benjamin, wanted him dead and had tried to kill him. Yet Will always wanted to live. He wanted to be happy and to let nothing deter him from a life on the frontier. A life he knew would be good.

Will pulled out the little pamphlet of Robert Burns' poetry. He admitted to himself that he knew nothing about poetry. The only poetry he had ever heard were dirty limericks that usually started with, "There was a young lady..." Yet a poem by Burns called "O once I loved a bonnie lass," caused Will's chest to feel heavy. The poem seemed to be the thoughts of a young man who had loved a young woman and now loved another.

Will wondered if this was what it meant to be educated. Was being educated the state of being constantly confused and wondering about things? Was being educated a state of being challenged and reading the thoughts of others as though they were your own? Was Abby the bonnie lass of Burns' poem, and was Mary the same as Nell, the new love?

Will wished he could ask someone who knew about these things. Someone who was a real teacher, not Mr. Tomlinson with his hickory stick that he tapped with each step. "Write the letters." Tap, tap. "Add these numbers." Tap, tap. It was never, "Do these words excite you? Do they take you to another place? Another world? Another time?" Tap, tap.

Will thought, "Ah, God! Why did I start reading? Life was easier when I was ignorant."

Two days later, Will, his new clothes carefully packed in a new leather bag designed to hold his clothing without damage, shook hands with Lieutenant Colonel Francis Marion.

"It has been a pleasure, Will. I hope to see you again. I know Elbert has offered you a commission as a major. I'm not sure if I can match that, but I fear we're going to see the British come south. We need good men like you."

Will said, "Kind of you to say, Colonel. And I will come back this way soon. I wish there were no war, and we could all pass pleasant times like the days at Yonge's Island."

Marion said, "Alas, twill be some years before we can have carefree days. Farewell. I hope the sea voyage is pleasant and safe."

Will said, "Best of luck to you, Sir. It has been my honor to travel with you."

Will led Old Tom up to the Schooner Athena. It's Master, Gus Panagiotis, was a Greek immigrant to North Carolina. The trip to New Bern was returning home for the Athena. Will paid $10 for his fare and $5 for Old Tom plus $1 for food for Old Tom. The trip was planned for three days.

Loading Old Tom was easier than when Molly had been put aboard *Beatrice*. There was a wide gangplank which would hold the horse and a ramp into the hold where Old Tom would be stabled. Will was afforded a small cabin and was told he was welcome to eat with the crew. Soon, Athena was past the bar and standing out into the Atlantic.

Master Panagiotis said, "We will hug the coast and put on all sail to try to avoid being waylaid by the British. For that matter, an American privateer would try to take us. We have only the two four-pound guns mounted and these two swivels, so our defense is speed. And we have that in good measure. Only another fast hull schooner can hope to catch us in a tail-chase. Our vulnerability is being intercepted."

On the morning of the second day at sea, a sail was visible on the horizon, but the ship carrying it was hull down on the horizon and never got any closer. Late the second day another sail was visible in the far distance. The ship that carried that sail was apparently on a southerly heading. Panagiotis watched that sail intently because a sudden tack to the west would have puts ship on an interception course for Athena, and running would have required reversing course to the south. Will and the rest of the crew held their breath waiting until the ship passed without incident.

Athena was not a bad ride as sailing ships go. She was as fast as Panagiotis had claimed and she seemed to barely touch the wave tops as she fairly flew across the water. On the third day Athena turned to a northwesterly heading south of Ocracoke and stood into the Pamlico Sound. Soon, the Sound gave way to the mouth of the Neuse River. Will had spent time as a child on the Neuse, but never this far down. His memory of the Neuse was a wide river, but not like this. Here, the river was a vast expanse of water that seemed like an ocean.

Will shook with excitement at soon arriving in New Bern. He hoped the Koontz's were well. How were Mama and Daddy in Halifax? Soon he would see Abby. Was she well? Did she still care? Did he still care?

It seemed forever since he had been home

Part II: Up Country

CHAPTER 20 – NEW BERN

Will and Old Tom trotted into the Koontz's yard. As Will approached the property his eyes swept over the family graveyard over to the edge of the land. There were no new headstones. He breathed a sigh of relief. He knew the freshest one belonged to Isiah. In the past year, even that marker had gathered dark mildew, attesting that the death was not recent.

Isiah. The disturbed young man who hated him. Son of Bert and Becky Koontz. Sad, ineffectual, nasty, mean Isiah. Isiah who had been intent on killing Will but who had been so crazed with murderous intent that he lost control of the musket he held and blew his own brains out with it. Poor, murderous Isiah. He accidentally killed himself in front of Bert who was awakened by the commotion in the barn and came to see what the racket was.

Becky Koontz, an inquiring look on her face, opened the side door of the small house. She saw Will and shrieked. "Bert! Bert! Come quick! It's Will! Will has come home!"

Will dismounted as Becky got to him and threw her arms around him. "Oh, thank God. Thank God you're home. Oh...my little boy. You look so good."

"Hello, Miss Becky. I'm so glad to see you!"

Bert walked around the side of the house. "Becky? Becky? What's the matter? Oh, my God! Look who's here!" Bert quickly crossed the yard and hugged Will.

Bert called, "Prince? Prince? Come take Will's horse." A concerned look spread over Bert's face. To Will, "Where's Molly."

Will said, "She's fine. I had to leave her in Georgia, but I will go back and get her."

"Georgia? What in the world?"

"Did you not get my letters?"

"No, Son. We've not had a letter from you in maybe six months."

"Oh, I'm so sorry. I wrote, but the mail must be not going because of the war."

"Aye. Well, you're here now. Let's go in."

Prince came around the corner of the barn and said, "Mr. Will. Welcome home. Is this your horse?"

"Hello Prince. It's nice to see you. You are looking good. Yes, Old Tom is my horse. Don't worry about Molly. She's fine. I just had to leave her in the care of good people in Georgia. I will go back and get her."

"Georgia? My, my."

Prince took Old Tom to the stable, and Will and the Koontzes went to the house.

Bert said, "I have some brandy. This calls for a taste."

Becky smiled, "I have a pot roast and potatoes. It will have to be our feast of homecoming."

They sat at the table. Bert poured three cups of brandy.

"Now, tell us everything."

Will said, "Tis a long story..."

Later, Becky said, "Oh, my, what a story. You were with Washington. What is he like?"

"As you might imagine. He's tall and imposing. He is commanding and yet friendly. He was kind to me."

Bert said, "It sounds like you've been rubbing elbows with the gentry, Will."

Will grinned, "Ha, they're just like everyone else, only rich."

Will relished Miss Becky's cooking for the first time in over a year. They talked for hours, well into the night.

Bert's business was doing well. He was tiring and his vision made working on small parts harder. But he managed. He had decided not to take on another apprentice. Miss Becky said she was feeling well, but Will could see she was slowing down.

Finally, all talked out, the three of them went to bed.

Miss Becky said, "This is your room, now, Will."

She pointed to Isiah's room. "We took out poor Isiah's things and made it up for you."

Will said, "I know it must have been hard for you."

Miss Becky welled up with tears. "I am so sad he died. But he was so ... afflicted. It is almost a blessing. He is at peace. And so are we. You are our only son now, Will."

Will hugged her and stroked her hair.

That night Will slept in a real bed at the Koontz's home for the first time. He was sad for their loss of Isiah, but Isiah had tried to kill him with great intensity, and he was not sorry Isiah was dead. Will fell asleep almost instantly.

The sun broke the horizon and peaked through Will's window. Will cracked an eye open and watched motes of dust dance in a shaft of sunlight that hit the opposite wall. For the first time in some months, he was not in a rush to get out of bed.

Will helped Bert in the gunshop for most of the morning. Then, he saddled Old Tom and trotted out and down to Aunt Patience and Uncle Ewan's farm. He visited their graves and told them how much he missed them. Wiping his eyes, he looked over the property.

A man came out of the barn and walked over to the small graveyard. "You'll be Mr. Yelverton, then?"

"Aye. Call me Will. You're Mr. Burdell?"

"Aye, call me George. It's an honor to meet you."

Will replied, "The honor is all mine. Looks like you're doing a good job of keeping up the place. Crops doing well?"

"Aye. And I do some fishing. My wife, Adele, takes in some washing and tends the livestock."

Burdell looked at Will appraisingly, "Would you be willing to sell?"

"Don't know. I suppose so. The war has made things iffy all around. Perhaps we could arrange something. I love the place, but what am I to do with it?"

"Aye. Tis a fine piece of land."

Will said, "Let me know what you propose, Sir."

"I shall speak to Mr. Ambrose, the lawyer who collects the rent. Would that be satisfactory?"

"Aye. I will be heading to Halifax in just a couple days, but I will be back this way in a few weeks."

"Very well. Until then, thank you for allowing us to rent your property."

"Thank you as well."

Will stopped at Cogdell's Tavern and ate a bowl of stew. He did not want to add much fuss to Miss Becky's life. Then he rode around to Caswells' townhouse.

He tied Old Tom to the hitching post and knocked on the door.

Moses, the butler, opened the door and registered shock and surprise.

"My goodness, Mr. Will. Get in here! The governor is at Tryon Palace, but Mr. Dicky is at home. He'll be as happy to see you as I am."

"You look good, Moses. Not a day older, I'll own."

"Ha, now you teasin' me. Please have a seat in the parlor and I'll go get Mr. Dicky."

Dicky Caswell burst into the room. "Will! Ha, ha! When did you get in?"

Will said, "I got in late yesterday and made it to the Koontz's for dinner. I'm pleased to see they're doing well. You're looking good, as well. Still in the militia?"

"Aye. I'm a major now. Don't know if I'll command the regiment. Daddy doesn't want to be seen as playing favorites."

"I understand that. But you're quite competent."

"Maybe. We have not been tested in a fight since Moore's Creek, thank God."

Will said, "I rode out to the MacNeill's farm and that looks good. The tenant, Mr. George Burdell, offered to buy the place. Perhaps we can get together on something."

"Do you want to sell the home place?"

"I know not what to do with it. I don't want to become a farmer."

"Aye. Farming has never been in your blood, Will. Speaking of what you'll be doing, will you go see Abby?"

"Yes, that's among the reasons for my trip to North Carolina. What have you been doing other than the militia?"

"We have invested in a couple ships. People are getting out of the shipping business because things are dangerous on the seas. I have made a couple runs to Charlestown and down to the Caribbean. Tis somewhat scary when you see a sail in the distance, but there is huge profit to be made. So long as the war is not in North Carolina, I think I shall be plying the sea lanes."

"Aye, I've been on a couple ships and can attest to the dangers."

"Have you, now? Tell me about your travels."

Will said, "How about we go see the Governor, and I'll tell you both at the same time?"

"I'll get my hat."

Will and Dicky walked to Tryon Palace. It was about a half-mile walk, but the weather was fine and not too hot. Will was wearing his new suit and, though it was black, it was not uncomfortable.

They walked into the palace. They were met by one of Governor Caswell's aides who said, "Ah, Mr. Caswell. The governor is available. I'll show you in."

Governor Richard Caswell was sitting at his desk writing a letter when the two young men walked in.

Caswell glanced up, smiled, and said, "Good morning, Dicky." Recognition dawned and he lit up. "Will! I'm so glad to see you! Come in, come in. Sit down. Refreshment?"

Caswell looked at the aide. "Please have some small beer brought for the three of us."

"Right away, Your Excellency."

Caswell said, "Will, again, I am so delighted to see you. Now tell us everything."

Dicky laughed, "Yes, do tell. The bugger refused to tell me the story until we were all together."

Will said, "I shall start with the trip to Philadelphia. My father manumitted Jack, the slave I grew up with, and Jack went with me. We rode north and slept rough several nights. One night we were accosted by slavers who claimed Jack was a runaway. They had an advertisement for him in the Pennsylvania Gazette. It seems my brother, Benjamin, had spitefully set the slavers on us to punish my father for not giving him more property. He felt the slaves should belong to him and not be set free. Father felt otherwise and that brought conflict."

"How upsetting."

"Indeed. But conflict with Benjamin is not anything new. I came here to live because he tried to drown me when I was but six years old."

"Yes, your father had told me that tale in confidence."

"We convinced the slavers that the advertisement was false, and they left, but it put us on notice that we were in danger. We pushed the horses hard, I fear, the rest of the way to Philadelphia."

"What a story that is, but I think there must be more."

"Oh, quite a bit. When I got to Philadelphia, I was lucky to be well received. The letters you provided to Dr. Franklin and General Washington were most helpful. In fact, the letters you wrote for me have saved me several times."

"But Dr. Franklin was in Paris by the time you got there, no?"

"Yes, but his daughter, Mrs. Sarah Brache, called Sally, was in residence and she was very gracious. She invited me to dine at the home of Mr. and Mrs. Samuel Powel where everyone treated me with great kindness."

"Tell me about General Washington."

"Well, sir, therein lies a tale..."

An hour later, Caswell said, "My God, but you have had an adventure. Couriered for Washington, threatened with hanging by the British, privateering, a river battle with the

British Navy. We should be drinking something more powerful than small beer!"

"Speaking of drinking, I spent the evening over a bottle of sack with Colonel Samuel Elbert of Georgia. He has been kind to me. We fought together aboard the galley *Washington* in the Frederica River. He has offered me a majority in the Continental Army, and he sends his regards as a brother Mason."

"Sam Elbert is a good man, and you may count upon him. I shall write him a letter if you are returning to Georgia?"

"I will certainly deliver it. Colonel Elbert and his wife, Liz, have taken me into their home on several occasions."

"You did not take the majority? That is quite an honor, Will."

"Aye. I am considering it. I still hold to my dream of the frontier, but it gets farther away every day. The British are laying waste to South Georgia with raids and rustling, burning plantations, indiscriminate killings. Colonel Elbert is on an expedition right now to invade East Florida. He has concerns about the various units and lack of a single commander. General Howe has tried to unify the command, but he is defeated at every turn."

Caswell said, "Aye. I know Bob Howe. He's not the finest commander we could have, but if he had complete control of an army maybe he could beat the British in Florida. I have not been there, and I imagine it is hot and malarial."

Will's face grew serious, "It is that. Men were dropping from sickness well before they could begin the march. Elbert sent me on my way here because he thought the expedition would become a fiasco. He said I'd be wasting my time, and I'm not in the military."

Caswell said, "Aye. Tis unnerving to go marching off to war with no confidence in the command."

Will said, "The funniest thing about the entire year is that I was most scared when we were accosted by the slavers. A night attack by British raiders on a riverbank in Georgia was nothing compared to the toothless redheaded man with a musket who was intent upon killing me and taking Jack."

"Aye. Scum of the earth, slavers. Something must be done, but I fear we won't see the end of slavery in our lifetimes. Too many monied people depend upon slave labor, both on the plantations and then in the mills and factories."

"There are slaves in factories?"

"Not many. But is not a New England cotton mill owner not an indirect slaver? Are not the British cotton, indigo, and rice merchants slavers? Tis imbedded and a terrible scourge. Yet, I must own slaves or go bankrupt. I know not what to do."

"Aye, my father owns slaves still, though he has pledged to set them free. Nevertheless, he will use rented slaves to bring

253

in his crops. That, too, makes him a slaver. Me, indirectly. Then, of course, I have stayed in the homes of monied planters who hold slaves. That makes me a slaver as well."

"Aye. It is a conundrum." Caswell brightened, "Where will you go next?"

"I go to Halifax this week. Then, to Kennedy's at Bear Creek. I know not how long I shall stay at either place. I have business at Kennedy's. Then, back here briefly before I hope to catch a ship south."

Dicky said, "I suspect the business at Kennedy's is named Abby."

"Ha. Yes. She has occupied my thoughts daily this past year. I hope she waits for me."

Caswell said, "Are you sure that is what you want? You mentioned reading books – and some weighty ones at that – have you changed? Perhaps she has changed. A year is a long time, Will."

"I know. And truth be told, I have been made aware of other ladies who are most attractive."

Dicky said, "Largesse, Sir. By the bye, I will soon be taking my ship to Charlestown, so perhaps the timing will work so that you can ride with me."

"If I can take my horse onboard that would be capital!"

Dicky grinned, "I believe that can be arranged."

Will looked at Governor Caswell. "May I ask a small indulgence in the form of perhaps a new letter of recommendation? Also, if I may, I have more funds to leave in your care and a new letter to that effect to your brother Masons would be sincerely appreciated."

Caswell said, "That would be my pleasure, Will. When will you need them?"

"I am not certain of exactly the date, but perhaps a month? Six-weeks?"

"I shall have them prepared and laid by for you. If I am not here when you come, my aides will have them."

"Thank you, Sir."

"It's good seeing you, Will. Be careful of our enemies...and, for that matter, some of our friends."

CHAPTER 21 – HALIFAX

Will and Old Tom trotted along the road from Halifax. They turned north at the post with three white stripes and trotted along the dirt track that led to Branchton, Will's parent's plantation. The air was heavy, for it was now June in North Carolina. Insects flew from the grass and weeds lining the road. Frogs croaked in the ditch that ran alongside the track.

Old Tom walked slowly. It was too humid to walk quickly, much less trot. Sweat shown on the horse's sides. A heavy scent of fresh crops and drying tobacco hung in the thick, unmoving, hot air. Sweat trickled down Will's back.

Shortly, they came in view of the white, two-story frame farmhouse that was Will's childhood home. Mandy was hanging wash with a black girl. Her back was to the road. Will did not see Zech. Old Tom blew as he came up into the drive before the house, and Mandy turned, a startled look on her face.

"Will? Will? Oh, my, oh, my." She dropped the laundry basket and started running toward him. She cried, "Zech? Zech? Will's home!"

Will had barely dismounted when the threw her arms around him and started crying into his chest. "Oh, Will. Oh, my baby! Oh, oh. You're home, you're home!"

Zech stepped out of the barn, a wooden mallet in his hand and a confused look on his face. "What's the matter....oh!

Oh, my GOD! Will!" Zech, too, set off at a run. He grabbed Will's arm with one hand and threw the other arm around Will's shoulders. Merciful heavens, you are a full-grown man, my son."

The little slave girl hung back at the wash line. Mandy turned and waived her over.

The little girl came reluctantly over to the family.

"Sarrie, this is Mr. Will our son."

Will smiled and said, "Hello, Sarrie."

Sarrie started to cry.

"There, dear. Will won't hurt you. Why are you crying? Run along and finish hanging up the laundry and then you can go rest at the quarters out of the heat."

Sarrie snuffled into her dress sleeve. She gave Will a frantic look and turned and ran to the clothesline.

Will said, "My goodness, what was that about."

Zech said, "Benjamin, as usual."

Will's face darkened. He said, "Oh. I have business with Mr. Benjamin." He brightened, "You are both looking well."

Zech and Mandy both blurted, "You look wonderful!"

Mandy said, "We're having chicken and dumplings for dinner. I must make that more often, for it seems whenever I make that you come riding up."

"Ha, ha. I must have a sixth sense for my Mama's chicken and dumplings!"

Mandy had, indeed, cooked Will's favorite meal. He ate with relish and, between bites of delicious chicken stew and soft, fluffy dumplings, told the story of the time since last he was at Branchton.

Will concluded, "And so that's the story of the past several months."

Mandy sat quietly wiping away tears. She snuffled into a small kerchief she kept twisting in her hands. "I'm so glad you survived all that. The Lord, our God, has watched over my baby every day. I would die if they had hanged you as a spy."

Zech looked at him thoughtfully. "You know, I always knew you would do great things, Will. I am so proud of you. My goodness, General Washington! Colonel Elbert. Being welcomed by leading people in Philadelphia, Savannah, Charlestown, and of course New Bern."

"Aye, Mr. Edward Telfair of Savannah sends his regards."

"Does he, now? How about that. Last I saw Eddie Telfair he was arguing with a merchant in Halifax. They nearly came to blows." Zech laughed at that memory.

"Aye. Telfair is now a leading merchant in all of Georgia. I understand he has a good deal of land, many slaves, and also has trade with the Creeks. He's still quite the dour Scotsman."

Zech smirked, "I think that might have been the source of the conflict in Halifax."

Will said, "We must talk about Benjamin."

Mandy twisted her kerchief again. "What has Benjamin done now?"

"I wrote to you and sent the advertisement where he used your name to sic slavers on me and Jack. Did you receive that letter?"

"No, son. In honesty, we received only one letter from you in the past year and that was the one you sent when you were about to flee Philadelphia. It was not truly clear exactly what was happening. The letter was obviously written in haste."

"I'm sorry that the letters were lost. It makes me worry that my letters to others have not made it."

"Aye. We're told that letters are slow at best, and many never arrive."

"The first letter I sent was to tell you I was well, and that Jack and I made it to Philadelphia. I also sent you an advertisement from the Philadelphia Gazette declaring Jack a runaway and signed using your name. The only person who could have done that was Benjamin."

Zech's face was like thunder. "Is that why the redheaded slaver was pointing a gun at your face?"

"Oh, aye. He couldn't read, but his leader could. Jimmy was that one's name. I showed them Jacks papers of manumission and Red, as he was called, didn't want to accept them. Jimmy had a cooler head and they left. He gave me two copies of the advertisement and I sent you one. This is the other one."

August 25, 1777

THREE POUNDS Reward.

RUN away on the 20th of August last, from the subscriber, living in Halifax, North Carolina, a Negro man, named JACK.

JACK, about 25 years of age, about 5 feet 7 inches high, of a dark brown complexion; he is very artful, pretends to be free, and will no doubt get a forged pass. He may be travelling with a white man of medium height and light hair. He is very fond of liquor. He had on, when he went away, a light hunting shirt, and breeches bound with green binding. Whoever apprehends the said Negro, and confines him in any jail, so as his master may have him again, shall receive the above reward, and reasonable charges, paid by ZECHARIAH YELVERTON.

Zech read the advertisement slowly and carefully, digesting every word. "Benjamin did this. No other could have. We manumitted Jack, and you left right away. It was not common knowledge in Halifax."

Mandy said, "He should be punished."

Will said, "I should beat him within an inch of his sorry life, but t'won't do any good. He's incorrigible. This was a betrayal of the whole family, and I could be bleached bones by a stream in Virginia. I'll bet Benjamin thinks me dead."

"We have not spoken to him about you. We don't often see him. I imagine he gloats that you're dead and gone and Jack is working a field somewhere."

In a quaking voice, Mandy asked, "What shall we do?"

Zech said, "I've good mind to get on my horse and ride over there and horse whip Mr. Benjamin. But, like Will said, that won't work. Something is wrong in Benjamin's head."

Will said, "I have an idea."

Three days later, Benjamin Yelverton, Esquire, as he now styled himself apropos of nothing, was trotting down the road on his black gelding. It was near dark and Benjamin Yelverton, Esquire, had been disporting himself at the Eagle Tavern in Halifax. Mr. Yelverton, Esq., enjoyed a tipple. Often. This evening was no exception. He swayed as the black gelding walked along in the waning light.

He laughed aloud at the thought of 'the waning light.' La penumbra he snickered rolling his Rs, enjoying his rudimentary knowledge of Spanish.

His horse shied and partially reared. It whinnied and jerked at the reins. Benjamin awoke from his drunken reverie to see two masked men with pistols holding the horse's reins and reaching to drag him out of the saddle. Benjamin Yelverton, Esq., kicked his heels back and tried to run, but the horse was held tight by the reins and could not move. It kicked its rear hooves, but to no avail.

One of the highwaymen dragged the horse to its knees while the other masked man dragged Benjamin Yelverton, Esq., from the saddle. Benjamin squealed, "I'm a rich man! I will pay you if you let me goooooo!"

One of the highwaymen said, his voice muffled through his bandit mask, "we're going to sell your ass into slavery."

"But I'm a white man! I'm a white man!"

"Yore name is Benjamin Yelverton, ain't it?"

"Yes...and I'm a white planter."

"We have an advertisement from the Pennsylvania Gazette that says you're part Black and a runaway slave. Your ass is ours! We gonna take you to Virginia and sell your ass. You'll be picking crops next week, and we'll be rich!"

Benjamin Yelverton, Esq., whimpered, "What? What? I'm not black. My mama and daddy are white."

"My mama and daddy are white," mocked one of the bandits.

"You piece of shit. We're gonna drag your black ass to Virginia, and that's all there is to it."

"Oh, no. Please...you must believe me. I'm not any parts Black."

"Huh...that curly hair of yorne sho' looks like a Black man's hair to me. Don't matter one way or t'other. We got this advertisement, and we're gonna get paid three pounds for yore sorry ass. Now git in that goddamn wagon."

Benjamin panicked...his hands were tied and he was being pulled to a waiting wagon hitched to a broken down mule. Suddenly, one of the highwaymen put a bag over his head and roughly dragged him onto the bed of the wagon.

"You hold still. If'n you move, I'll shoot your worthless ass and throw you in the ditch."

Benjamin Yelverton, Esq., whimpered but held deadly still. They would kill him if he moved. He vomited in the bag that covered his head. The effluent stank in his nostrils, and he gagged again.

The wagon set off with a jerk. Benjamin Yelverton, Esq., frantically thought about what he should do. He knew he must not move, or he would be shot. He thought he might escape if the evil slavers could be distracted. But how? Oh, God? How?

He began to pray. Benjamin Yelverton, Esq., had never been religious. In fact, he had scorned anyone who believed in God. God the creator. God the benevolent being that loved man.

Jesus who was crucified for Benjamin Yelverton, Esquire's sins. He had mocked all religion. People were such fools. But today? Today, Benjamin Yelverton, Esquire, was a Christian. He believed!

Benjamin Yelverton, Esquire, swore his soul to the God of the universe. "Please, God, get me out of this terrible mistaken situation and I shall be good for all time."

Hours went by as the wagon bounced and jounced and slammed along the rutted road to Virginia. Benjamin Yelverton, Esq., did not move. He urinated on himself. His bowels moved. He stank. He cried. He whimpered…he died a thousand deaths, each one more painful than the last. Each rut the wagon slammed through made his soul scream to his new God.

At length, the wagon stopped. He was dragged out of the bed of the wagon.

"Hoooo, he stinks. 'Bout like a goddam sorry-ass slave. Done shit on hisself! Git over here, you sorry ass sumbitch."

They dragged him, still hooded, and threw him against a wall. Benjamin Yelverton, Esq., was stunned. Through the stink of his own vomit and shit, he smelled hay and leather. He must be in a barn. He silently invoked the deity, "Thank you, God! We must have arrived."

The bag was jerked off his head, and a nasty little man stared at him. The man had a kerchief covering his face. It concealed everything except his pock-marked forehead and penetrating, black eyes.

"You sorry-ass thieving slave son-of-a-bitch. You stole from your master!"

"I didn't steal anything."

"Hell, yes you did! You stole your own sorry black ass."

"But look at my skin. I'm white!"

"All the high yellers say that. You are a thieving son-of-a-bitch! You're tryin' to pass, ain't ya? We're gonna sell you back to where you came from."

"Who says I was his slave?"

"Mr. Edward Jonas of PeeDee River. After we git you sold off in Virginy, you're a'goin' to South Carolina, boy."

"I've never been to PeeDee River."

"Shut up."

Benjamin Yelverton, Esquire, did not sleep for three days. His captors put the bag on his head and put him in the wagon, taking him farther and farther from his home. At night, they threw him in another barn and ripped the bag off. He was given a bowl of cold soup. He wore the same pants with shit in them for three days.

On the third day the nasty little man with the black crazed eyes and the pock marks snatched the bag off his head and asked, "Did you try to kill your little brother when he was just six years old?"

"I...yes, I did. But he survived."

"'Twas no fault of your'n he lived."

"You would have hanged the slave Caesar?"

"Yes."

"Did Caesar deserve your threat to hang him?"

"No."

"Did you take out an advertisement to get the former slave Jack sold back into slavery and possibly get your brother killed?"

"Yes."

"Do you know a slave girl name Sarrie?"

"I...uh..."

"I asked you a question, boy. DO YOU KNOW A SLAVE GIRL NAMED SARRIE?"

"Uh, yes."

"And how do you know this girl?"

"I ... uh...I used her."

A whisper, "Tell me."

"I made her lay with me."

"Oh...I see...you couldn't get a woman any other way, so you forced a slave child to give you pleasure. About like a damn slave."

Benjamin choked, "I, uh, I well, I had needs."

"She was a child. You used a child. You tried to kill your brother twice. You did what you could to have two other freed slaves sold back into slavery. I think maybe being sold into slavery is too good for you. I think maybe we just skip the reward for you. Jes' kill you and throw your sorry ass in a pig pen. Ever seen what pigs do to a man who falls into the trough? No? Them pigs'll eat your ass whole. 'Course, you'll be dead, maybe. Then, you'll be pig shit. Becoming pig shit is too good for you."

"Please. Please...don't. I'll be a good slave. Don't throw me to the pigs."

The terrible man with the black eyes said, "I'll have to think on it." He snatched Benjamin's bag back onto his head and shoved Benjamin against the wall. Benjamin slid slowly down to the floor.

Things got quiet. Benjamin Yelverton, Esq., slept with the bag on his head. Hours went by. He awakened hot. Through the bag he could tell there was sunlight. A sunbeam was hitting him, and it was making him sweat. He smelled his own vomit, shit, body odor, and a mix of horse shit, straw, and leather. He had to piss. Badly.

"Hello! Anyone? I have to pee. Anyone there?"

He reached up and pulled the bag off. That's when he discovered his hands and feet were no longer bound. Astonishingly, he was in his own barn! What was happening!? Was this a bad dream?

He peed out the barn door. Confused, he stumbled back into the barn. And met the terrible little man with the dead eyes and the pock marks.

"I have decided to give you another chance, Mr. Benjamin Yelverton, Esquire. You are a sorry example of humanity. Your face is a giant pustule. Don't you look at me, boy! Look to the heavens and fix your eyes there. If you look upon my face again, I shall smite you and send you to the Devil."

Benjamin quickly looked to the sky. He saw the rafters of the barn. Bending his head back made his neck hurt. But he believed God. For the first time in his life, he believed in God.

"You treat everyone like they're slaves. You used a little black slave girl for your pleasure. You should be a slave and work like one for all your days. But I heard you praying to your God and making promises. Were those true prayers, Benjamin?"

"Yes, yes! I have been such a terrible person. I will be better."

"Oh? How? Don't you eyeball me, boy! Fix them eyes on the heavens!"

Benjamin gazed at the rafters of the barn. "I don't know. I don't own slaves. I can be better to my family's slaves. Maybe I can free them? I can treat my family better? I can stop drinking and laying about and try to be more productive. I can work my land and try to be productive. I can find a wife and treat her well."

The terrible little man said in almost a whisper, his foul breath inches from Benjamin's ear, "Benjamin, I am the Lord, thy God. Do you believe in me?"

Benjamin whispered, "Yes, yes, I do."

"Do you swear those things you agreed to just now are what you shall do?"

"Aye, yes, I will."

"Do you repent? Do you repent from sin? Will you make amends for abusing that poor little slave girl? Will you repent from having tried to kill your brother for merely being your parents' other child?"

Benjamin Yelverton, Esquire fell to his knees, and bowed his head. "Yes, yes, I will. I will God. I dooooooo!"

"See that you do or the next time we meet will be the last time. And you won't know when I'm coming. And if you think I'm bad, next time you'll meet the Devil."

Benjamin looked up from his bowed posture and found he was alone.

He looked around. No one. The farm was dead quiet. There was no one anywhere. No hoof sounds of anyone riding away. Wind quietly moved through the half-planted crops that Benjamin had ignored.

Benjamin Yelverton, Esq., fell to his knees. "I will, God. I will be a better man. I could not be worse. Ahhhh, haha...Oh, God!" he cried from his soul. "I will, I will repent."

The next day, Benjamin rode his horse to Branchton.

"Hello, Mama. Hello, Daddy. Will, it is nice to see you. I didn't know you were home."

"I got in a few days ago, Ben."

"I'm so glad to see you looking well."

"Are you really."

"Yes. Mama, Daddy, Will...I have found God. I want to be a preacher. I want to help people who were lost like I was. Will you help me to do that?"

Mandy's knees went weak, and she sat heavily on a kitchen chair.

Zech said, "If you really mean that, Benjamin, then we will help you."

"Oh, I mean it. I had a visit from the Lord God. He showed me who I am."

Will rode quietly into the woods where he had hunted so many times as a child. The old broken tree was still there, but it had spouted some branches and surprisingly lived despite being snapped off by a strong wind all those years ago. Will walked Old Tom forward a little way.

Jimmy, the slaver from Virginia, stepped out from behind the broken tree. His penetrating black eyes and pockmarked skin were unmistakable. Behind him stood Red, the flame-haired man who, along with Jimmy and another man, had threatened Will and Jack in the Virginia woods almost two years ago.

"Hello, Jimmy."

"Hello, Mr. Yelverton. I hope we were successful."

"Aye. You'll be leaving now?"

"Yup. Red and me'll be getting on back to Virginy."

Will said, "Thank you for working to straighten out my brother."

"We rode him in that wagon across every rut in that old farm your father owns. I think I hit every bump possible. He

271

bounced around in that wagon for hours. The idea was to put the fear of God in him. I hope it worked."

"Here's the fee we agreed upon." Will handed Jimmy $50 in Spanish silver.

"If it had been up to me, I'd have fed his ass to the hogs. He coulda got me and Red hung with that fake slave advertisement."

Will said, "If it doesn't work, I'll come find you again and let you have him."

Jimmy and Red turned to go. As they walked toward their horses, Will heard Red say, "Did you see how much money he's got? Whyn't we just bust his head and take it all? That's a fine horse, too."

"Shut up, Red. We jes' made $50 for scaring the shit outta a rich boy. Let that be good enough."

Benjamin walked over to where Will sat on the porch. "Will, I...uh...I'm sorry for how I've treated you. I've done some – many – bad things, but I'm trying to repent and become a better person."

"Benjamin, I believe you. I've seen some terrible things in the past couple years. I've killed several men. I've nearly been killed, myself. It has made me see that we only have one pass through this life."

"I know that now. I will become a preacher. I am going to establish a church, but I also plan to ride where there is a congregation to hear me witness my conversion. Maybe I will ride with the militia and minister the gospel to them as they are to do battle. Perhaps I can bring peace to their souls."

"I hope you find peace, Benjamin."

"I already have more peace in my soul than ever before, Will."

Three days later, Will hugged Mandy close and held her for a long time. He shook his father's hand and mounted Old Tom. Mama cried and said, "So soon? I want you to stay."

"I know, Mama, but I need to go see Abby. Then, I need to go back to Georgia."

"Will you come back?"

"Yes, of course."

Zech said, "Give my regards to Governor Caswell as well as Mr. Telfair and the others in Georgia. Be careful with this war, Son. I want you to be able to keep your promise to your mother to return."

"Aye, I will."

Old Tom trotted down the road and turned at the post with three white stripes.

Will was heading to Bear Creek and Abby. He wondered how she would take his arrival. His letters had not made their way to Caswell or his parents. He had no confidence they had reached Abby. Had she waited for him?

The sun was hot, and insects buzzed. A thunderstorm was building in the west. The air tasted like rain.

Old Tom trotted on.

CHAPTER 22 – BEAR CREEK

Will and Old Tom trotted along the road heading out of Carthage. Last leg toward Bear Creek. This was their fourth day on the road, and Old Tom was tired. Will was tired too. After spending the night in a roadside tavern on his first night out of Halifax, Will had camped. His bedroll had been comfortable enough, but sleeping with one eye open looking out for bandits was tiresome. Last night he had tried to get a room at Lowden's Tavern in Carthage, but there were no rooms. At least he had eaten a decent meal before finding a place in the woods to sleep.

It had rained. Fortunately for Will and Old Tom they had found a rock out cropping to use for shelter. Will's oilskin had kept him mostly dry.

The road to Bear Creek was familiar, and wind rustled the trees near the spot where he had been ambushed by the highwaymen two years ago. The roadside ditch was running with water from an early summer rain. The humidity was so high that trees dripped as though it were still raining.

Will looked in the ditch and saw what appeared to be two small round boulders. They were the skulls of Caleb Johnson and his fellow highwayman, John. Water rushed around the skulls like little islands in a stream. Caleb and John's bodies had long ago been picked clean by buzzards, wolves, bears, maybe even a wildcat or two. Will allowed himself a tight grimace. There was no pleasure in having thrown their bodies in the ditch where they had been instantly obscured by high weeds and debris.

Will wondered how Elijah and his mother were doing. Elijah was the Lumbee Indian who happened along when Will was being held up. Caleb Johnson was about to shoot Will when Elijah put a knife in Caleb's back. Elijah had thus become one of Will's best friends. Will thought he should go see Elijah on his way back to New Bern.

Old Tom picked his way along. From well off the road, a bird sang. Will constantly watched for hints of an attack by bandits. As long as the birds sang and none flew suddenly out of their perch, it was likely that there was no danger. Sill, Will had ridden the entire way with the English Dragoon Carbine on his hip, it's sling holding it in place over his shoulder. The carbine and both Tarleton's Brander pistol and the huge old horse pistol in its bucket holster were all loaded with buck and ball, as well as an extra little measure of powder.

The mixture of buck and ball was a defensive load. It consisted of a both buckshot and a pistol ball. It would have been pure hell to be on the receiving end of such a load. If the ball missed, the buckshot would shred an enemy. Will could fire the carbine one handed, drop it, grab the horse pistol, fire, and toss it back in its bucket, and finally pull out the Brander. Will realized the increase in powder would make all three weapons kick like a mule, but the extra punch might just be the thing to depend on. He hoped it would all be enough.

Old Tom twitched his ears as a horsefly buzzed around them. The air seemed even heavier as the morning wore on. Soon, Will could hear the familiar sound of Bear Creek rushing along. In the distance there was the faint creek of Kennedy's waterwheel.

Will resisted the urge to make Old Tom trot. It was just too hot, and the poor horse had already walked about 140 miles across North Carolina. Fortunately, the two weeks at Halifax had rested Old Tom from his ride north from New Bern. Now he would need several days at Kennedy's.

Will smelled a cooking fire. Hint of some jasmine. He remembered that Irene Kennedy has planted some jasmine near the house and along the path just last year. It must have done well. Will came in view of Alexander Kennedy's little factory, its waterwheel splashing merrily in the noon-day sun.

Mr. Alex came out the door, paused and looked hard at Will. "Is that Will Yelverton?"

Will took off his hat and said, "Yes, Mr. Alex, it's me."

"Well merciful heavens! We thought you were dead."

"No, Sir. I am very much alive."

"Get down off that horse and come on in!"

Will dismounted and they shook hands. Kennedy grabbed him in a bear hug. "Damn, Son. We actually did think you were dead."

"Y'all didn't get my letters?"

"We had one when you were in Halifax saying you were heading north to Philadelphia, and that was it. You'll have to tell us all about your adventures."

"Tis an oft told tale!"

Kennedy laughed and pulled the door to the factory closed. "Let's go up to the house. Irene will faint!"

"And Abby?"

"Oh, son, Abby married and moved away."

The world shifted. Will put a hand on Old Tom. He couldn't breathe. "Oh, uh....oh. Well, uh, good for her. Is she happy?"

"She's as happy as she can get without you. Damn near killed her when it got to be months and no word."

"I, I wrote several times. But I was trapped in Philadelphia for much of the time and then at a fort in Georgia. I guess the mail didn't go anywhere. I'm so sorry."

"Irene will be thrilled you're here.

The went into the kitchen. Irene was bending over the hearth and when she stood up she was so startled she almost fell back into the fire. She put her hands to her face and exclaimed, "Oh, my lands! Will. My God, you're alive. You're alive! Oh, thank God." She rushed across the room and threw her arms around him. Hot tears wet his face as she kissed his cheek.

Will said, "Mr. Alex said y'all thought I was dead."

Through her tears, Miss Irene said, "Oh, Will. We just knew you must be dead. Lots of other men from hereabouts have gone off and never come home."

Alex said, "Tis a terrible time. First the Regulators running amok and burning anything that looked like a government building or tarring and feathering officers. Then, this war. Sometimes we get a band of Tory militia. That animal David Fanning is always skulking about."

"Other times, it's Patriot militia. They always want something." We also had Indian troubles after you left."

"Let's sit down. Davy is out hunting. He'll be thrilled you're here. You can have your old room in the barn, if that's ok."

Irene said, "Let me tell you about Abby" before she comes home. She married Ezekiel Carter who is another gunsmith. He has gone off with the militia to South Carolina. Her father-in-law, Micah Carter, took her to Carthage a couple days ago. They will be back here tonight or tomorrow."

Tears ran down her cheeks and Irene said, "I'm so sorry, Will."

"No, Miss Irene, please don't cry. Abby's happy."

"I did not say that. I don't know if she's happy or not. When you had been gone for months and no word, Zeke came a'courtin' and Abby didn't want to be a spinster. She's past 18, you know."

Will said "Oh, I know. I cannot complain about a thing. She has a life to live and, as you said, I could easily have been dead this entire year." Will said, "It will be nice to see Abby. We were friends long before I knew I was in love with her."

Davy walked in the door. He saw Will and lit up like one of the chandeliers in the Tryon Palace. "Will! You're alive!" He dropped the two rabbits he was carrying and grabbed Will around the shoulders.

Will grinned. "I see you're still a good shot."

"Aye. Tis how we eat. Is that your bay horse? I didn't recognize it."

"Yes. It's a long story, but to allay your fears, Molly is fine. She's in a stable at a fort in Sunbury, Georgia."

"Sunbury, Georgia? Never heard of it."

"Neither had I until the ship I was on put into port there after a sea battle with an English privateer."

"Oh, now, we're going to have to hear that story."

"Ha. I shall regale you all with my adventures."

Dinner was Irene Kennedy's wonderful rabbit stew with some root vegetables and boiled greens called poke salat. They were cooked with a piece of pork jowl. Will had not had poke salat since he had left Kennedy's for New Bern and then Pennsylvania. Miss Irene said she boiled the poke salat greens three times so they would not be poison. Will relished the food and loved the country style of cooking.

They asked about what all had happened in the past year. Will told them about being waylaid by slavers, and about finding Caesar. They were all riveted when he told them about Brandywine.

Davy exclaimed, "You met George Washington?"

Irene said, "Is he tall?"

"Oh, yes, I met General Washington, and he is very tall. He is also a courtly gentleman, but he is commanding. I was also honored to spend an evening with him socially when I chanced to stay at Mr. Potts' home in Pennsylvania and the general also happened to be there."

"My, my. Your last several months have been exciting."

"Well, twas exciting in a different way when a British officer in Philadelphia accused me of being a spy and threatened to have me hanged. Had I not run for my life, he would have succeeded in that endeavor."

Irene sucked in her breath. "NO!"

"Oh, yes. I ran across New Jersey on Molly's back and got passage on a privateer. We took a couple prizes before we ran into our match in the form of Captain John Mowbray aboard

Rebecca. Rebecca was a British privateer from Saint Augustine, British Florida. We had a running gun fight which *Beatrice*, my ship, won. We had heavier guns and shredded her mainsail, and then we ran for Sunbury, Georgia. I did shoot Captain Mowbray's hat off, which discomfited him greatly."

There was laughter all around at that.

"I chanced to meet him again in the Frederica River."

"Where is that?" Davy asked.

"Tis deep in coastal Georgia, behind an island that protects the land from the ocean. We met the British there. I was with Colonel Samuel Elbert of Savannah. We were aboard three river galleys with huge cannons on their bows. The British had seagoing ships, one of which was *Rebecca*. We fair shot them to pieces with the big guns and they could do nothing. Finally, they tried to run and grounded in the shallows. They abandoned their ships in little boats."

Alex Kennedy said, "I thought you were not going to join the army, Will."

"Aye. I have not joined. I was a volunteer. Both with Washington and with Elbert I could not say no. They are great leaders."

Soon, everyone was tired, and Will went to his little bed in the tack room in the barn. It felt like home to him.

He lay on his back and remembered Abby coming to him in this room. She had offered herself to him, but he didn't want to take advantage of her. They had kissed and held one another. She knew he was with Martha Black, and he told Abby that he must resolve that before he could be free.

He had written that he and Martha were no longer an item. Apparently, the letter never arrived, and Abby had no idea about Will's life since he rode off down the dusty track in front of the Kennedys' home. She had accepted another man, and that was that.

Will was sad in his soul. They had thought him dead. Abby had moved on with her life. She thought Will had forsaken her, when exactly the opposite was true. But Will was also grateful to Abby. She had given him a reason to live. The image of her gamine little face, bursting into a radiant smile, had given him hope. A goal. A cause to get back to Abby.

Now he had accomplished that goal, but it was too late.

Will knew he was not blameless. The afternoons with Frances Montravalle in the Philadelphia winter, while physically satisfying, were not exactly his finest hour emotionally. He felt deeply guilty about his weakness with Frances.

Then, there was Mary. His brief time with Mary was another source of guilt. He had hungrily kissed her, and worried about the effects later. Mary had started as a brief flirtation. Now...what would he call it? She had made clear that what started as fun had quickly become more to her.

Was it the same for him? Was Mary a part of his future? He wondered about how such a future might unfold. Mary had made it clear she was Will's friend. More, she made clear that she would be his supporter. But would she move to the frontier with him to live in a small cabin, threatened by Indians, privation, the weather, animals, poor harvests, and starvation? Would she? Or was Mary a spoiled little rich girl who was used to servants and finery? He had only known her for three days. Could two people build a future on just three days of brief chats and admittedly very strong physical attraction?

A tiny breeze floated through the small window.

The scent of jasmine wafted in.

He slept.

CHAPTER 23 – THE WATER HOLE

Will awakened to the warmth of a sunbeam coming through the tiny window of his little room in the Kennedys' barn. The smells of hay, leather and old wood were welcoming and made Will think of his time living there. It was a happy feeling of nostalgia tinged with loss. Loss of Abby because of the war.

Will had never hated the British. Until Tarleton accused him of being a spy in Philadelphia, Will had considered himself an Englishman. Even though he had been shot at by Loyalists at Moore's Creek Bridge and by British troops at Brandywine, he had not felt strongly one way or the other about independence. Part of him had felt things were going along fine without throwing the British out. Another part of him had resented the idea of heavy taxes and high-handed ways of British politicians and military officers. "Sure," he had thought, "Americans are provincials. What of it? We're still Englishmen."

Will realized his ideas had changed. He was angry for the burned-out homes and destroyed lives from British attacks in South Georgia. True, Georgia was not his home exactly, but he had been well treated by the Georgians and he sympathized with their plight of being constantly raided by people like Lt Colonel Thomas Brown and that disgusting criminal, McGirth.

Will lay in the little bed in the tack room and let his mind wander to what might happen if the British did take Savannah. What was preventing them? Georgia's militia and the few battalions of continental troops? Sam Elbert was a competent commander, but there were other, self-styled military men like Governor Houstoun who were not capable of leading troops in a fight. Will had not yet met General Howe, but he had picked up on Elbert and Lt Colonel McIntosh's lack of confidence in Howe. Then, Governor Caswell had made that face when Will mentioned Howe.

What would happen to Liz Elbert, Charlotte Jones, Eliza Wilkinson, and Mary Proctor? Would Savannah and Charlestown burn even further? Already both of those cities had suffered large losses in burned out buildings and lost commerce.

Will had recently discovered books. Would the British use beautiful libraries like Sam Elbert's as kindling? Would Mr. Robert Wells' bookstore be reduced to ashes? What a shame that would be. Will hated the idea of war and now, he realized, he hated the British and the Tories. Not so much the individual people, but the British and Tories as a group were destroying homes and threatening his home and those of his friends.

Should he accept the offer of a commission as a Major in the Continental Army? Would that help? Or should he continue his association with various leaders and allow things to develop. Maybe that was the best course. When he thought on it, Will realized he had already seen more war than many of the troops wearing the uniform of the Army or the militia. Few of them had ever fired a weapon in anger.

He rose from the little bed and stepped into the yard to wash at the trough. The water was cool, but summer was budding, and even just a after dawn it was already warm and muggy. The day promised to be scorching in up country North Carolina, and there would be little wind to cool things.

Davy went one way at the path and Will went the other. They carried their rifles and powder horns. A few bullets and patches were in a pocket, and each man had a hunting knife. Will no longer went anywhere without Tarleton's Brander Pistol, and as usual, it was loaded with buck and ball. The two young men were intent upon killing a deer, so the Brander was there simply in case someone decided to rob the hunters or worse.

They walked quietly and each instinctively knew where the other was. They had hunted together so often they were able to get inside one another's brains and know what each was doing and why. They also knew how the quarry was going to behave.

Will looked at the ground and saw tracks. The pointed hooves of a deer were unmistakable. These were not fresh. A few dry leaves lay over some of the tracks and the ground was equally dry. A deer had not passed this way in the last few days. Was the water hole dry? Will didn't think so. This water hole almost always had plenty of moisture.

Will quietly walked on. He looked on the other side of a log before stepping over it. That was always good policy in the woods. It was especially good policy today for a 4-foot Timber Rattlesnake lay sunning itself on the other side of the log, its black ringed tail lay quiet. The snake was not alerted to Will's presence, or it would have been rattling that tail. Had Will unwittingly stepped over the log the startled snake would surely have bitten him. A rattlesnake bite, especially from a large snake such as this one, would have meant an agonizing, slow death. The snake's head was the size of Will's palm.

Will quietly walked well around the snake's lair. No sense killing the creature. The racket would have alerted any game in the area. Will was not on a snake-killing hunt, although there had certainly been those in the past. No, today was about bringing home a deer.

Will watched for fresh signs of a deer passing this way to the water hole he knew was just over the little rise in the landscape. Will spotted a fresh deer track. And another. The soft, damp ground had plenty of recent sign. Will looked through the brush and saw Davy's hat move slightly. Will knew Davy was looking at the same deer sign. Will stepped over the tracks. He didn't want to leave human scent on the deer's path. There would be future hunts for Davy and no sense alerting the deer.

Will watched where he put his feet. He did not want to crackle a twig or cause the bushes to rattle. Another half step and the water hole came into full view. It was about 25 yards.

There was plenty of water in the soggy bottom land, and animal tracks abounded. Not just deer tracks. There were tracks of small game like racoons, possums, and rabbits. A profusion of bird droppings indicated the birds came here to bathe in the water and drink.

Will leaned against a tree and waited. He knew Davy was doing the same. Davy was parallel to Will. By silent agreement, they would not shoot away from the water hole. Neither hunter wanted to kill his friend.

Time slowly passed. Will's mind wandered to Abby. Would she be at the Kennedys' when he got back? She had her own home now. Would it be proper to visit her? She was a married woman. He did want to see her and let her know that he still loved her, but that she should live her life and not think about him. He would try to go on.

Will's practiced eye took in the subtle change in the woods. Where there had been green of leaves and gray of tree bark a gentle shift to a brown color had happened. The brown color was the back of a deer who had walked up to the hole from upwind of Will and Davy. That meant the deer was completely unaware of the hunters. The deer's sensitive nose would have instantly alerted the animal to human presence, but Will and Davy were downwind, and the deer did not catch their scent. It would be a fatal error.

The deer carefully picked its way through the thicket, pausing to nibble delicately on a couple green leaves. It was a buck. Will felt better about that. Spring, even late spring like June, was the time when fawns and does were foraging. It would be a shame to kill a doe and leave her fawns to starve.

Will quietly set the trigger on Josie and cocked the hammer. He waited.

The buck stepped into full view. It's new antlers still had velvet on them. This was a young buck, and it was cautious. The buck paused and twitched its tail. Testing the wind with its sensitive nose and looking in all directions to see if there were a threat. The deer took another step and then another. Now he was in full view. Will instinctively knew this was his shot. Davy could not see this animal.

Will waited until the deer looked over its shoulder and then leveled Josie. Will searched for the spot where the deer's heart was and touched the trigger.

WizCRAAAAK! Josie jolted into Will's shoulder, dropping the deer in its tracks. Will knew the ball had hit the deer's heart and shattered it, causing blood pressure to instantly drop and the animal was dead before it had completely collapsed.

Davy whooped from the other side of the water hole as he and Will quickly crossed the short distance to the dead animal. When they got to the dead animal, they both paused and reached out a hand to touch the deer's still warm body. Each man was briefly lost in a reverent pause of respect for the animal who had just given its life to sustain them and their family. For Will and Davy, this was not like slaughtering a hog raised for the purpose. This was the culmination of an ancient ritual of hunter and hunted. The deer was a noble beast, and its demise yielded no pleasure.

They dragged the deer some distance away from the muddy water hole, bled it out, and gutted it. They left the hide on the animal. They would skin it later and hope to sell the hide. They quickly tied its hooves together and put a green sapling through the tied legs, hoisting the carcass up to carry it home.

CHAPTER 24 – ABBY, AT LAST

Will and Davy walked into the Kennedys' yard carrying the deer. Although the animal was young, it was fat. It had been gorging on grass, leaves, acorns, and other food for over three months. Even better, the deer had died an instant death with no frantic running from dogs or other predators. The meat would be succulent and free of musk. The hide would bring top dollar, too. It was young and unscarred.

Miss Irene came out from the kitchen door and said, "Oh, my. That is a very nice deer. We shall have a roast tonight."

A wagon was parked by the kitchen door. An older man stepped out the door.

"Who might you be," he challenged.

Will, slightly irritated at the man's tone, replied, "My name is Will Yelverton. Who might you be?"

"I be Micah Carter, owner of the farm next door. What brings you to these parts, stranger?"

"I'm not a stranger, and what I'm doing here is none of your business, Sir."

"Well, now. I don't hold truck with a whippersnapper spouting off about my business!"

"That will have to be your problem to solve, Sir."

Irene said, "Now, now. Micah, Will is a guest in our home. Please treat him with respect."

"He has not respected me, Madame!"

"Oh, no, you don't Micah. You started this by acting as if this were your home and challenging Will."

"Well, he's a stranger in these parts, and there's too many of them for my liking."

"Will is not a stranger here, Micah. He's part of our family, and I expect you to treat him as such."

"Harrumph! I don't like the way he talked to me."

Will said, "That makes us even. I don't like your tone, Sir."

"Huh. Well, I suppose I can allow that I was a bit gruff. Still, we have too many coming around with bad intent."

"Indeed, you were gruff, Sir. But I will allow that there are bad actors abounding these days."

"If you're friends with the Kennedys then we shall be friends."

Will offered his hand, "Let us begin again. Hello, Sir. I am Will Yelverton. It is an honor to meet you."

Micah Carter eyed Will hard and saw the tempered steel in his soul. Taking Will's hand he said, "The pleasure is all mine."

Micah squeezed Will's hand. Hard. Will squeezed back harder. Years of working with small parts and squeezing gun springs had made his grip like iron.

Micah let go with a slightly pained look. That gambit had not worked, either. His hand would ache for a couple days.

Oblivious to the little silent contest, Irene said, "Good. That's settled."

From behind Irene, a soft voice said, "Hello, Will."

Will's knees went slightly weak. He had anticipated this moment for months, but in a different way. He had hoped to see Abby and the two of them rush into each other's arms. But that was not to be.

His mouth went dry. Will caught his breath and said, simply, "Hi, Abby. It's wonderful to see you again."

Abby said, "We thought you were dead."

"Aye. The rest of the family have told me as much. But here I am."

"Mama told me about your adventures. My goodness you have been quite a journey man."

"Yes, I have. Kind of like Odysseus."

"Who?"

Will smiled, "Oh, nobody. I better get this deer skinned and butchered. Will you and Mr. Carter be staying for dinner?"

Micah Carter said, "Aye. Then I'll have to get along to my farm. Can someone see Abby home to her place?"

Irene quickly said, "She can stay the night and then Davy and Will can take her home in the morning."

Will and Davy skinned the deer without the first bit of damage to the valuable hide. Then, they cut out roasts, steaks, and still had haunches to hang in the smoke house. The deer ham would be wonderful. There were plenty of small trimmings and other pieces that, mixed with some hog fat and some spices, would make excellent sausage.

Irene had some paper that she used to wrap some roasts and steaks for Micah to take home, and a smaller package of roasts and steaks for Abby. She put the meat in the spring house, a small building built over a natural spring that popped out of the ground a few yards down the slight hill behind the house. Even in June the spring water came out of the ground very cold, and the small building, built of thick mud brick, kept the temperature chilled. Food could be kept there, free of spoiling, for quite a while.

Will worked for a couple hours at the factory with Mr. Alex. It was more to stay out of the way of Micah Carter and to spend time with his mentor and friend.

Alex said, "Zeke Carter is a good man. Abby could do worse. His daddy, on the other hand, is a bit of a test."

"Aye, we got off on the wrong foot, but Miss Irene put that right."

Alex said, "Micah seems to get off on the wrong foot with lots of people. He has a big mouth. I suspect he is aware that you and Abby were once close. He's probably worried for his son's claim to her."

Will said, "I'm sure. But then, what does that say about his opinion of Abby if he thinks she would dump her husband for an old suitor?"

Alex said, "What does it say about his opinion of his son's ability to keep a woman?"

Dinner was a wonderful roast with gravy and fresh spring vegetables. There were some turnips called runups, immature turnip greens that sprouted early. A North Carolina delicacy. Irene pulled and washed some potatoes that she boiled and mashed with a little cream and butter. Abby went out into the woods and foraged for some spring ramps, a kind of wild green onion that was delicious mixed into the vegetables.

The entire group, Micah included, laughed, and chatted about everything except the war and Will's travels. They talked about the coming harvest. Alex thought that corn would do well this year. "Knee high by July," he said meant the crop would be good. Already, Indian corn in the fields was up to mid-calf height. But lack of rain could kill it.

They all talked about whether it would rain soon. There had been a slight drought where little rain had fallen for a few weeks. Will had seen signs of the drought in the existence of old tracks and then the profusion of tracks at the water hole. It meant there were not many watering holes for the animals. The drought did not bode well for crops.

The family adjourned to the yard where it was cooler and enjoyed the slight breeze. The chatting went on until it was almost dark.

Micah Carter rose, "I must be heading on toward home. My dear wife will wonder if I have not been waylaid by highwaymen."

Irene said, "Let me get you the meat from the spring house."

Alex said, "Thank you for taking Abby shopping. I hope there were sufficient wares for your trouble."

Micah nodded, "Aye, there were some shortages, but I think she got some cloth and other items on her list. She brought some things for Irene, too."

Micah looked at Will. "It was a pleasure meeting you, Mr. Yelverton. I hope you soon have safe travels."

Will replied, "The honor was mine. Traveling has become quite unsafe these days, no matter when undertaken."

Micah kissed Abby on the forehead. "I'll look in on you tomorrow."

"Thank you, father. I may stay here an extra day to help Mama. Do not worry about me."

Micah climbed aboard his wagon and put his parcel of meat on the seat. He said, "Walk on..."

The group sat by the fire for a while longer. Abby wanted to hear about Will's year of adventures, so he told the same stories again.

Abby said, "Oh, God. We thought you were dead, but you truly were almost killed. More than once, too."

Will said, "Oh, it was not that bad. Just a little scary. The worst was being chained up in a tent facing a hanging in the morning. If I had not had that small chisel in my pocket, I couldn't have opened the lock and then I truly would have hanged. It was a very lucky thing I had the chisel. I should frame it and hang it on the wall someday. When I have a house. Maybe my children will want to hear the story."

Abby made a funny noise and got up and ran into the house.

Will said, "Oh, my. Did I say something wrong?"

Irene quietly said, "No Will. You are your usual self and no worries there. It's just...well...uh...you see, Abby is with child, and she's upset with the situation."

"Upset how? I mean, it's wonderful she's going to have a baby."

Irene said softly, "Oh, Will. You are such a gentle, kind person. She's upset because the baby is not yours."

Will's face fell. "Oh. Oh, my. I ... uh, I... Oh."

Irene said, "Yes. It's that way, Will. You must be kind to her."

Will said, "Oh, Miss Irene, I'd never be cruel to Abby. I love her."

"I know that. And that's the problem."

Will's face twisted into a mask of pain. "Oh, God. I must leave soon. I'm hurting her being here."

"I fear that's true. Yet, Alex and I want you to stay. We'll have to see what can be done. Abby has her own home. Perhaps she can stay there and, in that way, reduce the pain."

"I shouldn't come here and upset the family. Micah clearly wants me gone."

"We must consider what to do. For now, I'm tired and I think Abby needs me."

"Yes, of course. I think I will go to bed as well."

Will washed at the trough and wiped off the water. The sweat of the day had made him feel grimy. He also felt grimy because he had been insensitive to Abby. He was trying to just be himself as though nothing had changed. But things had changed, and Will felt like a fool. He felt mean and unkind. He went to his little room. He looked at the room as a special place for him, and now he was not certain.

He stood looking at the room. Tears filled his eyes. He said out loud, "Ah, God. I'm such a terrible person."

A soft voice said, "No, Will. You're not."

Will whirled around to find Abby standing in the door of his little sanctuary.

"Abby. I...uh...I didn't know anything."

"I know you didn't."

"I'll leave in the morning."

"Don't you dare. Don't you dare walk back into my life like a ghost and then turn and leave without a word."

"But Abby, you're married, and nothing can change that."

"What if I ran off with you?"

"Oh, Abby. We can't even do that. I love you and I love your parents. They would hate me and disown you. Micah and Zeke would hunt us down. They'd kill me and drag you back. Or, worse, I'd kill one of them and then they'd hang me, and you'd have no one and a baby."

"Oh, Wiiilll. Oh, God. I'm glad you came back. I just knew you were dead. Dead, dead, dead. I'm so happy you are alive. I'm just so sad because I should have waited."

She lost control and ran into his arms. He held her close and stroked her back. "There, there. Not all is lost. We just have to know that we will not be together. I will always love you, Abby."

She turned her face to his. "Don't deny me, Will. Don't you dare deny me."

He kissed her and she kissed him back. She grabbed a handful of his hair. His hands ran up and down her back.

She whispered into his chest. "I cannot get with child."

Will said, "Miss Irene said you are already with child."

"Yes, that is what I meant. We can do as we please because I am already with child."

Will said, "I am not sure. I don't want to make you an immoral woman."

"Oh, God, Will. Don't you know that every time with Zeke I was with you in my heart. I wanted you so badly before you left, and you denied me. Don't...you...dare...deny...me...this...time."

Will said, "There have been others. I was so lonely."

Abby pushed back and looked at him hard. "I don't care. Did you love them? I can see in your eyes the answer is no. I don't care. I know you were lonely. Take me to that bed, Will. Now!"

Will fretted, "Won't it hurt the baby?"

"No, you idiot. For a smart man, you sure can be dumb."

She stepped back and, bending down, grabbed her dress at the hem. Straightening up she pulled the dress over her head. She stood in front of him nude, but for a pair of little shoes. Her belly stood out some, a tiny line of hairs running from her navel to her pubic area. Her breasts were engorged, and the nipples were dark red. She kicked off the little shoes and sat quickly on the bed. She laid back and ran her hands over her distended belly.

"Will, I have loved you since you walked into the kitchen the day you came to our little home. Come here."

Will walked on rubbery legs to the bed.

"Are you getting in the bed totally dressed?"

"Uh, no. I...uh...no."

Will pulled off his shirt and popped his breeches buttons. His erection popped out.

Abby said, "Oh, my. Just like I dreamed about."

Will said, "You are exactly like in my dreams."

"Liar. You never dreamed about me being a fat, ugly, pregnant woman."

Will said, "Oh, no. You are beautiful. You are in bloom. Your body is so perfect."

"Shut up, you liar. I want you in me, now!"

Will climbed on the bed and in an instant accommodated her wishes.

Abby threw her head back and said, "Oh, God. Oh, God! Ahhhh...this is what I wanted!"

Will felt her contract all down his member. He ejaculated hard. It was the hardest burst of semen he had ever felt. He spent until his muscles couldn't hold him. He collapsed next to her.

Will said, "I'm sorry."

Abby said, "I'm not. Not at all."

Will said, "Now what?"

"Now we make love instead of rutting like animals."

"But then?"

"I will go to my home, and you will stay with Mama and Daddy until it's time for you to leave and go back to your life."

"But..."

"No buts. Our lives will go on. I will know in my heart that you live and prosper. You will know that I am happy and raising my family. You will go and live your life. And you will not look back. Ever."

Will said, "Oh, but Abby...I..."

"Shut up and make love to me. I love you so much."

CHAPTER 25 – WHITE EAGLE

Will awoke to the heat of a North Carolina June morning. It was barely daybreak, and he was already sweating. The smell of hay, leather, and horse shit greeted him as it always had in the Kennedys' barn.

Sitting up, his feet hit the raw board of the floor and his soul felt both free and heavy at the same time. He would always love Abby, but circumstances had intervened. He felt loss. She carried another man's child. She belonged to another and nothing on God's green Earth could change that. Worse, Will felt like the coward that Eliza Yonge Wilkinson had called him. Zeke Carter was wearing the uniform of a North Carolina Militia Man somewhere in South Carolina, and Will was cavorting with Zeke's wife.

"God, I am a low-life." Will muttered to no one in particular.

He looked around at the bed and saw that the dent in the mattress was twice as big as usual. He and Abby had lain there nearly all night. They had talked and quietly made love. Abby had been responsive to his touch. She had eagerly, insistently, demandingly, gobbled up every moment.

Abby had said, "My God, but you are skilled at love, Will. You must have been taught by someone."

Embarrassed, Will said, "Aye, my darling. I was so lonely in Philadelphia. The equally lonely wife of a British officer took me to her bed. She was demanding."

"Well, I thank her. Not for taking you to her bed, the bitch, may she burn in hell. But for teaching you while you were there. Do that again...quickly! Ahhhhhhh....Goddddddd. Huhhh. I must be quiet or Daddy will hear."

"What about Miss Irene?"

"Do you not know that she sent me? Mama said I needed to get this out of me."

"Oh. I think your Mama loves us both."

"Oh, did you not know that before?"

Time and again, Will had done all he could to urge Abby on toward ecstasy. He was not sure if it was his love making or her desperate need that made things so successful. He thought about this some.

Frances had been appreciative and a good teacher. She ecstatically enjoyed love making and was responsive. She had strong climaxes and was clearly spent after each effort. It had made Will feel ... accomplished. That was a good word.

Will thought about Mary Proctor. Will also liked Mary immensely. Not because she took his side in the spat with Eliza. No, it was more. She made him feel good. Not just physically by sharing stolen kisses. She honored him. She looked at him with both kindness and lust.

Now came Abby. Abby loved him. There was no doubt. Her body was his and every touch lit her up like she had been struck by a lightning bolt. She loved him in her soul. Her eyes lit up when she saw him. Several times when he was apprenticed here, and then last night, he noticed that her eyes followed him. Everywhere. One, two, three…look at Will…four, five, six…look at Will. Will realized he could be a complete novice at loving and Abby would have been as ecstatic. That he knew what to do and how to do it merely added a layer of joy to an already wonderful friendship.

These things made Will feel light and happy. What made him sad was that he must leave. Abby was gone to her new home, and Will was not to cause her problems by visiting. They must appear to be chaste and not romantically involved, lest Micah discover it and make a scene. Someone would be hurt and that would be catastrophic.

Will knew he had to leave. And soon.

Will ate a wonderful breakfast of deer sausage and eggs from Irene's hens. Some of last night's potatoes shredded and pan fried added to the delight. Alex had eaten and headed to the factory. Davy was in the barn.

Will said, "Miss Irene, I have to go."

"I know, Will."

"Miss Irene, I…"

"I sent her to you, Will. I wanted the two of you to have last night. I know you love her, and she loves you."

"I know you sent her. You have always been kind to me. I know I have to go because I will not be able to resist going to her. And she is another man's wife, Miss Irene."

"Yes, she is. And Zeke is a good man. She could do much worse, and you leaving will let her be happy. As happy as she can be."

"I know, Miss Irene. It just hurts in my heart."

"I know. Imagine how much it hurts in her heart every time she lays with him and you're still in that heart."

"Aye, I can imagine."

Irene reached over an took Will's hand. Looking into his eyes she said, "No, you know. You have lain with other women since leaving here. You lay with them, but Abby was always there."

Will teared up. "Ah, God. Miss Irene. I wish my letters had arrived. I'm so sorry. Abby was the reason I didn't give up that cold night in the tent in New Jersey. I dug at that lock almost all night with the one goal to get free and come back to Abby." He buried his face in his hands. "Haaaa, haaaa."

Irene got up and came around the table. She put her arms around him. "It's ok, Baby. Go ahead and cry. Cry it out. Mama Irene is here for you. Abby cried like this, too. I will hold you both in my heart for all my life. Mama Irene loves you. Go ahead, Baby. Just let it all out."

Will cried until he had no more tears. Irene held him for what seemed like hours.

Sometimes a boy needs his mama.

Two mornings later Will stood by Old Tom. He was wearing his traveling clothes. His linen shirt and hunting shirt over hunting breeches and his high moccasin boots. His rifles and bedroll were strapped on Old Tom. Across his shoulders were his powder horn and shot pouch. The English Dragoon Carbine, loaded with buck and ball, was across his back. Uncle Ewan's dirk hung from his belt. Tarleton's Brander pistol was tucked in his belt. The Brander and the horse pistol were loaded with an extra measure of powder and buck and ball. Should a highwayman think to accost him, Will Yelverton would not die easily.

Miss Irene, Mr. Alex, and Davy all stood in the yard.

Alex, oblivious to events, said, "I wish you weren't leaving so soon, Will."

"Aye. But I have given my word to come back to Georgia. Plus, Molly is in a stable in South Georgia, and I have promised her to come back."

Davy said, "I want to go fight like you have, Will."

"No, you don't Davy. Try to stay out of this as long as you can. I have seen a man hit in the head with a musket ball. He was dead instantly, and it was not a pretty sight. Worse, when you're dead, it is forever. You have lots of good living ahead of you, Davy."

Miss Irene hugged him and whispered, "Remember what I told you. Find someone to love, and let your life move ahead. In time, you will heal. Know that I love you as if you were my own baby."

Will swung into the saddle. Will looked at the Kennedys. "I reckon we seem to do this every now and again. Perhaps I will come back this way. Somehow this seems like a place I should be."

Irene shook her head slightly, but Alex and Davy both said, "Yes. Come back and see us!"

Will and Old Tom trotted out of the Kennedys' yard and turned south toward Drowning Creek. He would go surprise Elijah.

Elijah Wambleeska Hammond was a Lumbee Indian, and he lived among his people at a small settlement near the headwaters of Drowning Creek. It was slightly south of Bear Creek. Half a day later, Will and Old Tom came trotting along a familiar path heading toward Elijah's home.

An Indian with a musket stepped into the road in front of Will.

"Where the hell do you think you're going, White Man?"

Will said, "I'm going to visit my friend Elijah. He's called White Eagle. Wambleeska. Know him?"

"I know him. What's he doing with a white man for a friend?"

"Just lucky, I guess."

"I'm not taking smart mouth from any white eyes!"

"Easy. He saved my life from a murderous highwayman up near Carthage."

"Did he, now?"

"Aye. He still live up this path?"

"Yup. Go ahead up thataway. If'n someone shoots you t'ain't my fault."

Will said, "Thanks. What's your name."

"Irving."

"Really?"

"Yup."

"Nice to meet you, Irving."

"Don't know about that."

Will trotted into Elijah's yard. The place looked the same. It was a log cabin similar to those White people lived in. A large barn stood where a smaller barn had stood a couple years ago.

"Ho! Elijah!"

Elijah Wambleeska Hammond stuck his head out the door of the cabin. "Really? Really? A damn white man comes just trotting in here like he owns the place? Damn! Didn't Irving shoot your ass?"

"Nope. Irving was quite pleasant."

"First time for everything. Get off that damn horse and get in here. Jesus...and I thought I was rid of your sorry ass."

"I love you too."

Elijah's mother, Aiyana, dithered over Will for the whole week he was visiting. Will was happy to see them as well as Elijah's friends. One or two were still wary of Will, but others accepted him. Good enough for Elijah...

They went hunting and Will killed a deer. He smiled to himself. Thought, "It must be my year for deer hunting." Aiyana was thrilled with the venison and the neighbors all came to eat roasts and steaks. Aiyana said she would make sausages with native herbs and the hot peppers she grew in the garden. She had a hot pepper that was so spicy that only one in a whole pot was almost too spicy.

Elijah and Will went fishing in Saddletree Swamp and in Drowning Creek. Perch and Bream abounded, and they brought home long strings of the fresh fish. Aiyana threw a fish fry and then the neighbors all agreed Will could return anytime. Being accepted made Will feel good, and he knew he had a friend for life.

Will and Elijah talked about events of the past year.

Elijah said, "I guess I shouldn't care about the white man's war, but I think if we win, maybe freedom will come to everyone, not just the whites."

Will said, "I hope so. My father is going to free the last of his slaves. He says if we're fighting for unalienable rights to be free, that should apply to everyone. Don't know if the plantation will survive without free labor, though."

Elijah said "Some of my friends have slaves. Unhappy subject, too. I mean, how can you be an Indian and hold slaves? But in past history we Indians had slaves long before white men brought Negroes."

Will said, "Yeah. I can see that. I also had some doubts about the war. I mean, I just want to go to the frontier and open me a little gunshop and fix guns for people. Maybe plant a garden, keep some chickens and a pig. Maybe a cow. Have some kids. But the British are brutal, and it's going to get worse before it gets better."

Elijah said, "I'm surprised they haven't come here yet. I mean, there are some Loyalist militia running around, but they don't come bothering us Indians. We got a reputation for scalping, and so on."

"Yeah, you're pretty fierce."

"Yeah, I've never scalped anybody. Neither have any of my friends. We Lumbee are kind of quiet, and we are accepting of lots of white man ways. Plus, you saw Irving. We keep a look out, you know?"

"Where did he get the name Irving?"

"His daddy is a Jew from Crosscreek."

"Ha. I was in Savannah for a time. Lots of Jews in Savannah, they have a big synagogue there."

"No synagogue's around here. Irving's our only Jew. He says Jews and Indians are alike in that white men attack us. So, he's happy to stand guard."

"Good idea. In Georgia and South Carolina there are banditti, that's what they call these armed bands of thugs. Some person gets a commission from the King to form a regiment and they use it as an excuse to plunder and burn farms. I understand that up country it's more of a civil war than just a fight between England and America. And there are some brutal, blood thirsty people on both sides of this thing."

One morning while Elijah was out tending the garden, Aiyana said, "There is heaviness in your heart, Will."

"Aye. How can you tell?"

"Women are sensitive to when a man is hurting. It is a woman, is it not?"

"Aye. Abby. I was gone a year and she married. Now she is with child."

"Even so, you lay with her before you left Bear Creek."

"How did you know that?"

Aiyana gave him a look. "Call it intuition. An Indian woman's sense."

"Oh. Well, yes. I feel ashamed, sometimes."

"Other times you feel good?"

"Aye. Miss Aiyana. I do feel good sometimes."

"This is the way of the world. Happiness turns to sadness turns to happiness. It is a cycle."

Will said, "I'm trying to learn some of the wisdom others have."

Aiyana said, "It will come with age. Know that there are others who will make you happy and your life will go on. Give it time."

Will looked at her and said, "Those are wise words."

"Yeah, I'm an Indian. I'm also a woman. Not sure which one is speaking just now."

Will grinned at her. He liked Aiyana very much.

Will and Elijah were sitting on the riverbank with a couple cane poles fishing. Tomorrow will had to leave.

Elijah said, "Last time you were through here you couldn't stop talking about Abby and Martha. This time, not a peep."

Will said, "Ah, God. I'm doomed to have what I heard a man in Georgia call 'woman trouble.'"

Elijah snorted, "Ha, we Indians don't have woman trouble. They tell us what to do and that's it."

Will said, "When last I was here, Abby had made it clear she loves me, and I was floating on a cloud. But I had committed to Martha, and I had to go see where that would go. As it happens, Martha was using me to distract her brother and her daddy from noticing she was caught up with a sea captain. She dumped me and almost immediately ran off with the sea captain."

Elijah leaned back and said, "Did she now?" After a moment, he spat, "Bitch!"

"Yeah. It was a surprise to get to Sunbury, Georgia, which is a little seaport, and that very night have Martha Black come walking into the tavern where I was staying. She had on a man's sea captain outfit and was buying a bottle of rum."

"You don't say? My God, but I need a woman like that!"

Will smirked, "She'd shoot you, I'm afraid. She'd probably shoot anyone other than her husband, the sea captain she ran off with."

Will continued, "I wrote to Abby several times, but it appears the mail does not run. She decided I was dead and married a neighbor. She's now carrying his child, and he's off with the North Carolina Militia."

"Damn, man. You surely live an interesting life."

Will said, "Yeah. I hear from some of the sea captains in Savannah that the Chinese curse a man by saying, 'may you lead an interesting life.'"

Elijah laughed and laughed.

Will got tickled and started laughing too. "I guess I am cursed like the Chinese say."

Will and Old Tom trotted out of Drowning Creek the next day. Aiyana said, "You're welcome here anytime, Will."

"Thank you, ma'am. I will come back. Watch out for those white men."

Everyone laughed, but Will knew it was a true caution. These people wanted nothing more than to live quietly following the ways of their ancestors. Will understood their desires. All he wanted was to get a little piece of land on the frontier and fix people's guns.

He hoped Elijah and Aiyana and the others would be unmolested.

Elijah and Aiyana waved from the dirt path in front of their humble little cabin.

Will looked back and smiled. In his heart, he knew his wish for their peace would not come true.

CHAPTER 26 – SAVANNAH, AGAIN

Five days later, Will and Old Tom trotted into New Bern. The Koontz's were doing well and were happy to have Will back.

Will spent a week renewing his gunsmithing skills with Mr. Bert. Actually, Will was helping to do things Mr. Bert could no longer do, but that was not spoken. It was good for Will, too. He hauled some heavy iron and kegs of swan shot. He pumped the bellows some, building a burn in the fire to match the burn in his muscles. It felt good to sleep at night, and Will was happy. Will knew he had to leave soon.

Over a supper of fresh fish that Will had caught in the Neuse River, just down from Koontz's, Will asked, "Can I leave Old Tom with y'all?"

"Sure," Mr. Bert said. "He's a good horse. Why are you not taking him?"

"Sea voyages are hard on horses." Will grinned, "They're hard enough on people. I have Molly in Georgia, and I don't know what I would do with a second horse. Old Tom is a good horse, and he's still young. If you don't need him, you can sell him."

"I'm sure we can find a use for Old Tom."

Will said, "I have been talking to Dicky about when he's sailing south. He's saying soon, perhaps next week. And this time he thinks he's going to Savannah. If that's the case, I can catch the express schooner there to go to Sunbury and collect Molly."

Miss Becky sat back and wiped her eyes on her sleeve. "You're leaving so soon? Oh, Will. We worry so when you are gone."

"I know, Miss Becky. I'm trying to find my way."

Bert said, "That brings up the question, 'what next?'"

Will said, "I don't know. My world has shifted. Abby is married and will soon have a baby."

Miss Becky put her hand on Will's. "Yes, sweetie. But the world is not at an end. There will be someone for you, my darling."

"Yes, Ma'am, I know. I am thinking I should go look at North Georgia. Colonel Elbert said he would help me to get a land grant there when we win our independence."

Bert said, "What will you do with your farm?"

"Mr. Burdell offered to buy it, but we have not settled on the details. I will see Burdell this week and work out a sale with our lawyer. There are no slaves. Uncle Ewan abhorred slavery, his experience as a Scotsman under the thumb of the English would never have allowed him to hold a slave. There are some 100 acres of land. I hear good farmland is worth perhaps £1 12 shillings per acre. There's that patch of wetland that is hard to plant, so I will talk to the lawyer about setting a price of £1 10 shillings per acre."

Mr. Bert said, "I'll be happy to help with all those details."

Will replied, "Good. Can we go see the lawyer together?"

Dicky confirmed the Caswell's ship, a top sail-rigged schooner named *Henrietta Alice*, was leaving on the coming Friday. The wonderful news was that *Henrietta Alice* was delivering a cargo to Savannah.

Will hurried and met with Mr. Bert, the lawyer, and Mr. Burdell about selling the farm. They settled on a price of £130 for the entire property including all the farm implements and other items.

Will left the £130 on deposit with Governor Caswell. He also provided Governor Caswell the $200 continental dollars from the *Beatrice*'s prizes

Governor Caswell had advised Will to convert the Pounds Sterling and Continental dollars to Spanish silver. Inflation was driving currency down very hard and converting to Spanish silver would at least preserve its value. The rate was some 4 Continental dollars to the Spanish dollar. Will banked $50 in Spanish dollars for his time on *Beatrice*. He smiled because the trip originally was to have cost him $10 Spanish.

The £130 converted to Spanish dollars amounted to an advantageous trade. The rate was 4.5 Spanish dollars to the Pound Sterling, netting Will some $585 Spanish.

Added to the $200 Spanish dollars he had placed on deposit before leaving for Philadelphia, and another $50 in Spanish dollars accumulated from his various gunsmithing jobs while traveling, Will's entire funds on deposit amounted to $885 Spanish.

Governor Caswell provided Will new letters of introduction as well as a new letter to Brother Masons identifying Will's funds on deposit. Will was not truly wealthy, but he was now well-off. He could afford a place of his own. Now to get the war over and find the home he always wanted. Perhaps he would find a wife to share it.

Mornings in August 1778 were already hot when the sun cracked the horizon. Sea spray cooled the air around the *Henrietta Alice*, but sweat still ran down the middle of Will's spine.

Dicky Caswell, Will's junior by a year, was already very competent as ships master. He was not born to sailing command, but he had a sailing master aboard who managed the trim of the sails and Dicky let him handle that task without interference.

Henrietta Alice mounted three four- pounders per broadside, plus several swivel guns mounted on the rails. But, as a fast schooner, her best defense against privateers was speed. The sailing master could set the sails in such a way that, with a following wind, the ship fairly flew across the water. Twice sloops attempted to intercept the *Henrietta Alice*. Those ship-rigged vessels quickly fell well astern, and within a few short hours each had given up, going off in search of easier prey.

The schooner was also a good ride. Not too much buck and wallow with a quartering sea. Even at speed, with all sail piled on, the schooner did not bang down into troughs, seeming to skim from one peak to another. Water hissed down the hull and left a creamy, white wake.

Will thought that it was pleasant being on a ship but did not relish the sea like some did. He did love the freshness of the air as it flew by the ship. The five-day trip to Georgia with a cargo of naval stores and rope served an opportunity for Will and Dicky to catch up. One evening they sat in Dicky's sea cabin eating a simple meal of dried beef and bread. They shared a splash each from a bottle of rum.

Dicky said, "Tell me about what happened at Kennedys' home. You have been close mouthed. I'm assuming things didn't turn out as well as you hoped."

Will told Dicky the story. Everything except Abby's visit in the night.

Dicky looked away. His voice husky, Dicky said, "Ah, life, Will. I, uh...I know you were hurt by Martha. Now Abby. But you're a handsome lad. I'm sure there are other women."

"Aye. A lady named Charlotte Jones in Savannah has signaled her interest. Truth to be told, I was not terribly receptive. Two young women in Charlestown have made clear they are available, and one has made her interest very clear."

"Oh? Very clear? My, my."

Will grinned. "Tis a distance from Savannah to Charlestown."

Dicky leered at him wolfishly, "Perhaps you can become a courier and travel from one city to the other on business. I'm sure they would provide you an escort."

Will laughed out loud. But he considered that such an idea might have merit.

Henrietta Alice stood into the mouth of the Savanna River on August 7, 1778. It was even hotter the farther south she sailed. The fresh wind Will had savored farther out at sea had become more languid with moisture and less refreshing. Will considered that the ship was moving forward creating a pleasant breeze. What must it be like to be out of the wind ashore in Georgia? At Fort Howe earlier this year someone had said September was the hottest month. Will would soon find out for himself.

The gray of the ocean water gave way to the copper-colored water in the river. Will looked at the snags and the few masts still protruding from the water, a strong vee in water behind each as the river ran swiftly to the sea. Those snags would gut a ship in no time.

Soon, the ship passed a place that Elbert had said was called Girardeau's. It was a wide spot with what appeared to be solid ground, a dock and a causeway leading to high ground. Will found himself idly thinking that it would be a good place to land an army. The *Henrietta Alice* came around a bend in the river and Savannah lay before them.

Will stepped onto the dock back in Georgia. It had been nearly 90 days since he had trotted onto the Rochester Ferry alongside Lieutenant Colonel Francis Marion. It had been a long, sometimes sad, sometimes joyous, trip. In the lee of the ship, the air was like a furnace. Will said to Dicky, let's go to the best tavern in town. Perhaps there will be people of my acquaintance.

They walked the few blocks to Tondee's Tavern where, as Will had expected, they found a friendly welcome. Lucy Tondee was putting a tray on a table just inside the entrance.

"Will Yelverton! I thought you were gone!"

"I have just returned from a long trip to North Carolina. This is my good friend, Dicky Caswell of New Bern, North Carolina."

325

Lucy appraised Dicky from head to foot. "You'll do. Do they make only handsome men in North Carolina?"

Dicky blushed, "I fear they broke the mold with my friend, Will."

"Not if you're younger."

"Aye, Miss Lucy, I am a year younger."

Lucy Tondee smirked, "Then the mold was still in operation for you. Y'all go on back to the long room. Several of the worthies have already begun gathering. Tis too hot to work this day!"

Will and Dicky stepped into the famous long room to find John Milledge and Edward Telfair sitting at one end of the center table, deep in conversation.

"It was a goad-dam cockup!" Telfair was sputtering.

"Aye, but what did you expect?" Milledge responded.

"What was a fiasco?" Will asked.

Milledge looked up, grinned and said, "Yelverton, old man! Back from the hinterland of North Carolina, I see."

Will smiled and shook hands. "Yes, t'was an arduous journey. My friend, Dicky Caswell brought me on his ship the *Henrietta Alice*."

Telfair boomed in his Scotish brogue, "You'll be Dick Caswell's son, then, Laddie?"

"Aye," Dicky said. "My father is Dick Caswell."

"Welcome to Savannah, and my regards to your father upon your return. Tell him Edward Telfair sends his best."

Handshakes all around preceded Telfair shouting, "Mistress Tondee! A bottle for the table. Our friends in from North Carolina are fair parched, Lassie."

Lucy Tondee came to the table with a bottle on a tray and two additional cups.

Will said, "Now, to my original question. What fiasco?"

Milledge and Telfair chorused, "Florida."

Will blanched. "Oh? I hope no one got killed."

Telfair "Oh, aye, Laddie. Several got killed. Elbert is alright and Houstoun is uninjured. But Howe struggled mightily without success to get overall control of the force. They took weeks to get to the Saint Mary's. Deaths from sickness and a good many deserters added to the misery. We had a courier come from Florida to say that they had gotten into a fight a few miles into Florida and were camped at Fort Tonyn on the south side of the Saint Mary's River.

Will said, "My goodness, that sounds like a terrible situation."

Milledge nodded. "I understand that rotten highwayman Daniel McGirth has been commissioned a Lieutenant Colonel in the Florida Rangers, and his band of shirtless, shoeless, unwashed crackers were there as well. Worst low-life cutthroats I've ever heard of."

Will asked, "What is the plan now?"

Telfair leaned close, "The courier said they're withdrawing. The fear is the British and the Tories will come north and attack into Liberty County. Sunbury and the fort there could be threatened."

Will replied, "Oh. I must travel to Sunbury. My horse is there."

Telfair said, "Think you should consider going sooner than later, me Laddie. Houstoun will probably be back directly to tell us about how he should have been the overall commander and that would have assured victory."

Milledge smirked. "Aye. I'm sure that'll be an interesting tale."

Dicky said, "You lead an interesting life, Will."

Will snickered, "The sea captains say that is a Chinese curse."

Will and Dicky hired a carriage and rode out to Rae's Hall. They could have stayed on the *Henrietta Alice*, but Will wanted to see Liz Elbert and learn if Colonel Elbert was truly uninjured.

The carriage crunched up the gravel drive to the mansion that was Elbert's home. Dust hung in the air, and insects flitted in all directions. Heat hung heavy in the early twilight, and gnats swarmed in a cloud around Will and Dicky's face, occasionally getting in their eyes. The gnats were particularly maddening when they found their way into the men's hair. As they slowed, a mosquito whined in Will's ear.

As the carriage crunched through the gravel at the front door, Liz Elbert stepped out the front door. "Will? Will! Oh, goodness! I'm so glad you are back. Come in, come in!"

Will alighted from the carriage and Dicky followed just behind.

Will said, "I have the temerity to bring a friend in hopes of learning that Colonel Elbert is well after the unsuccessful invasion and also to beg accommodation."

"Oh, Will, you don't have to ask about staying. And Sam is fine. And who is your handsome young companion?"

"Mrs. Liz Elbert, I have the honor to present Richard Caswell, Jr., Dicky to his friends. Merchant from New Bern, North Carolina. Son of Governor Richard Caswell."

"Dicky, this is my good friend, Mrs. Liz Elbert."

Liz said, "Welcome, Mr. Caswell."

Dicky bowed formally and said, "I am honored to meet such a lovely lady. Please, call me Dicky. Mr. Caswell is my father."

329

Liz grinned. "Are all North Carolina gentlemen so gallant? Do come in. I'll get someone to take your baggage to your rooms."

The three sat at the Elbert's table. Liz's cook had a pork roast cooking when they arrived, and she had the servants throw on some additional vegetables and had some fresh bread as well.

Will said, "The bread is so good. I love it with the cold butter from your spring house. What do you hear from the Colonel?"

"He will return during the week, I think. Sam is fit to be tied! T'was a terrible error for the forces to go south without a single commander. But he was not in command, and blame does not attach to him. Still, he is furious with Houstoun. Please don't repeat that."

"Oh, Liz, neither Dicky nor I will ever repeat anything we hear. I will tell you that my discussions with Johnny Milledge and Ed Telfair betray a similar displeasure with the expedition. Particularly the lack of a single commander. But that is something you already know."

That night, Will collapsed into his now-familiar bed at Rae's Hall and slept hard, the slight breeze drifting through the two windows cooling the room enough that Will finally needed the crisp, white sheet to cover up. The morning dawned warm and soon it was too hot to sleep.

Will cast off the sheet and lay on his back nude except for his linen drawers. He drifted, still drowsy from the heat. His mind wandered. He ached deep in his chest for Abby. He was so sorry for the fact that his letters had not arrived. He also floated in his mind to their last night together. His body betrayed him, and he became hard. Soon, his heart was pounding in rhythm of the stroking of his hand. He soon completed the act. It was both urgent from need and tinged with sadness.

Will washed at the small washstand in the corner and looked at himself in the mirror. How sad he looked! Despite being tanned from riding through the North Carolina summer and being at sea, he thought he looked pale and tired.

The smell of Liz Elbert's bread pulled Will to the dining room. Liz was drinking a cup of coffee. Dicky was still not down from his bedroom.

Liz said, "I detect a note of sadness, Will."

"Aye. I arrived in Bear Creek to find that my letters had never arrived. Abby has wed another and is with his child. Her husband is with the North Carolina Militia somewhere in South Carolina."

"Oh, my poor young friend. I'm sure you must hurt."

"Aye. The hurt is immeasurable. My heart aches."

"I hope you had time to say goodbye."

"She came to me in the night."

"Oh, my. I know that must have been bittersweet."

"Yes, Liz. I tried to feel morally wrong for that, but I cannot."

"Nor should you. The circumstances of this war have cruelly used you both. She is with child and her husband will not ever know of your relation. The goodbye was important to you both. What you must do now is move on. There is a life in the future for you, Will. I've told you that Charlotte Jones is quite taken with you."

Will said, "Yes, 'tis true, I should move on."

Liz paused. She looked at Will hard. "There is someone else?"

"Well, yes. I stopped at the Yonge's as you suggested."

"Eliza?"

"No. She was quite unpleasant to me. Called me a coward. But her friend, Mary, took pains to be kind to me."

Liz looked at him inquiringly. "She was kind."

Will was flummoxed. "I...uh...she...made her interest clear."

"Well, you had quite a trip. Did you not feel badly about this liaison when you were on your way to see Abby?"

"Yes, but as Mary said, it was entirely possible that Abby was married or had passed away. There is so much sickness."

"Aye. Tis true, Will. This is proof for you that you should move on to find your future. In that regard, I shall invite some of the Savannah gentry to come to a gathering to welcome Sam home. That will give you yet another opportunity to meet Charlotte Jones, as well as some other lovely young ladies."

CHAPTER 27 – ELBERT

Dicky grinned at Will. "These few days have been most pleasant. You have made some wonderful friends in Georgia, but don't forget your family and friends in Carolina."

The two men were standing in the sun on the dock next to *Henrietta Alice*. The air moved sluggishly in the mid-morning doldrums. The tide was about to turn, and there was hope of a breeze. Sweat popped and trickled as they said goodbye.

"Aye. I won't forget my Carolina home. Yet here is opportunity, and I think many of these men you have met will rise high in the leadership of this state, and perhaps others. Tis good to know such men."

Dicky smirked in mock wolfishness, "Their women are not bad, either. Two or three of the young ladies I had the pleasure of meeting at Mrs. Elbert's little party were quite comely and smart. T'was a delight to meet them."

Dicky glanced up at the trade buildings, some already rebuilt after the fire. "Trade was good. My cargo brought top dollar, and I shall have to work to open more trade with this fine city. After meeting the fair women here and becoming acquainted with the merchants, perhaps there will be more excuses to travel here."

Will said, "I worry that the war may come here soon. The failure of the latest expedition to Florida may open the door to British and Tory raiders coming north. I'm going to Sunbury soon to retrieve Molly. It worries me that she is stabled there, and the fort will fall under a sustained attack. It is naught but dirt and pine logs. I can't tolerate the thought of some miserable low-life riding Molly."

A slight breeze stirred, and Will saw a subtle change in the water. Now a slight ripple was evident around the pilings and running by the hull of the schooner.

Dicky noticed the change in the river, too. "I must take my leave. The tide has turned and 'tis time to cast off. Good luck, Will. And I'm sure someone will come along and help you forget about Abby."

Will looked down at his feet. "Perhaps. Good luck to you Dicky. Terrible pirates and privateers abound off the coast."

"Aye, but they'll have to catch me, and Miss Henrietta is quite fleet of foot."

They shook hands, and Dicky quickly walked up the gang plank. Bounding up the ladder to the quarter deck, Dicky stood back from the wheel where a Savanna River pilot stood waiting to take the ship out.

Will watched until the ship was well out into the copper water of the channel and headed downriver. The tide was right, and *Henrietta Alice* began to move at some speed as she picked up the freshening breeze from the west. Only a few sails were required for the quick little schooner to make good headway.

Will waived and went to the carriage to go back to Rae's Hall. He would miss Dicky.

Will walked into the entrance hall at Rae's Hall. Colonel Elbert came striding toward him from the dining room.

"Will! Tis good to see you."

"Colonel Elbert, I'm happy you're back. You look well. No injuries?"

"Nay. I'm unwounded except for my pride, which has taken quite a beating. Can't say the same for Elijah Clarke or Screven. They both were wounded, Clarke grievously."

"I have not had the pleasure of meeting those gentlemen. I do hope Colonel Clarke recovers."

"Aye, the coming days will tell. Come sit at the table and tell me of your trip."

"I shall be glad to tell you of my trip to Carolina, but first I must hear about the expedition. I understand command disputes caused problems?"

Colonel Elbert said, "Aye, Will. We shall not talk of this among others, but I can tell you that, in confidence, General Bob Howe did not want to invade Florida. He prefers a defensive posture. Alas, that position was not to be. The Continental Congress ordered an invasion, and off we went."

"It was, as I predicted, a terrible mess. His Excellency, Governor Houstoun, was most disagreeable, and a military genius he is not. The militia was utterly uncontrollable. Then, there were the South Carolinians. They have always been difficult when coming south to help us. The help is not truly help when it is conditioned upon being independent. General Howe begged the militias of both States to conform to his command. Had there been cooperation and unity of command, we might have prevailed."

"The army numbered some 2500 men and took quite a long time to march to Florida due to crossing many creeks and swamps. You were present for the sickness that raged in our camps. I can't tell you how many men we lost to that flux. Others simply deserted, and I know not where they went. We did hang a few at Fort Howe, or what was left of Fort Howe. That slowed the desertions, but not the sickness from the flux."

"On the march we were also hauling artillery that was a trial on the sandy, boggy, narrow roads. We had three brass field pieces, two iron two-pounders, and a pair of swivel coehorns. The field pieces rolled comfortably enough on their wheels, but the other guns had to be transported on wagons. Nevertheless, it was a struggle dragging those guns through swamp and marsh. Every mud hole was a fight, and the men were exhausted."

"The day we arrived at the Saint Mary's River we found Fort Tonyn abandoned and burned. Crossed right into Florida and started deploying our troops. The Georgia Militia got out in front as we completed the crossing."

"The next day during the confusion of getting organized on the south side of the river, the Governor let Colonel Jim Screven chase some of Brown's troops in a horse race for the British lines. Jim was over bold and very impetuous, and he dashed right out to where the British were encamped at Alligator Creek. Worse, neither our troops nor Brown's raiders were dressed in uniforms. That led to a vast confusion of who was who, and the ensuing melee was insane. At first the British regulars were hesitant to shoot for fear of killing their own. Then all hell broke loose, and the firing was intense."

"I think there may have been 500 British, Florida Rangers, and South Carolina Royalist Militia there under Major Marc Prevost, General Augustine Prevost's younger brother. Prevost ordered his troops to quickly take up positions and start shooting. They were dug in behind palm logs and an earthwork with a ditch. Screven got into quite a fight that he had not expected. Wouldn't be the first time he ran headlong into an ambush. He was wounded, too. I like Jim Screven personally, but he's quite a hothead and impulsive, too."

"Colonel Elijah Clarke gathered 100 mounted militia and attempted to support Screven by attacking the weakest flank on the British right. The entrenchments at the bridge and the soggy ground off the road bogged down Clarke. Clarke's men spurred their horses at the fort but found the ditch too wide to jump. Brown's rangers came up on the Americans' left flank and joined in on the fight. Clarke was shot through his left thigh, and barely escaped capture. Sixteen of his men went down. Elijah was bleeding all down the side of his horse and ordered his troops to withdraw. Fortunately, he did not bleed to death, and so far, he has escaped infection that kills so many with minor wounds."

Elbert said, "If Screven had not backed off when Clarke's attack failed, his entire command of maybe 200 would have been captured. As it is, Jim Screven himself took a grazing wound from a ball. They withdrew and camped at Fort Tonyn with nine dead and a good many wounded."

Elbert continued, "Governor Houstoun threw up his hands and took his escort and left. General Howe remained with the army for several days before deciding that the campaign was not going to succeed. The British were entrenched across the road and the area all around was swamp, reducing any chance of flanking their position. The defenses were simply insurmountable. It took us two months or more to march there for a two-day fight that we lost before we started."

"General Howe left Florida with his escort on July 14th. He is in Savannah. It took until August 10 for us to get back to Fort Howe. I came on here today. Screven and Clarke are in the area near Sunbury. Jim Screven's home is in Midway, near the Meeting House. Clarke needs to recover from his wound."

"John McIntosh continues to command at the Sunbury fort. A good many men are still in the area, White's battalion, Baker's unit, to name a couple. I still fear we are vulnerable to the British coming north from Florida."

Will said, "Aye. What of the French? And did you hear General Washington won a great victory in New Jersey?"

Elbert replied, "Yes, the war in the North appears to go better. And you ask a good question. The French have been active. I understand there have been some Naval actions. The treaty was signed in early February. The French pledged military materials, arms, and equipment, as well as funds and other support. I hope we shall soon see troops."

Elbert sat back and said, "I think we should get some brandy and you must tell me of your travels, Will."

Will said, "Very well, Sir. It is a short tale."

Three tots of bandy later for each of the men, Will's tale was told.

"I'm pleased you met Francis Marion. He is well liked and a good soldier. I know him slightly. I am, however, deeply sympathetic about your experience with Abby. What a tragedy."

Will looked at Elbert. "That is a word used about Shakespeare's plays."

"Aye. You know Shakespeare?"

"I did not until a young lady in South Carolina quoted Shakespeare and drove me to learn what she meant."

Elbert said, "Ah. Well, all of life is a tragedy, Will. But your situation where poor Miss Abby did not receive your letters and then wed another is, indeed, a tragedy."

"I have been reading your book by Mr. Gibbon about the Roman Empire."

"Aye? I have not had the time to read that book. You, Sir, are becoming an educated man, and I'm quite pleased."

Will blushed. "I felt a bumpkin when meeting society people in Philadelphia and again here in Georgia. South Carolina, too. I never had occasion to think of reading a book. I always saw myself as a craftsman repairing people's guns and running a small business. Learning was for others. I mean, I went to school for a time, but it was more like work than an interesting pastime."

Elbert refreshed their glasses and grinned from ear to ear. "Ah, and that, young Sir, is the beginning of wisdom. And now I shall press you about my offer of a majority."

Will sat back and took a sip of the brandy. An insect flitted by. He looked briefly at the ceiling and then leveled his gaze at Sam Elbert. "Ah, my life has taken the strangest turns, Sir. All I wanted was to go to the frontier, get a small plot of land and set up shop. I wanted simply to be of service to fellow pioneers and make a living. All that is for naught. The war has swallowed me up like Jonah in the whale. Tis upsetting that I have the means to own a small place, but not the opportunity. The British and the Tories have personally affronted me by pulling me away from the woman I love and by calling me a traitor and a spy. I am none of those."

"I know you're not, Will."

The insect buzzed by again, finding its way off the porch. Will took a deep breath, let it out, and said, "I shall accept your offer, Sir, provided some conditions are agreeable."

Elbert's eyebrows shot up. "Conditions? Will, when one joins the Continental Army, the Congress does not offer conditions."

"My conditions are reasonable. I wish to be allowed freedom to go places and do things that support our cause. Yes, it is now my cause. As I said, I have been accused of being a spy. I would have no problem with being a true spy. I also would anticipate acting as a courier. Perhaps without wearing the uniform all the time. I would prefer not to ride a horse in front of a group of men with muskets. I am not a coward, and I have been in a shooting fight. But there are others who are far more competent than I to lead men in a fight. As to being possibly hanged as a spy, I have nothing to live for, Sam."

It was the first time Will had ever used Elbert's Christian name.

Elbert gazed at Will. "Oh, you have plenty to live for. I think those conditions are reasonable. In many ways, you have already been doing exactly what you propose. You have stepped up to be a true patriot, and that rifle of yours has surely put the dot on the eye of the enemy in more than one instance. I shall talk to General Howe. I will insist you be assigned to my staff to carry out duties as assigned."

Will said, "Very well, Sir. I am always at your service."

Elbert laughed and said, "and to think, at our first meeting you threatened me with a pistol."

"You accused me of being a spy."

"Now you are one."

CHAPTER 28 – MOLLY

Will quietly walked into the stable at the fort at Sunbury. He had been gone for almost four months. Would Molly know him?

"Hello, Girl. I'm back."

Molly's head whipped around, and her eyes met his. She nodded her head, pawed the ground, and let out a loud whinny. Then she whickered and nodded vigorously.

Will stroked her neck. Molly nuzzled his hand and snuffled him. Excited, she whickered and pawed the ground.

"I bet you thought I had left you behind. I went off with that terrible other horse and you didn't get to go. But it's alright now. I'm back and we're going for a ride."

Molly nodded vigorously and, pawing the ground, whickered.

Getting Molly's saddle, Will said, "Want to go for a ride?"

Molly was shaking with excitement as Will led her into the stable yard and mounted up. He was wearing his hunting clothes, pistol, dirk, and carbine. The guns were loaded with buck and ball. He would not be gone long, and he didn't anticipate danger, but Will still took a dozen homemade cartridges of buck and ball as a precaution. He had carefully wrapped a charge of powder and a little bit extra with a pistol ball and half a dozen buckshot interspersed with some smaller swan shot in an oiled paper. The ends were twisted tight.

Will and Molly trotted out the main gate of the fort. The sentry glanced up, recognized Will, and stood to smart attention, saluting as Will rode past. Will did his best to return the salute and look military about it. After all, he was now Major Yelverton of the Continental Army.

Will and Molly rode through Sunbury and on up past the Cemetery. Dozens of fresh graves marked where military men from all over the southeast had been interred. Few from combat, many from malaria.

Will's mouth turned down as he passed these freshly turned piles of earth. He thought of Aunt Pat and Uncle Ewan, Peg, little Sally, his baby sister, and others who had died in the past few years. Even Isiah, who would have murdered Will, deserved a brief thought.

Trotting along, Will thought about Abby, too. Of course, Abby was not dead, but for him it was like she had died. She existed somewhere in his mind, but he could not conjure up thoughts of her daily existence. What did she do in the mornings? Where did she live? Was there a nice warm fireplace in the winter? Did she chop and split her own firewood? Did Micah come help her? These were unanswered questions. He simply did not know any answers. He could not see her cabin, the plot of land it sat on. It must be like other cabins, but he could not see it. Was there a stream where she could get water? Bathe? What would she do when the baby came?

Will was alone and he cuffed the tears from his eyes. He thought, "I have to stop acting like a baby and crying all the time. What's done is done. It is like Shakespeare. A tragedy."

The sandy road rose slightly, and Will and Molly trotted up the little rise. A wide meadow appeared. A startled bird flew from a thicket on Will's right. Insects buzzed in the heat. Will said, "Let's run, girl." He lightly touched Molly's flanks and she took off! They were at a gallop in no time, Molly's breath coming in whooshes and gasps as her body expelled air and dragged in oxygen. Molly's hooves kicked up a cloud of light beige dust in the September sun.

Will slowed Molly to a run. He thought she needed building up to galloping since she'd been in the stall a lot these six months. Six months! It was just September, and he had stepped off *Beatrice* at the end of February.

A lot had happened. Fort Howe, Frederica, South Carolina, Mary, North Carolina, Benjamin, Abby, a commission in the Continental Army, and now back to Molly.

Elbert had given Will leave to go to Sunbury and pick up Molly as well as to work with Colonel John McIntosh. "Learn how to be a Continental Officer, Will. John will teach you. Although you won't wear the uniform all the time, you should at least learn how to wear it and how to exercise the men in their drills, and so on. I'll see you back here in the fall."

"Very well, Sir. I will try to become a real officer."

Will had worn his new uniform to board the express schooner to Sunbury. He was dashing in the dark blue coat, major's shoulder epaulet, buff waistcoat and breeches, black boots, officer's hanger sword, and cocked hat.

He stepped aboard the small ship and the master said, "Don't I know you, Major?"

"Aye. I'm Will Yelverton. I have had the pleasure of being a passenger on your wonderful ship a few times."

"Indeed, but I don't recall the uniform."

"No, 'tis new."

"Congratulations are in order, then? I hope you wear it in good health."

"Thank you, Skipper."

The schooner fairly flew from Savannah to Sunbury and stood into the now-familiar little harbor. It nudged up to the quay and Will took his baggage and walked down to the wharf.

A private bustled up. Saluting Will, the private said, "I'll be happy to arrange for the major's baggage."

Returning the salute, Will said, "Don't recognize me, eh, Cuthbert?"

"My God! Will...er, I mean, Major Yelverton. Congratulations. The uniform suits you, Sir."

Will grinned, "Thank ye. I hope to do it justice."

"I'm sure you will. I'll have your baggage delivered to the officers' quarters."

"Thanks. I'm told I must have an orderly while I'm in garrison. Up for the task?"

"Oh, aye. And I'll be happy to do it. You've been kind to me in the past, and I learned a lot about gunsmithing. I've taken to being something of the fort's gunsmith."

"Well done! I shan't take you from the gunsmithing chores too much."

"I'm sure my sergeant will not complain. Welcome back."

Will walked into Lt Colonel John McIntosh's office and stood at what he hoped looked like the position of Attention. He rendered what he also hoped resembled a sharp salute and said, "Major Yelverton reporting, Sir."

John McIntosh glanced up, did a double-take, and returned the salute. He stood, and said, "What did Sam say to get you to become an officer? I thought you were adamant against being in the military."

"Aye, Sir. Circumstances..." Will trailed off.

"Oh, we all have those. I'm sure I'll worm it out of you over some brandy tonight. Care to join me at the Eagle for a bite this evening?"

"That would be excellent."

"Captain Pearre will get you a room. I'm sure we have a couple left open. Whichever one you get, air it out. We've had some sickness and death from a variety of fluxes."

"Thank you, Sir."

"You'll need an orderly. Field officers are authorized."

"Yes, Sir. Perhaps Private Cuthbert? He's agreeable."

"He should be. Comes with a promotion to corporal."

The next morning Will awoke with a somewhat painful head. Cuthbert tapped on his door and entered with a pitcher of hot water and some soap plus a towel.

"I will endeavor to steal, er...locate, a small mirror for you."

"Ah, God, but my head is exploding!"

"Bit of the hair of the dog, Sir?"

"I think I had the whole dog, Cuth. That corporal's epaulet looks good on you."

That's down to you, Sir. Happy to be of service."

"You may one day regret saying that."

Cuthbert glanced at Will. "Part of wearin' this outfit is the possibility of getting a small wooden box and a tiny piece of real estate for all time, Sir."

349

"Aye. We'll endeavor to avoid that real estate. Don't need to be a land baron quite yet, do you?"

Cuthbert grinned. "No, Sir."

Will said, "Cuth, I'm soon to be asked to drill the troops. It's not to be my primary function, but I must make a good showing of it. Can you give me some private lessons so that I don't look a complete idiot?"

"Of course. Let's do some stomping about down at the stable."

Over the next few days, Will learned how to bark orders like he'd heard real soldiers do. He learned how to draw his sword without injuring himself and to salute with it and how to carry it when marching.

The marching part was not hard. Will considered it a little like dancing the reel. You just had to step in time and not stumble. The hard part was learning the commands.

John McIntosh had a book that listed the commands as well as drills like how to load a musket. Will was surprised that there were specific, defined steps and hand movements to precisely load and fire a military musket. At the command 'Present!' Will read that the soldier was to "...step back about six inches with the right foot bringing the left toe to the front. Raise up the butt so high upon the right shoulder that you may not be obliged to stoop too much with the head, the right cheek to be close to the butt and the left eye shut and look along the barrel, with the right eye from the breech pin to the muzzle."

Will studied the book where he found several drawings of a soldier with a musket. There were several positions the men must know. They started with a drawing entitled, Position of a Soldier under Arms. The soldier was standing with his musket on his left shoulder. The steps of firing and reloading followed.

I. Poise the firelock. The soldier positions the musket vertically before his body.

II. Cock. The soldier quickly cocks the doghead holding the flint.

III. Present. The soldier raises the musket pointing it in the direction of the enemy.

IV. Fire. The soldier pulls the trigger briskly. After the firelock is discharged, the soldier is seen with the musket held across his body, ready to load for another volley.

V. Half cock. The soldier pulls the dog head cock to its half position and opens the pan.

VI. Handle cartridge. The soldier draws a cartridge from his cartridge box and bites off the top of the cartridge paper.

VII. Prime. The soldier shakes a small amount of the powder from the cartridge into the pan.

VIII. Shut your pans. The soldier closes the pan briskly and drops the musket onto its but plate, with the muzzle at the height of the soldier's chin.

IX. Charge with cartridge. The soldier puts the cartridge into the barrel, torn side down and shakes the powder down the barrel.

X. Draw rammers. The soldier draws the ramrod and starts the ramrod into the barrel.

XI. Ram cartridges. The soldier rams the cartridge well down the barrel and draws out the ramrod.

XII. Return rammers. The soldier places the ramrod into its channel under the barrel.

The soldier returns to the I. Poise position. Now the soldier was ready to fire again.

Will sat and thought about this entire set of steps that were natural to him as a gunsmith. He pondered why there were pictures and specific, exacting steps. It dawned upon him that while he could read, many men could not. A set of steps that were listed as must do items were probably set up that way so that the illiterate men could move in unison and achieve firing as one.

Will realized that muskets were more about volume of fire than they were about accuracy. There were no sights...just point and shoot. Rifles were about accuracy. They had precise sights. He wondered if the musket could be made more accurate with some training for the men and perhaps adding some kind of sight. He would have to consider that. But for now, he would simply be satisfied with appearing to know what he was doing leading men.

Now it was a month later. The men had accepted Will as Major Yelverton. He felt they respected him. Cuthbert had no doubt helped with that, telling the men that the new Major, though young, was a warrior.

Will conducted classes on how to maintain muskets. Correct cleaning and maintenance of the weapon might someday save a soldier's life. Will also did classes on marksmanship. While the muskets had no real sights to permit precision shooting, learning how to aim better than just pointing the musket was something useful for the men. The men instinctively knew that Will was a good leader and was concerned for their safety.

◇◇◇

Will and Molly were delighting in a ride in the woods and galloping across the meadow. It was getting late in the afternoon.

September in Georgia was brutally hot, and Will's sweat streamed. Molly was wet as well. They slowed to a trot and Will spotted a small stream. He let Molly drink.

A hint of wood smoke floated across the meadow. Will glanced to the west where the wind was drifting from. He could see a small tendril of smoke perhaps a mile away.

He turned Molly's head and moved his knees slightly. Molly began to trot and then to canter. The smoke grew stronger, and Molly cantered faster. They were on a small ridge of sandy soil that was bordered by marsh grass and spotted with grass and sandspurs, a kind of sticker that was maddingly painful should it get in the skin. Will could see the smoke was more of a column now, no longer a tendril. Something substantial was on fire.

Soon the strong smoke was cloying, and Will coughed. Still, Molly ran on. They slowed to a trot as they entered a farmyard where a small house was now fully involved in flames. A woman and a man were running back and forth carrying buckets of water from a small creek to throw on the fire.

Will shouted, "Get back! You cannot save the building and you might die trying."

The two people turned to look at Will and then returned to their task of getting water and running to throw it on the fire. Will dismounted and started running toward the farmers. The woman was bending over the creek while the man threw water on the fire. Suddenly, the fire burst into a larger flame and licking out like it somehow was a living thing engulfed the man in a roaring blast of flame. The man was instantly immolated. He exploded into a burning, human pyre.

Will reached the woman just as the man died in a screaming agony of flame and smoke. She tried to go to the burning man, but Will grabbed her arms and held her. She fought like a banshee.

"Let me go! I can save him."

"No. He is already dead. Please stop. You will die needlessly."

"Nooooooo! I'd rather die than be without him."

"No. Stop. There is no saving him."

The woman started to cough, a wracking, guttural, hacking spasm.

Will dragged her to Molly. Molly's eyes were running with tears and her nose flared. Will threw the woman up into Molly's saddle and mounted Molly himself. He turned her head and they hurried away from the conflagration. They soon got to a place where the smoke was blowing the other way.

Will got the woman off the horse and helped her to sit down in the grass. He ran to the little creek and soaked a rag in water. Running back to the woman he squeezed the rag over her head rinsing cool water over her face. Rummaging in Molly's saddlebag, Will found a small leather bucket he had often used to get water for Molly. He ran to the creek and filled the bucket. He poured the cool water over the woman and helped her to drink some.

She turned a soot-streaked face to Will and croaked, "Abner is dead! I could have saved him."

"No, you couldn't. He caught fire because he was too close to the burning house and when the fire roared to life it enrobed him. He was dead almost instantly."

"He was moving."

"Oh, dear lady, that was his muscles tightening from the heat. You could do nothing, but you would have died trying. Let me take you to Sunbury and get you to a doctor to be sure you are alright."

Tears streaked down her soot covered face. "I must go to Abner. He...he...haaaa, haaaa, oh, GOD! Abner..."

Will got the woman on Molly and mounted himself. They rode quickly to Dr. Lyman Hall's home.

Hall came running out when he saw the condition of the woman. "What happened?"

Will explained, "I was out for a ride and saw smoke. I rode to its source, and this woman and her husband were fighting a terrible fire in their farmhouse. He was immolated by a huge burst of flame. She has inhaled smoke and she's also quite distressed. Her husband was called Abner and he is quite dead."

Dr. Hall said, "Madame, please allow me to treat you. Let us get you into my surgery where I might help with your burns."

Will had not noticed the woman had burns on her arms and face.

Dr. Hall said, "Thank you, Will. I can handle this from here."

Will said, "Very well. She is quite distressed and would have died in the fire with her husband. May I call tomorrow to see how she is faring?"

"Yes. Now I must get her into the surgery and see if there are other injuries I must attend to."

Will and Molly trotted into the fort. The sentry rendered a sharp salute, and Will returned it. But he was not thinking of anything but the poor woman whose husband had exploded in flames before her very eyes. He reeked of woodsmoke.

Jim, the stable hand from The Eagle who had been taking care of Molly all these months, was waiting in the stable. "Took her for a ride did you, Sir?"

"Yes. I hope she's ok. We were at a house fire."

"Wooo. I can smell the smoke. I'll check her over, Sir. I'll also give her a good washing down and rub her coat. She's such a good horse."

"Good, thank you. I need to get cleaned up. I feel like a pig that's been over a pit for hours."

Will walked into the officers' barracks.

Lt Colonel McIntosh said, "My God but you reek of smoke. What happened?"

Will explained and McIntosh said, "Ah, but house fires are all too common. Everything is so dry this time of year and then a small spark gets out of the cooking fire in the hearth and the entire house goes up. You say the man died?"

"Aye. The woman said his name was Abner."

"That would be Abner Townsend. She is Edith. They are good people. I'm sad to hear Abner was killed."

"Aye. It was so fast. I tried to get them to get away from the building because I thought it was impossible to save. But they persisted. Edith was lucky to live because she was at the creek when the house went, taking Abner with it."

Two days later, Will rode Molly over to Dr. Lyman Hall's plantation.

Will said, "I came to check on the patient and ask if there were costs I might help with."

Dr. Hall said, "There are no charges. The lady is recovering."

Will stepped into the room where Edith Townsend sat next to an open window. Her hands were in her lap. She stared across the yard but there was nothing to see. There were bandages on her arms and soot still fringed her face. The edges of her hair were singed crinkly from the heat of the fire at her house.

She turned her eyes to Will. They were dull and empty. Her face was a mask of pain. Her eyebrows had been singed off. "I wish you had not saved me. I am nothing without Abner."

Will said, "Dear lady, that is not true. Life holds promise as long as you live. In my own case, my lady wed another after thinking me dead. She is as lost to me as Abner is to you. I thought I would die when I learned of this tragic turn. But you helped me to see that where there is life there is hope. There will be another for each of us, and I wish you peace and happiness. Please tell Dr. Hall if there is anything I can do to relieve your suffering."

Edith Townsend made a fluttering motion with her hand.

Will said his goodbyes to Dr. Hall and mounted Molly.

As he rode out of the yard he thought, "I actually spoke the truth. Life will go on for me. And Abby can live her life without my pain. I do wish her well and hope for her happiness."

Will leaned forward and whispered in Molly's ear. "You're the only girl for me. Ha!"

Molly leapt forward like a shot out of a cannon, and they were off for a spirit-filled, life-affirming gallop.

Life was good again, and Will was alive.

There was hope.

Will threw himself into his work as an officer. He worked on drill and commands. He learned how to order volley fire of the muskets and to manage a company-sized unit. He learned how to point his sword to issue orders in the din of battle.

He also spent time with Captain Tom Morris, commander of the artillery at Sunbury's fort. Will knew nothing of canons other than the rudiments of loading one. Morris had shown Will how to calculate and aim and accurately fire the most common 12-pound field guns that were mounted on wooden platforms behind the piled earth of the fort.

Will found the math challenging, but not impossible. Morris grinned and handed him a printed table which reduced the effort to determining the range and a few other factors and to produce the required elevation of the barrel. Will could figure out the azimuth – the left or right of aiming.

Morris said, "If we get attacked, it is not a wise place to be just beside these artillery embrasures. The enemy will almost certainly be shooting small arms at anything that moves near these guns. They will almost certainly have at least two or three pieces of field artillery. Those canons would also likely be aimed at our canons. Then, it is most dangerous to be near the guns."

Over the month, Will became more an officer and less of a private citizen. He had been in plenty of fights, but now he was ready to lead.

CHAPTER 29 – INVASION OF LIBERTY COUNTY

Colonel Elijah Clarke of the Georgia Militia sat uncomfortably in a straight-backed chair at The Eagle Tavern in Sunbury. Clarke's wound was clearly bothering him. His large, fleshy face and dark eyes flashed with pain when he adjusted his position.

With Clarke were Brigadier General James Screven, Georgia Militia, formerly Colonel in the Continental Army; Lt Colonel John McIntosh, Continental Army, Commander of the Fort at Sunbury; and Major William Yelverton, Continental Army. Two other men were at the adjoining table. Colonel John White, Commander of the Fourth Georgia Continental Battalion, and Colonel John Baker, Continental Army. It was October 15, 1778, and the men were discussing the buildup of British forces in East Florida.

Clarke said, "We need more information, but I hear they are gathering men near Cowford. That cannot be for defenses. Our last attempt at their defenses ran into the majority of their forces about 20 miles north of the Cowford."

Screven said, "We'd have beat them, too, had it not been for that bog and the ditch in front of their entrenchment at Alligator Creek. I'm happy you are recovering, Elijah."

"Thank you, Sir. This wound has been a trial, but I'm managing. Any ideas about where they will go if they come north? I mean, Savannah is obvious."

McIntosh said, "I am certain the path to Savannah involves Sunbury and Midway Meeting House."

At this, Screven nodded.

McIntosh continued, "But I think there will be two approaches. Land and sea."

All the men nodded in unison.

Screven's dark hair and swarthy complexion made him almost invisible in the shadowy tavern. His native South Carolina accent became more pronounced. "We must be sure Bowen and the galleys are in the rivers south of here to cut off any sneaking up the inland passage. We must also fortify Fort Howe once again as well as look at the various crossings closer in to Midway and Sunbury. That means Bulltown Swamp, the Newport River, and so on."

Again, nods.

Colonel Baker said, "I can take a unit to Bulltown Swamp and set up a blockade. I can send my brother, William with some horse troops to the North Newport bridge. I suggest John, you take the Forth Battalion of Continentals to Midway Meeting."

Colonel John White agreed and added, "I suggest we send some units to Fort Howe and attempt to at least block the ferry, and perhaps dig in with some entrenchments to replace the burned-out blockhouse and stockade. Twill be difficult to stop a determined crossing, as we learned with that wretch Brown, but we can hope to slow them down."

McIntosh said, "Surely, they will want to challenge the fort at Sunbury. But I don't think they'll come sailing casually into the harbor. I have had a word with Captain Morris, my artillery commander, and he's been working to re-site some of the guns for a landward threat. I will send a small detachment south along the shore to monitor for a possible landing and overland threat. Will, would you lead that detachment?"

Will said, "Yes, Sir. We can leave tomorrow. Do you think we should go to Yellow Bluff? It seems unlikely they would land on the other side of the North Newport River.

"Aye. Yellow Bluff at Colonel's Island is the most likely place where you would see them. They would have to pass there to come to the landward side of the fort. Colonel's Island has always been a weak point in our defenses."

Colonel Clarke and Brigadier General Screven nodded to one another, and the plan was set. There was not much likelihood of the British showing up immediately, but everyone agreed that not many days would pass before there was trouble.

Will led the 20-man detachment south along the creek and toward Yellow Bluff. The late October weather was wonderfully cool in the morning, and the breeze was fresh. By midday it would be uncomfortably warm in the sun. Mosquitos hummed and sand gnats swarmed at dusk. Still, things could be worse because the troops were not slogging through swamp and marsh. The area's name of Yellow Bluff was well earned. The ground was higher than its marshy surroundings and the walking was easy.

The detachment did have to cross one narrow spot of marshy land that cut off Colonel's Island from the mainland. It was boggy, but not covered by water, even at high tide.

Will rode Molly and was attired in his Continental uniform, complete with silver gorget and sword. He smiled to himself. "I couldn't use this sword to cut a piece of beef, much less defend myself. I need to learn how to use it if I'm going to wear it." Nonetheless, it was a symbol of his rank and so the sword dangled at his side and too often managed to get between his knees when he walked. He was learning to put his left hand on the sword hilt as he had seen other officers do. It was annoying, but a new fact of his life.

He did break with tradition and carry his own powder horn and shot pouch. He also wore a non-regulation belt where Uncle Ewan's dirk dangled, and Tarleton's Brander pistol was tucked. He carried the English Dragoon Carbine. The ancient horse pistol was in the bucket holster in front of his saddle. The carbine and both pistols were loaded with buck and ball and an extra dash of powder. His older .45 caliber rifle and Josie, his masterpiece rifle, were tucked into their scabbards on Molly's flanks.

Will reached down and ran his hand over Josie's deer hide scabbard that Abby had made for him all those months ago. The scabbard was soft, and his heart ached for Abby every time he touched it.

Will looked around the area. Scrubby palmettos made nearly impenetrable thickets under oak and some pines. Will had learned the spindly oaks with scrub palmettos so prevalent in the coastal area of Georgia was called Blackjack. He guessed it was because the small oak trunks were black.

He considered how he got to this pass. He had passed his 20th birthday on July 15 and was now a major in the Continental Army of the fledgling United States. He had never wanted to be in the military, but the war was to blame for every impediment to his life's plan. Will thought he should be trotting along with Molly in some backcountry locale, looking for his newly acquired plot of land and planning how he would set up his gunsmith shop. Yet here he was plodding along with twenty men under his command, kicking up dust and sand and swatting mosquitos and those misery-inducing little yellow deer flies. The deer flies seemed to be impervious to anything.

By four in the afternoon the small group had reached a spot where the ground was higher than the rest of the terrain and a few larger oaks among a clearing in the blackjack offered shelter. Will gazed around in all directions. He could see every reach of water from this vantage point. Will found the names of the creeks to be confusing. This was Blackbeard Creek, but the reach of the Medway near Sunbury was also Blackbeard Creek. That defied reason.

Corporal Charles Cuthbert accompanied the troops to Yellow Bluff. As Will's orderly, Cuthbert was of great value in setting up the camp, finding firewood, and cooking food.

Will assigned his 20 troops in two shifts to patrol near the two branches of Blackbeard Creek to assure any landing would be observed. Five men in each patrol served 12-hour shifts and exchanged out with their other five-man patrol. Will's mission was not to engage an enemy. The British would undoubtedly be far too strong for a small 20-man detachment. Rather, he was to keep watch and as soon as a landing was effected, march quickly back to the Sunbury fort and report.

Days passed. It was now November 17th, and the men were becoming restless. Worse, the last several days had been miserable weather with high winds and lashing rain. To add to misery, the provisions were running out and three men were sick with a flux. The men, Will included, had killed some small game. One man was quite a fisherman and he had caught several large bass and trout from the North Newport River. They were not starving, but other provisions, like grits and fatback, were running low. Will was contemplating sending a messenger to Sunbury to learn the situation and to ask for additional provisions when a rider galloped into the camp. "Sir,

Colonel McIntosh's compliments. He asks that you return to the fort but leave ten men here to maintain a lookout. A supply wagon is on the way to provide provisions."

Will said, "Very well. My compliments to Colonel McIntosh and reply that we will leave this afternoon. He may expect us tomorrow, mid-day."

The next day, a tired, but happy detachment marched into the fort at Sunbury. Will reported to McIntosh.

John McIntosh smiled and said, "Ah, good to see you, Will. We've had some activity with the British coming at Fort Howe the last day. Seems Lt Colonel Marc Prevost of His Britannic Majesty's Florida Forces has crossed into Georgia and is looting and burning. I expect he will force his way across the Altamaha in the next day or so if he hasn't already. I called you back because we've not heard a peep from the British navy or any forces coming up the inland passage. Of course, the weather must be in play."

"Aye, Sir. The wind and rain made the camp miserable for our little detachment. We were fortunate to find a sheltered location and to have some tarps and a few tents. The men were getting quite restless. I had them cut some small trees and pile them up against the wind so the tents would not blow away. The squalls were quite strong. I brought three sick men back with me. They were ineffective."

Will continued. "Still, I think it wise to have left a small contingent as a look out. I left a wagon and provisions and

368

horses so that they can send a rider if the British appear. They have strict orders not to engage the enemy but rather to alert us here of any sighting of the British."

The morning of November 20, 1778, dawned chill and with a fresh wind. Those who did not believe Georgia could get cold needed to stand on the ramparts of the fort at Sunbury face to the wind coming off the Medway River. The wind drove a light mist and moved the golden marsh grass in waves, making it look like an ocean of molten gold.

Will Yelverton looked out at the flow of wind on the marshes realizing that he loved this sight. He was feeling the morning chill and wondering what the day might bring. Reports were that the British were moving around burning and looting south of the Altamaha River. The fort was on alert. Men were drilling in the parade area, they were especially practicing loading and firing muskets. The goal was to fire three shots per minute. Will thought that it was good they didn't have rifles. Rifles have longer range, but their range was offset by the length of time it took to properly load a rifle.

The 200 men in the fort's garrison were as ready as any force could be for a British assault. Privately, John McIntosh had told Will that an assault with artillery would quickly breach the dirt walls of the fort. An infantry assault, without artillery support, would be less likely to prevail, but still, it would be a desperate fight.

A rider burst out of the woods and rushed to the fort. The sentry recognized the rider and admitted him. The rider rushed quickly to the officers' barracks, dismounted, and ran inside. Will hurried to catch up to him.

As Will walked in the door he heard the rider saying, "Colonel White's compliments, Sir. The British have crossed the Altamaha in force. Some 700 men under Prevost crossed and are burning plantations. They are killing or imprisoning the men. Women and children have not been molested, but their homes are being burned. Brown and the Florida Rangers as well as McGirth are with Prevost. They have brought Indians and other troops. Colonel White was forced to withdraw the company that was at Fort Howe, their number being too small to resist Prevost."

John McIntosh listened intently and then said, "Is Colonel White still at Midway Meeting?"

"Yes, Sir. He has some 100 men there."

McIntosh said, "Thank you. Please refresh yourself and rest your horse. Then return to Colonel White with my thanks for his message. If he has further orders for me, please return with them."

Two mornings later Colonel McIntosh send his orderly to ask Will to come to his office. "Will, please ride to Midway and ascertain the situation and report back to me. Ask Colonel White if he wants me to bring the garrison from the fort."

Will saluted and ran to the stables where he told Cuthbert to get Molly saddled. He ran to his room and gathered his equipment. He grabbed his saddlebag which had been packed for some days, his bedroll, and his weapons and rushed down to where Cuthbert waited with Molly.

Cuthbert said, "Can I go with you, Sir?"

"No, Cuth. I think I won't be gone long. Also, they need every man here. I think you'd be of great use to the men if you checked their weapons to make sure they're all in good repair."

Will and Molly shot out the gate.

Two hours later, Will and Molly cantered into the churchyard at Midway Meeting. Colonel White was sitting at a folding camp table in the shade of a huge oak tree. The cool breeze of the morning had given way to midday sweat. A listless breeze moved the huge beards of gray moss that hung from every tree, but especially festooned the oaks.

Will dismounted, strode up to Colonel White and saluted. "Good morning, Sir."

"Good morning, Will. I see you came in a rush. Have the British threatened the fort?"

"No, Sir. Lt Colonel McIntosh says since the British have made no move against the fort, perhaps you might need the troops here?"

"Nay. Things are quite fluid. And we don't know what the situation is with the British fleet. Best to hold the fort's garrison in reserve as well as to protect the fort."

Will went to get water for Molly. She was quietly cropping grass from the road verge. Will moved her to the shade and held the bucket for her to drink. In the distance came the unmistakable crackle of musketry. Will put the water bucket down where Molly could reach it and walked over to Colonel White.

White said, "Sounds like Bulltown Swamp. Baker and his men are mounted, and I'll bet that is a fight between Baker and Brown and his Florida Rangers plus that gutter rat McGirth and his band of trashy, Cracker low-lifes. Please ride that way and bring back a report of the situation. Meanwhile, I think I shall prepare a surprise for Lt Colonel Prevost at Spencer's Hill, just over there."

Will and Molly cantered out of the Midway Meeting area and then broke into a run toward Bulltown Swamp. As he rode, Will glanced at the horse pistol, touched the butt of Tarleton's Brander pistol, and put his hand on the hilt of Uncle Ewan's Scottish Dirk. His heart pounded with both excitement and fear. Memories of his rides at Brandywine flooded back. "Here I am again," he thought.

Will and Molly heard sporadic firing just ahead. The rice fields at the edges of Bulltown Swamp gave way to the impenetrable morass of a cypress swamp, and Will slowed to a trot along the sandy, dirt road. He did not want to ride headlong into a fight. As he rounded a slight curve in the road – a path really – he saw yellow-gray gunsmoke drifting in the trees. The sound of musketry was louder, but still sporadic. Will swung the English Dragoon Carbine up and rested it across his saddle.

Will walked Molly over to the trees along north edge of the road. He hoped he was on the Patriot side of the road. Molly walked quietly forward toward all the firing. The hairs on the back of Will's neck rose and tingled as he and Molly got closer to the shooting.

Molly nodded and whickered. She was nervous and pranced a little. Will leaned forward and said, "It's ok, girl." He patted her neck. Molly looked around at Will and rolled her eyes. He patted her neck again and she settled down.

Will picked his way through the edge of Bulltown Swamp and soon he saw two men he recognized as Georgia Militia. They were on horseback. Three others were dismounted and leaning against the trunks of giant cypress trees, muskets at the ready. Will got close enough to speak in a normal voice.

"Where is Colonel Baker?"

Pointing, the man said, "Sir, he is thataway. I think maybe they're pinned down."

Will nodded and walked Molly toward where the man had indicated. Baker and two men were in a swale where water collected in a small, muddy puddle. The swale offered protection from the occasional musket ball that whizzed past. The stink of mud and rotted vegetation were strong here. Mixed with the sulphureous stink of gunsmoke the area was ripe with cloying stench that stuck in Will's throat.

Will said, "Colonel White's compliments, Sir. He inquires about the situation. He also asked me to inform you that he has set something of a plan in place at Midway Meeting."

"Hello, Will. This is Captain Quarterman and Lieutenant Crowls. Gentlemen, Major Yelverton of the Continentals. Will, I think we're going to pull out of here. There are at least three hundred of Brown and McGirth's men over yonder, and it won't do to stay here."

Will said, "Aye. What is your plan?"

"We will move back to North Newport bridge where my brother, William, has a small detachment. I hope to hold these murderous swine there long enough for White to make his plans."

Will said, "Very well. I will return to Colonel White with your plans."

Just then, two horsemen came crashing across the dirt track that was the road to Fort Howe. One held a pistol the other had a musket. They rode straight toward Baker and Will and the two other officers. The musket owner leveled his weapon and Will shot him with the carbine. The buck and ball with extra powder hit him all over the torso and he flipped backwards off his horse.

Baker and the other two officers fired at the man with the pistol who ducked down behind his horse's head and kept charging. Will drew the Brander, cocked it and waited a couple heartbeats until the man was coming down the slight slope of the swale. Will shot him from less than ten feet away. Again, the load of buck and ball was devastating, and the Florida Ranger collapsed off his horse, falling face first into the cypress swamp mud.

Baker looked at Will, "Damn, Son. You hell on wheels, ain't ye?"

The other two officers looked at one another. Quarterman said, "What did you load with?"

"Buck and ball plus a little extra powder."

Baker said, "Damn sure worked! We're pulling out of here." To Crowls and Quarterman, "Please order the men to back out through the edge of the swamp and head down the road to North Newport River Bridge."

Will trotted into the Midway Meeting House yard. It was now three pm. Molly was exhausted, and Will was not far behind her. Will tied Molly up at a shade tree and got her some water. Will trudged over to where Colonel White's tent was set up.

"Good afternoon, Sir."

"You look tired, Will."

"Aye, Sir. What can I do to help?"

White said, "Get some sleep and tomorrow morning I have a task for you."

November 23rd dawned muggy and hot. Not a surprise for Georgia. One day the temperature was in the 40's with damp cold pervading, the next day sweat poured from the humid heat. Will poured water over his head and scrubbed his face in the trough beside the church. He had slept on the floor of the church along with a good number of other troops.

He ate a scrap of bread and some dried beef washed down with ale. Will smiled to himself wryly. "This seems to be my usual fare these days."

Will stood beside Colonel White's folding desk. He was happy to be out of the broiling sun. It was not yet eight of the clock, and already the day was promising to be miserably hot.

"Will, I want you to ride to Baker and tell him to bring his troops back here. He must quit the bridge because he'll be overwhelmed there."

Poor Molly rolled her eyes when Will walked up.

"It's ok, girl. Just a little five-mile ride down to North Newport Bridge to see Colonel Baker. We're not running, we're going to walk it."

Will rode with the loaded Brander in his belt and the carbine across his lap. The buck and ball loads had proved perfect for close self-defense. Things were getting tense, and Will was worried that he could easily be jumped by British or Loyalist troops.

Will arrived at North Newport River Bridge and found Colonel Baker.

"Colonel White's compliments, Sir. He requests you withdraw to Midway Meeting."

Baker and his troops plus Will trotted into Midway Meeting. Will rested Molly in the shade and got her some water. A slight commotion down the road had Will reaching for his pistol. He relaxed when he recognized Militia Brigadier General Jim Screven's dark, aggressive, pug-nosed face riding at the head of a troop of about 20 militia.

The Americans set up camp behind their lines. White had two artillery pieces and 100 men. With Baker's 50 men and Screven's 20, White now had about 170 men.

Nothing to do now but wait. Will wondered if tomorrow would bring his death. Will dozed off laying on his bedroll on the floor of the Midway Meeting House.

The morning of November 24th dawned brisk. Will made a face. Would this weather ever settle down? Chilly one day, with donning a coat a must, sweating and shirt sleeves the next. Some days cold in the morning, sweltering by mid-day. A man would catch his death in this. And many had.

Will reported to Colonel White.

White said, "Not much to do. We're going to set our lines here. Screven has heard from some of the local people that there is a perfect ambush location at Spencer's Hill. Spencer's hill is not really much of a hill. It was more a high spot near the edge of the road to Sunbury. There is a dip there and some heavy brush. Jim is intent upon setting an ambush."

"You look skeptical, Sir."

White said, "Aye, the old saying is 'if the attack is going well, it's probably an ambush.' Similarly, if it looks like a good place for us to set up an ambush, the enemy will like it for similar purposes. But Jim Screven being Jim Screven, wants to jump them and thrash them good. I want you to go with General Screven and be my liaison with him. Try to keep him from doing anything stupid."

Will said, "Aye, Sir. I'll go join him now."

Will tied his bedroll and saddlebags on Molly. He checked his two rifles, paying special attention to Josie, and checked the horse pistol, the Brander, and the dragoon carbine. He reported to General Screven.

"Welcome, Will. Glad you're here. We'll have us a fine day today. We're going to surprise them sumbiches!"

The little group trotted down the road toward the selected site for the ambush. Will was alerted by what White had said about a successful attack actually being an ambush and a good place for an ambush was good for the enemy, too. His time on the road these many months caused him to also be wary.

They trotted along. Will scanned constantly. His carbine was on his hip, and he had cocked it. This just felt wrong! Thirty or so yards ahead, birds flew out of the thicket on the right. Will reigned Molly in and said, "Sir! Watch out on the right!"

Loyalist troops burst from the thicket and started firing. Jim Screven went down hard from his horse. Loyalist troops gathered around Jim Screven's inert form. One of them fired a musket right into his body. Another one followed suit, shooting General Screven again, from close range.

Will nudged Molly with his knees and she jumped forward. Will leveled the carbine and killed one enemy. He let the carbine dangle and drew out the ancient horse pistol. Riding forward to where Screven lay in the dust, Will shot another enemy at point blank range, the buck and ball shredding the man's face. Will dropped the horse pistol in its leather bucket holster and drew the Brander. Cocking it he put a load of buck and ball into two enemy who were cavorting over Jim Screven's body.

Will looked hard at Screven. He was unmoving, and Will thought he was dead. A ball whizzed past Will's head. One of the loyalists grabbed at Molly's reins, and Will dragged the sword out of its scabbard. He whacked at the loyalist's head and succeeded in knocking off the man's hat. Perhaps he hit the man's skull, too. That man let go of the reins and grabbed at his head. Seeing that the situation was hopeless, Will turned and said "Ha!" Molly bolted toward the Militia who were milling about on the road and firing at the loyalists. A ball plucked at Will's sleeve.

Then it was over. The sudden quiet was disconcerting. One moment there was chaos and confusion, muskets popping and bullets flying. The next instant, no banging of guns. A few moments of no human activity, and birds started singing in the brush.

Will and Screven's troops rode dejectedly back to the Meeting House and reported to White that Screven was down and likely dead. Will had seen him shot off his horse and then shot at least twice while prostrate in the dust.

Screven's second in command, a Major Martin, said, "You should have seen this one," nodding at Will. He raced over and put his horse between the loyalists and the General. I saw him kill three with his guns and cut one of them with his sword before it became so damn hot that he had to come back."

Will looked down at his feet. "I saw the ambush coming, but before I could say anything the General was in the midst of the enemy. This is my fault."

White said, "Nonsense! You tried to warn him at the time. I tried to warn him last night. You defended him even when it was likely that Jim Screven was dead, you waded into the fight, Will. No, this is not at all your fault."

Martin said, "It was General Screven's choice to set the ambush there. We all thought it could work, but they beat us to it. Major Yelverton is blameless. Your defense of General Screven was honorable, Sir."

Will nodded, but he felt sick.

Two hours later, Prevost and his men marched into view. There were quite a lot of them.

Will stood near Colonel White behind some trees that had been felled. Their limbs had been cut off to about four feet and sharpened. The trees were dragged horizontally to make what someone told Will was a defense called an abatis. Will guessed that was some kind of French word for sharpened tree limbs. It was one hell of a good, improvised defense. His carbine was on his back, the Brander and the horse pistol were in his belt. He held Josie on his hip. The .45 caliber rifle leaned against a tree.

The British made a great show of marching around, the East Florida Rangers, less so. Clearly, the British regulars were well disciplined and well drilled. A man in a red officer's coat riding a white horse trotted around observing his troops. This must be Lt Colonel Marc Provost.

Prevost and his men continued to mill about smartly as they aligned for battle.

Handing Will a sheet of paper, White said, "Read this."

The paper was a letter from Colonel Samuel Elbert to Colonel John White. In clear terms it directed White to withdraw his 400 men northward from the Midway Meeting house. The letter went on to direct Colonel Baker to assemble his 300-man cavalry force north of Darien and attack Lt Colonels Prevost, Brown, and McGirth from behind. White was then to pause and attack south, completing a pincer movement.

Will looked at White. "What is this?"

"It's a little surprise for Prevost."

"Uh, Sir, it's a surprise to me as well. We don't have those troops. Why would Colonel Elbert order such a thing?"

"He didn't. This is what we call a ruse, Will. I made up that letter. If we have to quit this place, and I think we shall, we will leave that letter among some unimportant papers where Lt Colonel Prevost can find it. Perhaps it will buy us time."

About 1 pm the British launched a frontal assault.

Prevost rode his horse out front and waved his sword. Somewhere a bagpipe squalled. Some drums began thumping.

382

The British and the Florida Rangers began to move forward. They had no artillery, which was probably a godsend for the Americans.

Will idly thought about how much he hated the dying cat sound of bagpipes. That thought was cut short by the crash of White's two cannon. The balls bounced and ripped through the ranks of the enemy. When the smoke cleared Will could see a few men were down.

The swampy land on either side of the road and the thickets forced the British into a narrow front and the American gunners took advantage of this, pouring cannon fire into the enemy. Prevost roared out in front and appeared about to order a charge, when Will shot him.

Actually, Will shot his horse. Will had intended to kill Prevost, but his horse reared just as Will touched Josie's trigger and the .40 caliber ball that was moving at 2000 feet per second hit the poor horse just below the right eyeball. The horse was dead, and Prevost was down hard. Will felt sick. Poor horse. It had been harmless.

The bagpipes skirl stopped, it's squalling dying off to a whisper. Quiet settled over the battlefield as both sides wondered what was next.

"Somebody get this bloody horse off me!" shouted Prevost.

Two men ran out and pulled the horse so that Lt Colonel Prevost could get up. He picked up his sword and limped over to another horse. Prevost mounted the horse and swung his sword around his head. The bagpipes started squalling again like an annoyingly hungry baby with the colic.

White ordered, "Withdraw! Withdraw!"

The American troops pulled back from their abatis and melted into the woods. Will and White along with the several other officers all mounted and trotted north. Will noticed that White carefully tossed down a dispatch case as they left.

Once they were away from the field where the fight had happened, White said, "Will please go to the fort and tell McIntosh what has happened here. I am going to withdraw up the road and set up to block an assault on Savannah. I will send word when we know more of the situation.

Will saluted. "Good luck, Sir."

White said, "How did you know that shooting Prevost's horse would stall their advance."

"I didn't. I was trying to kill Prevost, but the poor horse stuck its head in the way."

CHAPTER 30 - FORT MORRIS

Will reached the fort before nightfall. The November day was growing colder by the minute. Molly's breath huffed in a white cloud as she walked along. Will was very happy that Molly seemed completely recovered from her confinement on the *Beatrice*. She had been ready to ride when Will returned from North Carolina, but he had been careful not to push her too hard. These last few days of rushing from one fight to the other had been tiresome, but Molly had done well. Will would be happy to get the saddle off her back. He was sure she felt the same.

Corporal Charlie Cuthbert saw Will and Molly come through the gate and came hurrying over. "I'll take care of her for you, Sir. I'll also take your personal effects to your room."

"Thanks, Cuth. Everything alright around here?"

"We had riders in from Yellow Bluff saying that the British have landed a great many men and some field guns. I'm sure they're headed this way."

"That is not good news."

"No, Sir."

Will hustled over to Lt Colonel John McIntosh's office.

"Will! Glad you're back. Did you hear that Screven is not dead?"

"No. Tis a pleasant surprise, for I saw him shot, point blank, at least three times."

"I fear there were more shooters. After our men were forced back, apparently the Loyalists shot him several more times. Yet, he's alive. Prevost sent a letter apologizing for the mistreatment of the General and offered to let our physicians take care of him."

"Nice of them," Will said, his voice dripping with sarcasm.

"Aye. Bastards. I don't know how anyone would survive being shot point-blank several times."

Will said, "He was crumpled in the dust unmoving when last I saw him, Sir."

"I heard you tried to defeat them all single handed, Will."

"I had no idea how many enemy troops there were. I thought to defend the general, but the numbers were simply overwhelming."

McIntosh said, "We have a British force coming toward us. Incidentally, this handsome edifice is now called Fort Morris in honor of Captain Tom Morris."

Will grinned. "Tom Morris is an excellent choice. Very capable gunner."

"I suspect the British will arrive here tomorrow and demand our surrender. On a good note, a rider was here just ahead of you with an express from Colonel White. Prevost has marched south. He apparently believed the letter White left for him."

Will smirked, "That was an inspired idea. Colonel White casually dropped that dispatch case as though it had fallen by accident. Yet he dropped it where they could not fail to find it."

McIntosh said, "Thank God for small favors. Best get some rest. Tomorrow will be very difficult."

November 25th dawned crystalline and cold. The men's breath was visible and many who lacked coats were wrapped in their blankets as they stood near the ramparts or waited by a fire in the parade ground.

Several hundred Sunbury residents had come to the fort for protection. Will thought that was foolish. The fort would not hold out long under cannon bombardment. If the British stormed the fort the killing would be widespread among the civilians. There was only one entrance to the fort, and Will thought that made the citizens more trapped than protected.

Toward noon, skirmishers in green jackets appeared in the edge of the woods. Some trotted down the streets of Sunbury. They set up, weapons at the ready, covering the road to the only entrance to Fort Morris. Clearly, they were advance elements awaiting the arrival of the main body. A few muskets popped in the town.

The officers gathered in McIntosh's office.

McIntosh said, "The British appear to be encamped in the town and are enjoying the hospitality of the people, like it or not. Occasionally, someone has showed their displeasure by taking a random shot at the British. I don't know if any of the shooting has been accurate."

Soon, the fort's defenders heard the rumble of drums and the unearthly squall of bagpipes. In the distance Will could see the redcoats of the British Army, flickers of red through the trees along the street into Sunbury.

Colonel McIntosh said, "Gentlemen, please man your posts."

Captains and lieutenants spoke with sergeants who shouted, "Man your posts! Load!" Two hundred men rammed cartridges down the bores of their muskets. Those that had a second musket available loaded that weapon and leaned it against the dirt of the fort's wall. Officers checked their pistols and loosened their swords in their scabbards.

Not every man had a bayonet, but those that did checked that they could be pulled and fixed quickly. An all-out assault would quickly mean a breached wall and bloody hand-to-hand fighting. Will remembered the British bayonets at Brandywine. The Redcoats were simply masters of that fight, and Will thought things would not go well for the fort if the walls were breached.

Captain Morris ordered the guns to be charged and run out of their embrasures so that the British could see the fort was not to be taken lightly.

Will checked his English Dragoon Carbine and his Brander pistol taken from Banastre Tarleton all those months ago. Cuthbert had cleaned Will's weapons last night, and Will had personally loaded them this morning. The carbine was across Will's shoulder and the Brander was in his belt alongside Uncle Ewan's dirk. Will's officer's sword hung from a cross belt on his left side. Will's right side cross belt carried his powder horns and his shot pouch. Cuthbert had Will's .45 caliber rifle, and Will carried Josie.

Will was not in command of troops. He would act as a rifleman today. It was possible that Will could be demanded to assume command, should McIntosh and his deputy, Major Lane, fall, but that was unlikely.

As the British force marched out of the trees, they began to marshal into ranks just out of musket range. Swords and bayonets glittering, the companies wheeled and turned and stamped to a halt. An eerie silence descended over Sunbury and Fort Morris.

A British Major with a white flag rode out to some 50 feet from the Fort's gate. He shouted, "Sir, I bring a letter from the commander of His Majesty's Forces to the commander of this fortification."

McIntosh shouted back, "Please advance to the gate, Sir."

The British major slowly walked his horse forward. An American private stepped out the gate and took the white flag and held his horse. An American lieutenant stepped outside the gate and, saluting, accepted the letter. The British major remounted his horse and walked it back to the assembled Redcoat army.

In the distance a couple musket pops could be heard, followed by the more strident crack of a rifle.

McIntosh motioned to his senior staff, including Will, to join him in his office to review the letter.

To Captain Thomas Morris November 25, 1778
Commander of the Fort in Sunbury
Sir,
You cannot be ignorant that four armies are in motion to reduce this province; the one is already under the guns of your fort and may be joined when I think proper by Col. Prevost, who is by now at the Meetinghouse. The resistance you can or intend to make will only bring destruction upon this country. On the contrary, if you deliver me the fort which you command, lay down your arms and remain neuter until the fate of America is determined, you

shall as well as all the inhabitants of this parish, remain in the peaceable answer, which I expect in an hour's time, will determine the fate of this country, whether it is to be laid in ashes or remain as above proposed.

I am, Sir, your most obedient,
L.V. Fuser, Lt Col.
60th Regiment and Commander of
His Majesty's Troops in Georgia
On His Majesty's Service
P.S. Since this letter is closed, some of your people have been firing scattering shot about the town. I am to inform you, that if a stop is not put to such irregular proceedings, I shall burn a house for every shot so fired.

Lt Colonel John McIntosh looked around the assembled officers. "Well?"

Everyone stiffened. One man said, "We'll kill them in the hundreds with the cannons. Canister will cut through their ranks like a scythe. They have those two small cannons, is all."

Several other officers nodded in agreement. Will said, "Are they not aware that Prevost has left for Florida."

McIntosh said, "Aye. They have fewer men than they expected. Prevost has left, and I think Colonel Fuser knows it. He's bluffing. I shall tell him no." Looking around the group, McIntosh said, "I am proud to serve with you all. You may return to your posts. Major Yelverton, please stay a moment."

When they were alone, McIntosh looked at Will, "If they set about storming this fort, I want you to kill Fuser. Then, to the extent you can, kill his officers."

"Yes, Sir."

McIntosh said, "Take a seat and please wait to read my reply." He sat at his desk and began to write.

After a brief few minutes McIntosh looked up at Will. "Here. Tell me what you think."

```
'Lieut. Col. L.V. Fuser
Fort Morris
     Of His Britannic Majesty's Troops in
Georgia
     November 25, 1778
     Sir,
     We acknowledge we are not ignorant that
your army is in motion to endeavor to reduce
this state. We believe it entirely chimerical
that Colonel Prevost is at the Meetinghouse;
but should it be so, we are in no degree
apprehensive of danger from a junction of his
army with yours. We have no property, compared
with the object we contend for, that we value
a rush and would rather perish in a vigorous
defense than accept of your proposals.
     We, Sir, are fighting the battle of
America, and therefore disdain to remain neuter
till its fate is determined—As to surrendering
the fort, receive this laconic reply --- Come
and Take It!
     Major Lane, whom I send with this letter,
is directed to satisfy you with respect to the
irregular loose firing mentioned on the back of
your letter.
     I have the honour to be, Sir, your most
obedient,
     John McIntosh,
     Lieutenant Colonel to the Continental
Troops.
```

Will smiled, "Either they will be infuriated and attack immediately, or they will burn the town."

McIntosh said, "Let's hope they pause long enough to realize Prevost has left them and they don't have the forces to reduce the fort. I counted about 400 troops out there. We will kill a tremendous number of them with the canister and rifles before they get to the walls of this fort."

McIntosh called out, "Major Lane?"

McIntosh's deputy, Major Lane, stepped in the door. "Sir?"

"Please take this reply to the British commander. Inform him that his threat to burn a house for every shot fired is meaningless. Tell him, as soon as he burns a house, we will light a fire at the other end of town and allow the flames to meet in the middle by mutual conflagration. Mention that he will bear the blame for that unfortunate circumstance."

Turning to go, Major Lane said, "Very well, Sir. I shall leave immediately."

McIntosh grinned at Will. "I hope I don't have to burn the town, but I will not be intimidated by some jumped-up, self-important pipsqueak in a red uniform."

The situation settled into a stalemate. In addition to occupying the town, the British set up camp in full view of the fort. Some cattle from the town were slaughtered and roasted by the men of the 60th Regiment of His Britannic Majesty's forces. The smell of roasting beef made everyone in the fort ravenous. Worse, it was their cattle that were being roasted for the pleasure of the British.

Morning broke around seven am and the chill of the night before still hung heavy in the air. The ocean could be seen from the fort and the sea air was moist, making the cold penetrate the men. Blankets barely dented the deep chill. Will noticed the British, being from Florida, fared no better in the cold.

Drums began to beat, and the British troops fell into their ranks. Shouting, stamping, and some huzzahs from the British caused considerable distress among the civilians crowded into the fort. McIntosh strode across the fort and mounted a ladder to a wooden firing step on the side of the dirt rampart next to the fort's only gate. Will checked his weapons and took Josie to the far corner bastion where he had been assigned by McIntosh.

Presently, a captain with a redcoat and Highlander kilts stepped out in front of a company of troops. He drew his claymore, an evil looking, basket-hilted broadsword like the ones Will saw at Moore's Creek Bridge. A black man stood just behind this Scottish officer. Another officer hurried out to the Scottish captain and spoke to him urgently.

A man next to Will said, "That is Captain Roderick McIntosh. "Old Rory" they call him. He is Colonel McIntosh's older cousin. He's frequently at the glass, and I think today is no exception. That's his slave, Jim. Jim is devoted to the old drunken bastard."

Old Rory presently advanced, with claymore in hand. He approached the gate of the fort, stopped, and stamped his foot at attention. Old Rory shouted, his Scottish accent thick in the morning air, " Surrender, you miscreants! How dare you presume to resist his majesty's arms! "

Will watched as Colonel McIntosh ordered the gate thrown open, saying, "Walk in, cousin, and take possession."

"No," shouted Old Rory, with great indignation, "I will not trust myself with such vermin, but I order you to surrender."

Uncommanded, some of the British troops began to fix bayonets and Will saw a couple sergeants begin walking about carrying their spontoons, the long spear-like symbol of their authority which was used to dress ranks as well as communicate commands. The British ranks began to dress and cover. Suddenly they looked smart and purposeful.

Will looked at the artillery officer in charge of this portion of the battery. The lieutenant said, "He's whipping them in to a frenzy, and I think they're getting ready to assault the fort."

Will watched closely. McIntosh had ordered him to kill Fuser if it appeared there would be an assault. Fuser was nowhere to be seen, but this drunk Scot was having an effect on the Redcoats.

Old Rory shouted out, "Surrender, Damn yer eyes! If ye d'no surrender we will storm the fort and put ye all ta' tha' sword."

Old Rory turned to the Redcoats and brandished the claymore. The troops let out a loud huzzah in response.

Will cocked Josie and set the trigger. He leveled Josie at Old Rory. It was not a long shot, perhaps 100 yards, but Will's location was at almost 90 degrees to where Old Rory stood.

Old Rory opened his mouth to shout again.

WizCraaaak! Josie bucked against Will's shoulder. And Old Rory sat hard on his rear.

Old Rory used his claymore as a cane, thrust point-first into the sandy soil, and levered himself back to his feet. The ball had passed through his face below the eyes. Blood spewed from both wounds and drained out of Old Rory's mouth. Jim, his slave, hurried forward and reached to help him. Old Rory shrugged Jim off and stood facing the fort, still flourishing his sword.

A few muskets popped from the ramparts, bullets kicking up sand near Old Rory. Jim spoke rapidly, obviously begging Old Rory to run.

Old Rory, still facing the fort shouted, blood spraying with every word, "Run yourself, poor slave, but I am of a race that never runs."

With that, Old Rory flourished his claymore one last time and backed into the ranks, continuing to face the fort, blood cascading down his uniform, soaking his black silk stock and his waistcoat. A couple more muskets popped.

Quiet descended over the fort. Will could hear the wind soughing in the trees, the marsh grass rattling softly. The British ranks relaxed. Soon British sergeants were heard dismissing their men to attend to a morning meal.

The fort's defenders relaxed somewhat, and men went in shifts to eat grits and fatback for breakfast. Will walked over to Lt Colonel McIntosh.

Will said, "Sorry about shooting your cousin."

"Aye, how did you manage to shoot him in the mouth?"

"I was trying to shoot him in the brain, but he was so animated that he put his mouth in the way of the bullet."

John McIntosh said, "Largest part of Old Rory, his mouth."

"Aye, I feel bad about shooting a drunk old man, but I think he was having an effect on the Redcoats."

"He's always been a hot head, and this was going to get out of hand."

That day passed without further incident. Will wondered what the British were planning.

That evening Lt Colonel John McIntosh held a council of war in his office.

"I don't know what is happening among the British. Lt Colonel Fuser seems content to sit quietly. They have not burned the town, despite Major Yelverton shooting my errant cousin through the mouth. Biggest target on him, methinks."

Laughter all around. A couple officers slapped Will on the back.

McIntosh said, "If they're going to attack it will be at first light tomorrow. We must be vigilant and stand to an hour before dawn."

Major Lane asked, "Do we know if Prevost is still in the area?"

McIntosh said, "That rider who raced in a couple hours ago brought a message that Prevost is now south of the Altamaha and still stealing cattle and burning farms. I'm sure that bastard, McGirth, and his army of unwashed trash are looting and pillaging everything they can find. But the damage to our friends down south is the price our state is paying for keeping this fort intact. I fear Savannah is next, and this fort won't stand long."

The next morning the British formed ranks. Fort Morris' defenders stood to, anticipating a huge fight. But bagpipes skirling and drums thumping, the British Army marched away.

Old Rory, his head a mass of bloody white bandages, was reclining in a wagon along with the supply train. From the fort's walls Old Rory could be heard shouting, "I'll be back, cousin. And I'll have yer goots for garters! Whoe'er shot me is a bluddy coward. I demand satisfaction! Pistols at 20 yards! By God...I'll make ye pay!" He spat blood over the side of the wagon.

Old Rory was still shouting and spitting blood as the British disappeared around the bend in the road to Yellow Bluff, their ships, and Saint Augustine.

CHAPTER 31 – RETURN TO SAVANNAH

Will and Molly rode alongside Lt Colonel John McIntosh. McIntosh was leading most of the 4th Battalion toward Savannah. The threat to Sunbury had abated when Fuser and Prevost pulled out and went back to Florida. But there remained quite a threat to Savannah. Nothing definite, just hints and fears.

They trotted into Savannah. The stink of burned wood and destroyed lives still hung heavy in the air from the fire almost a year ago. Will ached over that loss. He liked the city and her people. It was now full-on winter in Georgia. Though the season was not the killing cold of the Middle Atlantic colonies, those who had been unhoused by the fire were suffering if they did not have a house to protect them from the elements. Will saw some tents and lean-to's that housed the less fortunate. Many scavenged unburned timbers from damaged homes to build fires for what warmth and cooking they might do.

Colonel McIntosh said, "Will, Colonel Elbert has assigned you to his personal staff. I'm sure you can find your way to his home."

"Yes, Sir."

"It has been a pleasure serving with you, Will. You are brave and reliable."

"Thank you, Colonel McIntosh. I have learned a lot from you."

Will saluted and turned Molly's head to go west, down the River Road to Rae's Hall. It was also the road that went to Ebenezer, a small community of Germans. The road went on from Ebenezer past well populated farmland to Augusta, a town that was almost the end of European civilization in the colony. Will knew Augusta was also a place of contention. Lt Colonel Brown of the Florida Rangers was from South Carolina, just across the river from Augusta. Brown was frequently in the neighborhood of Augusta. When he was present there was always potential for a fight.

Corporal Charles Cuthbert rode along with Will on a horse Will had requisitioned from Colonel White.

As he trotted along, he looked at the trees and plants. It was fall but still there were leaves on the trees. True, some were turning colors, but it was not like the riot of color he was used to in Western North Carolina where the Kennedys lived. The air smelled different, too. It was thick and cool, but not cold. Insects still buzzed and flew. Will wondered if there was ever a season in Georgia without bugs.

Will trotted up to Rae's Hall where Ephrem, the butler, came out to meet him.

"Hello, Mr. Will. You look fit as a fiddle!"

"Thank you, Ephrem. You look well. It's nice to see you again."

"I'll get the stable hand to come and take your horse. That's a fine animal."

"Yes, thank you, Ephrem. Her name is Molly, and she has been everywhere with me. This is Corporal Cuthbert, my orderly. Can you find him a room?"

"We shall take good care of you both."

Will smiled, "I know you will." Discretely handing Ephrem a shilling Will said, "Thank you for everything."

Elbert said, "I understand you rode into the middle of the ambush that killed General Screven and singlehandedly tried to ward off the enemy. Is it true you killed three of them?"

"I don't know if they died, but I shot three of them. I think a fourth got a dose of the buck and ball I had loaded in my pistol."

"Did you actually saber another?"

Will said, "I suppose you could call it that. I clubbed one poor fellow with my sword. I'm not sure if I hit him with the edge. I was so frantic I just lashed out with the bloody thing."

Samuel Elbert threw his head back and laughed. "Not many of us provincials have been trained in swordsmanship. The English, especially the gentry, are trained with a blade from early age. It is not wise to get into a sword duel with an English gentleman."

Will turned glum, "I'm afraid that when I ran out of loaded pistols, I cut and ran."

Elbert said, "Nonsense! I have been told that the troops were begging you to quit the fight long before you came to your senses and realized you, too, would be badly wounded if you stayed."

Will said, "Still, I was sick when I heard the General died."

"It is hard to imagine surviving eleven musket balls fired at close range. Also, it is no ones' fault but Jim Screven's that he got into that predicament. By every report, he charged into the middle of an ambush, and that was his mistake alone. He was always impetuous. You risked all to try to protect him."

Will said, "Tis true he suddenly trotted forward just as I was trying to say to wait. Apparently, Brown also thought the place a good ambush site and got there before us."

Colonel Elbert said, "Jim Screven was a good man. There will be others. Perhaps none with the verve he had for the attack, though."

Will and Elbert sat on the veranda overlooking the Savannah River. It was cool, but the evening shadows had not yet lengthened onto the porch. Soon, a chill would be in the air pushing them indoors. But for now, they were enjoying the end of the day. They sipped on sack, a fortified wine with a light golden color, and chatted.

Crickets began to sing. When darkness fell thousands of the little insects would be making a powerful racket. Will thought the crickets were a good alarm system. Anytime an animal or human got near the house the crickets stopped singing, creating a sudden silence.

Will was reflecting on his reading of Shakespeare and Christopher Sly, the drunkard in Taming of the Shrew. Will smiled as he realized Christopher Sly's claim to have never drunk sack was an outrageous lie.

Elbert shattered Will's reverie when he said, "There are frequent hints that the British will try to take Savannah. Nothing definite, yet. But we must be vigilant. I've said so to General Howe. He is in the city and plans to direct the defense personally, if it comes to that."

Will reluctantly left his thoughts about Shakespeare and asked, "Are we prepared? I mean, do we have defenses erected?"

"No. I've wondered if we should not move the guns from Fort Morris up here. Most of them, anyway. But that would require we put them on the galleys and build emplacements for them here. So far no one is listening to any of that, and we don't really have a true fort to defend the city."

Will said, "That's surprising."

"There are a few places where an army would be able to land. As you know from being there, they were scouting Savage Point and the plantations down there. We should fortify that area and garrison it with troops. They also could try to land at Wormslow Plantation. You've seen that location from the river. If they landed there, they'd have to march a long way across a good bit of marsh to get to Thunderbolt and then into the city."

Will said, "Aye, tis boggy there from what I've seen. Savage Point is rice fields and would be a similar problem. Too much well-watered bottom land and too few roads."

Elbert said, "Aye. That leaves John Girardeau's Plantation at Brewton's Hill the only suitable landing spot. You saw it from the schooner."

Will said, "Aye. I wondered why there is not at least a battery there. You said Wormslow has a battery."

"Yes. There's a landing and a causeway across Girardeau's rice fields that leads to the bluff. It is maybe 600 yards to the bluff from the landing. A few cannons in some earthen embrasures would make landing hell. As it is, there are no cannon and once a landing force makes the bluff, it's a walk into Savannah on the Sea Island Road."

"Can you not prevail on General Howe and Governor Houstoun to place men and artillery there?"

Elbert snorted softly, "Would that either of those two would listen to anyone save themselves. We only have the little fort at the eastern end of the bluff in town. No attacking force would be impeded by that puny defense."

Liz Elbert hosted a small get together that evening to welcome Will back to Savannah. Governor Houstoun and Major General Robert Howe, Major James Jackson, Dr. Noble Wymberly Jones, Miss Charlotte Jones, Colonels White and McIntosh, John Milledge and Edward Telfair, along with several others, were in attendance.

The military men wore their uniforms and Samuel Elbert wore his militia Brigadier General Uniform. Will was quite pleased that his uniform was appropriate to the gathering.

Charlotte Jones thought so, too. "My, you are quite resplendent, Major Yelverton."

"Please call me Will. I'm the same fellow you met last time I just have a different coat. It's nice to see you. You are as lovely as a spring day."

Charlotte's laughter tinkled like crystal goblets tapped together. "How gallant of you to say. I hear you tried to save dear Jimmy Screven. Poor Jimmy. He was so intrepid, and I hear he was ferocious in battle."

"Aye. General Screven dashed into the fight, and I failed to save him."

"I heard you took on an entire rabble of Tory militia singlehanded."

Will grinned wryly, "Nearly got killed for it, too."

Governor Houstoun stepped up, "Good evening, Miss Jones. You are looking lovely this evening." Without waiting for an answer from Charlotte, "Major, may we confer with General Elbert and the others?"

Ignoring Houstoun, Charlotte smiled at Will and stepped back. "Perhaps we might chat a bit later."

Will bowed, "I will count the minutes." He turned to go with Houstoun.

Houstoun said, "Making headway, were you?"

"Aye, Sir. I fear the war creates headwinds."

"Yes, we must talk about the possible invasion of our fair city."

The men gathered in Elbert's study. Will loved the smell of the books and leather. The press of soldiers in one room brought body heat and wool to the mix of scents. Will stationed himself near an open window where the chill night air helped with the closeness of the room.

Houstoun cleared his voice. "Gentlemen, today a man stumbled into Savannah claiming to be a deserter from His

Majesty's transport Neptune. His name is William Haslem, and he claims the Neptune is anchored off the Tybee Island light."

Houston continued, "Mr. Haslem further claims that there are some 20 ships headed our way with about 5000 men aboard. The naval force is commanded by Captain Hyde Parker, also a capable officer. I believe Parker is in overall command, at least until the Army is landed."

Elbert said, "The Army force is commanded by Lieutenant Colonel Archibald Campbell, a well-respected Scottish officer. The units consist of three battalions of Campbell's 71st Regiment, the Jersey Volunteers, and another corps of Loyalists. There is a Royal Artillery detachment along, as well. Neptune, it seems, was separated from the other ships, and forced to sea by a storm. Haslem knows not when the remainder of the fleet sailed."

Howe nodded and said, "It seems we'll soon be facing the enemy. The governor and I both have been in contact with my replacement, General Benjamin Lincoln, to request assistance. We must also be wary that perhaps Haslem is a spy planted to distract us. It is possible the actual objective is Charlestown."

Elbert said, "We must also be vigilant to the south. Governor Tonyn in Florida has the regulars and Florida Rangers. Worse, the scum banditti under McGirth pose a threat to the back country. I have alerted Colonel Dooley and other militia colonels at Augusta and in Wilkes County."

Houston said, "Yes. However, General Lincoln has promised assistance. I do not know when that assistance will arrive. Regardless, we must consider an attack imminent. Accordingly, we will meet tomorrow at my headquarters at Tattnall House to make plans."

As the others turned to leave, Elbert said, "Major Yelverton, please remain with us a moment."

When the room was empty except for Governor Houstoun, Major General Bob Howe, Elbert and Will, Elbert said, "General Howe, I am honored to present Major William Yelverton of your home state of North Carolina."

"Yelverton, is it? Your Pa named Zech?"

Will bowed slightly, "Yes, Sir. Zechariah is my father."

"Good man!"

Elbert said, "As is his son, Sir. Will here did everything he could to save General Screven at Midway. He personally shot four of the attacking Rangers and slashed another one with his sword. Alas, the enemy was too numerous."

Howe looked at Will hard. "Well done. You were at Moore's Creek, I hear?"

"Aye, Sir. I was."

Howe said, "Heard about your court-martial. Dick Caswell said you were wrongly accused. Not even a member of the militia, too."

"Yes, Sir. The supply train I was with was taken by the Loyalists. The brother of my sweetheart at the time accused me of cowardice and of losing the supply train. He was not in favor of my suit of his sister. Colonel Caswell allowed the trial to proceed to clear my name and to expose the other party's accusation for what it was."

"Having known Dick Caswell for several years, I can see that he would do exactly that. I heard you saved the wagon train with the captured muskets and powder on the way to Brunswick Town. And now I see you're a major in our service. We're glad to have you."

"Thank you, Sir."

Will excused himself and returned to the party.

Charlotte Jones was waiting discretely near a door to the veranda. "Please escort me outside where we might get some cool air, Will. It's very stuffy in here."

They stepped outside onto the porch and immediately the cool air was a wonderful rush of freshness. The crickets were in full voice and a light breeze rustled the leaves in the oaks and stirred palmetto fronds in the distance. A mosquito whined in Will's ear.

Swatting the insect, Will said, "It seems there are bugs here all year round!"

Charlotte said, "Oh, yes. In summer we usually go up the river to our small cottage on higher ground to get away from the heat and bad air that brings disease. It also seems to reduce the number of insects."

She leaned toward Will. "Have you considered taking up the gauntlet, Major Yelverton?"

"Gauntlet?"

"The one you said I threw down when last we met."

Will kissed her. "Does that answer your question."

"Why, how forward of you, Sir." Charlotte Jones teased.

"I have lately learned that this war might quickly end our lives, so I am not as reticent as I once was."

"I see. Perhaps you will visit my home at Wormslow soon."

"Aye. I would enjoy that. But you must know that the British may be threatening us soon. It may be a good idea for you to evacuate Wormslow for a safer location."

"Oh, my! Well, you are among the bright spots of vigilance for our little city. I hope the enemies of our freedom do not attack us before you and I have a chance to become better acquainted."

"I hope so, too."

A week went by and another.

Will and Colonel Elbert trotted east on Sea Island Road heading toward Brewton Hill one morning. Although it was

December the air was merely cool, not cold. Molly pricked up her ears, and Will saw a snake dart across the road into the weeds. A bird sang in a tree near the side of the road, only taking flight when the horses got close.

The wind drifted the smell of river water and salt marsh. Will found he did not tire of the humid, salt air. Will smiled to himself. Christmas was just two days away, and it was still warm. Yet, he knew that tomorrow could dawn frigid.

This morning was one of several trips out to Brewton Hill where Will and Elbert sat on horseback, surveying the area around Girardeau's house. Even a military novice like Will could see that a few cannon and supporting troops would wreak havoc on an enemy attempting a landing and crossing the rice fields.

Elbert said, "Houstoun and General Howe continue to bash heads over who is in charge. It's clear to me that there must be only one commander. True, Howe has been replaced by Lincoln, but Lincoln is not here, and Howe has sufficient rank to make a reasonable case for command. Still, Houstoun refuses to give him the militia. That, I fear, will be our undoing."

As they crossed a bridge on the Sea Island Road heading back to Savannah, Elbert said, "We can't just destroy this bridge while we have troops on the east side of it. General Howe wants to set up the defenses here on the town side of this bridge. Still, he has not considered moving some guns from Fort Morris."

Will said, "So, he would allow the British to land and collect their forces, make dispositions of men and equipment, and then let them march here?"

"Aye. He claims the marsh on one side and the bridge in front make a good defensive position. It does have advantages, but I cannot prevail upon him to understand the value of emplacing guns at Brewton Hill. Having guns on that bluff would make a landing very costly. I venture to say that they simply would refuse a landing there."

Will and Elbert took the day to travel to Wormslow to check the battery there and visit with the Joneses. Will noticed that Isle of Hope, where Wormslow was located, was an excellent piece of property. It was high ground and would withstand storms, Will thought.

Will admitted to himself that the Isle of Hope was not a likely landing spot for the British. True, they would quickly occupy the land of the plantation, but getting an army across the small creeks and marshes that surrounded the island would prove difficult at best. Then, there was the slow movement across several miles of islands and roads.

Elbert said, "I doubt they would try a landing here, but I did want to inspect the battery that guards the Ogeechee."

They trotted down the seemingly endless bower of giant oaks into the yard at Wormslow. Dr. Jones himself came out to greet them.

Jones shouted from the door, "Welcome! I suspect you came to inspect our battery."

Elbert said, "Yes, but we also enjoy your company, Sir."

"Bah, you flatter me. My daughter, on the other hand will be quite pleased to have visitors."

Elbert and Will dismounted and handed their reins to a stable hand who came out to take the horses. Will surveyed the expansive two-story house covered in white stucco. Where the stucco had broken off there was a grey muddy-looking substance that was studded with oyster shell.

Elbert saw Will looking and said, "We call this material Tabby. Tis a mix of sand, oyster shell, lime, and water. Turns into something like stone."

Will said, "It looks rough, but seems quite sturdy."

Will looked up to see Charlotte Jones sweeping down the steps from the entrance to the spacious home. Charlotte trilled, "Welcome Colonel Elbert and Major Yelverton. How exciting that you are visiting our humble home."

Colonel Elbert bowed and said, "It is a delight to see you again, Miss Charlotte. You always brighten one's day. I regret we won't be staying long."

Will smiled and bowed formally. "Good day, Miss Charlotte. You look lovely."

Charlotte lit up and said, "Come along, gentlemen, and we shall have some tea. Please don't tell anyone that we have tea in our home!"

After tea, Will and Colonel Elbert rode out to the gun battery that sat on Dr. Jones' land. The guns were attended by men recruited by Dr. Jones and the guns were in excellent condition. The grounds of the battery were well kept, and the powder was dry. All was in order.

Elbert congratulated the captain commanding the battery and discussed the potential British landing. "I wish you a happy Christmas, captain. I regret it will not be a warm and pleasant one by a fire with your family."

Over a pleasant dinner with Dr. Jones, his brother Inigo, and Miss Charlotte, Elbert filled everyone in on the potential for a landing and likely loss of Savannah.

"I fear we do not have sufficient troops. After our loss in Florida, we have only about 1000 men and little artillery. The men are armed with an admixture of rifles, muskets, and fowling pieces. We have a few artillery pieces, but General Howe has been hesitant to commit those few pieces to the obvious landing place at Girardeau's Plantation."

Dr. Jones said, "I'm aware that Governor Houstoun is not cooperative in the slightest."

Elbert said, "No, Sir. The relations between the governor and General Howe have been terrible at best. Tis worse than just bad relations. Tis foolish decisions. Colonel Mordecai Sheftall, whom you know is Deputy Commissary General of Issues to the Continental Army, begged to know whether he should remove the provisions stored in Savannah. General Howe told him not to worry. When Colonel Sheftall replied that he could not agree, General Howe told him if he thought it proper, then he could remove the provisions. However, there has been no attempt to do that."

Jones looked skyward. "Oh, my God."

"Indeed. The Lord is perhaps the only Being that can help our situation."

Will sat on the porch overlooking the Ogeechee River. Thousands of crickets chirped in unison in the evening air that finally had acquired a hard chill. Charlotte Jones, wrapped in a woolen shawl, sat with him.

Charlotte said, "It was nice of you to come courting in the middle of a possible invasion."

Will said, "Not to be ungallant, but Colonel Elbert is quite beside himself trying to get motion on the defense. He asked me to come with him. But I was quite delighted that I would get to see you. I fear things will be very bad these next few days."

A shadow crossed Charlotte's face. "Perhaps you will be injured? God, please say that is not possible."

"Miss Charlotte, there are no assurances of anyone's safety. The British are surely coming."

Charlotte said, "Let's take a walk."

They descended the steps and walked past the edges of the grass and out toward the river. At the river there was a bench shielded from the wind by a close hedge. One side was open to the water view. They sat on the bench.

Charlotte said, "I'm freezing from the chill." With that she moved close, and Will put his arm around her shoulder. Charlotte turned her face to Will, and he kissed her.

Charlotte whispered, "We could die this week. I would entertain your suit very favorably, Will, if we should live. Would you court me formally?"

Will said, "Yes. I would. But I fear we won't see one another for some time. Will you and your family stay here?"

Charlotte looked out to the river. She knitted her brows, "Where would we go? If we go up country, we simply will be vulnerable to the banditti. Maybe we would go to Charlestown. Daddy could practice medicine there, I suppose."

Will said, "I worry for you and your family. I also think you and your family should be ready to evacuate immediately, should that become necessary."

"Do not worry about us. You have plenty to worry about with all the shooting to come. It is I who should worry about you."

Will tottered off to bed. He was tired and Charlotte had given him a lot to think about.

He looked out the glazed window. A light frost had formed on the panes, distorting the moonlight, and making the stars look like streaks instead of tiny dots.

Will dozed. Abby, radiant in full blossom with her baby, intruded into his thoughts. She smiled and asked if he was happy.

Charlotte's exquisitely beautiful face floated before him in his dream-like state. He told himself to forget Abby.

But he could not.

CHAPTER 32 – DEFENDING SAVANNAH

Will and Elbert rode out of Wormslow at a pace to get to Savannah by mid-morning. Elbert said, "Liz will kill me if we do not have a small feast at Rae's Hall and at least celebrate the birth of our Savior. But I must report to General Howe and the Governor and make one last attempt to do something about this coming invasion."

They rode hard to get to Tattnall House, Fair Lawn, to confer with General Howe by noon. They stormed into Howe's headquarters about 12 pm on December 24th. Elbert strode past the secretary and the sentry straight into the study where Howe had made his office.

"Sir, we must reinforce the detachment at Girardeau's. We can move the guns from Wormslow and have them there by morning. A lookout at Tybee Light says he has seen many sail. That seems to confirm the possibility of over 5000 British troops. It won't be long before they cross the bar."

Howe fixed Elbert with a hard stare. Colonel, "The enemy's army is composed of raw boys from the Highlands and Delancey's green-coats, who will not fight. I don't care if they have double the number."

Elbert said, "But, Sir, should we not tell the people and advise evacuation? Should we not move the provisions as Colonel Sheftall recommended?"

Howe said, "It is surely not my province to dispirit the people. It is impossible to remove the public stores from Savannah. We have neither carriages nor vessels to conduct an evacuation. I have suggested to many private citizens that their goods be removed as a precautionary step for fear of accident. I have seen little response in that regard, Sir. Besides, I have this day sent an express to Major Lane at Sunbury explaining the good situation we find for ourselves and the force of the Army as well as the expected reinforcements from South Carolina."

Elbert paused and gathered himself. "Sir, we must reinforce Captain Smith at Brewton Hill. I insist we send a company of men. He does not have tools to entrench. He needs workers and tools. Better would be to move at least a small battery of cannons to oversee the landing."

Howe looked out the window across the grass that gave Fair Lawn its name. "I will send some negroes and tools to dig in."

Elbert said, "Thank you. And the artillery?"

Howe said, "We cannot afford artillery when we must defend the bridge across the creek on the Sea Island Road."

A muscle in Elbert's jaw jumped but he said nothing further.

Will and Elbert trotted toward Rae's Hall.

Elbert said, his voice dripping with disgust, "Raw boys from the Highlands and Delancy's Green-coats who will not

420

fight! My eye! Howe's lack of vision and inability to face facts tells me we must evacuate our home day after tomorrow. We shall have a pleasant Christmas Day. I'm sure Liz has a delightful feast planned. Then, the day after Christmas, we shall have the servants and some hired men load wagons with anything of value and take it to my farm out in the countryside. Liz will be distraught, I'm sure."

Will said, "How can I help?"

"I need you to go out to Brewton Hill and do everything we can to be prepared. The day after Christmas will be soon enough. I will continue to try to get you artillery. I will come there if the British land."

Will said, "Very well, Sir."

Christmas day passed quietly with a delicious roast goose and a variety of vegetables. Although she had servants to do the work, Liz made a stuffing for the goose that was based on cornbread with sage. Will reveled in the yeast bread from Liz's kitchen.

After Christmas dinner, Will and Elbert sat on the porch. The weather had warmed considerably, and they sat quietly in the late afternoon.

Elbert said, "Hell is about to break loose, Will."

Will said, "Aye. But the British are not gods. They are but men."

"Yes, but they are men with bayonets and iron discipline. The man, Haslem, says there are Hessians with the British. They are professional soldiers and very dangerous. I am going out to the stables to talk to the stable hands about moving the horses and wagons. I've already talked to Ephrem about marshalling the others to load and remove the household tomorrow."

Elbert left the porch and Will sat quietly, contemplating the beauty of the land before him. What would it look like next year? Ten years? A hundred? Would all this survive? Would there be a United States of America?"

Liz interrupted Will's reverie. "It could all be yours." She sat quietly in the chair that Elbert had left.

"Huh? What do you mean?"

"Wormslow. It could all be yours. Charlotte is taken with you. Smitten, more like."

"Uh, yes, I suppose."

"Will, you passed a pleasant evening at Wormslow. True?"

Will blushed. "Yes. She said she would entertain my suit."

Liz said, "You realize that Dr. Jones has quite an estate, and Charlotte is among those who will inherit. Dr. Jones likes you. Inigo is not truly competent to take over. The estate will flow, at least in part, to Charlotte. If she has a strong, smart husband she will be well placed to inherit a great deal."

"I had not considered that. I like her."

"Ah, but you do not love her, do you."

"No. But tis hard to know what I feel."

"Aye, Will. These days tis hard to know what is real. But you could do worse than Charlotte Jones. She's beautiful, rich, and connected. She would bring a rich dowry. Think on that."

A light breeze was moving the bushes as Major Will Yelverton and Corporal Charles Cuthbert trotted up to the house at Girardeau's Plantation at Brewton Hill. The breeze drove some moisture that hung heavy in the air making it seem colder than the actual temperature. It was Saturday morning, December 26th.

"Captain Smith, I am Major Yelverton." Nodding his head at Cuth, "My orderly, Corporal Cuthbert. Colonel Elbert sent me to oversee the situation here. His orders are that we attempt to build some entrenchments if possible. If the British land in force, we are to resist. Should it become clear that we will be overwhelmed we are to withdraw without delay."

"Welcome, Sir. I have some 40 men here. Would you care to inspect the men?"

"Yes. I would like to be sure their weapons are in good order."

"Aye, Sir. I don't know what we'll do if a weapon is not workable."

"The good news, Captain, is that I am a master gunsmith and Corporal Cuthbert is a skilled apprentice. Perhaps Cuth and I can repair any weapon that is not workable."

Smith grinned. "Best news I've heard in a month."

While he got along with the men and found them willing, Will was disheartened over the condition of their weapons. Two men had adequate rifles that Will hoped would be accurate. There were ten fowlers scattered among the men. The rest were an admixture of muskets, mostly somewhat battered English Brown Bess Muskets. He identified a few weapons that would not have worked. Fortunately, his small stock of parts allowed repair of all the weapons, and between Will and Cuthbert, the weapons were soon in working order.

Will insisted that the men all clean their weapons thoroughly. They would foul quickly enough when the shooting started, but at least they could be clean to begin with. That might make it possible to fire ten more rounds. Will asked Cuthbert to make sure the weapons were clean.

Will checked the supply of cartridges. He was pleased to see the cartridges and the loose powder were dry despite the moisture hanging in the air. Will showed the men with muskets and fowlers how to create a buck and ball load like that in his pistols and carbine.

"Load the buck and ball when it seems they enemy might get close. Otherwise, use the regular cartridge loads. Remember to shoot low because these muskets have a tremendously heavy trigger pull and when you jerk the trigger the musket will tend to ride up. I know you all know how to shoot, but let the enemy get close enough for your volley to do some damage when you do fire."

Will continued with the men. "Who has a bayonet?" Four hands went up. "Don't plan to use it. The British will slaughter us in a bayonet fight. If it looks like they are going to overwhelm us, we are simply going to withdraw. I will make that decision early."

"Now, we're going to dig a couple trenches overlooking the rice fields. We're also going to set up a defensive position in those woods where we can shoot at the British. Anyone have a question?"

Will sent one of the men with a message to Elbert explaining what he had done and asking if there was any movement on getting some tools and artillery. The rider returned about dark with a note saying there was no movement on either need. Will simply nodded in the knowledge that Elbert was frustrated and angry.

Sunday and Monday passed quietly with the men digging with the few tools they had available. The provisions for the men were only grits and fat back. Two of the men went down to the landing and caught fish and crabs. One man used a cast net to catch dozens of shrimp that were boiled with the crabs in salt water. The fish were roasted over the open fire. Girardeau allowed the men to milk the two cows he had, so there was a little variety in the food.

Girardeau invited Will and Captain Smith to lodge in his home. The men were sleeping in Girardeau's barn, so the living was not terrible. The camp settled into a monotonous routine.

On Tuesday, December 29th, the monotony was broken when the British arrived. Over 20 ships dropped anchor in the South Fork of the Savannah River. At dawn, they began landing using flatboats to navigate the shallows and disgorge the troops at Girardeau's landing.

Will knew the sails from the ships were visible from Savannah, it was only about two miles distant. But he sent Cuthbert to Colonel Elbert with a report confirming Girardeau's was the target. Will also looked at the size of the force and told Girardeau he should take his wife, livestock that could walk, and any high value items, and evacuate to Savannah. The men checked their weapons and waited.

Will said to Captain Smith, "We won't be able to hold them for very long, but I think we should make them pay as much as we can. It will be hard to climb up that causeway under fire. Maybe we can delay them long enough for General Howe and troops to arrive."

Smith snorted, "I don't think we can count on General Howe."

"Colonel Elbert, then."

"Aye, if Howe will let him come help us."

As the British gained the landing an energetic Redcoat Lieutenant Colonel set about forming ranks. It would not be long before a sizeable force of Redcoats would march up the causeway. Will considered shooting the British Lieutenant Colonel, but the landing was some 600 yards distant. "Better to hold our fire a bit, anyway," Will considered.

All morning the British unloaded their troops and artillery. Will estimated their numbers to be about 2000.

Will passed the word that the detachment would hold fire until the British were in musket range. Except the men with rifles would be free to fire when Will fired his rifles.

They waited.

About noon the bagpipes began their nerve-wracking squall and drums began to pound. For the 400th time, Will checked the prime on Josie, his other .45 caliber rifle, the Brander pistol in his belt, and the English Dragoon Carbine. As had become his custom, the Brander and the Dragoon were loaded with buck and ball. So was the horse pistol which remained in its bucket holster in front of Molly's saddle.

Will looked at Captain Smith. "This is it, I'm afraid. They're coming up the causeway soon with all that piping and drumming. We're going to fire once and move to the woods. I think we might get one or two volleys there and then we're going to run. I count 2000, maybe more."

"Aye, Sir. I'll tell the men and remind them we're not firing until the Redcoats get to musket range. One volley and we head to the woods."

The bagpipes squalled and the drums pounded, and the Redcoats marched. Will and the other riflemen nodded to one another. They had agreed to shoot the officers.

WizCraaaak! Josie thumped against Will's shoulder and a Redcoat officer collapsed. Crack! Crack! The other two rifles snapped. Will saw a couple more Redcoats fall. Will stuffed Josie into the deer hide case Abby had made for her and picked up his .45 caliber rifle.

A portly sergeant with a spontoon was upbraiding his men to maintain ranks or some other such detail of discipline. Will smelled the sulphureous stink of the gun powder, saw the noon-day light glinting on ranks of hundreds of bayonets, heard the tramp of British boots. Then he heard the Crack! Crack! as the two other rifles popped close by.

Will took careful aim at the fat sergeant. WizCraaaak! The sergeant paused, swung his spontoon to put the point in the air and the butt against the ground. The sergeant leaned against his spontoon, looking down at his uniform where a red blotch was appearing just below his collar bone. The sergeant slowly lowered himself to the ground, using the spontoon as a kind of cane. A corporal took the spontoon out of the fat sergeant's hand, stepped into his place with the troops, and Redcoats continued to march. The fat sergeant collapsed, and the Redcoats stepped over his inert body.

Will stuffed the .45 into its scabbard under Molly's saddle and, mounting Molly, shouted, "Captain Smith? You may fire, and then we must leave this position."

Muskets thundered. Sulphur stink roiled the air. A half-dozen Redcoats fell.

The Redcoat army continued to march, the uninterrupted tramping of their boots making an eerie sound, thumping in time with the squalling bagpipes and rumbling drums.

The Patriots got out of their shallow trench and ran to the woods. They ducked behind trees and jumped down into hastily half-dug trenches. Everyone reloaded as quickly as they could. Will put a ball down the bore of the .45, primed the pan, and cocked the hammer. He rested the rifle on his right thigh, holding Molly's reins in his left hand.

Sulphur stink wafted and the sky turned a strange yellowish-gray from the gunsmoke that now eddied and obscured the position just abandoned by the small band of Patriots. Will looked at Captain Smith, who stood 30 yards away. "One volley and we leave."

"Aye, Major." Smith shouted to the troops, "Did you hear the Major? One volley and then we leave here at a run. We're staying to the woods until we get far enough to take the road. Then, we are going to run until we cross the bridge."

The Redcoats burst out of the acrid cloud of smoke and continued marching directly toward the Patriot positions. It was unnerving that they didn't seem phased by the deaths of officers, sergeants, and their fellow soldiers.

WizCraaaak! Will's .45 jolted his shoulder and another sergeant spun and sat on his rear, his spontoon tripped a half-dozen men who quickly got up and resumed marching.

Smith shouted, "Fire!"

Brrramm! The Patriot volley thundered out, and another few Redcoats went down. Will was not sure if they were dead or merely wounded.

Will sheathed the .45 rifle and said, "Let's go!"

He turned Molly's head and waited, watching his troops get up and start running in the woods. The British had still not fired a shot. The last of his troops had pulled out and started running pell-mell, keeping to the cover of the woods.

A glance over his shoulder told Will that the retreat was timely. The Redcoats were now about 70 yards away and still advancing. Will nudged Molly with his knees and she trotted along, making chuffing noises, her eyes rolling.

Will leaned forward and patted Molly's neck. He said in a soothing tone, "I won't let them hurt you girl." His knees urged Molly to a canter and soon he caught up to the slowest troop.

Looking back, Will saw the Redcoats were now some 200 yards behind him, and it appeared they had stopped. Will thought that perhaps they were consolidating and planning the next phase of the operation. Will wryly thought that it didn't take a military genius to know that the next phase was undoubtedly a march down the road directly to Savannah.

Cuthbert came galloping up. "Sir, Colonel Elbert's compliments. He says there is a defensive position set up just beyond the bridge about a mile toward the city. He asks that the troops withdraw there. He intends to burn the bridge."

Will said, "Thanks, Cuth. Ride back and tell him we fired on the British and inflicted some wounds and are withdrawing to the bridge. As you can see, we're at a run. The British have paused, I think to gather the rest of their forces and march on us. I make their numbers to be at least 2000. Can you remember all that? Aye? Good. I'll see you shortly."

Cuthbert turned his horse and lit out at a gallop, back toward Savannah and Colonel Elbert.

Will and Molly trotted into the Patriot defenses as his 40 men along with Captain Smith also shuffled into the defensive lines. One man paused to vomit copiously, the stink of his meal of seafood from the night before pervaded the defensive lines. Others lined up at a barrel of water and drank desperately, quenching the thirst from running, and rinsing out the gagging taste of gunpowder.

Will saw that there were two lines of troops set up in a shallow V, one arm on either side of the road about 100 yards back from the bridge. In the near distance, Will could see the small barracks building where the troops had lodged. Four field pieces were set up facing the line of approach the Redcoats must take. Will also saw that light infantry companies had been arrayed to the left and right flanks of the main defense line.

On the left, Elbert commanded about 300 Continentals. The right was made up of a similar number of militia commanded by a South Carolina Militia colonel named Isaac Hugger.

Will and Molly trotted over to where Colonel Elbert was sitting astride his horse. Will saluted and said, "I regret to inform you that we were forced to withdraw from Girardeau's Plantation. We fired on the Redcoats, but aside from wounding several, there was no real effect. Captain Smith and his forty men are here. Some of the men are exhausted from running near two miles."

Elbert returned the salute and said, "Glad you're back safe, Will." Turning slightly, to acknowledge a militia officer, Elbert asked, "Have you met Colonel George Walton?"

Walton walked his horse a little closer. "Hello, Major Yelverton. Colonel Elbert speaks highly of you, Sir."

"Thank you, Colonel. Your reputation precedes you, Sir. I am honored to be in the presence of a man who signed the Declaration of Independence."

George Walton said, "I hope someday I am known for more than scribbling my name. Care to join me? I'm going to have a look at our flank."

Elbert nodded, and Will turned Molly's head to follow Colonel Walton. As he was leaving Elbert said quietly, "He thinks there is a dry pathway to our rear and wants to go see if the Redcoats have learned that such a path exists." Elbert smirked, "Walton says he used to bring ladies here to dally."

Will grimaced, "Perhaps his dalliances will help us to avoid disaster."

Elbert nodded and said, "General Howe convened a council and believes we can hold the British until General Lincoln arrives. No one knows where Lincoln is exactly, and Moultrie recommended we retreat up country to preserve our troop strength. Howe might have entertained that notion, but he is not entirely at liberty to decide. Several of the other commanders and staff have money and business interests in Savannah. They are too concerned with protecting their financial interests to render a sound military judgement. Thus, here we are."

Will and Colonel George Walton trotted over to some stunted piney woods some few hundred yards to the south. The woods gave way to swampy bottom land, and Will and Walton saw the British light infantry hurrying through the swamp toward the American right flank. The British troops were jumping from one dry hammock to another, making quick work of the swampy land.

Walton turned to his second, a Colonel Leonard Marbury, and said, "quickly, Mar, go to General Howe and, with my compliments, ask for reinforcements. The British are bearing down upon us in force! We've been flanked!"

Will drew Josie from her scabbard. He had reloaded both his rifles upon arriving at the American lines. The British got past the final watery edges of the swamp and woods and formed ranks quickly. As Will drew a bead on the sergeant at the forefront of the British lines, the British lines erupted in smoke and flame as they fired a massive volley.

WizCraaaak! Josie jolted Will's shoulder and the Redcoat sergeant spun around, staggered three or four steps and flopped on his face.

Will was sheathing Josie when he heard Walton exclaim, "Damn!"

Startled, Will looked at Walton who slid from his saddle. A musket ball had broken Walton's thigh and a sheet of blood was running down the horse's side. Will looked right and left. There was no one to help get Walton up, so Will swung a leg over Molly and dropped lightly to the ground. He got Walton to his good leg and helped push him up into the saddle as best he could. Remounting Molly, Will grabbed Walton's reins and slowly walked the horses away from the British assault.

The British huzzahed and began to rush the small unit of Walton's militia.

Walton drew his sword and waived it at the British. He weakly shouted, "Stand up to them, men. Hurrah! Hurrah! Hurrah!"

The militia broke and ran. Will saw several drop their muskets and run full tilt toward Savannah. Worse, Will heard cannon fire from Howe's main defensive position. He tugged on Walton's horse and moved with as much speed as he could while taking care not to cause Walton another fall. As he cleared the edge of the woods, Will saw the Americans in full retreat. It was just after 2 of the clock. There were three hours of daylight left. Plenty of time for the British to complete their rout of the Americans.

Elbert's Georgians were in formation and marching in good order, but they were somewhat behind the less-organized South Carolina troops.

Walton said to Will, "Leave me, man! I will fare well, but you must save yourself. I will surrender to the British."

Will hesitated.

"Go! Go!"

Will said, "Very well. Good luck, Sir."

Walton replied, "And good luck to you, Sir."

Will nudged Molly to a run to catch up to Elbert's Georgians.

Will rode up to Elbert.

"Colonel Walton was badly wounded in the thigh and insisted upon being left behind. His militia troops broke and ran before a determined rush by the British light infantry over in the woods."

Elbert said, "Damn! Marbury asked for reinforcements, but General Howe ordered a retreat the instant the British opened with their cannon. You no-doubt heard their fire."

"Aye. Look there!" Will pointed toward Spring Hill.

"We cannot go that way," Elbert said. "The Ogeechee Road is our last chance!"

At that moment, Colonel Francis Harris galloped up saying, "There are logs over Musgrove Creek at Yamacraw."

Turning to his Georgians, Elbert shouted, "Follow me, soldiers, and I will conduct you to a safe retreat!"

Elbert and Will turned their horses and hurried toward Musgrove Creek. But a safe retreat was not to be. Will immediately saw that the creek was inundated with the tide and there were no logs. Worse, the British were bearing down on the creek from the American right. Elbert, Harris, and several others guided their horses to the creek and plunged in. Will and Molly plunged in just behind them. Others without horses started swimming.

Still others balked at water's edge. Major John Habersham, who was without a horse, was one of them. He shouted to Elbert, "I cannot swim. I shall surrender and give you time to get away."

Will shouted, "Johnny, I'll come get you, and you can ride."

Habersham shouted back, "Tis too late, Will. Good luck!"

Will waived a salute and turned Molly's head to continue swimming the creek.

Corporal Charles Cuthbert plunged his horse into the water and swam up to Will. "I'm here, Sir."

Will grinned at Cuth. "Good man! Let's get moving and get out of this water."

The water was frigid. Georgia had not yet had a hard freeze this winter, but the water temperature had plummeted with the arrival of December, and Musgrove Creek was life-threateningly cold.

A body floated by, Will recognized the poor soul who had lost his life in the creek as one of the brave troops who defended Girardeau's that morning. Looking down the creek, Will could see other bodies floating toward the Savannah River. He was not certain, but there appeared to be thirty or more dead men.

Did they all drown or was it the effects of being plunged into the chill water? Will realized he would never know. As it was, Will's legs were numb, and Molly was shivering by the time they reached the other bank of the creek. Will unrolled his heavy Pennsylvania coat and threw it over his shoulders covering Molly as well as his own legs.

Will caught up with Colonel Samuel Elbert, Colonel Harris, and several others. Elbert said, "Howe delayed as long as he could to let the people evacuate, but it didn't do much good. We will go to Zubly's Ferry and then into South Carolina. I hope we can meet up with General Lincoln and the rest of the army."

Will asked, "Where is Liz? Is she safe?"

Elbert smiled, "Aye. I sent her up country with the servants, the plate, and as much livestock as can be managed. She will be well."

Elbert continued, "I do worry about the Negroes. The British have been enticing them to revolt. James Jackson said it was a slave named Quamino Dolly, called Quash, who gave up the secret path through the woods to the British. I doubt we could have resisted their direct approach to Savannah, but the treachery of helping the British to flank us sealed the city's fate."

The ride around Savannah had been frantic, and the crossing at Zubly's Ferry was fraught with fear that the British would arrive at any moment to catch the Americans on the Georgia side of the river. Joachim Zubly, himself, was a reluctant patriot. Though he had served as a delegate to the Continental Congress, he had commented often about opposition to the revolution. Today he had grumbled to Elbert and Will and any others who would listen that he would be punished for aiding the rebel cause. Elbert had soothed him, saying that the British could not punish everyone in the colony. They wanted the colony to function now that they had taken Savannah.

Molly was tired. Her head hung as she plodded, one hoof after the other. Will looked at Colonel Samuel Elbert. Here was a man who was as tired as Molly. His head nodded with every step of his horse.

As dark fell, a dejected Will Yelverton threw down his bedroll on the sandy South Carolina soil. The bedroll was wet from the dousing in Musgrove Creek, but Will did not care.

Will's heavy coat would be wonderfully warm tonight, but he had draped it over poor Molly. He had taken the cruel saddle from her back and rubbed her down with grass as best he could and had given her an apple he had in his saddlebag. He would not eat, but at least Molly was fed something. She was too tired to crop any of the grass she stood on.

Elbert had his wet coat and huddled under a blanket a few feet away. Several others had neither blanket nor coat. There was a campfire, but there being no food to cook, it was not large. Some men huddled around the fire anyway, desperate for the small warmth cast by its dying glow.

Will smiled in wry self-deprecation. Just a few days ago he had slept in wonderful feather beds at Dr. Jones' and at Rae's Hall. Even the days at Brewton Hill in Girardeau's house had been pleasant enough, sleeping indoors against the fresh, chill sea breeze.

Tonight, he would listen to the frogs and insects and shiver in a wet bedroll in Carolina's cold night air. Tonight, he would see the plastered hair, white eyes, and blue face of the dead soldier floating in Musgrove Creek. Tonight, he would see the British sergeant trying to support himself on his spontoon, Will's fatal bullet in his chest and his life blood running out and onto the Georgia soil.

But Will was in South Carolina, and he was alive.

CHAPTER 33 – ESCORT

Will awakened to the jingling sounds of bits, bridles, saddles, and other horse furniture being put in place. Horses stamped and whickered. He rolled over thinking it must be quite late, but it was still dark. He rubbed sleep from his eyes and sat up. His body ached from too many hours in the saddle and sleeping in a wet bedroll on cold ground. Will wryly thought, "I'm hurting, and I'm only 20. Wonder how bad it must be for the older fellows?"

Stooped with fatigue, Elbert ambled over. "We're taking the 4th Regiment up north to be ready to cross the Savannah River if needed. The British will almost certainly move on Augusta, and soon. Having a force ready to threaten the Augusta Road may make them think twice about that expedition. Also, I need to go see that Liz and the servants made it safely to the farm. Liz's sister, Isabella Habersham, is with them. Joe is beside himself with worry about her. So, once I get the regiment settled in, I am going over to Georgia to check on Liz and Isabella."

Will said, "Aye," the cotton taste in his mouth from sleep, thirst, and lingering gunpowder, making it more of a croak. He coughed to clear his throat. "Of course, I'll go with you."

"Aye, I'd like to have you. But I need you to take a special mission to escort Dr. Jones and his family as well as some of the other notables. They're evacuating to Charlestown. Dr. Jones would surely be arrested if he stayed. Colonel Sheftall, Colonel

441

Walton, and several others are no doubt already in British custody."

Will saw a carriage behind one of the wagons. "Is that Dr. Jones' carriage?"

"Aye. He really wanted me to escort him personally, but that is just not possible. I should send a lieutenant, but I would be criticized for ignoring such a prominent citizen and patriot. So, you're elected."

"Happy to help. I have been on the road to Charlestown this year, so I know the way. Will I have a detachment?"

"Aye. Twelve men?"

Will nodded.

"Good. Joe Habersham is going as well. I have told him you are in command. He is senior, but he is on the run, and you are coming back."

"Yes, Sir. And then what would you like me to do?"

"Come back to meet up with me. I must settle the men properly into camp. Lincoln and others think Brier Creek on the Georgia side offers a very defensible position with the creek providing protection on two sides. There's one bridge so, if necessary, it can be destroyed should the British threaten. We have problems presented by Augusta and the Loyalists. The Tories are active in the back country, and the state government is relocating to Augusta. That means we'll have fights with

Brown and McGirth, not to mention the Indians. The backcountry could turn very dangerous very quickly."

Will said, "Seems like things are going to be different."

"Aye. This will require we become more rapid in responding. We must learn to fight like Indians. Hit and run. At least for a while."

"What of General Howe and General Lincoln?"

"Howe has departed for the north, thank God. Lincoln will be marching into Purysberg. His camp there – just down the road from here, really – will be safe from the British as he decides how to take Savannah back."

Will rubbed his face. Said, "A siege, then?"

Elbert made a slight scowl. "Perhaps. Time will tell. I have had a message that North Carolina militia will be joining us. They've marched across South Carolina to Charlestown, and I had word that General Lincoln will soon dispatch them to meet up with us at Brier Creek. On the other hand, the Virginians have backed out of their commitment to defend South Carolina."

Elbert sighed, stretched his back, looking heavenward, "After Governor Lowndes made an ass of himself about not releasing South Carolina troops and funds, he has relented. South Carolina militia troops under Colonel Andrew Pickens will soon be moving into the area north and west of Augusta. God be praised, someone made sense to Lowndes."

Will nodded. "I will leave this morning with Dr. Jones, and Major Habersham. I suspect it will take several days with carriages and all the servants and various other refugees. I will try to be back as quickly as possible. I do think the men should rest a few days in Savannah after all this."

"Aye. Do as you see fit, Will. See you when you get back."

Will shook out his bedroll and threw it over a bush to air a little before he would put it on Molly's back. Cuthbert saddled Molly.

"Cuth, we're going to Charlestown. Is your horse up to that kind of ride?"

"Aye, Sir. She's a good horse. I regret I have no bedroll, but I do have a blanket."

"Very well. I think we'll be leaving soon. Probably within the hour. And I'll get you another couple blankets."

Will walked over to Dr. Jones' carriage.

"Good morning, Dr. Jones. I'm pleased you are safely away from Savannah. Colonel Elbert has asked me to escort you to Charlestown."

"Ah, Will! Excellent. I feel we're already in good hands."

"Thank you, Sir. I understand your family are with you?"

"Only my daughter, Charlotte, and my wife Sarah, both of whom you have met. Inigo stayed to look out for the house at Wormslow. He's never been much of a revolutionary."

444

"I hope the ladies are prepared for a bit of a ride."

"I have told them this will be quite a rush, Will."

Will said, "Very well. I'll gather my troops and we will leave as soon as everything can be arranged."

Will and Molly trotted along with Corporal Charles Cuthbert. There were two riders well out front, two guarding the rear, and the remaining eight in close formation near the carriages that held Dr. Jones' family and a couple other notables fleeing Savannah.

Dr. Jones, Sarah, and Charlotte rode in the Jones's carriage.

A dozen less-notable people in a couple wagons and on horseback brought up the rear of the little wagon train. Joe Habersham's horse trotted alongside Molly.

Habersham said, "Bloody business, this."

Will said, "Aye. Your brother held back at Musgrove Creek to surrender to the British while the rest of us escaped. T'was a brave thing to do."

Habersham said, "Aye. Johnny can't swim."

"I offered him to climb on the back of Molly and ride across with me, but he refused."

"Sounds like Johnny."

Will asked, "Where are you going beyond Charlestown?"

Joe Habersham said, "I have relations in North Carolina. I feel a coward running away from Georgia."

Will said, "Nonsense, Joe. The British are liable to hang you just for sport. Trust me when I tell you that I've been accused of spying and thought certain they would hang me in the morning. Let me see if there is a ship for you. I know Dicky Caswell frequently sails between New Bern and Charlestown. I'll make inquiries, if you wish."

Habersham shrugged off the possible hanging, saying, "I would be honored if you could arrange passage."

The trip was much like the ride toe Charlestown earlier in the year for Will. The landscape was the same sandy soil bordered by palmetto scrub, blackjack scrubland, and soggy wetland infested with bugs, reptiles, and woodland animals. Occasional farm fields; rice paddies. Insects buzzing, but less so because it was December. Days were cooler and nights were frigid. Ditches bordered the roads. Despite the cold, frogs jumped from the bank into the water as the little caravan approached. At night, the same frogs sang in a deafening chorus.

The farther into South Carolina they went the colder it became. A couple nights even the frogs were dormant. One morning Will woke to a two-inch layer of snow on the ground. Will had last seen snow in New Jersey when he slept in his bedroll next to a bank of snow on the edge of the pine barrens. Then, he had welcomed the snowbank because it gave him cover. Here, the snow merely meant the road would be sloppy as the day wore on and the sun melted the snow. Still, it had the unearthly quiet that always seems to accompany freshly fallen snow.

On the third evening, Will sat by the campfire. Cuth and another trooper had killed a deer, and now the meat roasted on a stick over the fire. Some of the men had jerked the rest of the meat, making it into thin strips hung in a small tripod made of green sticks over a hickory fire that smoldered and smoked the meat. Will was eating a piece of venison that was quite good and perhaps the best food he had eaten since standing guard at Girardeau's. That had been seafood, this was red meat. The venison filled his stomach and warmed his bones.

Charlotte Jones walked over and looked expectant.

Will moved over so she could have some of his bedroll and oil cloth and said, "Please sit here. Would you like a piece of venison?"

Charlotte smiled shyly, "I've already eaten." She hooded her eyes and then looked at Will directly in the eye. "Are you avoiding me, Will?"

Will said, "Not at all. This has been a most trying time, and I'm charged with getting your family safely to Charlestown. I've thought of little else."

"Ah. Then, you're forgiven for ignoring me these two days."

"Oh, Miss Charlotte, I was not at all ignoring you. I just thought it politic not to disclose our friendship unnecessarily."

"Ah. My father and mother are aware that we are friends. So, no need to be circumspect."

"Aye. But there are the men."

Charlotte smirked, "Oh. I see. You're concerned that being in charge might be somehow compromised if you are seen to be my friend."

"The thought had crossed my mind, aye. We are a bit on display here."

Charlotte became mock serious, "So, should I leave?"

Will smiled, "Not at all. Are you sure you won't have a piece of meat and some of the brandy one of the men found in that burned out farmstead we passed a few miles back?"

Charlotte Jones' face was innocent, but her eyes were full of mirth. "I'd love a tot of brandy, if you promise not to tell Mama and Daddy that I've been drinking."

The fire was warm, and an icy rime of snow still clung to sheltered areas of grass. Will and Charlotte leaned against the wheel of a wagon that carried some of the Jones's valuables. They were wrapped in Will's winter coat and the bedroll under them kept away the chill.

Charlotte said, "This is a wonderfully warm coat, and this bedroll keeps away the chill."

"Aye, the bedroll was made for me by Mrs. Koontz, my master's wife when I was an apprentice. I bartered for the coat in Philadelphia for a king's ransom. But it has saved me more than once. I fear it stinks of horse. I threw it over Molly's back a few nights ago when it was chill, and she was exhausted."

"The coat smells fine, Will. I'm glad you took care of your horse before yourself. It confirms for me that you are the man I thought you were."

The next day the little caravan rolled into Charlestown. The sun was warming against the biting cold of a winter day on the coast. In the shelter of the trees Will could still see crusts of snow where the sun did not reach.

Will talked to the local commander about housing his men and was told they would have to pitch tents. Will checked with McCrady's and found accommodation for himself and Cuthbert. Will left a lieutenant named Robinson in charge of the small detachment and said they would be resting for a few days before returning to Georgia. Robinson had strict orders that the men must rest and not be carousing in town.

In the press of things, Will lost track of the Jones's. He satisfied himself that they must have found accommodations and were safe. Still, he would have liked to say goodbye to Miss Charlotte Jones.

Will went to see the bookseller, Mr. Wells on Meeting Street. The walk from McCrady's was as pleasant as he remembered from last spring, only harshly colder as the wind brought dampness from the harbor. Will stepped into Wells' shop. Once again, the smell of leather binding, paper mold, ink, musty dust gathering on old volumes, moisture, and newsprint assailed his nose. Will had come to associate that oddly comforting odor with libraries like those at Caswell's and Elbert's. The bell over the door tinkled as Will entered.

"Ah, Mr. Yelverton. I mean, Major Yelverton. I see you have joined the fight formally. My congratulations, Sir."

Will laughed, "Hello, Mr. Wells. Kind of you to remember me."

"Aye, Sir. I remember everyone who is interested in Rabbie Burns."

"His poems moved me. Today, I am looking for something you think I might like to read. I have read Mr. Gibbon's book on Rome, and I'm still working on the Shakespeare you let me have last time."

"Ah...come this way, Major." Wells dithered his way down the stacks. Pausing, Wells pulled a small beige pamphlet from the shelf and handed it to Will. "First, Sir, have you read Mr. Paine's Common Sense? No? Tis a must for a patriot officer. Also, tis dangerous to be caught with a copy. And here is Mr. Paine's other pamphlet, The Crisis. I believe you will find them enlightening."

450

"Now, Sir, let us see. We have several works of fiction to go along with Mr. Paine's politics. Here is Mrs. Frances Brooke. Her novel is called *The Excursion*. Tis *au courant* all about life in London society. Perhaps more a story for the ladies? Of course, we men might learn from Mrs. Brooke."

Will said, "I'm not sure I need to know about London society just now."

"Aye. I know what will be perfect, Sir. *The Odyssey*. Tis an epic story of a Greek warrior and his ship's crew returning home from a war. An educated young man like yourself will find it verra entertain'. This version was published just a few years ago, translated from ancient Greek by Mr. Pope. Tho' the original was written hundreds of years ago by an ancient Greek named Homer, this English translation is verra current."

"What is it about?"

"Odysseus is the hero of the story. He is a great Greek warrior and king. After a ten-year war far from his land, he tries to return to his home. He has angered the gods, and he has many adventures on his journey: women, a cyclops – a monstrous creature with only one eye – a whirlpool that threatens his ship. Some say tis a true story, but we dinna really ken. Twas verra long ago in a land far awa'."

Will said, "I must read it. I know how Odysseus must feel."

"May I also give you this short book on the Greeks. It will explain their gods and other myths they held. Twill make it easier to understand *The Odyssey*."

Wells also provided an oilskin that would protect the books from wet while Will was traveling. Will paid Mr. Wells and waited while Wells wrapped his new books in brown paper tied with string.

Will settled in on McCrady's piazza to read Mr. Paine's books. Though a harsh chill continued in the air, the sun warmed the bench and Will was comfortable. Instantly captivated by the words, "The cause of America is in a great measure the cause of all mankind," Will was fascinated. He was not sure he fully understood all the words, even those in the Foreword. He wondered that perhaps that was a trait of an educated mind: the lack of surety in the details, of content, of the author's intent? What exactly did Mr. Paine mean? Was an educated man supposed to constantly question everything?

Putting aside Common Sense, Will picked up The Crisis. Will could immediately tell that this pamphlet had been written during a more stressful time. He read, "These are the times that try men's souls..." Will smiled, "This I can understand, and tis important to know. Having been in a war that I did not want, and seeing that the future holds more war, it certainly has tried my soul." As he read, he wondered if he was one of the people Paine deplored. Was he a summer soldier? A sunshine patriot? Could Mr. Tomlinson and his hickory stick answer those questions? Tap, tap. Will doubted it. He needed to speak with Elbert or another educated person about these matters.

As Will was considering these questions, a distinguished Black man in livery walked up on the piazza. "Sir? Are you Major Yelverton?"

"Aye, I am he."

Producing an envelope, the tall, dignified man said, "I have a letter for you, Sir."

Will rose, accepted the envelope, and discretely handed the man a tuppence. "Thank you. Were you asked to await a reply?"

The man smiled and bowed slightly, "No, Sir. I will take my leave."

The envelope contained an invitation:

```
Major William Yelverton, Continental Army
             Is Invited
                to
           A Gathering
                on
      Saturday, 9th January 1779
        At 7 of the Evening
                at
   The Home of Mr. Homer Proctor
           Broad Street
      Charlestown, South Carolina
   Supper and Refreshments will be Served
```

Will smiled. The gathering was tomorrow night. Miss Mary Proctor was in Charlestown and apparently had learned of his presence. This was quite fortunate. Will had been trying, and failing, to contrive a reason to visit Wadmalaw Island. Will also thought that Miss Mary had shown quite a resourceful turn in learning he was now an officer in the Continental Army and that he was staying at McCrady's.

Will would certainly go to the gathering. But for the moment, he would investigate the exploits of Odysseus.

Will wondered if Miss Mary Proctor was one of the adventures on his own *Odyssey*.

CHAPTER 34 – A GATHERING IN CHARLESTOWN

Wearing his major's uniform, suitably cleaned and pressed by Cuth, his boots polished to a bright gloss, Will arrived at Mr. Homer Proctor's Charlestown townhouse. Will smiled to himself. Homer was the author of *The Odyssey*. "Coincidence?" he wondered.

Will mounted the steps trying to keep from tripping on his sword. "Infernal thing!" he fumed as he controlled the sword with his left hand and tapped on the knocker with his right.

The door opened immediately held by the same dignified Black man in livery who had delivered his invitation. "Good evening, Major Yelverton. Please come in. May I take your hat and coat?"

"Thank you. I regret I did not get your name when you came to see me at McCrady's."

"I am Adam, Sir, Mr. Proctor's butler."

"Very nice to meet you, Adam. Please call me Will."

"Thank you, Mr. Will. Please follow me."

They walked a few paces and stepped through a large door into the beautifully appointed home. Will noticed the floors were wide heart pine polished to a deep patina. They mounted a beautifully polished oak stair with hand carved banister.

Will thought Mary had said her family were not as well off as the Yonges. "Hummm...apparently not exactly true."

Adam stepped into the large ballroom on the second floor, announcing: "Major William Yelverton."

Everyone turned to look to see this new arrival.

Fluttering over toward him, Mary said, "Will! I'm so glad you could come."

Mary was wearing a light gray night gown with pink ribbons and lace over a white petticoat, Will smiled at the way the pink ribbons complimented the natural pink in her cheeks.

Just behind Mary was Eliza.

Will smiled and bowed formally. Said, "Hello ladies. I'm delighted to see you both. Thank you, Miss Mary, for honoring me with this kind invitation."

Eliza wore a gold night gown that hung from her shoulders, emphasized her bosom, and offset a pale green petticoat. The green and gold picked up the hazel color of her eyes.

Eliza smiled shyly. "Hello, Will. Or should I say, Major? I hope it does not offend you when I say I am proud of you in that uniform."

Will smiled and said, "Not in the least, Miss Eliza. You look lovely tonight."

Mary turned to Eliza, "I told you he has been in the highest society in the land in Philadelphia. Unlike many of these bumpkins here, regardless of their high birth or blue uniform."

Eliza said, "I think you are the real gentleman here, Will."

Will said, "Oh, to be sure, I'm quite the bumpkin, myself."

Mary said, "I think not. You are quite a fine gentleman. May I introduce you to my father?"

Homer Proctor was a middle-aged man, portly, sweating, and with thin hair barely disguised under his powdered wig which sat slightly askew.

Proctor's rheumy eyes took in Will at a glance. He spoke with a staccato rhythm. "Welcome to our home, Major Yelverton. I am delighted to meet you. You are staying at McCrady's? Well, please decamp from there and plan to stay here with us for the rest of your visit to Charlestown. We have plenty of room, and you are most welcome. Do you have a servant? A horse?"

"Yes, my orderly is Corporal Cuthbert."

"Well, we have room for him in the carriage house and your horse is most welcome to be stabled here."

"Very kind of you, Sir. I shall have my things moved tomorrow."

"Nonsense. I will send my man tonight. Your man is Cuthbert, you say? I will have your things moved here straight away. Tell me, Sir. How goes the war."

"I'm afraid we lost badly at Savannah. The British outnumbered us greatly, and then treachery showed them a path to flank us. We lost some men swimming a freezing cold creek. The retreat should have been more orderly."

"Have you met General Lincoln?"

"No, Sir. I have not."

"Well, no time like the present."

Homer Proctor took Will by the elbow and worked his way through the crowd to a corner where a tall man in a general officer's frock coat and a sash across his heart, called a ribband, stood in conversation with several other men, one of them another Continental general.

"General Lincoln, General Moultrie, I have the honor of presenting Major William Yelverton, late of the fight in Savannah."

Lincoln's fleshy face and sharp, pouchy eyes took in Will immediately. "By Gaad! You were at Savannah, Sir?"

"Good evening, General. Yes, I had the honor of serving with Colonel Elbert and briefly with General Howe during that unhappy affair."

General William Moultrie, tall, slender, with a hawk nose, narrow-set eyes, and a cleft chin, said with what Will would learn was characteristic bluntness, "What happened?"

Will started, "We had a difficult time."

His story took several minutes.

Will concluded, "And so we escorted some of the more notable patriots here to Charlestown. No one knows what the British might do to those who participated in things like deposing the Royal Governor or plundering the powder magazine."

Lincoln's Boston accent was pronounced when he said, "We will be marching in the next few days to Purysburg and then, I'm not certain, perhaps Augusta. The situation is fluid. General Moultrie will retain command here in Charlestown."

"Aye, Sir. I have given my detail a few days to rest and then we are to return to find Colonel Elbert. I last heard he would be encamped in South Carolina across from a place called Brier Creek along the road from Savannah to Augusta."

One of the men in the group said, "Yelverton, eh? North Carolina?"

"Aye, Sir."

"Your Pa named Zech?"

"Aye, Sir, Zechariah is my father."

"You're damn welcome, then. Your Pa is a good man. A brother mason, truly. Are you a mason, as well?"

"Thank you, Sir. No, I am not yet a member of the Freemasons, though I do intend to join when this war is over."

Another man said, "I believe I heard you are a marksman who shot the hat from Captain Mowery's head at sea."

"I regret I missed."

Laughter abounded at Will's jest, and back slapping followed. Will quietly reflected that he had not been jesting.

Someone thrusted a glass of thick orange syllabub laced with sack into Will's hand and guided him over to a group of field officers. The discussion raged over the fight at Savannah and what would be the next move.

Sometime later, Will extricated himself from the group of officers and made his way back to Mary and Eliza.

"Your father has insisted that I move in here to stay a few days while I'm in town."

Mary smiled knowingly, "Of course he did."

Eliza said, "You must forgive me for my rude behavior when you came to my home. I have no excuse."

Will said, "I quite understand. I know you have suffered, Miss Eliza."

Eliza lowered her eyes.

Will's heart went out to her. He, too, had suffered from unrecoverable loss.

Adam, the butler announced, "Dr. Noble W. Jones and his family."

In the doorway stood Dr. Jones, his wife Sarah, and Charlotte. Charlotte locked eyes with Will, her glance making it clear he was expected to attend to her.

"Pardon me ladies. I will be right back."

Will walked over to the Jones's. "Good evening, Dr. Jones, Mrs. Jones, and Miss Charlotte."

Dr Jones said, "Hello, Will. I have not properly thanked you for seeing us safely to Charlestown."

"Twas my honor, Sir. I regret we were separated immediately after we arrived. Have you found comfortable accommodation?"

"Aye, we are staying here with Mr. Proctor. He is most kind."

Will said, "Ah, wonderful coincidence! Mr. Proctor has invited me to stay as well. I had the pleasure of meeting his daughter and Mrs. Eliza Wilkerson last spring."

Charlotte, wearing an emerald-green night gown over a light-yellow petticoat, looked across the room at Mary and Eliza, daggers flashing out of her eyes. The green in the gown emphasized Charlotte's auburn hair. "They are such lovely creatures, Will. Let us go visit with them."

Will grinned at Dr. and Mrs. Jones, "Please excuse me. Duty calls."

Mary smiled at Charlotte. "Hello, my dear. Have you rested after your trip? You looked so tired."

Charlotte smiled and said, "Oh, I was not at all tired. Major Yelverton saw to my every need. I love your dress. With the shortages tis no surprise that it's last year's color."

Eliza said, "Isn't he dashing in his uniform. It was wonderful having him visit my home earlier this year. Your dress is lovely. Isn't that heavy velvet a bit warm in this room?"

Mary said, "I think he is quite dashing. He was kind enough to escort me on a ride at Eliza's plantation. I felt so safe!"

Charlotte's eyes flashed hard. "He has visited my home as well and has been kind enough to escort me at gatherings of the gentry in Savannah. Will is a wonderful escort."

Will smiled and said, "Ladies! I am right here. I enjoy a pleasant friendship with each of you."

Charlotte said, "Hush, dear Will. This is girl talk."

Seeking escape akin to a retreat from a bayonet charge, Will said, "May I get any of you lovely ladies a drink?"

Will did not understand much of the rest of the evening. The ladies seemed to be complimenting one another on their dresses and hair. They tittered away with comments about how much fun each had enjoyed with Will. Even Eliza, who had never had the slightest of pleasant times when Will was present, went on at length about how she had enjoyed his visit to her home.

Will struggled to catch any of their meaning. Several times he saw them snap their fan closed and drag the closed fan across their palms. Every time Will glanced at one of the ladies, the others would change hands with their fans. Will knew there was some secret language among women involving the fan. The business with the fan confounded Will. You open it and use it to cool off. You close it when you're not feeling warm.

The party quieted down, and soon the guests left. Adam quietly came to Will and said, "If you will follow me, Mr. Will, I'll show you to your room."

"Thank you. Permit me to thank our hosts, and I'll join you.

CHAPTER 35 - SIRENS

Will liked the corner room he was given. It had two windows which he threw open, relishing the cold breeze after the stuffy ballroom. Looking down he saw he was over the courtyard made by the piazza side of the Proctor's home and the blank back wall of the neighboring house. Though it was dark he could make out palm trees and ornamental plants bordering a brick walk and a small seating area with a bench. Will pondered if that would be a good place to sit and read the next section of *The Odyssey*.

Will leaned against the windowsill, dragging in deep breaths of chill night air, thinking about *The Odyssey* and the confusing array of Greek gods and the fickle nature of Odysseus' fate. He was happy to have the little book from Mr. Wells that explained the pantheon of Greek pagan gods. There certainly were a great many, each more despicable than the last.

Charlotte Jones stepped out into the courtyard and put her face in her hands. Her shoulders heaved. Will realized she was crying. He wondered why. He felt it wrong to watch her, so he stepped back from the window and quietly pulled the window closed.

Will's room was well appointed with a comfortable bed and two windows to provide ventilation. A washstand with a silvered mirror stood in the corner. Atop the washstand was a pitcher, bowl, and towel.

Will removed his shirt and boots. He washed his face in the bowl and pawed for the towel. It was not there. When he opened his eyes to find it, he found Miss Mary Proctor standing there holding the towel out to him. She wore a garment Will had been told was a bedgown. It was abundantly clear that the bedgown was the only garment Miss Mary wore.

"Oh, I..uh...Miss Mary. Uh...I ... I mean...should we be here alone?

Mary said, "Do you not like women?"

"Oh, I ... uh...women...uh, yes."

"Yes, you don't like women or yes you do like women?"

"Yes, I do like women."

Mary smiled faintly. "Good. After our afternoon in the meadow, I was pretty sure you liked women. Now that that's settled, we could all be dead tomorrow. Perhaps the British will attack Charlestown tonight and kill us all? Will you reject me?"

"Uh, well...I mean, I would be a terrible guest to take advantage of your father's hospitality."

Mary stepped still closer. "Who do you think arranged for you to stay here?"

Will could now feel her breath on his chest. Each word made the hairs on his chest tickle. Something sweet floated in the air from Mary's hair. She turned her face to Will's, and he kissed her hard.

She kissed him back and her tongue darted, tickling his. She broke the kiss and put her lips on the skin of his neck and on his chest. She tongued his nipple as her fingernails raked his back. Will's breath was roaring in his throat. He leaned down and kissed her again.

Mary broke the kiss, spun around and taking his hand dragged him to the bed. She quickly sat on the bed and demonstrated amazing dexterity in popping the buttons of his breeches.

Mary whispered, "Ooooh...I see it's been some time for you, Major Yelverton."

Will pulled Mary up by her arms and bending down he caught the hem of her bedgown and, straightening up, pulled the gown up and over her head. In the same motion he dropped the gown and stepped out of the breeches that had puddled at his feet. They were both now nude.

Will took in her body. In the light of his single candle, he could see she had beautiful, heavy breasts tipped with rosy nipples. Her nipples were hard and had little bumps where the skin was pulled tight. He gazed down her body further. Jutting pelvic bones framing her smooth, flat belly. Hips and thighs well shaped, perhaps a trifle heavy to match her ample breasts. Her feet were delicate and pink. His gaze moved back up to her sparse thatch. He could tell it was light brown to match the curls on her head.

She looked at him through hooded eyes. "Do you like what you see, Major Will Yelverton?"

"Oh, yes. Very much. You are quite beautiful."

"You don't need to say that."

Will said, "Oh, but tis true."

Mary grabbed his hands in hers and sank back on the bed, pulling him with her. The bed made a groaning sound under their weight.

Mary giggled softly. "Perhaps we should be careful not to break the bed. That would be hard to explain."

Will ran his hands over her breasts and she shuddered. His hand ran up the inside of her thigh and found her soaking wetness. She moaned softly, turning her head, and biting the pillow to stifle a cry.

"Quickly, Will, quickly!"

Will thought "quickly what?" Then it occurred to him that she desperately wanted him inside her. He got on his knees between her legs and, putting a hand under her hips, lifted her, and they were joined.

Will was just 20, and his body begged for release. But Frances had taught him well, and he unlocked his mind to allow him to maintain his composure for a short time.

And a short time it was! Mary threw her head back, her breath whistling through bared teeth. In no time he emptied himself into her. It was so exquisite he did not want it to stop. Will continued to stroke his hips extending the sensation until his legs collapsed and he rested his weight on Mary.

Mary, for her part, whispered, "My God! I had no idea..."

Will quietly said, "Your first time?"

Mary breathed, "Yes. Others have tried to entice me, but I did not trust them. We may not be together forever, and I do not expect that. But you are a trustworthy man of honor, Will. You would never betray me."

Will whispered, "Of course not."

Will was worried he was hurting her and went to move. Mary said, "No, no...stay, stay."

"Hush, now. I must have more," she whispered.

Will felt her right-hand sneak between them. Her fingers began to dance. Soon she threw her head back again, gritting her teeth, her eyes rolling up. She made tiny sounds that soon became more insistent. Her left hand held onto Will's neck with surprising strength. Will was both participant and observer. She was in her own little world for a few moments.

A few minutes later, Mary quietly muttered, "I had...uh, I had...it was...God, I'm quite exhausted." She made little puttering sounds with her lips as she slipped into a deep sleep.

Will dozed, too. As he drifted off, his mind floated to Abby. He felt ashamed. Then he thought: I've been so alone for so many months and Abby is married and with child. For that matter, her baby is probably born by now. He resolved to put Abby out of his mind.

He was in the war now, and life was uncertain. The young woman in his bed was quite beautiful, gentle, and kind. She had been open to him every time they had met. She cared for him.

Will realized he cared for her too. Not like Abby. There would never be another Abby. But Abby was gone, and Mary was right. They could all die tomorrow under the heel of the British. She was here and warm and made him feel good in his heart.

As Will drifted off to sleep he thought, "For now, that is all I can hope for."

◇◇◇

The morning dawned with clear skies and a light breeze. Warmer. Will marveled that a bird sang in the tree outside his window in Mr. Homer Proctor's Charlestown townhouse. It was January and the tree was bare, but a bird still sang. There was a slight indentation in the bed next to Will. Soft, flowery scent — a hint of roses - on the pillow.

Will washed and dressed in his uniform. He left the infernal sword leaning in the corner. Probably would trip him down the stairs. He walked quietly downstairs to find a little hubbub going on in the dining room. Several people were moving around the large table and the buffet. Dr. Jones was there. His wife and daughter were apparently not early risers.

Will found eggs, grits, bacon, some sausage links, toast, biscuits. Honey, jam, and other condiments adorned the left side of the buffet. The right side had a pot of coffee and fine China cups.

Will ate with abandon. He was careful not to shovel food into his mouth as had become his habit while with the army in the field. When he was in the field, every meal seemed to be a gift, and things could always change and interrupt the food. As Cuth had once said, "Never miss the chance to eat, sleep, or pee." Here, Will was quite aware he was in polite company. He tried hard to be genteel and avoid making himself a spectacle.

He planned to leave three days hence, having rested his men and their horses as well as allowing his mental and emotional states to calm. Meanwhile, he was looking forward to sitting on the courtyard bench in the sun and reading his books. *The Odyssey* was a bit intimidating, but he was making his way through it. He considered that becoming an educated man was not without pain and effort. But he was determined to not only own books but to actually read those books.

Will also had decided he needed to talk to Colonel Elbert about becoming a freemason. It seemed that every notable man he had met in the past several years was a freemason. Caswell, Washington, Elbert, his own father. Clearly, these were successful men and freemasonry seemed to be a linking condition they all shared. He resolved to speak with Elbert on the matter.

A satiated Will sat on the bench in the sun. The sun was almost hot, offsetting the slight chill in the air. Will thought that later it would be cold here since the sun would go behind the house and the courtyard would be in shadow. That would be nice in summer, though. He turned in *The Odyssey* to his last page and began to read.

It seemed that Odysseus and his crew were being beckoned to an island by three singing women called the Sirens. It was clear that the Sirens were up to no good and that being enticed by them meant great danger.

A soft voice broke Will's concentration. "Good morning, Will."

It was Charlotte Jones. She wore no cap and her auburn hair glowed in the morning sun framing her smooth, oval face.

"Good morning, Miss Charlotte."

Her dark eyes glittered. "It appears I have lost."

"You have?"

"Yes. It seems that Mary Proctor has cut you out of the herd and is intent upon branding you her own."

"Oh."

"There are plenty of other fish in the sea, Will. But I did so want you."

"Oh, I uh...I mean..."

Her eyes became icicles. "I had hoped for a better response than that."

"Please sit down, Miss Charlotte."

"Harumph! I will, but only because the sun is very nice."

"I don't want to belong to anyone, just now. The war..."

"Oh, pooh! The war, the war, and the war! That's all we women hear as an excuse for every damned thing. Yet, when you men want something, it's also the war."

"Please. I do not wish to offend anyone. It's just, well...it is the war. Over a year ago, I left North Carolina on the way to Pennsylvania to buy sufficient stocks for my future gunshop. I had every intent of procuring those supplies and then going back through Carolina, collecting my things, stopping in Bear Creek to marry Abby, and moving on to either Tennessee or North Georgia. Here I sit in a garden in South Carolina almost two years gone. No gun parts, no frontier, no gunshop. Caught up in the middle of more than one battle. Shot at, killed people, threatened with hanging. Frantically ran from all that and landed in the middle of more war. Abby is married and with child. And you tell me the war is just an excuse. No. It *is* the war! And no, I don't want to become someone's man and have that on my conscious on top of all this other."

Charlotte sat back slightly, her gaze cast around the courtyard. "Oh, Will. You had not told me about Abby. You really loved her, didn't you?"

"Yes. I will always love her. But she is gone. Good as dead. I was away so long, and my letters never reached her. She decided I must be dead, and she rightfully did not want to be a spinster. She married a young fellow who is from a decent family, and by now I'm sure she has his child."

"I'm sorry about Abby, Will. Truly, I am. The other two are both simply smitten with you, Will."

"The other two?"

"Yes, you ninny. Mary and Eliza."

"Oh, I like them too."

"That's all you can say? You like them too? I know Mary came to your bed last night."

"Oh. I uh...well..."

"I won't tell. I actually like Mary and Eliza. Be careful with Mary's heart, Will."

"Uh, I will."

"I hope so. In spite of myself, I like you an awful lot. I think it's because you are a rare thing: you're a good man who has character."

"Uh, thank you, I think."

Charlotte growled in her throat. "Grrrr. You frustrate me no end! I shall go find something to do like knit or embroider to get my mind off this. I wish you well, Will. I shall always be your friend."

"I am your friend, too, Charlotte."

"Dammit, I know that."

Will sat quietly, thinking about his conversation with Charlotte. He felt sad that he must have hurt her somehow. He thought, "Maybe we shouldn't have kissed and talked about courting. I don't know how I should have acted."

"Good morning."

Startled, Will jumped. It was Mary. "Good morning." Will stood up. "Would you like to sit?"

Mary sat on the bench and Will returned to his seat.

Will said, "It's beautiful out here this morning. You are beautiful, too."

"You are sweet to say that, Will. You look troubled."

"Charlotte just came to chat and said that she has lost. I was not aware there was some competition."

"Oh. Huh. Well, all women want to think that every man belongs to them. I know you have not gotten past your feelings for Abby."

Will looked up at the bare tree outside his bedroom window. "I have not had a moment to tell you about that, and last night didn't seem the right time."

"How about now?"

"Certainly. It's pretty simple. I was gone for many months, and my letters did not reach anyone in North Carolina. When Abby did not hear from me, she decided I must be dead. So, not wanting to be a spinster, she married a fellow who lives nearby her parents. When I saw her she was with child. I think by now she has had the baby. Her husband is somewhere near Charlestown with the North Carolina militia. I wish them and their baby well, but I feel empty."

"Have I not filled you, Will?"

"Oh, Mary! Yes, you have made me happy."

Mary's eyes darted around the courtyard. "I hear a 'but' coming."

Will looked at Mary. Her eyes were round and wet. "The 'but' is this war. Charlotte said that men are using the war as an excuse for whatever they want to do. But it *is* the war. The war has made everything uncertain. What kind of man would I be if I married someone and went and got killed?"

"You were willing to marry Abby."

Will held Mary's gaze. "Yes. But the plan was to gather sufficient parts for a gun shop, marry Abby and move to the frontier. Of course, I could get killed on the frontier, or Indians might kill me and my family. I understand that. Tis true that dangers are everywhere in our young country. But the frontier is more controllable, I think. At least I would be in control of me. The war seems driven by others, and there seems to be a great deal of uncertainty about where the British will strike next."

Mary looked at Will. "I understand."

After last night's party, dinner at the Proctor's was a quiet affair. The cooks were wizards with fresh fish, and there were root vegetables kept buried in the back garden. A wonderment of the winter, there were fresh greens from a small hot house on the south side wall of the carriage house.

Will enjoyed the fish. He also relished the bread which seemed to be a feature of every high-end home. Will complimented Mary's mother, Hannah, on the wonderful dinner.

Homer Proctor asked Will penetrating questions about the war and the chances of Charlestown staying independent of British control. Will was forthcoming saying that Savannah had fallen in a matter of hours. Homer was disconcerted when Will said Charlestown might hold out just a little longer. Dr. Jones observed that there was neither sufficient money nor troops to defend Savannah, and Charlestown was no better.

They talked for two hours by the light of candles, fueled by excellent rain-water Madeira wine. Everyone began to yawn. Will wondered if he had bored his hosts or if the wine had made them sleepy.

Will went to his room, urinated in the chamber pot, covered it, and washed up. He sat on his bed in his underwear and pulled out his copy of *The Odyssey*.

The room was even more pleasant tonight. A small vase held a gardenia flower which perfumed the air. Perhaps a servant had put the flower there. Will considered that the hothouse was good for more than just vegetables. Maybe one day he would have a hothouse like that and experiment with growing vegetables and flowers, even in the cold of winter. Perhaps the cost of glass would be prohibitive?

The door silently opened, and Mary stepped in. As with last night, she wore a soft white linen bedgown. It hung from her shoulders and the shadow of her body was accentuated when she moved. Every soft step held promise, and Will was instantly erect.

Will watched silently as Mary quietly walked to the bed and pulled a small blue ribbon at the throat of the gown, letting the garment fall from her shoulders to puddle in the floor. She was young, firm, and every curve was perfect. Will's breath caught in his throat.

Still lying on his back, Will tugged his long shirt up and over his head. Before he could move, Mary swung a leg over him and guided him into her. Frances had done this, and Will had loved it. He was surprised that Mary knew how as well. Mary had proved herself an excellent horsewoman when they went riding at the Yonge's plantation, now she posted away as though in a formal competition for best rider.

They lay quietly talking.

Will could see a slight sheen of sweat reflected in the moonlight on Mary's chest. His own sweat cooled in the slight night breeze.

Mary said, "Damn, you, Sir. I fear you have stolen my heart."

Will replied, "You are quite important to me, Mary. I was thrilled to be invited to the party here. I was expecting to have to make up a reason to visit Wadmalaw Island when I led my troops back to Georgia. All these months I thought we would not see one another again."

"I know there are many impediments, and that is true. But I shall remain faithful to you while you are away at war. I will certainly pray for you. Is that acceptable?"

"Remaining faithful or praying?"

"Both!"

"Hahaha. A small jest. Of course, I welcome you praying for me. But do not ignore others because you will not know if I live or die."

"Yes. These are troubled times. So many people do not see their adulthood."

"I have no designs on others. I am an honorable man."

"That you are. Tis why I lay here with you last night."

"And tonight?"

"Nay, Sir!" she snickered, "This is pure wanton. I am shamelessly using you to my purposes."

The next two days passed swiftly and suddenly it was morning and Will packed to leave. Yesterday he had sent Cuth to Lieutenant Robinson with news that the detachment would be riding south to Purysburg this morning. Will dressed in his Continental Army officer's uniform.

As usual, he added his belt with Uncle Ewan's dirk and Tarleton's Brander pistol. He hung his shot pouch and powder horn across his shoulders. Though not common for an officer to carry any of these items, Will was not about to be without his protection.

Mary quietly stepped into the room. "I came to say a proper goodbye."

Will swept her up into his arms and kissed her hard. She clung to him. "I will not cry. You must be safe and come back soon. You must!"

"I would promise to write but I know not how to get a letter to you."

"Perhaps you can send a note with a courier bringing important papers, and we can correspond that way."

"I will try. I do have writing paper and a pen and ink."

Mary said with mock severity, "Good! See that you use them."

Will grinned. Then he turned serious. "These past few nights were delightful. I worry that perhaps you might be with child. What will we do if that is the case?"

"I am not with child, Will. Educated women know how to avoid falling pregnant until we are ready, and I have taken precautions. Worry not."

"I do not worry for myself, but for you and any possible child marked as illegitimate. If you say you are safe from unwanted motherhood, then I am content. But also, I do not want to feel I used you for my own pleasure."

"I came to you, remember? Now, let us not speak of this further."

Will pulled her close and they kissed one last time.

Mary cracked the door open, quickly stepped into the hall, and was gone.

The scent of the gardenia in its little vase wafted in the room. The flower had been fresh just two days ago.

But this morning the gardenia's petals had already started to fade.

Part III: The Battle

CHAPTER 36 – STORM IN THE BACKCOUNTRY

Major William Yelverton and Lieutenant Henry Robinson led their small troop of twelve men plus Corporal Charles Cuthbert jingling along the road into Purysburg, South Carolina. The Continental Army encampment there was well established, and General Lincoln had moved many of the troops there from Charlestown. It was not far from Savannah and Lincoln was considering how he would take that city back from the British.

As he dismounted, Will said to Lieutenant Robinson, "Take the men and find some place to pitch camp. I'm sure someone here is in charge of all that. I'm going to see how to find Colonel Elbert."

Cuthbert came over and took Molly. "I'll make sure we get a good place, Sir."

"Know you will, Cuth. I'll be back shortly."

Will spotted a large tent with many officers coming and going. He walked over to the source of all the hubbub. As expected, it was General Lincoln's headquarters and there he found Lieutenant Colonel McIntosh, and several others including Major James Jackson." Jackson looked up. "Ho! Will! Welcome back to chaos, old boy."

"Hey, Jim. Haven't seen you since the fight in Savannah. Looks like you are unhurt."

483

"Only me pride, old boy, only me pride. I have a message from Colonel Elbert for you. He says he wants you to join him up north of here in South Carolina across the river from the Augusta Road. I think he is camped across from Brier Creek or thereabouts. Burton's ferry is near there."

Will said, "Thanks, Jim. I'm glad I stopped here. Colonel Elbert had told me to seek him out. I had thought he might be across the river at Brier Creek. That's too close to Ebenezer for comfort."

"Aye. Are your men bedded down for the night?"

"My lieutenant was seeing to that as I came over here."

As they chatted, several hundred men led by General Moultrie were forming up to march.

Will asked, "What's that about?"

"The British have made a move toward Carolina. They dragged a derelict old ship into Beaufort's harbor. It's not seaworthy, but they've mounted guns on it and anchored it to bombard Fort Lyttleton. Captain John DeTreville commands there. He's competent but doesn't have sufficient men to defend Lyttleton. The British mean to take Beaufort and Port Royal Island. Those men there are our response. Things are heating up, Will."

"Aye, it seems they will push for Charlestown itself soon."

"They'll have to get past our forces here, first. I'm concerned they will try to land near Stono River and flank us. They are masters of flanking, and we are amateurs at nearly everything."

The troops began marching to the east. Will watched as the mix of militia and a few Continental troops plodded out of the camp. The somewhat shambling appearance of the troops did not fill him with confidence.

Two days later, Will and his detachment trotted into Elbert's camp about three miles east of the Savannah River and across from Brier Creek, a strategically useful spot along the Augusta Road. Burton's Ferry across the Savannah made for a possible quick access or escape.

Stepping out of his tent, Elbert smiled. "Will! Glad to see you. Dr. Jones and his family are safely in Charlestown?"

"Aye, Sir. They were staying with Mr. Homer Proctor at his townhome as I left, but I understood Dr. Jones has found a home to rent. I believe as soon as they are settled Dr. Jones will open his medical practice."

Elbert lowered his voice. "Good. Liz will kill me if I don't ask. How goes it with Miss Charlotte."

Will dropped his eyes and said, "Alas, I somehow transgressed by being friends with some other young ladies who were also present in Charlestown. I do not understand the ways of women, but apparently there was a duel of sorts and Charlotte lost. Now she is...distant."

"Too bad. But know that understanding women is beyond the ken of mortal man."

Will smirked. "I'm reading Homer's *Odyssey*. While the story frequently confuses me, and I get lost in the poetry, there is a part where women called the Sirens sing sweetly trying to get Odysseus to dally at their island. If he visits the island, the Sirens will eat him and his crew. I think that's some kind of cautionary tale for men in general."

Elbert snorted. "Gad, young Sir. You are learning."

Elbert's face turned serious. "Will, I need you to go up to the area on this side of the river across from Augusta and find General Pickens with his band of South Carolinians. Elijah Clarke has recovered from his wounds in Florida, and he will be there along with Colonel John Dooley and other Georgia Militia officers and troops. Tell them that the British are marching on Augusta and to be aware of any movement of other British forces moving to support that. You'll need to wear your hunting clothes. Take your orderly and two soldiers with you. They also should wear their civilian clothing."

Will's eyes went wide. "The British are marching on Augusta? So soon? Tis only three weeks passed since their taking of Savannah."

Elbert met Will's gaze. "Aye, t'was to be expected, Will. But they've moved even faster than we expected. Campbell took Ebenezer two days after we lost Savannah. We did not go to Brier Creek because the situation changed so quickly. The British immediately set about building redoubts along the River Road to Augusta at Ebenezer. I plan to cross the Savannah River in the next couple days and set up to impede Campbell. Tis late today, so rest your horses and leave tomorrow."

Will looked up into the trees. "Yes, Sir. Do we have anyone who can guide us?"

"Aye, it's mostly Indian paths in this part of both Carolina and Georgia's back country. I'll get one of the men from Wilkes County to go with you."

"We'll leave at daybreak."

Elbert said, "Good. Come find me when you've finished to your satisfaction with Pickens. And Will, this should provide you a chance to see what the frontier in this area looks like. I hope you like it."

"Aye, Sir. Seems that no matter how much I might like it, tis just out of reach."

Will sat on a stump next to a pinewood campfire. The pungent woodsmoke floated up and occasionally wafted over him. The heat from the fire warmed his front, but his back was chill from the cold upland South Carolina winter. A crust of snow was visible in the grass near the edge of the clearing where Elbert's rag-tag army had made its camp. Watching the dancing flames and the rapidly burning pitch pine, Will thought about how pine burns hot but is quickly consumed. He wondered if his experience with women was akin to a pine log fire.

A voice interrupted his reverie. "Are you Major Yelverton?"

"Aye."

"Sir, I am Bartleby Ashmore. I'm from Wilkes County, Georgia. They want me to go with guide you to Colonel Pickens. I also know this side of the river as well as the back country above Augusta."

"Good! You'll make our fifth. Aside from you, there's me, Corporal Cuthbert, my orderly, and two troopers who are assigned to make us feel safe, regardless of how inaccurate that feeling may be."

Ashmore grinned, "I know the area well enough that I think we can avoid the British and the Tory's with no trouble."

Will stood and shook Bart Ashmore's hand. "You're most welcome. You have a horse, weapons, provisions? Good. We'll set off at first light."

Ashmore went back to his tent, and Will turned to roast his backside. Evenings outdoors by a fire like this always made him think of sitting with Abby by the firepit at Kennedy's. He sighed and looked up at the stars. His coat and breeches felt like they would explode into flame any minute, and he moved away from the fire. The bittersweet memory of Abby faded into the background. Will wondered if that melancholy memory was a forever thing. Part of him wanted it gone; another part clung to the imbedded joy that had been his time with Abby.

Will wore his hunting shirt and breeches with Uncle Ewan's dirk dangling on his right side with Tarleton's Brander pistol tucked into his belt. The English Dragoon carbine rested butt first on his right thigh, a thigh that was tired and bruised from days of supporting the small, but still heavy, carbine. Josie and Will's .45 caliber rifle rode in their scabbards under Will's right leg, and the old hog-leg horse pistol rode in its leather bucket, close to hand. As was his habit, both pistols and the carbine were loaded with buck and ball with an extra dash of powder. Will hung his officer's sword from the left side of his saddle. Useless, infernal thing.

Two exhausting days of trotting through reddish orange sandy soil overgrown with what Ashmore called wire grass, and shaded by tall pines and tangled with briars, brought the little detachment to the last hundred yards before Colonel Elijah Clarke's camp. Late afternoon shadows made strange shapes along the Indian path as Molly picked her way daintily along, stepping around small obstacles and snorting at unfamiliar scents. Will breathed in the fresh pine odor and shifted in his saddle. A covey of quail startled the small troop when they burst from their cover and flew a hundred yards before setting into the brush. Will's thighs and buttocks were tired from all the time in the saddle these last four weeks. He thought wryly, "More of this to come."

"Will Yelverton! Welcome." Clark called out from his seat by the campfire, his breath popping little clouds in the cold air. "Come eat something." Over his shoulder, "Lieutenant Mullen? Ho! Dan? Please see that Major Yelverton's men get a place to bed down."

Swinging out of the saddle, Will saluted, and said, "Tis good to see you, Sir. I hear the leg wound has healed."

Clarke waived a half-hearted salute. "Aye, but it still aches on cold days like this. Worse when it's damp like it has been the last two days."

Stretching his back and lower legs, Will said, "I was sent to provide you an update on the situation with Augusta."

Clarke's eyebrows shot up. "What situation with Augusta?"

Will said, "The British marched from Ebenezer up the river road toward Augusta on the 24th. That was three days ago. Colonel Elbert wanted me to inform you of that and to say that he predicts the Royalists and British will be hard to dissuade from taking the town. Colonel Elbert is heading to cross the Savannah at Brier Creek with about 400 regulars and some militia. The remnants of our Savannah defense. He asks that I find out the status of Colonel Pickens of South Carolina and warn that other British Units might be moving toward Augusta from South Carolina."

"Damn! I thought it would take Campbell longer than this to get his delicate British ass in motion. Him being an aristocrat, and all."

Will said, "I was told he has been replaced by General Augustine Prevost from Florida as overall commander of the British Forces in Georgia. That freed Campbell up to move inland. Lt Colonel Thomas Brown's Florida Rangers are in the lead with the British Regulars in the center and Robinson's Carolina Royalists bringing up the rear. I understand the Royalists' commander, Colonel Alexander Innes left for England and has not yet returned to resume command."

Elbert spat in the fire. "That Brown is a bandit and no two ways about it."

"Aye. Colonel Elbert says that Campbell is a force to be reckoned with and may be trying to get behind our troops at Burke County. That may not work since we hold some Loyalists in the Burke County jail. Our spies tell us that Brown has broken off from the Augusta Road at Brier Creek and is likely headed for Burke County. The obvious conclusion is that Brown intends to rescue the Loyalists in the jail."

"Hmmm...sounds like the British are having squabbles about command." Clarke's voice dripped with sarcasm. "Of course, we never have such disputes."

Will grinned. "Do you know where Colonel Pickens might be? I'm asked to confer with him and his South Carolina militia."

"Aye. He's not far. We will go meet with him in the morning. North of Augusta that scum McGirth controls all the bluffs on the Georgia side of the river. Fortunately, Pickens controls the bluffs on this side!"

The morning dawned bright, clear, and cold. It was that hard cold that makes fingernails feel brittle and harshens each breath. The grass crunched as Will walked over to Molly. A light breeze soughed in the tops of the trees, more hardwoods here: bare, stark, gray slashes against the azure of the sky.

Everything Will touched crackled with electricity. He smiled to himself as he thought that Dr. Franklin would require neither kite nor key this day to prove interesting facts about electricity.

Molly pawed the ground, whickered, snorted, and blew. She looked around at Will expectantly. Then she crunched happily on the apple that Will produced from his shot pouch. He had been keeping it for just such a morning. At least Molly had not been cold. Cuthbert had thrown a blanket over her back. Will smiled. Cuth was a good man.

Clarke mounted his horse stiffly. Will thought it was from both the cold and the wound in Clarke's leg. The two officers trotted the three miles to Pickens' camp in companionable silence, the muted clop of the horses' hooves on crusty, near frozen ground the only sound. Will enjoyed the silence of up-country Carolina.

Elijah Clarke said, "Gentlemen, this here is Major Will Yelverton from Elbert's staff. I've had the pleasure of serving with Will at Sunbury. He's a deadeye with a rifle. Served with Elbert at the Frederica Naval fight."

Colonels Andrew Pickens, John Dooley, and Clarke all looked at one another and then to Will. Dooley spat tobacco juice. "Bit young, ain'cha?"

"I was one of Washington's couriers at Brandywine."

Dooley said, "Were ye now?"

Clark continued, "Don't let his youth confuse you. Will's here to pass along that the British are marching in force up the River Road from Ebenezer. Clearly, they intend to take Augusta."

Dooley, his rough, backcountry tones clouded with tobacco, growled, "Glad to have ye, young feller."

Will nodded his thanks, "Happy to be here, Sir."

Pickens, his voice cultured, educated, asked, "Can you provide more information? What's Elbert doing?"

Will said, "Aye, Sir. Colonel Elbert was two days ago camping a couple miles into South Carolina across the Savannah River from Brier Creek. I'm sure you know that Brier Creek is a defensible strategic location along the River Road to Augusta. Colonel Elbert said to let you know he was going to cross the river and position himself in hopes of impeding the British march to Augusta."

Will continued. "He also said that Loyalists are being held at the Burke County jail with a small force of some 200 Georgia militia guarding them. His spies have said that Brown and the East Florida Rangers broke off from the main British column and were last seen heading toward Burke County. Colonel Elbert said he would work to put some of his forces between Brown's Rangers and Burke County."

Dooley said, "They's a problem here. If Elbert fights them Rangers at Burke County, and the main British force keeps a'goin' to Augusta, that puts the British behind Elbert. We know they's good at flankin' maneuvers. 'Course they want them loyalists outta that jail, but I'd say they's tryin' to distract Elbert, and open him up to being attacked in the rear."

Clarke looked thoughtful. "Aye, we're in quite a pickle. We're keeping an eye on the British in Carolina, too. The British have sent a Lieutenant Colonel Boyd to recruit loyalist militia all over the middle part of South Carolina. Our spies believe

Boyd will take his men across the river north of Augusta and threaten the good people of Wilkes County and other areas in the Georgia backcountry. I suspect that will include reinforcing the British in attempting to take Augusta. Either way, I'm afraid Augusta will be surrounded."

Dooley said, "Aye, them's my people in Wilkes County. My men'll want to be a'goin' home if they homesteads is attacked."

Will asked, "What is to be done?"

Pickens said, "We're watching Boyd. But I think we should cross the river and try to cut the British out of taking Augusta. We didn't know Campbell was moving so soon, so that may present problems."

Dooley spat tobacco juice, glanced at the trees as if for inspiration and said, "Tis hard to know where Boyd may be a'goin' and if'n he intends to meet up with Campbell. Maybe he don't know Campbell has marched so fast?"

Pickens spoke, "We've all agreed I will be overall commander in this area. I think we're in agreement, too, that we must cross the river and threaten the British. And soon. I think we should move tomorrow at first light to cross the river."

Dooley and Clarke nodded.

Dooley said, "That rat McGirth controls them bluffs on tha' Georger side o' tha' river up yonder north of Augusta. I think we should go across a bit south of them bluffs and see if we kaint get into Augusta thataway."

Pickens said, "Very well. South of the bluffs it is and to Augusta. Prepare to move first thing tomorrow morning. I want the men to travel light, so leave anything that requires wagons or pack horses, and bring personal bedrolls, ammunition, and the like."

Nods all around ended the conference.

Will and Elijah Clarke rode back to Clarke's camp. Again, the silence of the ride was pleasant as each man was lost in his own thoughts. The crunch of frozen grass under the hooves and the soft whisper of the biting wind were the only sounds.

CHAPTER 37 – KETTLE CREEK

Dawn broke to dry, frigid air made colder by a light breeze from the north. The sounds of breaking camp invaded the silence of the backcountry. Jingle of horse furniture, creak of wagons being loaded, men cursing, sneezing in the cold, urinating, and bitching about the lack of hot food. Pickens had ordered that the units step off as soon as the trees were visible, so there were no fires. The wagons were going south to hold in a rear area until a location in Georgia could be secured. The men were going slightly north to cross the Savannah at Cowan's ferry. The ten-mile march would take them all day. Moving the army across on the ferry would take hours.

Dooley rode up, "We's ready. That British Major Hamilton is camped at Water's Plantation near the mouth of the Broad River. I'd like to kick his ass after he done run us outta Georgia last month."

Pickens replied, "Aye. He's an obstacle. As soon as we get across and form up, we will jump him at first light. The men'll be tired, but they would like revenge on Hamilton."

Clarke said, "We're ready to march."

Pickens looked over the troops arrayed in loose squares of about 30 men each. Three files with ten ranks made up each company.

Pickens called, "Regimennnnnnnt...."

Subordinate commanders echoed, "Battalion...." and "Compaannnyy..."

Pickens shouted, "Attention!" The ranks stood more or less at a position of attention.

Pickens shouted, "The regiment will advance by companies! Forwaaaaaaarddddddd....

Subordinate commanders echoed, "Forwaaaaaaarddddddd...."

Pickens shouted, "March!" and the men stepped off.

There was neither fife nor drum.

Will gave silent thanks for the lack of a bagpiper.

The day passed with no incident. The warmth of the sun finally overcame the frigid morning air and the men gradually removed heavier layers of outer clothing. The route march stretched out to a gaggle of loosely formed companies, men carrying their bedrolls, canteens, and coats draped over the muzzles of their muskets which the men balanced on their shoulders. They looked like a huge line of heavily laden hoboes. Though the muskets were heavy, and the coats, canteens, and bedrolls added to the weight, the ability to balance the load was helpful in the long, ten-mile march.

The odor of the army was pungent. Will thought horses stank, but this was utterly putrid. Unwashed bodies in the hundreds, compounded by miserable hygiene and weeks in the field in the same clothing created a cloud of stink that was breathtaking. Some men were clearly sick and stumbling along, pausing to vomit or spray liquid from their bowels by the roadside, adding to the reek of humanity on the way to war.

Despite the chill and the damp that pervaded everything, the little army began to kick up a cloud of choking dust. It was not as bad as the aftermath of Brandywine where late summer dust had been like a wall, driven by the feet of thousands more men, horses, and wagons moving along the narrow road to Chester. In both cases, Will counted himself lucky to be in the lead elements of the army. Will thought to be at the rear must truly be brutal.

The army arrived at Cowan's Ferry about 4 pm. Many of the men collapsed by the roadside, eager to throw off the weight of their bedrolls, haversacks, coats, and muskets. Will watched as many men filled their long-empty canteens in the river and proceeded to drain them, refilling yet a second time. Will wondered how safe the water was to drink, it being already the dark copper color of Georgia clay Elbert had explained those months ago. Were there bugs of some kind in that water? Someone had told him boiled water was safer. Maybe that killed bugs, or some such, whatever it was that made men sick. Will thought better of drinking it and resolved to boil any water he might drink, though building a fire and boiling water might be somewhat difficult if there were men shooting at him.

Almost immediately, lead elements of Pickens' little army began boarding the ferry and shuttling across. The first of the troops dispersed into the edges of the woods and the road –

more of a lane or Indian path, really. These men were not lounging and drinking. They were alert, muskets ready, in case enemy troops might be lurking. Fortunately, all was quiet. Still the advance elements kept a vigil, guarding the small bridgehead as more and more troops crossed.

It was fully dark by the time the entire regiment was across. Pickens signed a voucher to pay for the many trips of men and horses. Will wondered if the ferryman, presumably Mr. Cowan, would ever get paid. Will was one of the last across the river and he led Molly over to the group of senior officers.

Clarke was saying, "This is Mr. Watts who lives near the mouth of the Broad River above Petersburg, a small settlement near the Waters Plantation. He has news for us."

Watts, a wizened little man with a wispy white beard and equally wispy hair, spoke with a surprisingly strong bass voice. His right eye drooped along with the right side of his face. His breath gusted foul from rotted teeth, tobacco juice, and probably some form of stomach ailment.

"Them Tories wuz a'campin' at ol' Waters Plantation, but they done left a couple days gone. I heared they was a'goin' to visit they forts up yonder and demand loyalty oaths frum everbody they seen."

Dooley paused in the act of packing a plug of tobacco into his cheek and asked, "Mr. Watts, do ye have an idee of whur they wuz headed first?"

"Yup, looked to me like they wuz headed to Carr's Fort up the Broad near Long Creek."

Pickens said, "Thank you, kind Sir. You must guard against being arrested by those thugs. Especially, watch out for that brigand McGirth."

"Oh, aye. McGirth is a bad 'un." Pausing to spit a copious squirt of tobacco juice, Watts continued, "He done let his Injuns scalp my wife's cousin over to Wilkes County. We got a cave up in the hills where we can run if'n they start nosin' around."

There were nods all around, and Watts accepted a shilling for his trouble. He shuffled off down the lane, his gait awkward as he half dragged his right foot with each step. Will thought it hard to imagine that such a bent, tired-looking man was going to walk several miles back to his home.

After Watts had gone, Pickens said, "I need someone to go with a flying column to take Carr's Fort and hold it against Major Hamilton."

Dooley said, "I have a good man. I'll send him right quick-like to tell them men at the fort to hold out against the Tories."

Dooley went and spoke to a young captain who left at once, riding at a canter so he would get to Fort Carr quickly but not kill his horse in the doing.

Pickens said, "I had hoped to rest the men, but we must strike when the opportunity presents itself. The British are unaware that we are on this side of the river, else they would not have gone on a walk in the woods to check their positions. They would be entrenched and waiting on us."

Dooley spat a glob of tobacco juice, swiped the back of his hand across his brown stained lips, and said, "They got the big-haid raht now. We ort ta' kick they asses while the kickin's good."

Clarke said, "Hell yes, let's go!"

The men had enjoyed a couple hour's rest on the South Carolina side and another three hours on the Georgia side of the river. Still, it was near midnight when the army stood up to march off. Though they were still bone tired from the march, they were somewhat refreshed, and the army set off at pace in the hopes of catching Major Hamilton and his Tories unaware.

Four hours later, still dark, a scout thundered back from a mile ahead of the column. He reined in his horse in front of Pickens and shouted, "The British are inside the fort. Appears there were not many of our defenders there and the ones that were there refused to defend the fort because they feared the British would take the fort anyway and hang them in the bargain. Our captain said the British had to leave their horses and other baggage outside. We can take them if we hurry!"

Pickens spun his horse around and shouted, "Captain Peters? Captain McCrackin? Take your companies and hurry to the fort. Load muskets before you leave. As soon as dawn breaks, attack the British. We will follow quickly."

A thin line of light was just peaking above threatening clouds in the east. It was not as cold, but the air was heavy with damp, making the chill dig through a man's bones. Will wore his heavy Philadelphia coat and was glad of it.

As before his time in the army, Will wore his hunting clothes. Long linen shirt, breeches with several patches even though they were bought new in Charlestown just a few short months ago, a frock hunting shirt that reached his knees. Soft moccasin boots with buttons. A neckerchief kept his throat warm, and his Continental Army Officer's cocked hat served as his symbol of rank. The hat was turned to the side in case Will had to shoot, it's red major's cockade plainly visible.

Will's belt held Uncle Ewan's razor-sharp Scottish dirk and Tarleton's Brander pistol, loaded with buck and ball. His powder horn and shot pouch completed Will's complement of weapons for war.

As always, the English Dragoon carbine rested its butt on his thigh. The carbine irritated the small bruise that marked its frequent resting place. The bruise seemed permanent after months of riding in this manner, a familiar ache. The carbine, too, was loaded with buck and ball, as was the horse pistol resting in the leather bucket holster just to Will's right front. The carbine was clipped to a sling that crossed Will's chest. The hated officer's sword was in its scabbard mounted on the left side of Molly's saddle. Josie and the .45 caliber rifle were carefully loaded and rode in their scabbards on Molly's right.

Will trotted along a couple horses behind Colonel Pickens. Clarke and Dooley were just in front of him. As Pickens and the rest of the army were drawing near Fort Carr, a bursting crackle of musketry rang out from about a quarter mile in front of the column. Pickens spurred his horse and the rest followed suit. As Molly picked up to a canter, Will heard company commanders behind him ordering men to pick up the pace to a double time. The fight was on!

The leaders arrived to see a brisk exchange of musket fire. Patriots on one side blazed away at British in the block house of Carr's Fort. The British fired back, their musket barrels protruding from loopholes in the wall. Balls whizzed past patriots sheltering behind a fence and behind a small building. Pickens and his commanders hunkered down behind the small building, musket balls smacking into the opposite walls adding to the din of the firefight.

Pickens asked, "Where is the water supply for this fort?"

A major said, "Tis that small stream running just by the edge of the fort out the back."

"Cut it off. Take men upstream and divert that stream with rocks, dirt, tree branches. Dry it up."

The major ran to get a small group of men and they trotted off up the hill, out of range of British musket fire. Soon, the stream, just visible beyond the edge of Carr's Fort slowed to a trickle and then not at all. Thirty feet away, a small rivulet picked up and soon was running as a stream, the water being diverted there.

Pickens looked over to Clarke, "That'll fix their wagon! They'll have to give up soon. I have allocated their horses. Tell the men to plunder the baggage, they can keep what they find. If they find papers, I want to see them."

Hours passed with occasional, desultory musket pops. The situation was just dangerous enough to keep the patriots' heads down while they waited for Hamilton's men to realize their situation was hopeless with no water. It was no matter to Pickens. His men were mostly resting from the march, fixing a bite to eat, keeping watch against an attack from the rear.

Five in the morning came early. The wind had picked up and Will breathed in the harshness of winter in the Georgia piedmont. The piedmont was not quite mountains and not quite coastal plain. The cold rushed down from the mountains to the north. This close to the rushing waters of the creeks and the Broad River, the cold was multiplied by the damp.

Will had slept sitting up, back to a low rock wall that protected against any errant musket balls, face to a campfire that reflected off the natural river rock to his back. He had supped on some dried beef, water, and a potato that he had thrown into the coals of the fire. He wasn't sure which he liked best, the potato or the beef. Will considered that drinking the water here was likely safe, it rushed down from the hill, and the chance of it being fouled by animal waste was small. The water was certainly crystalline and though cold, it was refreshing.

A rider on a nearly exhausted horse trotted into the camp. Several musket balls whizzed by as the rider dismounted and duck walked over to where Will and Dooley were sitting in the glow of the campfire. Light cracked the distant hills as dawn sneaked into view.

The rider said, "I have an express for Colonel Pickens from his brother."

Dooley said, "Pickens is over yonder," indicating the back of the small barn with his chin.

The rider duck walked over to the edge of the barn and stood up to walk to Pickens.

Pickens, his long, hooked nose wagging in the early light, fixed the rider with a glare. "You have a message?"

"Aye, Sir. Your brother sends his compliments and begs me to inform you that Lt Colonel Boyd is on the march to enter Georgia and make trouble north of here. The details are in this letter, Sir."

"Is he now? I'll read this. You go get some rest and rest your horse."

The messenger duck-walked back to his horse and, taking its reins, moved well away from the miniature siege.

Will and Dooley scuttled over until they could stand up behind the barn and then walked over to where Pickens and Clarke were looking at the message. Will smiled to himself. Neither Clarke nor Dooley could read, so the pretense of looking at the message with interest was probably for show to the troops.

Pickens said, "Damn and blast! We were going to take this bloody little fort and run these Torys to ground. But my brother says Boyd is on the move and we can catch him if we hurry. These bloody cut-throat Tories in this little fort will undoubtedly rush to Augusta and claim a victory! But we must go back across the river and try to intercept Boyd's blood thirsty rabble. Joseph says no man is safe, every woman is subject to rape, and even the humblest little cabin is subject to being fired. Boyd has left a trail of destruction with his rabble."

Within the hour, Pickens had issued orders to move, and the small army had up stakes and marched off to cross the Savannah River back to the Carolina side. There they would wait for Boyd and his 800 Loyalist militia.

A rider thundered up to Pickens to say that Boyd had tried the river north of Pickens' position and been turned back by a lieutenant at a small crossing called Cherokee Ford. The lieutenant had fired swivel guns mounted in his little fort at the British and made it generally too hot for Boyd to cross. Pickens called this lieutenant, "Horatius at the gate." Will was astounded when he immediately understood the reference to the defender of Rome against the Tuscan horde in ancient times.

The rider said Boyd had swum his horses and forded his men a few miles north of Cherokee Ford and made the Georgia side without loss, his baggage crossing on rafts quickly made from poles and twisted bark to tie them.

Another rider informed Pickens of this crossing and the valiant defense of a Captain Anderson who slowed Boyd on the Georgia side before dropping his resistance and withdrawing to join Pickens. The rider said Anderson had done what he could despite dealing with impediments like canebrakes and heavy river rock along the muddy shore. Anderson reported some 30 wounded, killed, or missing in the fight in the muddy, rocky mess along the shore. Anderson reported that he believed he had killed or otherwise injured some 100 of Boyd's men.

Meanwhile, Will was following along with Pickens as the Americans recrossed the Savannah. They chose Cedar Shoal, a low spot in the river where the patriot force quickly crossed the now narrow river and rushed toward intercepting Boyd before he could link up with McGirth. The Americans were now south and east of the British column. Elijah Clarke's one hundred dragoons caught up with the main body and added to their strength. Pickens ordered the troops to double time to catch Boyd.

Pickens, Dooley, Clarke, and Will conferred at a rest pause for the men. Dooley said, "Ah know jes whur he's a'goin'."

Pickens' narrow eyes flashed, and his long nose waggled. "You do?"

"Yer, I do." Dooly spat a glop of tobacco juice, wiped his mouth with the back of his hand and said, "He's a'headin' fer Kettle Creek. They's a cow pen there, and he's a'thinkin' thur's food fer his men. I'll lay odds he's a'plannin' to butcher some cattle, get a rest, an' feed them troops. Thets whur I'd go. He's a'plannin' to link up with that butcher McGirth who's camped jest up from Kettle Creek!"

Pickens said, "This makes great sense to me. Is there a way we can catch him there?"

Clarke said, "Yer. If we hurries along this here path, we might catch 'em unawares. They's acting like they don't know we're here. This path is beneath thet hill yonder, and our noise will be heshed."

The next morning, they passed through the British camp from the night before. Will noticed that only a few men slowed to pick through Boyd's camp from the night before. There was not much to be had anyway. Soon, the Americans arrived at a spot looking down at a cattle pen where Loyalist soldiers were busily butchering cattle and building a fire to cook the meat.

The Loyalists were intent upon their tasks. Will considered this was the kind of situation where the enemy troops were exhausted, hungry, and focused only on their bellies and rest. Sadly for them, they would get neither.

Pickens and the commanders briefly conferred. Pickens said, "I'm going straight up the middle. Elijah, can you and your horsemen take the left? John, the right?"

Nods all around.

"Very well, we will advance as soon as the men have loaded their weapons. Elijah and John step off smartly and keep an eye out. You'll know when we advance, and you can close on the flanks and their rear. Everyone clear on the plan?"

"Very well. I will give it a brief time and then give the order to advance. Will, I'd like you to stay with me as we engage. If necessary, you will be my courier."

Soon, the mounted troops under Clarke could be seen quietly moving along on the left. Dooley's men were in position on the right. Pickens stood up, looked around at the disposition of his troops. Muskets loaded and at the ready. He shouted, "Advance!"

The troops in the middle moved forward in skirmish order. Pickens and Will stayed on horseback along with a few other officers.

The British troops looked up, saw the Americans marching toward them, and raised the alarm. Soon the enemy camp was panicked, running in all directions. A small group, maybe 100 men, raced to man a makeshift breastwork of fallen trees. Musket fire erupted, and Will could see a Redcoat Officer issuing frantic orders.

Pickens observed the rate and accuracy of the enemy fire from the makeshift breastwork and led his men from the center toward the high ground on the right, flanking the breastwork. Americans fired on the breastwork with great effect. Several Tories fell in just a few minutes. Pickens' troops reached a commanding spot on the high ground.

Will looked across to Clarke who was struggling with a muddy canebrake. The Redcoat officer was looking that way and ordering troops. It was clear to Will that Clarke would be quickly in trouble if something were not done. Dropping the dragoon carbine to dangle from its sling, Will reached for Josie.

Musket balls whizzed past, but mostly they were spent by the time they reached Will and Pickens. One man a few feet away was unlucky and took a ball in the forehead. The ball was not traveling very fast when it hit him, but it caved in his head and he collapsed, dead before he hit the ground. Smoke floated all around, obscuring the view across the battlefield. Will coughed from the pungent stink, the cloying smoke catching in his throat.

Will peered through the dense, yellow-gray sulphury-stink. Molly was agitated at all the shooting, and she whinnied and pawed the ground. She pranced a bit, but Will nudged her with his knees. Holding Josie in one hand he leaned forward to Molly's neck, patter her, and said in soothing tones, "It's ok, girl. I'm here with you." Molly rolled her eyes at Will but stopped fidgeting.

Will returned to looking across the field. There! There was the Redcoat officer confidently standing among the flying bullets issuing commands. Across the little valley, maybe 100 yards, Clarke was still struggling to get though the dense canebrake. Will pulled Josie's set trigger and cocked the doghead. He quickly checked Josie's prime. Perfect, finely ground powder. Dry. Ready. Deadly.

A moment to locate the busy Redcoat officer. 200 yards? Perhaps. Setting Josie's sights on the Redcoat officer, Will ignored a musket ball that plucked at his sleeve. He settled himself. Gently, gently...he touched the trigger.

WizCraaaack! Josie thumped into Will's shoulder. The Redcoat officer paused in the middle of issuing a command. He looked down at his shirt, looked up. Directly at Will. His knees buckled as a second ball slammed into him. A third ball hit the Redcoat officer's leg and he collapsed.

British resistance began to collapse along with the wounded Redcoat officer. Clarke's men broke through the canebrake on the left, and Dooley's men plunged down the high ground on the right into the swirling melee that had engulfed the British camp.

A small group of British on horseback under command of another Redcoat officer broke free and raced up the hill behind the British camp. Will saw Clarke and his men clear the canebrake and race after them.

Will's heart stopped as Clarke's horse went down hard, taking Clarke with it. Will thought, "Oh God, he's been hit again." But, no...Elijah Clarke was up, and another horse was brought to him by one of his troops. He remounted and then charged up the little incline after the small group of Tories trying to escape. Clarke's men saw the charge and joined in.

The Tories on the hill cut and ran. The battle was over.

There was still thick smoke from musket fire mixed with the British cooking fires that had been scattered. The stink of butchered beef offal mixed with human blood and effluent from the voided bowels of dying men clung in Will's nostrils. Men sweated profusely from both effort and fear. It was still cold, and the air had a hard, February bite, but no one noticed.

Will followed Pickens down to the center of the British line. The Redcoat officer Will had shot was on his back, color drained from his face. Will thought him dead. But Lt Colonel Boyd half sat up, fixed Will with a hard stare, and said, "You have killed me, Sir."

Will said, "I'm sorry. Tis war."

Boyd coughed. "Indeed, it is. And you, Sir, are?"

"I am William Yelverton of North Carolina. Please accept my apologies for your injury."

"T'was an astonishing shot."

Pickens said, "Can we make you comfortable, Sir?"

"Aye, well, I'm dyin', that's the point, is it not?" A wracking, gurgling cough and a trickle of blood from Boyd's mouth emphasized his words.

Pickens said, "I fear so, Sir. I would not have had it this way."

Boyd said wryly, "Aye. Neither would I. But your young fellow put an end to me."

Pickens said, "I see other wounds, Sir. Are you in pain? Would you like some refreshment? I have Madiera in my bags."

"T'would be a blessing."

Pickens glanced at his orderly who quickly went to get the wine.

Boyd drank a deep draught. "Ah, God, but I'm going to miss living. Sir, would ye give me wife me brooch? Tis here in me pocket? T'was hers given me for luck. I appear to have run out."

"Aye. T'will be my honor to return her brooch. I shall tell her you met your end bravely with honor."

"Will ye now? Well, tis probably more than I'd have done in yer place, so I thank ye for that."

Boyd's face went gray, and his eyes fluttered.

Will looked away, feeling sick. It was one thing to shoot an enemy. Quite another to have a civil chat with that enemy while he died.

When Will looked back, Boyd's face was slack, his eyes unseeing.

CHAPTER 38 – THE NEW BERN BOYS

Will rode next to an exultant Elijah Clarke. Clarke whooped, "We whupped their ass! Yes, we did!"

Dooley said, "They's on the run, now! Now we gonna run they asses outta Augusta." He pronounced it 'Aww-GUS-ter.'

Pickens smirked and said, "Gentlemen, we got very lucky in that they were overconfident, and they did not pay attention to their surroundings. We had the high ground. Even so, without the element of surprise, we would have had a very hard time. They did outnumber us by at least twice our number. Beating the British out of Augusta will not be easy."

Dooley said, "Say what you Will, Andy. We done whupped 'em good, and we'll whup 'em again."

Will watched Molly's hooves plop one after the other, cracking the frosty grass and stirring little whirls of dust with each step. Will felt glum. He had killed men before. When necessary, it did not bother him to take a life. He had seen the face of the Highlander he killed at Moore's Creek. That man was his first. Will often woke in the night, bathed in sweat, heart pounding, reliving that instant when he shot a man dead for the first time. The grimace on the Highlander's face was etched in Will's brain. But that man was an enemy, intent upon killing Sam Hawks or Noah Harris, Will's childhood friends who were

North Carolina Militiamen. The Highlander also would have killed Will if he had the chance.

But Will had never had a polite chat with a man he had killed as that man lay dying. Shooting Lt Colonel Boyd and then discussing his impending death with him was macabre and confusing. Earlier men that Will had shot were the enemy who meant harm to Will or his fellow American soldiers. Even the man at Moore's Creek was clearly an enemy, and it was not so much the Highlander's death that disturbed Will as it was the up close, personal, and startling nature of that death. Sometimes Will wondered what that man's name was and whether he had a family. Was he a pleasant companion? What did he do? Was he a farmer? A hunter? Did he have a son? A daughter? If there were children, they were without a father. Will mourned that.

In the case of Lt Colonel John Boyd, Will had answers to all these questions. John Boyd was a pleasant man. Under different circumstances, Will and Boyd might have been friends. Boyd was married, and his wife and children would mourn him. Boyd was intelligent and a capable person who was certainly a contributor to society. As with Will's Highlander, Boyd's children would grow up fatherless.

Will also considered that Boyd was a Tory, intent upon subjugating the patriots who simply wanted to be left alone in freedom to pursue happiness. Reports were that Boyd's troops had left a path of destruction in their wake. Was this true? Did they kill, rape, burn, and steal their way across South Carolina?

517

Will was not sure. But Boyd was surely the enemy. A pleasant, sociable man who died with Will's bullet in his chest. Will was sure he would think of Boyd often. He would always see Boyd's eyes looking at him in death.

The small column that was Colonel Pickens' command marched up to the outskirts of the frontier town of Augusta. A small farmstead on the side of the well-traveled road seemed deserted until an old man tottered out of the cabin and shuffled over to the road. He put a shaky hand on a post by the drive into his farmyard.

"Y'all Whigs? Patriots?"

Pickens and the other commanders pulled over to the side of the road. The column continued marching toward Augusta.

Pickens said, "Aye, Sir. Who might you be?"

"I'm the man who owns this little tract of nothin' that's done been swarmed by Patriots, Tories, British, and Injuns. I ain't got nothin'...y'all intend to steal what little I got left?"

"Not at all, good Sir. I will hang the first man who intrudes upon your property, and no doubt."

"Alright. But you won't have to hang nobody. I'll kill the first sumbitch who steps into my yard."

Pickens said, "I hope it won't come to that, Sir."

The old man snorted. "Heard that a'fore. Y'all goin' into Augusta?"

Pickens said, "We are going to take Augusta from the British."

"Don't have to. They done left a couple days back."

"They have?!"

The old man hacked a deep, wet cough and spat a pink glob of mucus. He dragged the back of his hand across his lips. "Aye. They wuz here for about a fortnight. Ran around actin' like they owned tha' goddam place. Threatened folks. Skeered hell out of everybody. Got fed up with whatever they couldn't git, and they's done up and gone. Marched off down the road back ter Savannah, I hear."

Pickens smiled around his long, hawk nose. "Thank you, good, Sir. I hope you fare well."

"I ain't gon' be here come spring. Got this cough. Next sumbitch who comes to take my stuff is gonna die. I might die doin' it, but I don't give a shit. I cough blood all day." The old man tottered around to face toward his cabin. "Y'all be keerful with them Tories. They's bloodthirsty."

Pickens looked at Dooley and Clarke. "I'm sending a scout into the town." Turning to his orderly, "Have Captain Baxley put a guard on this man's home until the column has passed. Shoot the first man who trespasses."

Dooley and Clarke nodded, and Pickens called out, "Captain Johnston? Send Sergeant Boortmann to confer with me."

Two minutes later a husky man with shoulder-length gray hair tied in a que trotted up on a bay horse. His uniform consisted of a pair of patched breeches, stockings, beat down shoes covered with a long shirt and a short vest. A musket was slung across his back.

Boortmann waived a salute toward Pickens. "Ja, herr Colonel?"

"The old man who lives in that cabin says the British have left Augusta. I want you to scout the town. Take whichever men you need and find out if the British have left. We will camp on the outskirts up the road near the creek."

"Ja! Ich vill leaf sofort."

The column began marching again. Less than five minutes later, Sergeant Boortmann and three other South Carolina militia cantered by, a focused expression on their faces.

The column continued moving forward for an hour and more. Soon, Boortmann and his two troops thundered up and reined in in a cloud of dust. Will saw Boortmann throw a salute at Pickens and overheard his report.

"Zir, zey are gone. Nicht a Britisher to be zeen. Ve ask several pippl und zey all zay der British are gone."

Pickens said, "Excellent. Thank you, Sergeant. Please rejoin the column." Then to Dooley and Clarke, "We should skirt the town and go south. I'd like to try to catch the British from behind as we did with Boyd. On the other hand, the British may have outdistanced us, and we have these prisoners from Kettle Creek to take back to Carolina to face justice for their rampage."

Clarke and Dooley nodded, and Pickens pulled out a map. They conferred and turned the column right at the next road. Soon, there was a clearing where the column stopped to camp for the night.

Pickens turned to Will. "Can you take your men and scout out ahead and try to find the North Carolina Militia? I had an express a few days back saying that General Ashe was leading men to take positions south of Augusta."

Will said, "Yes, Sir. I will send a rider back immediately upon contacting the North Carolinians."

Pickens said, "Fine work with us, Will. You can stay with General Ashe until Colonel Elbert joins him. Let Ashe know we're going back to Carolina unless there's some immediate need for us to join him."

Will saluted and turned Molly's head. He trotted back down the column. He spotted Cuthbert and his three troops. "No rest for the weary. We've been ordered to scout ahead to find the North Carolina Militia and report back to Colonel Pickens. Get some food and make sure you have full canteens.

Cuth, please get enough for both of us. You should load your muskets. We don't know what we will run into."

Ten minutes later, Will and his small troop trotted out of the camp headed for the road to Savannah, south of Augusta.

At midnight on February 16th, Will found the North Carolina Militia camp along the Georgia side of the Savannah River. General Ashe had pursued the retreating British on the 15th and had camped here on the sixteenth. Will told one of his men to rest himself and his horse for a few hours and then at first light ride with speed back to Colonel Pickens to inform him of General Ashe and his 1100 North Carolina militiamen's position. He sent Cuthbert with Molly and his other men to find a place to camp.

Will reported to General Ashe.

Ashe looked at Will owl eyed. "You look familiar, Major... er...Yelverton. Do I know you?"

"Aye, Sir. I was the armorer to the expedition to take Fort Johnston."

Ashe said, "Damn me! Of course! Ain't you a bit young to be a major in the Continentals?"

Will replied, "It's been near four years since Fort Johnston, Sir."

Ashe snorted, "Aye. We've all aged. What brings you to my camp?"

"I am on Colonel Samuel Elbert's staff. I was on detached assignment to Colonel Pickens who sent me to find you enroute to my returning to duty with Colonel Elbert."

"Colonel Pickens' compliments, Sir. He wishes me to inform you that we defeated the Tories soundly at Kettle Creek northwest of Augusta on 14th February. Lieutenant Colonel Boyd commanding the Tories was mortally wounded and has died. Boyd's force is now scattered with perhaps 200 dead and as many captured. Colonel Pickens is south of Augusta and returning to South Carolina with the prisoners. Some two hundred Tories escaped the fight and are possible wandering the countryside looking for British units to join."

"Damn good news! Who killed Boyd?"

"Uh, Sir, well..." Will squared his shoulders, "I fear it was my ball that inflicted the mortal wound."

"Did it now? Shot him in a close fight?"

"No, Sir. 200 yards."

Ashe looked at Will hard. "Two hundred yards, ye say?"

"Yes, Sir. We were on the high ground and surprised the Tories. I observed Boyd beginning to get resistance organized while Colonel's Clarke and Dooley worked to flank the enemy position. Clarke bogged down in a canebrake, and it appeared Boyd might be successful. So, I shot him."

"Shot him with what?"

"As you know, Sir, I am a master gunsmith. My masterpiece is a .40 caliber long rifle that is very accurate."

"It must be. Pleases me no end that a Tarheel killed him." Ashe grinned and slapped his knee. "Remind me not to make you angry!"

Not waiting for an answer, Ashe continued, "As to Elbert, we expect to see him joining us shortly. We are pursuing the British but not hotly. Williamson is bringing some 1100 troops from across the river. I am set to meet with Generals Lincoln and Rutherford over in Carolina next week. We will finalize plans to push the British and then re-take Savannah. Meanwhile you are welcome to ride with us. My adjutant will find you a tent."

Will was bone tired. The adjutant, a young lieutenant from Wilmington, looked at him skeptically when he heard Will's rank. Will was still dressed in his hunting shirt. He collapsed into his bedroll in the tent he was assigned. The chill night made it nice to sleep in a tent.

Will opened his eyes before dawn, momentarily confused as to where he was. The noises of a military camp coming to life answered his question. He sat up, looked around and wondered where Cuthbert was.

In answer to that question, Cuth stuck his head in the tent flap and said, "I got you some warm water if you want to shave. I also brought your uniform."

"Bless you, Cuth. I must be getting old! My back and bottom are tired, and I ache all over."

"Tisn't age, Sir. Tis too much riding! They're getting victuals together."

A wolfishly grin spread across Will's face. "Good! I'm also starved, there was no food last night."

Will shaved and emerged from his tent in his Continental Major's uniform. He stretched his back and tried to flex his legs some.

"I knew I'd see you again," said a voice from over Will's shoulder.

Will turned to see Major Roger Adams. "Roger!"

"I see you did as well as I expected, too, Major Yelverton."

"And you."

"Aye, well, they got desperate for experienced leaders."

"Ha, I doubt that's the reason."

"Come eat. How did you come to be here?"

"Tis a long story. It's been three years since we took that weapons train to Brunswick town. I ran into Flora and Allen MacDonald a year later in a tavern in Halifax. They admitted they set the Tories on us. MacDonald apologized for that but said it was, and I quote, 'the vicissitudes of war.' After that we had a pleasant lunch. She's still acting high and mighty."

"I'll bet."

Will and Roger ate grits and fatback from a boiling cauldron in a central clearing. Will gratefully accepted a piece of bread with butter on it. Will noticed that there must be some eleven or twelve hundred men camped here.

Roger listened to Will's story. "God! But you have had a trying three years! Highwaymen, Brandywine, accused of being a spy, privateering, and now battles all over Georgia. As for me, I've been with the militia all this time when I wasn't farming my little place. We have not had much worrying about the British or the Tories. Sure, they've been some small uprisings and some Indian trouble whipped up by the British. When the British took Savannah, that's when the Assembly ordered us to march."

Will asked, "When are we moving?"

Roger said, "I think we'll be here a few days. I understand several units are marching to join us."

"Aye, General Ashe said Williamson is bringing 1100 men and Rutherford may cross from Carolina."

Roger looked around at the camp. "We don't need to sit around here for long. The more you sit the more desertion and sickness you get. Having the river just over there," Roger jerked his chin, "cuts down on desertions because to get to Carolina you either have to ford the river or get on a Ferry. Drown if you try to swim. No place else to go. Easy to get caught."

Will nodded. "Aye, we lost a great many to desertion when Colonel Elbert took the Army to South Georgia. Worse was sickness. Men were dropping like flies. T'was hot and malaria afflicted so many. Fortunately, here the weather is cold, and that seems to keep the malaria and other fevers down."

Will said good morning to Roger and was walking toward Ashe's tent when a familiar voice said, "Good God! A major? My God, but I must be feverish and having deliriums or something!"

Will turned to see Chuck Black smiling at him. Chuck rendered a salute. He was still a lieutenant. "Hello, Chuck."

"Hello, Will, er, Major Yelverton. You, Sir, are the last person I expected to see here."

"I could say the same thing, Chuck. Are you well?"

"As well as I can be. I should have mustered out of the militia after Moore's Creek, but I perversely stayed on. I should be captaining one of my father's ships, but I have been shanghaied to Georgia. On the other hand, captaining a ship these days is fraught with danger. Truth to tell, I have found I'm actually a patriot, and I like it with the men."

"I saw Martha."

"You don't say? How was she? Father disowned her. I disagreed with that, by the way. I tried to tell Father that he drove her away, but he would not hear it. So, she's gone from our lives. I hear she's a ships mate?"

"Aye. She walked into a tavern in Sunbury, Georgia, just down the coast from Savannah. She was dressed in trousers and a shirt with captain's boots and a pistol. She was looking to buy a bottle of rum. Beautiful as ever. Surprising. We talked for a few moments. She's happy with Manoah something."

"Compton. He's one of my father's best captains. Was, anyway. He's lucky to be alive as furious as Father was."

"Martha said they married, so perhaps your father should re-consider. I wish her well. She said Bet was sold."

"Ah, Will. I had to sell Bet to protect her. Father was going to beat her, but I talked him out of it. He was then going to put her on a ship where she would have been subject to…well, you can imagine."

"Aye. I spent some weeks on a privateer, I can imagine. Rough lot, privateers. Martha said Wilmington?"

"Aye. A gentleman named Josiah Harlan. He's a planter. I hope he treats her well. None of this was Bet's fault, but Father was looking for someone to blame, and she was it."

"It's good seeing you again, Chuck."

"Aye. I'm glad we're no longer enemies. I regret a lot about my past."

"I was never your enemy, Chuck."

"I know that now. And, much as I am surprised, the Major's uniform looks right on you. I don't mean that in a backhanded way."

"Thanks, Chuck. It's pleasant seeing you. We've both grown up."

"Aye. More's the pity." Chuck grinned and walked off with his usual swagger. Some things don't change.

Will checked in with Ashe's adjutant. He learned there would be no march today. Likely none for a few days. Ashe wanted to let Williamson catch up. The adjutant said General Lincoln had 'suggested' Ashe and the Carolina Militia move toward a camp at Brier Creek on the way to Savannah. Lincoln thought it would be well protected by water on two sides.

Will smiled at the thought of a couple days respite from riding. He would relish a couple days to sit and read, allowing his body to recover and his mind to refresh. Molly could use a rest.

Will ate some boiled pork and beans. Glop, but at least fresh. The pork must have been butchered just before Ashe and his command started marching. The boiled meat had plenty of salt and pepper and a few hot peppers thrown in, and the beans were cooked with some smoked hog jowl. This was the best food Will had eaten in the past fortnight. It was not as delicious as the food in Charlestown, but after mostly grits and fatback on the campaign trail the pork and beans was a welcome change.

Will sat in the sun, his copy of *The Odyssey* on his lap. He farted copiously every few minutes and smiled. He was not the only member of this command who was bilious from the beans. He had been somewhat constipated since leaving Charlestown, fatback and grits with an occasional slab of bread were not conducive to regularity. He smiled in anticipation of the beans remedying that uncomfortable situation.

Will had just finished reading about the Sirens when another familiar voice, dripping with sarcasm, said, "I will be completely goddamned!"

Will looked up to see Sam Hawks and Noah Harris standing at attention, saluting.

Will jumped up and the three boys hugged and laughed.

Will said, "Oh, my God, but I'm so happy to see you two."

"Aye. We're thrilled you're here. And you're going to have to catch us up as well as explain who you're blackmailing to get that major's suit."

His two friends from childhood were unchanged. They were still great fun and they reminisced about their adventures. Sam and Noah's past few years had been much like Roger Adams'. Mostly being at home, farming, or fishing with occasional call ups to deal with some small Tory activity or Indian trouble.

Sam said, "Tis been three years since we were at Moore's Creek. Then you said you were never joining up and you were going to go to the frontier. Yet here you are."

"Aye. A great many things have happened since I last saw you." As with Chuck Black, Will had not seen his friends in three years. He told them of his travels, the road to Philadelphia, Brandywine, and George Washington, his time in Philadelphia society, the threat of hanging as a spy, privateering, and his adventures in Georgia with Colonel Elbert. He related that Elbert had all but demanded he become a Continental officer. Besides, without gun parts there was no hope of the frontier, at least not now. Will mentioned that what he had seen of the Georgia frontier looked promising.

Will did not share that he had fallen in love with Abby and losing her had prompted him to accept Elbert's offer of a commission. He also did not share his failed romance with Charlotte Jones, nor did he mention his warm liaison with Mary Proctor.

Sam said, "'bout like you to be hob-knobbing with the gentry."

Will snorted, "Yeah, I learned that they're just like us. Only rich."

Noah said, "I'd rather be miserable and rich than miserable and poor."

Will laughed, "They do eat better!"

Noah said, "Oh. And you have supped with George Washington, I suppose."

"Uh, actually, I have."

"Liar!"

"Nope. After Brandywine Washington gave me a safe passage letter, and I rode to a town called Lancaster where there are lots of gunsmiths. I wanted to buy some parts, but I got there and learned that all their parts have been confiscated by the state government for the Pennsylvania militia. I left Lancaster and got caught in a huge thunderstorm. Lucky thing because if I hadn't been forced into a night at a tavern by the weather, I'd have been smack in the middle of another huge battle."

"Next day, I went to a place called Reading Furnace. Again, to buy parts. No luck. Washington's army had been in the battle I avoided during the thunderstorm, and his staff showed up at the furnace. I spent a few days earning some coin repairing the army's muskets and then headed back to Philadelphia."

Will continued. "Along the way I went to the home of a man named Potts. It is quite a mansion in the Pennsylvania countryside. Potts is an iron monger, and I hoped he might have parts I could buy. It was my last chance to get the parts I needed to set up shop. Again, no luck, but Mr. Potts read my letter of introduction from a Mr. Willcox of Crosscreek and invited me to stay the night. I went to wash and rest. When I came down for dinner, General Washington was also a guest for the night.

We had a pleasant meal. I didn't see much of him other than at dinner because he was frantically planning where his army would go next."

Sam and Noah looked at each other and then at Will. Sam said, "You're really serious, ain't you?"

"Yup. I've had some good luck and some terrible luck these past three years."

Later, Will smiled to himself. He was delighted to see Roger, Sam, and Noah. Chuck Black, less so, although Will admitted that Chuck seemed genuinely friendly. His friends were all astonished that he was a Continental officer. He couldn't blame them. Every time he donned the uniform it seemed odd. Yet here he was: Major William Yelverton. He laughed in self-deprecation. "I doubt I could command my way out of a cocked hat!"

The next four days passed pleasantly with Will, Noah, and Sam having plenty of time to sit and chat or venture into the woods hunting as they had when they were boys. Twice they brought back two deer to put in the pot. They also found wild ramps, a kind of green onion. The cooks were pleased to have those to add flavor to the meat.

Several of the men in Noah and Sam's company remembered Will from Moore's Creek and from New Bern. Despite his rank and position, Will was accepted by these men. They were proud of his success. One was a man named Zeke Carter who was pleasant but quiet. Will thought that name seemed familiar, but he could not place the man. Carter kept mostly to himself.

On February 24th word was passed that the regiment would march tomorrow on the way to a new camp at Brier Creek. A brief chat with the adjutant yielded the information that Lincoln had grown impatient with Ashe's pause and ordered him to Brier Creek, that no longer being a suggested course of action. Ashe would be meeting with the other generals across the river in South Carolina in the next few days. The adjutant also said the spies had reported the British encamped at a redoubt just northwest of Ebenezer, some 15 miles below Briar Creek and Old Freeman's Bridge that linked the road across the creek of the same name.

The next morning, the camp came alive with activity as the troops broke camp and got ready to march. At eleven of the clock, the units formed up and began to march. The column of eleven hundred men plus two hundred newly arrived dragoons spread out over a mile. The baggage train trailed the rear element of the soldiers, making the column almost a mile and a half long.

Once again, Will counted himself lucky to be a field officer and to be invited to ride with the senior officers at the front of the column. Otherwise, the dust and stink would be choking. He felt bad for Roger, Sam, and Noah marching in the dust and stepping over horse droppings. He smiled to himself. He didn't feel terribly sad for Chuck Black having to eat the dust of the column and smell the horse shit from the lead elements. But then, Chuck had said he liked this life. Good for him.

All along the way to Brier Creek, Will noticed that the settlements were mostly abandoned. Farmsteads had been looted, and what was left had been neglected for some time. Many were ruined and would need a lot of effort and expense to return them to useful purpose.

One abandoned farmstead had a broken-down gate to a hog pen. The hogs had either escaped or had been stolen. Will's jaw tightened. The hogs were likely feeding the British army. The front door to the once-neat little farmhouse banged listlessly in the wind. Beyond the door, Will could see shattered crockery, a broken chair lying on its side. The family must have left in a frantic rush. A bell on a post in the front yard dinged when the wind gusted. It's deep, rich bong an empty call to no one. A heavy sadness filled Will's chest.

The land was dry and sandy, but the further toward Savannah they marched, Will noticed more swampy land to either side. The smell of pinewoods, swamp, and sandy dust mingled with the odor of the army. The dust was worse now as there had been no rain for a few days.

At two in the afternoon on February 28th, the column had begun to straggle some, the weather becoming slightly warm for February. An hour later, the lead elements marched into the spot the adjutant said was the planned camp.

It was Sunday, though Will didn't think anyone felt especially Godly this day.

CHAPTER 39 – THE CAMP

Will and Cuthbert trotted up to where Ashe's adjutant stood. Will dismounted, leaving the horses with Cuthbert, and walked over to where Ashe and the other senior leaders were gathered under a water oak near the edge of the swampy creek. An advanced scout rode up from the south, dismounted and hurried over to General Ashe and the staff.

The scout saluted. "Sir, the British have burned Freeman's Old Bridge south of here. We are bottled in here between Brier Creek and the river."

Ashe gave the scout a hard stare. "Is the bridge completely destroyed, or can it be rebuilt?"

"I fear it is destroyed, Sir. I also must report that there is considerable swamp some three miles wide around the bridge, and the creek there is too deep to wade. It must be eight feet deep, and fast flowing."

Ashe said, "We're going to have to rebuild that bridge immediately. Also, if the swamp is that large, we'll have to put in a road."

A major said, "I will get a party of men together to build a bridge. We will start immediately, Sir."

Ashe said, "Very well. Proceed."

Ashe then looked around the gathered staff officers. "General Lincoln ordered that we camp here. I am not over fond of this place, but we will follow orders. I will leave it to my adjutant to determine campsites and those details, but I think we should keep units together. So, New Bern Militia to the south of the road, Edenton Militia to the north. We'll put Elbert's Continentals near the road here. That way I can confer with Colonel Elbert when he arrives. Wilmington Militia to the east of the Edenton troops. Halifax Militia to the east of New Bern. I think that will give us depth should the British come out of their camp at Ebenezer and cross the creek."

Ashe continued, "Major Yelverton, you command the Continentals until Colonel Elbert arrives. I know it's not many men, but you can work with my adjutant to get your camp established. Tomorrow I am going across the river to meet with Generals Lincoln and Moultrie. I hope Elbert arrives tonight. We will plan how we're going to eject the British from Savannah."

Major Roger Adams asked, "Sir, as close as we are to the British camp, should we issue cartridges?"

Ashe said, "I don't see a need to do that. The bridge is out. That blocks the only approach from the south. Colonel Marbury? Please ride to the Paris Mill and check that bridge. If it is still intact, destroy it. There will then be no approaches to our position. We'll be protected by the river and the creek which are just like moats around a castle."

Will had last seen Lt Colonel Leonard Marbury at the debacle that was the brief defense of Savannah. Will thought he must be on detached duty from the Georgia units.

Marbury saluted and hurried to his horse. Rounding up his men, Marbury and his dragoons set out at a canter. Their objective was the mill owned by a man named Paris. He had installed a stone dam on the creek and a bridge. Paris' home, built of sawn wooden planks, was nearby, but abandoned. The bridge Marbury was to burn connected the north-south Old Augusta Road to a back road to Augusta on the east.

Will found Sam and Noah. "Can you two go hunting? We could use something other than the tired beef we've had. This looks good for deer."

Sam said, "We're under orders to pitch tents, and so on."

Will said, "Well, I'll go and hope to bring back some meat. Tomorrow we'll all go hunting. I feel certain I can prevail on your captain to let you go."

Sam smirked to Noah, "The major feels certain he can prevail upon our good captain to let us accompany him on his expedition."

Will said, "Mock away...but I'll bet you'd rather be hunting than digging a shit trench."

Will and Molly trotted off to the south toward the swamp that bordered Brier Creek. He let Molly pick her way quietly along the muddy edges. Will looked at the swamp and thought about how nearly impenetrable it looked. Molly walked ten or fifteen feet and stopped, pausing to listen and twitch her ears. Will, too, was listening and watching. A nudge of his knees and Molly walked another few feet.

A buck was delicately nibbling at the few green leaves still on a sapling. Will and Molly were downwind from the deer and Molly was quiet as she picked her way just on the dry ground. This was just what Will had hoped would happen. Will quietly pulled Josie from her deer skin scabbard and checked the prime. He set the trigger and cocked the doghead. Will carefully aimed at the deer's chest just behind its front leg.

WizCraaaak! Josie jolted Will's shoulder and the deer collapsed as if struck by a hammer from God.

Will quickly put Josie back in her scabbard and drew out his .45 caliber rifle. It was possible that there was another deer nearby. The sound of the shot was startling, but then all was silent as Will and Molly quietly walked to where the first kill lay. Will listened for the crashing sound of a deer running through the scrub. Nothing.

Somewhere a squirrel barked a warning. Molly was a bit jittery with the smell of the freshly killed deer, but she was quiet. She pinned her ears and then twitched them. Will sat still in the saddle, the .45's butt on his right thigh. The wind soughed in the tops of the tall pines that occupied the high, dry ground. Water oaks swayed in the breeze, their roots in the soggy mud of the swamp.

There! A second deer, only just visible because its brown back was higher than the surrounding thicket. Only when the deer moved could Will see it. The deer raised its head once and Will noted there were no antlers. Possibly a doe, but maybe a buck since winter was a time when deer shed their antlers. Will cocked the doghead and leveled the .45, waiting. It seemed an eternity, but then the deer stepped into view and died.

Will quickly cut each deer's throat and tying them to Molly's saddle with a thin rope, dragged the heavy, bleeding bodies back to the camp. He dragged them by their front legs so the grain of their hair did not catch on the wire grass.

"Hoooo! That's what tha' shootin' was about. Major done kilt us a brace a deers! That'll be dinner. Uh, begging the Major's pardon, Sir, but you 'bout to feed us bettern' we ever et afore a'joinin' up in this here army."

Will grinned. "Aye, that's what I brought them for. Someone skin and gut these for us. I'm sure we won't lack for volunteers to do that and also to build a fire. I'm going to do some scouting before dark."

Will quietly trotted along, Josie and the .45 reloaded, his English Dragoon carbine on his thigh as usual. This time he was not hunting, though if a wild hog showed up, he would certainly kill it and add pork to the pot. No, now Will was looking around the entire area. His years of hunting made him uneasy about the triangular tip of land between the river and the creek that Lincoln had directed Ashe occupy for the camp. While it appeared impregnable because of the two watercourses that met in a point where the creek mouth met the river, it was also a kind of trap for those inside.

Unlike a castle where defenders might see the enemy from all sides, there were, to Will's mind, blind spots. Like a castle, though, there was no easy escape. Will remembered Moore's Creek, Brandywine, and Savannah. In all three cases, the British had shown cunning and guile in executing masterful flanking maneuvers. In all three cases, water had not deterred the British. How would the British come at the Americans? Will wondered this. Was it possible for the British to somehow flank this position?

Will rode the length of Brier Creek from the burning bridge at Paris Mill all the way to Freeman's Old Bridge, the one that Ashe had ordered rebuilt. Ashe certainly intended to cross there with his army on the way to relieving Savannah of British occupation. Will wondered what if the British used the reconstructed bridge to attack the Americans?

When he got to Freeman's Old Bridge, a quarter mile below Ashe's camp, he saw that a company of light infantry had established a small defensive position. Two field artillery pieces were also placed to cover the bridge approach. Will wondered about this. Could the British negotiate that swamp, somehow ford the creek that was too deep to wade, and then come at

Ashe's forces head on? No. There were several hundred feet of swamp on either side of the bridge. The roadway was actually a wooden causeway with a couple bridges in addition to the burned main span over Brier Creek. Here, Brier Creek was some 100 feet wide and eight to ten feet deep. The only way to cross was if there were a bridge over that creek, and the British had burned that bridge. Will wondered how long it would take to build a new bridge. He wryly thought that the entire war seemed to be about rivers, creeks, and bridges.

Back at camp, Will enjoyed the venison stew that one of the better cooks had made. A few potatoes thrown in, plus some onions and carrots and other root vegetables that were in the supply wagon rounded out the flavor. Fortunately, there was sufficient salt and black pepper to keep the stew from being bland. Will noticed a few sliced long peppers and some fatback. Fatback was a good idea since the deer meat was almost devoid of fat.

Will was still pondering the tactical position of Ashe's army when Samuel Elbert's 200 men marched into camp. Will stood up and walked over to Elbert and saluted. "Good evening, Sir. I am glad to see you. We have venison stew for supper."

"Ah, good. I'm starving. We crossed the bridge at Paris' Mill just before they burned it and have been on the march. The men are exhausted. I will report to General Ashe and come back to join you for a bite."

Will and Elbert sat, their backs against logs from a couple felled trees. The warmth from the fire reflected from the tree trunk and made the cold winter evening almost pleasant. Will was finishing telling Elbert about his trek up to find Pickens and then the events of attacking the blockhouse with Hamilton inside, and finally the Battle of Kettle Creek.

"Shot Boyd, did you?"

"Aye. Not proud of that."

"Didn't think you would be, Will. Tis war, and that's the whole of it."

Will asked about Elbert's actions. Elbert related that he and his 200 men had successfully thwarted Brown and his Florida Rangers from rescuing the prisoners at Burke County Jail, but then not much else had happened. He had visited Liz and made sure she was well before rejoining his troops and receiving orders to proceed to Brier Creek and link with Ashe. Elbert reported many burned out farmsteads and a good number of murdered Georgians.

Will told Elbert about the old man outside of Augusta saying the Tories had taken everything. He also related the desolation he felt looking at the abandoned farmsteads on the road to Brier Creek.

"Aye. This has become quite a terrible tit-for-tat kind of fight with murder and mayhem at every turn. People who used to be good neighbors, even friends, are slaughtering one another without a second thought."

The next morning, Ashe and his immediate subordinates left for Black Swamp on the South Carolina side of the Savannah River. Will and Elbert rode along with the rather large entourage to Burton's Ferry at the end of the road where Ashe had ordered the burning of Paris's Bridge. Will and Elbert watched as Ashe and his escort of dragoons rode the ferry to the South Carolina side of the river.

Back at the camp, Elbert and General Bryant, the other major commander at Brier Creek, agreed to move the camp a mile north to be on higher ground and not be bottled in the angle between the river and swamp. After the move, Will sat in the sun reading *The Odyssey*. He admitted that he did not understand much. He wondered if being camped between Brier Creek and the Savannah River was not a bit like trying to sail between Scilla and Charybdis – the monster on the rocks and the whirlpool.

Late in the afternoon, a courier rode into the camp, saluted Bryant and Elbert, and handed over a message. Later, Elbert ambled over to Will and sat on a stump that doubled as a camp stool.

Elbert said, "It's from Ashe. General Lincoln has sent express messengers to Williamson up near Augusta to bring his 1100 troops to Brier Creek. General Rutherford will decamp and cross the river at Mathews Bluff – that's the high ground you can just see across the river. That will be another 1100 or so men. Lincoln means to march down the Old Augusta Road and retake Savannah. I think tis a fool's errand."

Will raised an eyebrow.

"Aye. Of course I want my home back, but tis hard to have confidence when our troops have not been truly tested in battle, our equipment and funds are very low, and the men are not truly disciplined. The men have no bayonets, or mostly so, and even if they did, they're not trained in the bayonet. As you know from working on the guns, we have several calibers and many different kinds of muskets. Tis a quartermaster's nightmare, Will."

Will nodded. "The weapons Captain Smith had at Girardeau's Plantation were a mixed bag of everything. Couple rifles, several muskets, some fowlers. Many were in poor repair. I tried to put them right, and we did kill some British, but t'was not truly effective."

Elbert nodded. "Worse, we're camped between two boggy swamps and water ways with no way out. Listen to me, Will. If we get attacked and it looks like we will lose, regardless of what happens to me, you must attempt to rally the troops. If it is hopeless, then get them to safety. There are a couple crossings — Burton's Ferry and the ford at Mathew's Bluff. You must get out with whoever you can if things go badly."

"Aye, but I don't want to be seen as a coward."

"Will, you're no coward. Also, our troops have already shown a lack of confidence in battle. A bayonet charge at the right moment, and our troops will collapse and run. Of course, don't share that with anyone. But tis true. You saw it at Savannah."

Elbert glanced around. They were not near the others in the entourage. "We're led by fools, Will. Lincoln is alright, though I can't fathom why he ordered Ashe to camp here. Nonetheless, he's certainly better than Howe. Between us, Ashe is an idiot. I hope Rutherford can get across that river and get to our camp where they might sort out command and put Ashe as second. Ashe is a hot head and not really prepared for a fight."

Will said, "Aye. I saw him come unhinged at Fort Johnston."

Elbert's eyebrows shot up. "Did ye, now? That's been four years. You were just a boy then."

"Aye. I was 16 and hired on as armorer for that campaign. We arrived at Fort Johnston to find Governor Martin gone and the fort deserted. Ashe had a near apoplexy and ordered the fort burned. I might have done the same, but he was surely unglued."

"Damn! That's not good to hear."

"Aye. He's been pleasant enough to me, but I am concerned about being hemmed in between the two waterways. Certainly, the creek and the river are impenetrable for an enemy to try to cross, but they also are impenetrable for us."

"You have it exact, Will. This will not go well if we don't march out of here soon. Tis critical for Rutherford to arrive and for Williamson to get here, as well. That said, I'm not too keen on Williamson. He's always seemed...reticent. I think he's not sure if he really is a revolutionary. Understandable. Some among us still struggle with loyalty to the crown. But tis not a good quality for the commander of a rebel army."

Elbert paused in thought, then continued, "To our immediate position, we've placed ourselves here with our backs to Freeman's Old Bridge. Thus, we're near the water on our left. We need water for the men and animals. But that leaves us short on the right with about 200 yards between the end of our line and the swamp before the river. Bryant ordered a unit of 100 men out front there as a picket guard. They're commanded by Major Thurston. We've got a chain of sentries along the front. I don't understand why, but the four pounder is placed near Freeman's Old Bridge where there is almost no possibility of the British crossing. We're bottled in here, and vulnerable on the right, Will."

That night, after an unsatisfying meal of watery corn meal mush that was not even grits and wet, gummy bacon, Will went to sleep in his bedroll.

At least he was warm.

CHAPTER 40 – BRIER CREEK

Will woke early. There was not yet a hint of light in the eastern sky. A milky wash of cloud made the sky look starless and empty. He had slept poorly, and his mouth tasted foul. Days of not washing added to his distress at being unclean and having foul breath. Although he had never had a heavy beard, Will's face felt scruffy. He felt fortunate to have a tent. It kept out some of the wind and damp. He rose and stretched his back, bent, and stretched his tired legs. His legs and buttocks were still sore from so many days in the saddle.

Will stepped outside the tent and looked around. The camp may as well have existed in peacetime. It was dead quiet, a few crickets sang, but the cold of the past few days had even them quiet. Wind rustled the trees and made the beards of moss flutter. A couple sentries were visible in the distance at each end of the road that went through the camp. Will knew there was a unit of 100 men out front as a picket in addition to the line of sentries. He hoped they were alert.

Acknowledging that he was not a trained military man, Will wondered if General Ashe had sent out any patrols before leaving for Black Swamp. Will had seen a small group of light infantry guarding the south end of the camp at Brier Creek and Freeman's Old Bridge. And there were men there rebuilding the bridge. Will did not know when the bridge would be complete. A few men were stirring, mostly people kicking up fires and getting food cooking. Otherwise, it appeared as if the rest of the entire camp was sleeping soundly. A bird made a trilling sound. Will wryly smiled. Birds singing in February. Georgia was quite a place.

Will walked over to Elbert's tent. "Sir, are you awake."

A hoarse voice, "Aye, I haven't slept a wink."

"I was thinking about taking a ride around the edges of the camp."

Elbert said through the tent flap, "Let me get my breeches on and I'll join you."

Will and Elbert quietly saddled their horses. Cuthbert saw the activity and hurried over. "Can I help?"

"No, Cuth. We're done saddling. But saddle your own horse and get our things together. Get the colonel's orderly to saddle his own horse as well. Load your musket and pistol. Get us some cartridges for our long guns. I don't know what's going to happen today, but I keep getting feelings that this has been too quiet. We could be surprised as I have seen so many times before, and then it's 'Katie bar the door.'"

"Aye, Sir. I'll saddle up and then see about some food for you and the colonel."

"Thanks, Cuth. If something starts up with the British, I want you to be holding my horse and be with the colonel's orderly. We may need to get on horseback to direct a fight. Don't mention this to the others. We're just being prepared."

"Very well, Sir." Cuth headed over to the cooking fire.

Elbert said, "Good man, that one."

"Aye. I've been teaching him some gunsmithing, and he's most willing as an orderly."

"I see that."

"Aye, he has family in Sunbury and since the British took it, he's been worried. No wife, but brothers, mother and father, a sister. All living with the occupation. I understand some houses were burned in addition to the fort being bombarded."

"Aye. Tis scary to have one's family captive or displaced like Liz. I worry about her constantly."

Sam Elbert and Will trotted out of the camp and went south toward Freeman's Old Bridge. The sun had cracked the horizon and the dawn's light began to reveal the landscape. Still there were black trees and dark shadows. A startled bird flew, and Will heard a fish jump in the creek. Wood smoke wafted from the campfires.

Elbert pulled out a map. "What worries me is this back road to Augusta. Suppose the British rushed up that road and came in our back door up here?" He put his finger on the map.

Will asked, "But didn't Len Marbury's men burn that bridge?"

Elbert scowled. "Aye, but we've both seen the British take tremendous initiative to do unpredictable things. Right now, we are to believe they are snug as a bug in their camp behind the redoubts at Ebenezer. Not sure about that. Not sure at all." He looked pensive and glanced up to the sky. "No rain. Chill, but not frigid. Perfect day to march an army, Will."

"Aye. At Brandywine the British marched several miles in the heat and dust, crossed two creeks, and flanked us. Meanwhile, the Germans were making quite a lot of noise and gunfire at Chadd's Ford to our front. That kept us focused on Chadd's Ford. Marching from Ebenezer to Paris' Mill would be less of an effort than Brandywine."

"But you spotted them at Brandywine and warned Washington."

"Aye, and I was not the only one. Washington hesitated for quite a long time before believing me and the others. He finally acted when it became clear that the British had flanked us and were coming in from our right. It was almost too late."

Elbert was silent for a few moments. They trotted along Brier Creek. The swamp was extensive and very boggy. "Tis not like that swamp in Savannah that Howe called impenetrable and then that treacherous Quash showed them a path to flank us. There's certainly no path here, just a mud bog and cypress knees."

Will said, "Aye. I think this one is truly impenetrable."

Elbert mused, "And what does that mean? To us?"

Will answered, "If the British come, t'won't be through that bog. Boats won't do on the river, either. They'd be rowing up stream and that current is flowing. Yet, as I say, they have shown us they are masters of flanking maneuvers."

Elbert looked hard at the road. "Where might they flank us? I mean, there is no bridge, and the creek is too deep to wade. The river is not an option because of the current. This creek and swamp are impenetrable. That leaves the road."

Will said, "Aye, but Marbury's men burned the bridge at Paris' Mill."

Elbert slapped his thigh. "Damn! This is just impossible. I keep thinking the British will not just idly sit by and let us build up over 3000 men and then come after them like it's some afternoon at the races. They always strike first. Always!"

"And they are masters of the flanking maneuver."

They rode up to Paris' Mill and observed that the bridge was nothing but cinders. Cinders, except for the support piers which seemed mostly intact. But there being nothing left of the bridge surface it seemed an impenetrable barrier to the British as well.

As they trotted back toward the camp Will said, "At Moore's Creek the British had to cross Black River. They went well north, found a crossing, raised a bridge, and crossed. They then rushed toward Caswell's camp. I was fortunate to get wind of that and got to Caswell ahead of them. He had the good fortune to have time to withdraw across Moore's Creek Bridge and damage it. That slowed down the Highlanders. I worry about that bridge at Paris' Mill, Sir."

"Aye. Why Ashe has not placed the four pounder there and assigned at least a company of men to guard that approach, I don't know."

Will and Elbert got back to camp and had some breakfast. Mushy peas someone had brought from last year's harvest. They had been dried months ago. Now they had been soaked in river water. Will found a stick and a leaf in his. Congealed grits with some fatback rounded out the meal. Will choked it down.

Will sat in the sun, half-heartedly reading *The Odyssey*. Will thought. "What more could happen to Odysseus?" He carefully wrapped the book in its oil cloth wrapper and placed it in his saddlebag. Poor Molly was still saddled. Will patted her on the neck, and she nuzzled him. He mounted and nudged her out onto the road and trotted up toward Paris' Mill.

Riding toward Paris' Mill, Will passed Ashe's entourage arriving back from Black Swamp. Will saluted and moved off the solid road to wait for the column to pass.

He arrived at the burned-out bridge hulk and dismounted. Looking at the water Will could see that the current in the creek was fast-moving and the water was deep. A look at the bend in the creek just downstream showed white sand under the far bank. Will's trained hunting and fishing eye told him that there was a deep hole on this side of the river and the sand was scoured out from there. This creek could not be forded. Anyone getting in that water would be quickly rushed into that hole and drowned.

That left the bridge. But it was burned. Could the British cut logs quickly enough to make some kind of bridge surface? Not likely. At least not likely without being detected. So...what?

Will scanned across the creek past the bridge. Where was Paris, anyhow? His house was abandoned like so many other farmsteads Will had seen on the ride south from Augusta. The mill was still there, and the wheel was turning. Quite a sawmill...could the British fell trees and saw them into lumber and re-build the bridge? Again, unlikely without detection. The whine of the huge saw would be heard at the camp.

But...the house. Could they dismantle the house and use the boards to build a bridge? At first thought it seemed quite unlikely. But, where else might the British quickly get lumber? Where else could they do it without the Americans hearing the sound of axes and the toppling of trees?

He turned and cantered back to camp. Dismounting he hurried over to Elbert. "The creek is impossible to ford at the bridge. Paris' Mill Bridge. There's a deep hole where tis easy to drown. White sand."

Elbert looked at him like he was deranged. "Aye. We looked at that this morning."

"Aye, Sir. But...Paris' house is standing abandoned and tis built of plank lumber. The British could dismantle that house quickly and build a new bridge surface. T'would be imperfect, but passible."

Elbert sat back and thought, his eyes flicking left and right as he mentally tore apart the house and reconstructed the bridge. "Damn! I think you have something. Let's go see Ashe."

Ashe was sitting on a camp stool behind his portable camp desk. "I left most of my baggage up at Burton's Ferry but had to have this desk. Tis useful, no?"

He dithered with some papers, a map, his ink pot. Ashe continued, "I'm quite tired after all that riding over to Black Swamp and back. Tis a good 15 miles up to Burton's Ferry, another 15 to Black Swamp. Sixty miles in two days!"

He looked at Elbert then Will, owl-eyed, "Now, what's this about the burned-out bridge?"

Elbert told him what Will had surmised.

Ashe thought for a few seconds, smiled, and looked at Will. "Well, you're young yet. The British are never that smart. Plus, who says they are on the move? You know I'm whipped after riding sixty miles in two days. Imagine what it must be like for infantry marching. Then, this camp is a veritable fortress, Sir. A veritable fortress!" Ashe grinned. His smirk said, "leave the war to the adults, sonny."

Elbert said, "But, Sir, should we not at least place our four pounder and a company of men near Paris's Bridge? Shouldn't we issue ammunition and drill the troops?"

"Naw! They'll not be coming that way, Sam. I don't think they'll be coming anywhere. They're safely behind the walls of those redoubts down toward Ebenezer. Y'all quit worrying so much, now."

As they walked out of earshot of Ashe's tent, Elbert sputtered, "Jesus! I should not blaspheme, but God in Heaven! That man is a bloody fool! I'll grant we have no intelligence that the British are on the move, but it feels right. We both have seen the British pull a rabbit from a hat, and you're right that they're masters of flanking maneuvers."

Will asked, "What shall we do?"

Elbert gritted his teeth, "I can't get him to put even a modest company of men up by that bridge. But there are some gaps in the trees along Brier Creek. I can put some men along there to watch for movement on the far side of the creek." Late in the day one of the scouts watching through the trees hurried into the camp. He hustled over to Elbert.

"Sir, I saw movement through the trees. It was difficult, but I thought I saw green jackets and some redcoats as well."

"How many?"

"Impossible to say, Sir. Tis very hard to make out anything through the thick trees, even with no leaves on most. The brush is very dense."

Elbert said, "Go check with the other scouts up that way. Take my orderly's horse. Come back and tell me if they have seen anything."

Soon, it was dark. The wind picked up from the north and the air was again chilly with arctic cold dropping into the southeast. Will and Elbert sat in front of a roaring campfire waiting for the scout to return. The wind occasionally eddied, swirling smoke in their faces. Will was tiring of the stink of wood smoke.

The scouts came back into camp. The first scout came to Elbert, saluted, and said, "Sir, the other scouts thought they saw something, but tis too dark now to tell. More, there has been no noise of any kind. Marching men make a tramping sound."

Elbert said, "Aye. But the wind's not right. It's shifted 'round to the north and that's against us hearing from the other side of the creek. Go get some rest and food, and good job."

When the scout was gone and they were alone at the fire, Elbert turned to Will, "They're coming, and they're going to tear down that damn house and make a bridge out of it. I'm going to see Ashe."

An hour later, Elbert, his head down and his shoulders slumped, walked back to the fire. He flung himself onto a stump used as a seat. "Tis nothing to do. He's like an ox. No amount of urging will get him off the belief that this camp is a fortress. I think it's a bloody damn trap!"

CHAPTER 41 – MARCH 3, 1779 – BLOOD AND STEEL

March 3rd dawned cold. Hard cold. Will had learned over the past year that Georgia was mostly pleasant, but broiling hot summers and harsh, arctic cold in the winter sometimes dropped down from the north like a frigid blast. Men jumped around trying to ward off the chill. Frost clung to the grass and there were places in the edge of the swamp where ice had formed on shallow pools. Everything looked brittle. Every step crunched as the grass broke underfoot.

Will was warm in his bedroll, but knew he had to get up. Digging himself out of the bedroll and shaking it out, he quickly got dressed. His uniform was cold and putting it on chilled him to the bone. He scrubbed his hands on his legs trying to warm up the cloth. He shook out his heavy Philadelphia coat and threw it over his shoulders. There was just enough light filtering into the tent for Will to see.

He stepped outside to even greater cold. Someone had brewed coffee, and Cuthbert was saddling Molly and his own horse. Elbert's orderly was saddling their horses. Other men were stirring quite a bit by the time Will, looking like a huge bear in his brown coat, shuffled over to the fire and got coffee. The mug warmed his hands, but he knew it was temporary.

Will thought, "No one will ford a creek in this cold. They would die from drowning, or if not that, then from exposure once out of the water. The British must build a bridge if they are to cross. For that matter, so must we. Except for the ferry to Carolina, we're trapped here."

The coffee warmed his guts and Will urinated behind a tree. Then he went looking for Sam Hawks and Noah Harris.

"Let's go kill a deer. I can't eat that disgusting mess again."

Sam said, "I'll go, but the deer ain't gonna be moving around in this cold."

Noah, said, "I've got a gripe in my belly. Y'all will have to go without me."

Will and Sam walked over to the horses. "Cuth, Sam and I are going hunting. Ok to take your horse?"

"Aye, Sir. I've packed your bedroll and put it on Molly. Your rifles and so on are also there."

"Thanks. We're going to try to kill a couple deer. Might be hard with this cold, they're probably bedded down for a while. But they have to get up and move sometime. I think when the sun gets up some it's going to burn off this frost, then they'll move."

Will checked Josie and his .45. He also checked the Brander pistol in his belt. Every time he checked it, he thought wryly about the night he took it out of Major Banastre Tarleton's hand. That was a cold night in Jersey, just like today. He grinned. That was a little over a year ago.

Will and Sam mounted their horses at mid-morning. As Will predicted, the sun was out. The frost was quickly burning off. There were still icy puddles and pools in the swamp. Maybe the deer would be stirring, looking for food.

They trotted down to Freeman's Old Bridge. Some small progress had been made on building a new one. The captain in charge of the light infantry said, "Sir, there's some activity down the road."

Will peered down the road and could see some men moving around. Had to be the British! But what were they doing?

Will said, "I'm not in command here, but perhaps you should have your men load muskets. Seems to me the British are up to something."

"Aye, there were campfires down that away last night. Haven't been any before."

Will and Sam trotted back to camp where Will spotted Colonel Elbert sitting on his customary tree stump. "Sir, the British have set up a camp south of Freeman's Old Bridge. The captain down there said they were burning campfires last night. He thinks they're down at Buck Creek. That's maybe three miles at most."

Elbert said, "That's to get our attention and keep it. Ride to where you can see through the trees and let me know if you see movement on that back road."

Will and Sam hurried along the edge of the swamp, pausing to look through any opening that seemed to offer a view of the other side of the bog and the back road. Will and Sam had the advantage of being on horseback as opposed to yesterday's scouts who were on foot. Will could occasionally see the road. Nothing there.

Sam said, "Seems to me we'd be better off killing a deer."

"Aye, but Elbert and I both are worried about the British getting behind us. Every battle I've been in with the British, they've flanked our position. Why would this be any different?"

Sam said, "Damned if you ain't actually thinkin' like an officer, Will."

Will grinned, "You may kiss my ring."

Sam snorted, "You know what you can kiss."

Will grinned. Same old Sam.

Will and Sam trotted back to Elbert. "We did not see any activity on the road. The British moving around openly down past Old Freeman's Bridge, showing themselves and lighting campfires last night makes me think of the Germans at Chadd's Ford."

Colonel Elbert paused to think, "Aye. Ride up to Paris' Mill and see if there's anything going on there."

As they trotted along Sam said, "This makes me feel important."

"Yep. I've felt that before, too. Somehow, it keeps you from feeling helpless. I got roped into being a courier for Washington at Brandywine. I resented it at first. All I wanted was him to sign a safe passage letter for me so I could get out to Lancaster and get some gun parts. But, when the British showed up and started shooting, I felt like I was contributing."

"I can see that."

"Yes. And when I got on top of that hill and saw the British coming through Jeffreys Ford, I was both excited and scared. Rode poor Molly almost into the ground to get back to Washington and tell him we'd been flanked. It got worse from there."

Sam looked hard ahead. "You're going to get that chance again! Look!"

British soldiers were forming up on the south side of Paris' Bridge. Several hundred at first glance.

Will said, "Damn! Tis just as we thought. Sam, ride back and tell everyone. Hurry!"

As Sam turned to go, Will said, "Sam, be sure to tell Elbert there are hundreds of them and it looks like they're regulars." Will emphasized, "Especially, tell Colonel Elbert. I'm going to try to get a little closer and see how many there are."

Sam turned Cuthbert's horse and spurred him into a gallop. Will turned hard left and trotted over to the bushes and brush. He skirted along the swamp, leaning forward with his body aligned along Molly's neck. He hoped no one would notice him if he moved slowly, his brown coat camouflaged his blue Continental uniform. He hoped.

Will edged closer. In the distance, Will saw that the British had captured three of the scouts Elbert had sent out yesterday and again this morning. This meant that the British probably knew the arrangement of Ashe's camp.

Will counted and stopped when he got to 900 men. It was an estimate based on counting eight square formations that looked to be about 100 men each. Then, there was the mounted militia milling around in the background toward the road over to Burton's Ferry.

Will saw a Highland regiment, probably the same men he had fought at Savannah. He thought, "God, bagpipes again!" He also saw grenadiers in addition to some mounted militia. Worse, Will saw several artillery pieces, at least five.

It was about noon, and the British would be in the American camp in between two and three hours. Time was short!

Will edged closer. Nothing else to report, so he backtracked cautiously down the edge of the swamp. When he was a good half mile away, he let Molly get into a good canter.

Behind him he heard a shout. Turning to look he saw mounted militia spurring up their horses to chase him. He had been seen!

Will paused for a moment. Need to give them something to worry about. He pulled Josie from her deer skin scabbard and checked her prime. Cocking the doghead and setting the trigger, Will drew a bead on the lead militia man.

WizCraaaak! Josie jolted Will's shoulder and the leader of the militia fell out of his saddle.

The mounted Loyalist militia reined in and paused to look at their wounded leader. Will calmly put Josie back in her scabbard, and nudged Molly with his knees. She turned and cantered toward the American camp. Will thought, "God, what a wonderful horse. She reads my mind." He nudged her slightly and she stepped up to a full gallop.

The Americans were in pandemonium as Will and Molly galloped into the camp. Sam had obviously arrived a few minutes before and delivered the news. Ashe was shouting orders forming the New Bern Militia on the left with the Halifax Militia behind them. Elbert and the Continentals plus a small number of Georgia Militia were in the center. Their numbers looked woefully inadequate. On their right, the Edenton Militia was backed by the Wilmington Militia. A light horse company was forming up to the right and rear of the Wilmington Militia. Men were running back and forth to the supply wagons. Out toward Paris' Bridge, Will could hear faint pops of sporadic musket fire as Ashe's inadequately manned picket skirmished with the advancing British light infantry. The British were on the move!

Will rushed to where Ashe and Elbert sat on their horses. "The British have least 900 troops. Some of the same Highlanders that we fought in Savannah. There were at least 100 mounted militia. The worst thing is that there are five artillery pieces that they got across the creek."

Ashe demanded, "Where are they?"

"Sir, they're about ten miles down the road, marching this way. The main element is six abreast. The Highlanders are in the middle. There are some skirmishers along the road to Burton's Ferry. They have cut off that route of retreat. The mounted militia is on their left."

Ashe turned to look for the quartermaster. "Damn! Where is that man?"

Elbert said, "Sir, he is by the supply wagon handing out cartridges."

Will looked to the supply wagon where there was a near riot of men trying to get cartridges. Other men were rushing to the water on the left to fill canteens. Company commanders were screaming at men to get in formation. Forming companies into line was chaotic at best, impossible at worst. Will saw that Elbert's assessment of the lack of bayonets was accurate. Men were bartering cartridges to fit their muskets. Some men were screaming that they didn't have the right cartridges. Will saw several men carrying cartridges in their shirttails for want of cartridge boxes. One man was stuffing cartridges in his pockets. The quartermaster was desperately trying to get the right cartridges handed out, but it was slow. Disorganization and chaos ruled.

The wind from the northwest drifted the faint stink of gun smoke. It was not yet cloying, nor did the smoke reduce visibility, but the wafting sulphury odor was the soft wing beat of the angel of death. The air was still chill, and the wind had a bite, but the sun was beginning to beat down. Sweat popped both from the sun and from fear. The sporadic crackle of musketry was a reminder of impending doom. The sound of bagpipes was the squall of the tortured souls in hell.

And the bagpipes were getting closer.

The British marched out of a copse of trees bordering the road about 200 yards in front of the Patriot front line. They put on a display of marching and forming line. Will watched with rising alarm as the British artillery moved into place in the center and swung around to point at the Americans. The sun glinted on the brass cannon barrels. Even from this distance Will could see the black holes of their muzzles. Soon they would spit death. And nothing could be done but to stand and bear the brunt of their hellish fire.

Still the bagpipes squealed. Will idly wondered if the pipes were actually playing a tune or was it just a random collection of annoying sounds laid over hum of the drone pipes.

Elbert looked at Will. "Stay with the General. If he needs to communicate with me, you're the courier."

Will nodded as Elbert edged his horse closer. Elbert lowered his voice. "This will not go well, Will. Stay with Ashe and try to get him to safety. I'm dismounting to be with the men."

"How will you escape, Sir?"

"I won't. Tell Liz I love her." Elbert fixed Will with a hard stare.

Will swallowed hard and nodded. He did not trust himself to speak.

Elbert dismounted, handing the reins to his orderly. Will saluted, and Elbert returned the courtesy. They briefly smiled at one another. Elbert turned and walked swiftly to the few Continentals and some Georgia militia that formed the center of the American line.

The British artillery belched smoke and flames and round shot bounced through the American lines. The blood spray from a decapitated soldier briefly made Will flash on the death of John Watkins, the sailor decapitated on *Beatrice*. Another man was lying on his back, shrieking in agony as his severed leg spewed blood. Another artillery volley produced similar results, the round shot bouncing and careening through the ranks like an insane game of lawn bowls.

Will pulled Josie from her scabbard, checked her prime, set the trigger, and cocked the doghead. He carefully lined up on a British artillery sergeant...

WizCraaaak! There was a spray of blood and brain matter, and the sergeant spun around and landed face first in the dirt behind the line of guns. Will had shot him in the head on purpose to rattle the other artillerymen.

The pace of artillery fires slowed somewhat as the gunners reacted to the sudden, horrific death of their sergeant, killed at over 200 yards by a Yankee bullet. Will calmly reloaded Josie and slid her home into her deer hide scabbard. Watching the enemy line, Will rechecked the prime on the Brander, his horse pistol, and the English Dragoon carbine. He loosened Uncle Ewan's dirk in its scabbard.

The British line advanced and still the cannon fire continued. Will saw the mounted militia milling around on the British left. He worried that they might charge down the American right which did not reach all the way to the boggy swamp before the Savannah River. It would be hell to pay if the British cavalry got behind the Americans. Once more, Will drew Josie from her scabbard.

Setting the trigger and cocking the doghead, Will took careful aim at the mounted militia man who was farthest out front of the rest of the gaggle of men and horses. They were some 250 yards away.

WizCraaaak! Josie jumped in Will's hands and a second later the militia man jerked upright in his saddle. He slowly slumped forward until his head lay on the neck of his horse. Then he slid off to land on the turf in a lifeless heap. Other militia men in the horse troop looked around to see if there were some nearby Americans. Then they looked at the American line. The horse troop moved back some 50 yards and milled about, temporarily leaderless.

Ashe looked at Will. "Damn, Son. You hell with that rifle!"

Will said, "I wanted to serve them notice that t'won't be easy to come at us."

"Damn sure did that. Here come the damn Highlanders. Wish they'd quit with that infernal bagpipe music, if you can call it that."

Will swung his gaze to see the British 71st Regiment of Highlanders marching in perfect step, muskets leveled, bayonets flashing sunlight and death. The artillery went silent.

Elbert shouted, "Fire!" and the American line erupted in gunsmoke and sulphury stink. Will picked out a Highlander at random and killed him with the .45. Then, he hurried to reload both the .45 and Josie. He would not use them again when the British closed with the American line, but he wanted them ready. From here on in, it was carbine and pistols, buck and ball, and that damn sword that he tripped over all the time. Bloody thing might save his life, though.

The American line burst into a blaze of fire and hell-stink of sulfur as a second volley took down a few more Highlanders. But the Highlanders marched on.

Ashe shouted, "Sam! Close up the middle!" and to Bryant on the right, "John...quick, move up some men on the right that cavalry looks threatening."

In response to Ashe's command, Elbert led his men toward his right and a few paces forward, but in so doing he blocked the line of fire from the New Bern Militia. Will looked around and spotted Sam Hawks and Noah Harris. Beside them was that flax haired young man named Zeke. They were in the second rank of the New Bern troops. Will saw Chuck Black, sword in hand, running back and forth dressing the line and looking over his shoulder at the oncoming Highlanders.

Without warning the Highlanders stopped, dressed ranks, fired a volley which killed three or four Americans. The Highlanders shouted "Huzzah!" and charged into the gap left by Ashe's faulty command to Elbert. The New Bern Militia could do nothing. Other Americans were in their line of fire.

The Highlanders flooded into the American line, now the New Bern troops could fire, but they only had time for one volley, and that was inaccurate. Smoke and flame, tartan-kilted Redcoats mixed with randomly clad American militia.

Will looked at Ashe who edged his horse back and, looking horrified, watched in morbid fascination as the New Bern Militia, with no bayonets and no time to reload, broke and ran for the swamp. Will spun around and looked for Sam and Noah. He quickly saw Sam and Zeke Carter. They were running full out, their empty muskets thrown aside as being ten pounds of useless weight that would only slow them down. He couldn't find Noah. Struggling to remember what Noah was wearing, Will remembered he had a gray shirt, black tricorn, white breeches.

The sun flashed off metal as fallen New Bern militiamen were bayoneted where they lay. The professional Highlanders were almost nonchalant in their killing strokes, only pausing briefly to administer an almost surgical plunge of the 16-inch triangular-bladed needle. Will cried out when he spotted Noah. Noah who had been sick all week with intestinal cramps and had tried to run but was too slow. Noah who now was crawling on hands and knees as a Highlander casually jammed his bayonet between his shoulder blades. Noah who was now dead.

The Highlander put a foot on Noah's lifeless back and wrenched his blade free to a gout of Noah's blood. Noah, Will's life long friend. Will pulled Josie from her scabbard, set the trigger, cocked the doghead, and with cold, furious precision, almost as casual as the Highlander's, shot the Scotsman in the back. The Highlander collapsed on his face, his killing musket flopped on his back, the blade of its bayonet visible even at this distance, still red with Noah's blood.

Ashe said, "Elbert has been forced to retreat to the swamp. Come with me!"

Will turned to follow Ashe to the New Bern Militia who were now getting into the boggy part of the swamp before Brier Creek. The Highlanders continued to press them as well as

Elbert's Continentals and Georgia Militia. Will saw Colonel John McIntosh, his friend and former commander at Sunbury, clubbed with a musket butt. Elbert in front of his men, was swinging his sword holding three Redcoats at bay, one of them an officer. Will thought momentarily about shooting the officer, but Ashe interceded.

"Quick, Son. Let's get where we can rally these troops. We can still win this thing!"

Will saw instantly that Ashe was deluded. The fight was already lost. The only hope for the Americans was to get to the path to the ford to Mathew's Bluff. Already a great many Americans were rushing through the swamp to the Savannah River. He followed Ashe and drew his own sword. Damned useless thing!

He whirled the sword around his head and shouted, "New Bern! To me!" A few men paused and ran to Will. Two of them were Sam Hawks and Zeke Carter.

Will turned to look for Elbert who was in a fight for his life. A Highlander stepped forward, parried Elbert's sword thrust and swatted Colonel Sam Elbert with the butt of his musket. Elbert landed flat on his back. Will thought "Oh, God, no!" The Highlander drew his musket back to drive the bayonet into Sam Elbert when Elbert made a Masonic hand sign to a British officer standing just left of the Highlander with the bayonet. The officer issued some sharp words to the murderous Highlander who immediately lowered his musket and then stood guard over Elbert's prostrate form. There was no hope of rescuing Colonel Elbert.

Relieved that Elbert was alive, Will swung back around to see Elbert's horse had followed along with Ashe and Will. Elbert's orderly was nowhere to be seen. Will shouted, "Sam! Get on that horse!"

Zeke Carter, his eyes wild with fear and confusion, looked around at Will. Will held out his hand and Carter grabbed it. Will pulled and Carter grabbed Will's bedroll with his other hand and swung up onto Molly's back. Molly jumped a little at the extra weight and looked around at Will, her eyes rolling in fright.

Will leaned forward and said, "It's alright, girl. We're going to get you out of here."

Ashe finally had realized the impossibility of the situation. He looked around at what had been the American right. The gap between the line and the Savannah River was still open. That direction lay the path to the ford and the only means of escape for the Americans.

Will looked back at the New Bern Militia. Astoundingly, Chuck Black was in the middle of a fight with three Highlanders. Jamming his sword back in its scabbard, Will spurred Molly and in three strides was next to Chuck and the Redcoats. The dragoon carbine blazed out its load of buck and ball, knocking two of the three Highlanders to the ground, one bleeding from a headwound, the other with a mangled arm. The third Highlander turned and ran toward the swamp.

"Chuck, get on the horse with Sam!"

Chuck Black looked blankly at Will. "I say, old boy, do what?"

"Get on the bloody horse with Sam!"

"Oh. Of course." Chuck looked at his sword and carefully put it in its scabbard. Then he walked quickly to Sam and accepted a hand up onto the back of Elbert's horse. They all turned to follow Ashe who was now hurrying toward the right and the path to the ford.

Dropping his carbine to dangle from its sling, Will said to Zeke, "Hang on!" and for the first time ever, put his heels into Molly's flanks. She shot forward.

As Will, Zeke, and Molly caught up to Ashe, the mounted Loyalist militia started closing in. Will pulled out the ancient horse pistol that had killed the bandit named John on the road to Bear Creek, thumbed back the doghead, and shot two militiamen from their horses. Once again, the load of buck and ball and a dash of extra powder made for a fearsome blast of hot lead and death.

Will threw the horse pistol in its leather bucket and dragged the Brander out of his belt. Molly was running fast, not a full gallop for that might have thrown Zeke from his precarious perch on the back of the horse. Zeke held on to Will with a death grip and they plunged into the last of the enemy cavalry. The river was some 300 yards ahead.

A Loyalist on a white horse charged over toward Ashe, leveling his musket as he rode. Will cut by him, and at point-blank range nearly blew his head off with Tarleton's pistol. Will shoved the Brander into his belt and cursing his bad luck, snatched the sword from its scabbard. Ashe was now ten feet ahead and there were no militia between the small group and the river.

Will saw Americans running through the swamp toward the river. "Please God, I hope they can swim." To Zeke, "Can you swim?"

"Aye, I can dog paddle some!"

"Dog paddling won't do in that river! Stay with the horse. Don't get off. You hear?"

"Yes, Sir, Major."

"It's Will, and just don't let go."

"Aye. I'll hold on."

Will heard hoofbeats and turned just in time to swing his sword at a Loyalist militiaman who was rushing to catch up to Ashe. Will's sword cut the enemy across the face and neck and the man looked astonished. He reined in his horse and looked at Will. The militia man asked in a blood-strangled voice, "Why'd you have to do that?" Then he turned his horse and trotted off, holding the bleeding cut with his free hand.

Will and Zeke, Sam and Chuck plunged after Ashe who was nearing the water. A musket ball whizzed by. Will nudged Molly to move left then right as another ball zipped near Molly's head. Will did not have to urge her again. She was full out running, still not a gallop. Zeke hung on tightly.

They got to the water's edge. Will pulled up short to look at the bottom. No luck, the mud had been churned by dozens of other Americans who were desperately trying to swim the river. It was cold, the water was fast, and Will knew men would drown. Sam and Chuck plunged into the frigid water, their horse swimming hard before finding purchase on the bottom.

Sam Hawks turned and shouted, "There's solid bottom about thirty feet out, Will."

Turning Molly, Will reached for the .45 caliber rifle and shouted, "I'm going to give them something to think about before they follow us.

The .45 jolted Will's shoulder and a loyalist flung back out of his saddle. The other loyalists stopped and looked at the wounded man. Will shoved the rifle back into its scabbard.

Zeke said, "Now I know you. You're Will Yelverton. You were at Mr. Kennedy's. I married his daughter."

Will said, "You're a lucky man, Mr. Carter."

Zeke said, "I know that. She speaks fondly of you. Thinks of you as a brother. Now I do, too."

With that Will turned Molly's head and the three of them plunged into the frigid, copper-colored murk that was the Savannah River.

CHAPTER 42 – GENERAL ASHE'S LETTER

Matthews' Bluff, March 3, 1779.

Major General Lincoln
Purysburg Encampment
Sir, -

I am sorry to inform you that at three o'clock, P. M. the enemy came down upon us in force; what number I know not. The troops in my division did not stand fire five minutes. Many fled without discharging their pieces. I went with the fugitives half a mile, and finding it impossible to rally the troops, I made my escape into the river-swamp, and made up to this place. Two officers and two soldiers came off with me. The rest of the troops, I am afraid, have fallen to the enemy's hands, as they had but little further where they could fly to. Luckily Major Grimkie had not got the artillery out of the boat, so that I shall keep them here with General Rutherford's brigade to defend this pass until I receive further orders from you. This instant Gen. Bryant and Col. Perkins arrived. Col. Eaton was drowned crossing the river.

Since writing the above a number of officers and soldiers have arrived. We have taken a man who says he was taken by them, and he would not take their oath and was formerly under Lee to the northward. He informed that there were 1,700 Red coats in the action, also a number of new levies from New York, Georgia militia, and Florida scouts: that 1,500 men had marched up to Augusta to fortify that place: that they are fortifying Hudson's very strongly: that the day before they marched off, 7,000 men had arrived from New York. Gen. Bryant and Rutherford are of opinion that it is better to retreat to your quarters: therefore, I am inclined to march tonight when we get all our fugitives over.

I am &c,

John Ashe

EPILOGUE – MIDNIGHT, MARCH 3, 1779

Will Yelverton sat on a fallen tree looking back across the Savannah River. The darkness obscured all but the white glimmer of the moon's waning light on the water. Will wept. His tears were hot with anger and loss.

Noah Harris, his lifelong friend, was dead. Brutally slain by a professional British soldier. Expertly stabbed through the heart with a razor-sharp bayonet. Noah of the great sense of humor. Noah who was an excellent hunter and fisherman. Noah who had stuck up for Will when Chuck Black and Isiah Koontz had bullied him. Noah who could never understand arithmetic but could write his name. Noah, the subject of many of Mr. Tomlinson's tirades, rapidly tapping the hickory stick when he caught Noah looking out the window, dreaming of hunting squirrels rather than making perfect letters. Tap, tap.

Noah Harris would never have a grave. Noah's memorial would be in Will's heart. Will had no satisfaction from killing the bastard who had bayonetted Noah. Will would tell Noah's parents of their child's death. No letter. He would do it personally. It would mean a trip to North Carolina.

Colonel Samuel Elbert. Captured, and Will hoped, unhurt. Will wept tears of rage for Ashe's miserable command decisions and intractability which led to Sam Elbert being in a British prison somewhere. The last Will had seen of Sam Elbert he was about to die when the British officer stayed the hand of the bayonet-wielding Highlander. Where was Sam Elbert?

Savannah? Not yet, but probably he would be held there as a high-ranking prisoner and therefore valuable in an exchange. Will resolved to find out. Will also knew he must go to Liz Elbert and tell her of her husband's bravery and good fortune to be alive. It would mean a trip into Georgia where the Loyalists now ruled completely.

Will wept for Abby and their lost love. Will had rescued Abby's husband. Had he known that Zeke Carter was the same man named Zeke who had married Abby? No. Well, maybe. Would he still have rescued him? Of course. Zeke Carter was an American in peril in a furious fight to the death. Zeke Carter, father of Abby's baby lived. Zeke Carter who now called Will Yelverton his brother.

Will had lost two friends and a lover. Brier Creek, this whole damn war, was a tragedy. Just like Shakespeare, except, Will thought, "you can't make this up like Shakespeare did." He would let Abby go and wish her happiness. He would be Zeke Carter's friend.

Major Roger Adams had come across the river with only a cut on his upper arm, but Corporal Charles Cuthbert was nowhere to be found. Cheerful Cuth who always seemed to be available to help. Will had last seen him sitting on his horse, waiting to do whatever needed to be done for Will or any other officer for that matter. Will was sick with worry that Cuth had drowned or been killed. Perhaps he got away in the aftermath of the killing. He had a horse. On the one hand, that meant more mobility and speed on dry land. On the other hand, a horse was useless in a swamp. Will uttered a silent prayer for Cuth.

Molly. Of all the people Will knew, Molly was his best friend. Poor Molly had been worn to the bone. Half frozen from the river, she was so tired her head hung as she shambled into General Rutherford's camp. One of the men had taken her and rubbed her down with some straw and given her food. Molly had always been there for him, and he took without giving back. He didn't even have a treat for her. He did throw his Philadelphia coat over poor, tired Molly's back. It was the least he could do. He felt ashamed and he wept for that shame. He would make it up to Molly.

Georgia was lost. Will was sick with grief because he had come to love the place. T'was true it was hot in summer and unpredictably cold one day and hot the next in winter. Boggy, malarial muddy swamps, glorious golden marshes, rivers laden with fish. The place was insect-ridden and positively floored with snakes and other dangerous wildlife. But the people were good, and the State teemed with opportunity. Already there was talk in Rutherford's camp of Lincoln's plan to lay siege to Savannah.

Ashe had ordered that what was left of the North Carolina Militia, the few Continentals and Georgia Militia who had come across the river, and Rutherford's brigade would march for Purysburg.

Will thought, "Marching! Again!" The words of a marching song he learned three years ago on the road from Moore's Creek Bridge to Crosscreek came back to him:

It's 40 shillings for the man
Who'll stand up tall and raise his hand,
So come and join us, enlist today,
Over the hills and far away!

Will let out a shuddering breath. "Yeah, well, I stood up and raised my hand, and look what it got me."

Will listened to the quiet gurgle of the Savannah River as it rushed headlong to the Atlantic. This river had run for eons from mountain to sea. To the river, this war was but a brief moment in time. Will thought about the timeless hills and forests, the land of the frontier and his plans to go there and make a life. Those things, that life, would have to wait. They would wait for Will and the others to win their freedom.

Will dried his eyes and squared his shoulders. Self-pity simply would not do for an officer in the Continental Army. He realized he was now in command of the few Continentals who survived the terrible onslaught of the bayonet charge. Will wondered what was required to be truly in command? The words of another song came, unbidden, into his head. The answer to what he must do was in the words of the song:

Hark! Ye hearts of tempered steel
Come and leave your sweethearts and your farms,
Your sports and plays, and pleasant days,
And march away to arms....

He would lead his men.

They would march away to arms.

They would have hearts of tempered steel!

Look for Book III of the Journeyman Chronicles coming in November 2022:

Journeyman: Honor Fades Not

BIOGRAPHIES

I wish there were time and sufficient ink to provide biographies of each historical character featured in Heart of Tempered Steel. Alas, I must be satisfied by noting the following important people are well covered in sources such as Wikipedia, and other easily accessed online sources. The brief comments for each of the following are offered to clarify any detail which may help the reader to understand the person.

John Ashe – Was a North Carolina militia leader who rose to Brigadier General. His major command was over the Wilmington, North Carolina Militia which he led to join General Benjamin Lincoln's forces in South Carolina. Sent to Georgia, he was in command of the American forces at Brier Creek, which occurred as written in the novel. General Ashe was court-martialed for his failure at Brier Creek. Acquitted of cowardice, Ashe was convicted of poor placement of sentries leading to his defeat. While he was not the strongest of military commanders, the historical literature makes clear he was ordered to occupy the untenable position at Brier Creek (Davis, 2016). Moreover, Davis (2016) observes clearly that British Lt Colonel Marc Prevost's attack on the Americans at Brier Creek was slightly premature given that Williamson and Rutherford were hurrying to consolidate forces at Brier Creek. Had Prevost been a day later, the entire American forces in the South could have been destroyed, making the taking of South Carolina a near *fait accompli*.

Ashe returned to Wilmington, North Carolina where he was captured and imprisoned by the British. While in prison he contracted smallpox and died in October of 1781.

As an aside, General Ashe's letter to General Lincoln, reproduced in Chapter 43, is ironic in that while writing the story I was not aware of this letter. I stumbled across the letter in an academic paper that had been overlooked. Will's gathering of his two soldiers (Sam Hawks and Zeke Carter) and Lieutenant Chuck Black was part of the story. That General Ashe's letter mentions coming away from Brier Creek with two officers and two soldiers was coincidental, but one of the delicious ironies of writing fiction.

Reference

Davis, R. S. (2016). Civil war in the midst of revolution: Community divisions and the Battle of Briar Creek, 1779. *The Georgia Historical Quarterly 100* (2), pp. 136-159.

John Boyd – Information is sparse on Lt Colonel John Boyd, Loyalist commander at the Battle of Kettle Creek. He is believed to have been a South Carolina landowner who received a commission and orders to form a loyalist regiment. He is most likely buried in one of the unmarked graves at the Kettle Creek battle site. According to Wikipedia, Colonel Andrew Pickens did converse with the dying Boyd and accepted a brooch to deliver to Boyd's wife. Pickens eventually delivered the brooch in keeping with Boyd's dying request.

Thomas Brown – Thomas Brown was a South Carolina loyalist who became hardened against the revolution by his poor treatment at the hands of the Sons of Liberty in Augusta, Georgia. Brown was tarred and feathered, burned, and severely beaten for refusing to sign the patriot association. The mistreatment resulted in a fractured skull and burned feet, and once recovered from these terrible injuries, Brown journeyed to Florida and quickly gained the confidence of Governor Patrick Tonyn who commissioned him a lieutenant colonel of Loyalist militia. Brown raised a regiment of loyalists called the Florida Rangers and led that unit in successfully defending Florida against three separate invasions of American troops. Later, Brown's Florida Rangers became a major force in the fight for Georgia and, still later, South Carolina. Brown was intrepid and his audacious swimming of the Altamaha River to take Fort Howe was as described in the novel. Brown was instrumental in recruiting Indians in Georgia's backcountry to fight for the crown. Brown raided South Georgia and made life miserable in the backcountry, rustling cattle, burning farms, killing men and dispossessing women and children.

References

Cashin, E. J. (1999). *The King's Ranger: Thomas Brown and the American revolution on the southern frontier.* Fordham University Press.

Olson, G.D. (1970). Thomas Brown, loyalist partisan, and the Revolutionary War in Georgia, 1777-1782. *Georgia Historical Quarterly 54* (1), pp.1-19.

Sir Archibald Campbell – Lieutenant colonel of the 71st Highlanders, assigned to subdue Savannah, Georgia, in 1778. Ultimately, Major General and successively Governor of Georgia, Governor of Jamaica, and Governor of Madras. Successfully attacked Savannah, and led British troops in subduing Augusta, Georgia, after being relieved by General Augustine Prevost. Campbell was a capable officer and leader and did not remain in the Colonies for the end of the Revolution, being assigned as Governor of Jamaica. He was named a Knight of the Bath and is interred in Westminster Abbey.

Elijah Clarke – A key figure in Georgia's Revolutionary War effort, in addition to his exploits detailed in the novel, Clarke led a group of some 700 men, women, and children to safety in the Carolina mountains after Loyalists engaged in a backcountry terror campaign. He served in the Georgia legislature and fathered a governor of Georgia.

Samuel Elbert. Samuel Elbert was born in 1740 in Savannah, Georgia. His parents were William and Sarah Elbert. William was a Baptist minister. By 1754, Samuel Elbert had become a merchant in Savannah, working for successful planter and merchant, John Rae. Elbert owned several tracts of land and many enslaved Africans.

In 1769, Samuel Elbert married Elizabeth Rae (1745-1788) daughter of Samuel's employer, John Rae. They had six children together, one of whom was named Samuel de Lafayette Elbert after his Elbert's good friend, the Marquis de Lafayette.

<u>Elizabeth Rae Elbert</u> brought the home at Rae's Hall to the marriage. Elizabeth Elbert's sister, Isabella, married John Habersham, another important figure in Colonial Georgia history. As mentioned in the novel, Lt Colonel Robert Rae was also a member of the Georgia militia, commanding the infantry deployed on Saint Simons Island during the Frederica Naval Action. Thus, Elbert married well, and his family connections were politically and financially rewarding.

From 1766 to 1786, Elbert served as provincial grand master Mason of Georgia. He established a Masonic Lodge in Savannah. Although born into the Baptist faith, Elbert's later years were spent as a member of the Anglican Christ Church parish in Savannah.

Samuel Elbert's military career spanned several years, dating from well before the American Revolution. In 1772, Elbert was commissioned a captain in the grenadier company of Savannah's 1st Regiment of Militia. As part of this post, he attended military training in England, making him one of the few militia leaders with formal military education.

Elbert was elected a member of the Savannah Committee of Safety, and in January 1776 assumed command of the Georgia militia. Commissioned a Lieutenant Colonel in the Continental Army when the Continental Line was formed in Georgia in early 1776, Elbert held dual commissions in the Georgia Militia and in the Continental Army. He was promoted to Colonel and led three unsuccessful invasions of Florida, the last of which was described in the text of Heart of Tempered

Steel. As noted in the novel, lack of unity of command resulted in failure of all three of these invasions.

Elbert commanded the troops aboard three river galleys, *Washington*, *Bulloch*, and *Lee*, of the Georgia Navy at the successful Frederica Naval Action in 1778. This action and its resulting capture of three British Navy ships occurred as described in the text of *Heart of Tempered Steel*. Elbert did consider challenging HMS *Galatea* in the St Simons Sound, but wisely delayed. Regardless of Elbert's decision making, *Galatea* slipped her moorings and sailed before the Georgia Navy could be brought to bear (Wood, 2006).

Although he was nominally in command of about half the troops at the defense of Savannah, failures of command by General Robert Howe led to the fall of the city after only brief resistance. The engagement was a fiasco, as described in Heart of Tempered Steel (Lawrence, 1952).

Elbert was wounded and captured at the Battle of Brier Creek, Georgia. The events surrounding his capture were as described in Heart of Tempered Steel. After several months of captivity in Sunbury, he was exchanged in 1781. Immediately upon his release he went to Washington's headquarters where he was welcomed. Elbert commanded a brigade at Yorktown where he was present for the surrender of Cornwallis' army (Wikipedia, n.d.).

He returned to Georgia where he became active in State politics and was elected governor in 1785. He briefly was sheriff of Chatham County (Savannah).

Elbert suffered from a long, but unspecified, illness and died, at age 48 on November 2, 1788. The November 6, 1788, edition of the Georgia Gazette carried a lengthy obituary which included the following statement:

"His death was announced by the discharge of minute guns and the colours of Fort Wayne, and vessels in the harbour being displayed at half-mast high."

Samuel Elbert's remains, along with those of Elizabeth, were interred atop Irene Mound, an Indian mound on the grounds of Rae's Hall overlooking the Savannah River. The grave was later disturbed, and the bones therein presumed to be Native American. However, military buttons found with the bones helped to identify the remains as those of Samuel and Elizabeth Elbert. Their remains were reinterred with military honors in 1924 Colonial Park Cemetery in Savannah.

As best as can be discerned from map coordinates and satellite photos, the site of Elbert's home, Rae's Hall, is now under a concrete parking lot associated with the Savannah Maritime Terminal.

Although the novel was about Will Yelverton, a fictious character, if any actual historical figure depicted in the story deserves the title of Heart of Tempered Steel, it is General Samuel Elbert of Georgia.

References

Diamond, Beryl. (2014, September 17). Samuel Elbert. *New Georgia Encyclopedia.* https://www.georgiaencyclopedia.org/articles/government-politics/samuel-elbert-1740-1788/

Lawrence, A. A. (1952, December). General Robert Howe and the British Capture of Savannah in 1778. *The Georgia Historical Quarterly 36* (4), pp. 303-327. Stable URL: https://www.jstor.org/stable/40577396

Wikipedia. (n.d.). *Samuel Elbert.* Retrieved from: https://en.wikipedia.org/wiki/Samuel_Elbert

Wood, V. S. (2006). The Georgia Navy's dramatic victory of April 19, 1778. *The Georgia Historical Quarterly 90(2)*, pp. 165-195. Stable URL: https://www.jstor.org/stable/40584908

The Habershams. The Habershams were a distinguished family in Colonial Georgia. James Habersham, a successful merchant and loyalist, had three sons all of whom were patriots. Two became revolutionary leaders.

John Habersham was a major in the Continental Army who was captured twice and exchanged both times. He served in the Georgia Assembly and in the Continental Congress.

Joseph Habersham was a Freemason and, in addition to serving as the Speaker of the Georgia Assembly, served at United States Postmaster General and Mayor of Savannah.

Joseph Habersham was a colonel in the Continental Army. He married Isabella Rae and was thus Samuel Elbert's brother-in-law.

John Houstoun – It is not known exactly when or where John Houstoun was born, but the best information available suggests he was born in Georgia between 1746 and 1748. His father was Scottish nobility and was among the first settlers of Georgia. Houstoun was twice governor of Georgia, and served as one of Georgia's representatives to the First Continental Congress. Houstoun's insistence upon being commander of the Georgia Militia during the third invasion of Florida was as described in the novel.

Robert Howe – Major General Robert Howe (c.1732-1786) was a wealthy North Carolinian from a prominent family. He fought in the French and Indian War and commanded the artillery at the Battle of Alamance in the War of the Regulation. Howe became a revolutionary and was commissioned a Brigadier General and assigned to command the Southern Forces of the Continental Army. His poor performance in the third invasion of Florida and contentious relations with southern political leaders, not to mention his reputation as a womanizer, led to his relief before the British invasion of Savannah (Wikipedia, n.d.). Howe's replacement, Major General Benjamin Lincoln had not arrived before the British landed at Savannah, so Howe commanded American forces in that engagement. Historian A.A. Lawrence, writing in the Georgia Historical Quarterly (1952), makes clear Howe's ineffective leadership caused the loss of Savannah when well-placed artillery could have stopped the landing of Lt Colonel Archibald Campbell's 71st Highlanders. Howe served throughout the war, notably sitting as senior officer at the military tribunal that sentenced Major John Andre' to death for spying. Howe put down several late-war mutinies. Howe has been accused of attempted treason in his late-war role as spymaster of the Hudson Valley (Wikipedia,n.d.). These allegations are not supported by evidence (Wikipedia, n.d.).

References

Lawrence, A. A. (1952, December). General Robert Howe and the British capture of Savannah in 1778. *The Georgia Historical Quarterly 36* (4), pp. 303-327. Stable URL:

https://www.jstor.org/stable/40577396

Wikipedia. (n.d.). *Robert Howe (Continental Army Officer).* Retrieved   from https://en.wikipedia.org/wiki/Robert_Howe_(Continental_Army_officer)

James Jackson – Born in England, Jackson immigrated to America at age 15 in 1772. He was known for being a duelist, taking offense easily. Jackson was a member of the Georgia Militia and was at the Defense of Savannah and the Battle of Cowpens. He served in the state legislature and was elected governor of Georgia but declined the position citing his inexperience. In 1989, James Jackson was elected to the First United States Congress.

Noble Wymberly Jones – Dr. Noble Wymberly Jones was one of the first settlers to arrive in Georgia on the Ann, the first ship of immigrants from England. His father was Noble Jones, an early key leader of the Georgia Colony. Noble Wymberly Jones was politically active for most of his life and was an early patriot who was among the group of Liberty Boys who, in 1775, broke into the Royal Magazine in Savannah and stole 600 pounds of gunpowder. As depicted in the novel, Jones escaped to Charlestown upon the fall of Savannah where he practiced medicine until the fall of Charlestown in 1780. Jones was captured and imprisoned in St Augustine, Florida until 1781 when he was transferred to Philadelphia. Jones had several children, though the record does not include the fictional Charlotte.

Jones' descendants changed the family name to DeRenne, a maternal surname considered more elegant than their original Jones. DeRenne Avenue in Savannah is a major thoroughfare. Wormsloe Plantation, the ancestral home of the Jones/DeRennes is a Georgia State Historical Park well worth a visit.

Bragg, W. (2014). Noble Wymberly Jones. *New Georgia Encyclopedia.* Retrieved from: https://www.georgiaencyclopedia.org/articles/history-archaeology/noble-w-jones-ca-1723-1805/

Francis Marion – Brigadier General Francis Marion of South Carolina, also known as 'The Swamp Fox,' is a legendary figure of the American Revolution. Though Marion never led a large unit in a major, consequential battle, he pioneered guerrilla warfare after the fall of Charlestown, South Carolina. Marion was fortunate to have been injured and evacuated from Charlestown before the British siege of that city. Thus, he was free to create a small unit of patriots who harassed the British at every turn. Banastre Tarleton tagged Francis Marion reportedly saying, "...as for this damned old fox, the Devil himself could not catch him." Francis Marion will be a major player in *Journeyman: Honor Fails Not*, Book III of the Journeyman Chronicles of the American Revolution.

John Milledge – Born in Savannah in 1757, John Milledge fought in the American Revolution, and served as aide to Governor John Houstoun in the failed third invasion of Florida in 1778. Milledge was among the Liberty Boys who broke into the Royal Magazine and stole 600 pounds of gunpowder in 1775, as well as taking Royal Governor Sir James Wright prisoner in that same year. Milledge was governor of Georgia and served in the US House of Representative and the US Senate, where he succeeded James Jackson upon Jackson's death. He died in 1818, and is buried in Augusta, Georgia.

John Mowbray – Little is known of John Mowbray beyond his command of the *Rebecca* as part of Governor Patrick Tonyn's Florida Navy. He was not exactly a privateer, though he was seen as such. Rather, Tonyn had a lease in 1776 for *Rebecca* with Mowbray remaining as captain under Tonyn's auspices (Wood, 2006). On the other hand, Siebert (1943) holds that Tonyn's 1776 lease letter to Mowbray was a letter of marque, making him a privateer. Wood (2006) disputes this claim citing US Naval documents. Regardless, Mowbray was a known raider of commerce along the South Carolina and Georgia coasts. For at least a brief period, Mowbray commanded the only vessel, *Rebecca*, in Tonyn's Navy and was instrumental in foiling the second American invasion of Florida in 1777 (Buker, 1979). According to the website *Three Decks*, Mowbray passed the British Admiralty Lieutenant's examination in 1780 and commanded HMS *Germain* in Florida and Georgia waters thereafter. Mowbray was apparently a good commander and well respected by friend and enemy (Wood, 2006).

References

Buker, G. E. (1979). Governor Tonyn's brown-water navy: East Floirda during the American Revolution, 1775-1778. *Florida Historical Quarterly.*

Siebert, W. H. (1943). Privateering in Florida waters and northwards during the revolution. *Florida Historical Quarterly 22(2).*

Wood, V. S. (2006). The Georgia Navy's dramatic victory of April 19, 1778. *The Georgia Historical Quarterly 90(2),* pp. 165-195. Stable URL: https://www.jstor.org/stable/40584908

Andrew Pickens – Was a South Carolina planter, military officer, and politician (1739-1817). He was promoted to Brigadier General in the South Carolina Militia and fought in several of the major battles of the Revolutionary War in South

Carolina. He served as a member of the South Carolina House of Representatives and was a delegate to the Constitutional Convention. He was a delegate to the Third Congress.

Augustine Prevost - Major general Augustine Prevost, originally from Switzerland, was commander of the British troops in East Florida. He, and his younger brother Lt Colonel Marc Prevost, successfully defended Florida from three separate American invasions. He led his forces in a successful attack on Sunbury in January 1779. He subsequently replaced Lt. Col. Campbell in Savannah, where he was in command of all British troops in Georgia for the remainder of the war.

Jean Marcus Prevost - Lieutenant Colonel "Marc" Prevost commanded British troops from East Florida in the 1778 campaign against St. John's Parish (by that time, officially Liberty County) and Midway Church. He accompanied General Prevost, his brother, in the January 1779 attack on Sunbury. The reduction of Sunbury by British troops in 1779 was not covered in the novel; however, the destruction of the officers' barracks essentially ended the useful life of Fort Morris. Prevost's occupation of Sunbury as well as the fall of Savanna rendered the Georgia Navy's galleys useless, and they were beached and burned by their crews. As an aside to Prevost's conquest of Fort Morris, Charles Cuthbert is a fictional character; however, there were several Cuthbert's from Sunbury. Alfred Cuthbert (born 1785 in Sunbury) was a United States Senator from Georgia. In an additional twist to the story of Sunbury, the author's fourth great-grandfather was a private captured at the 1779 fall of Fort Morris.

James Screven. James Screven, a famous name in Coastal Georgia, was commissioned captain of the St. John's Rangers, a volunteer company, in 1776. During June of 1776, Screven was commander of the First Battalion, Third Regiment of Georgia Militia. From July 1776, until March 1778, he served as the commanding colonel of the Third Georgia Continental Battalion. He resigned his US commission in 1778 and was then appointed brigadier general of the Georgia militia. He was mortally wounded in a skirmish during the defense of Midway Church and died on November 22, 1778. Known as an aggressive commander, Screven's death was largely as reported in the novel. It was reported that he was shot 12 times by Loyalist Militia and lingered near death for several days. Lt Colonel Prevost allowed Screven's doctor to treat him and apologized for the murderous treatment of him after his initial wounds.

Edward Telfair – A prominent businessman in Savannah, Edward Telfair was born in Scotland in 1735 and immigrated to the British American Colony of Virginia in 1758. He moved first to North Carolina and then to Savannah in 1766 where he established in business with his brother. Telfair was among the Liberty Boys that, as outlined in the novel, broke into the Royal Magazine and made off with some 600 pounds of gunpowder. Telfair was father to six children. One of his children, Mary Telfair, bequeathed the Telfair mansion in

Savannah to the Georgia Historical Society and this property ultimately became the renowned Telfair Museum of Art. Edward Telfair was elected to three terms as governor of Georgia. He died in Savannah in 1807.

Reference

Johnson, C. (2015). Edward Telfair. *New Georgia Encyclopedia*.

Eliza Yonge Wilkinson. Born February 7, 1757, on Yonge's Island, South Carolina, Eliza Yonge Wilkinson was widowed when her young husband died suddenly. That same year, her newborn baby died. She moved to live with her parents on Younge's Island. An ardent rebel, Wilkinson was noted for being charming, attractive, feisty, self-assured, witty, and engaging (Chamberlain, 2016).

Eliza Yonge Wilkinson became famous after her death when, in 1839, Caroline Gilman published a portfolio of Wilkinson's letters during the period from just before the British occupation of Charleston, SC, in 1779, to Cornwallis' surrender in late 1781. Notable were her vivid descriptions of depredations by invading troops – in particular, banditti or Tory militia – who raided plantations hanging men and threatening women while stealing property. Her letters present a vivid picture of life under the occupation.

Reference

Chamberlain, E. (2016). Wilkinson, Eliza Yonge. *South Carolina Encyclopedia*. University of South Carolina, Institute for Southern Studies.

LANDMARKS

Tondee's Tavern: A Savannah Landmark

According to the New Georgia Encyclopedia, Tondee's Tavern stood at the northwest corner of Broughton and Whitaker Streets. The tavern was founded by Peter Tondee who arrived in Georgia on the second ship to bring settlers. In addition to his work as a builder and minor government official, Peter Tondee and his wife, Lucy, ran the establishment for many years.

Tondee's Long Room served as the seat of government for the State of Georgia during the revolution. The tavern also served as meeting place for Masonic lodges, the Union Society, and numerous other clubs. Tondee's Tavern was a hotbed of revolution prior to and during the war. Several meetings of patriots, including the Second Provincial Congress of 1775, met in the Long Room.

When Peter Tondee died in October 1775, Lucy Tondee continued operating the tavern until the British occupation at the end of 1778. When the revolutionary government returned to Savannah in 1782, it occupied Tondee's.

Lucy Tondee died in 1785 and the building was sold. The tavern, sometimes called the Cradle of Liberty in Georgia, burned in the Great Fire of 1796. The location of the original Tondee's Tavern is commemorated by a plaque on the building at the corner of Broughton and Whitaker Streets in Savannah.

References

Weeks, C.S. (2003). *Peter Tondee*. New Georgia Encyclopedia.https://www.georgiaencyclopedia.org/art icles/history-archaeology/peter-tondee-ca-1723-1775/ 3/3

Sunbury, Georgia

Once a bustling seaport, the town of Sunbury no longer exists. There are a few condominiums near the Medway River and a couple excellent seafood restaurants. Fort Morris still stands as a Georgia State Historic Site, and the Sunbury Colonial-era graveyard still exists. Otherwise, a few historical markers and some roads that follow the original paths are all that remain.

The death of Sunbury was driven, in part, by the Revolutionary War and in part by commercial concerns. Other ports were simply more important as time went on. Hurricanes devastated the area further, and the little town withered away.

The following attributed to Dr. James Holmes in the Darien Timber Gazette, December 21, 1877 is quoted in Sheftall (1977, p. iv.):

In its palmy days, Sunbury was a beautiful village with its snow-white houses, green blinds, and a red roof here and there. From the fort to the point was a carpet of luxuriant Bermuda grass shaded with ornamental trees on either side of its wide avenues. Today it is a cotton field with one or two dilapidated buildings.

Thus, in 1778 Sunbury was a bustling little city of some 1000 residents, many of whom were very well-off members of the Georgia gentry. Dr. Lyman Hall, a signer of the Declaration of Independence, owned property nearby. Many other famous Colonial-era Georgians frequented the town.

The Eagle Tavern in *Heart of Tempered Steel* is a fictitious location, but its proprietor, Abraham Williams existed and owned an unnamed tavern in Sunbury. Andrew Darling was, as were many Sunbury residents, a Congregationalist who moved south from Dorchester, South Carolina. The three public squares mentioned in the novel existed (Sheftall, 1977), and the area was a hotbed of strong revolutionary sentiment. Note: the parish was renamed Liberty County on February 5, 1777, in honor of its strong revolutionary fervor.

After the British occupation of Georgia, many captured senior American officers were held on parole in Sunbury. Not allowed to leave the city except for occasional approved visits to Savannah to buy provisions, they were given free rein within Sunbury. Paroled captured officers included Colonel Samuel Elbert, Colonel George Walton (after he recovered from his leg wound at the capture of Savannah), Major John Habersham, Colonel Mordecai Sheftall (deputy commissary general of the Continental Forces in Georgia and highest-ranking Jewish officer of the Revolutionary War), and several others. The reader will note these names from *Heart of Tempered Steel*.

For those who are interested in more fine-grain detail of the life and times of the Town of Sunbury, Sheftall (1977) is an excellent read –see list of references below.

References

Anonymous. (n.d.). *The ghost town of Sunbury, Georgia.* Retrieved from:

https://www.exploresouthernhistory.com/sunbury1.html

Corry, J.P. (1930, Sept 3). The houses of Colonial Georgia. *The Georgia Historical Quarterly, 14 (3)*, pp. 181-201. Stable URL: https://www.jstor.org/stable/40576053.

Eliott, D. T. (2010). *Ebenezer and Sunbury: Revolutionary War landscapes of two dead towns in Georgia.* The Lamar Institute. PowerPoint Presentation to SHA, January 7, 2010. Retrieved from https://Ebenezer_and_Sunbury_Revolutionary_War_L.pdf.

Midgette, G. M. (1976). *Fort Morris at Sunbury: Survey and first excavations.* [Master's Thesis], University of Georgia, 1976.

Sheftall, J. M. (1977). *Sunbury on the Medway: A selective history of the town, inhabitants, and fortifications.* State of Georgia Department of Natural Resources Office of Planning and Research Historic Preservation Section.

BATTLES AND MILITARY LOCATIONS

Fort Barrington (Top center of the map) –The location of Fort Barrington (later Fort Howe) is clearly important due to vast tangle of waterways to the east. Fort Barrington/Howe was perfectly located along the King's Highway at the shortest route to crossing the Altamaha River when traveling north to south.

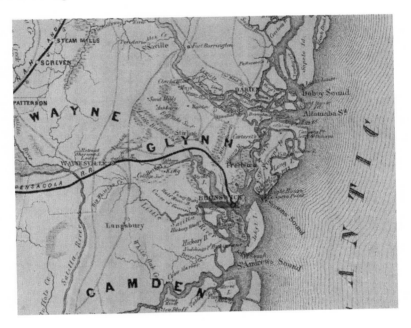

Source: Wikipedia. This image is in the public domain.

Battle of Brier Creek Map

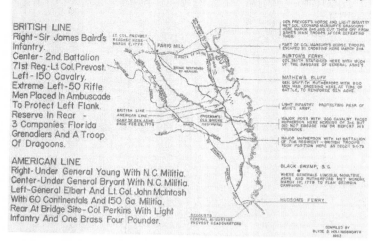

Source: Wikipedia.

According to Wikipedia (2022), there is no apparent copyright associated with this map.

Coastal Georgia during the American Revolution

Source: Wikipedia.

Romans, B., De Brahm, J., Gerar W. Robert Sayer, and John
   Bennett (Firm) -
   https://www.loc.gov/item/gm71005467/, Public
   Domain,
   https://commons.wikimedia.org/w/index.php?curid=1
   16739495

Frederica Naval Action

See map above of Fort Barrington to note location of
Frederica.

Source: Wikipedia.

Per Wikipedia (2022), this image is in the public domain.

The Frederica Naval Action was much as described in
the text of Heart of Tempered Steel. From the map of the coast
of Georgia, it is easy to see that the 'inland passage,' now called
the Intracoastal Waterway, was a critical waterway for
movement of military and commercial traffic. Naturally, both
the Americans and the British wanted to control this vital line
of communication.

The illustration above depicts the Georgia Navy's galley
Washington with its lateen sails reefed as it engages with the
Hinchinbrook.

ACKNOWLEDGEMENTS

In any written work, especially one of historical fiction, there is research into the works of others. I have attempted to capture the main references I used in recounting the American Revolutionary War in Georgia. Of necessity, there were many episodes left out. The story is told from Will Yelverton's point of view, and it would be impossible for Will to have been at every action that occurred. I acknowledge the work of so many historians and apologize for those references that might have been missed.

Every novel, and for that matter, every research effort, academic or otherwise, needs readers to offer critique, commentary, proof reading, question the logic, and offer encouragement. This list is getting to be the 'usual suspects:' Bob, Darryl, John, Karen, Rick. Special thanks to Karen, who has become my *de facto* editor. Each of these wonderful people, my friends and colleagues, gave of their time and brain power to push this effort across the finish line. The words 'thank you' are insufficient, but they're simple and heart-felt.

AUTHOR'S BIOGRAPHY

Frank A. Mason

Frank A. Mason is the pen name for a retired US Air Force Lieutenant Colonel who also served as a college professor for 25 years. As an officer in the USAF, Mason flew B-52's during the Cold War, served as a flying training instructor, and directed high-level staff organizations over 22 years of his early adult life. A college professor from the late 1990's to the present, Mason's alter ego earned a PhD from one of the nation's top 10 public institutions and had the privilege of mentoring hundreds of doctoral students at three respected higher education institutions.

The Journeyman Chronicles is Mason's series of novels about the adventures of a young master gunsmith caught up in the American Revolution. The Journeyman Chronicles is available on Amazon.com and other booksellers.

Frank A. Mason is also author of a series of modern suspense novels that will also be available in summer, 2022 on Amazon.com and other booksellers.

Mason lives in Florida with his wife, who is a university professor and author of a forthcoming series of children's books. They share three adult children who are each successful in their own right.

Contact information:

Frank.a.mason.jr@gmail.com

frankamason.com
904-460-7919
C&F Creatives, LLC
2800 N 6th Street, Unit 1, PMB 301
St Augustine, FL 32084

Made in the USA
Middletown, DE
08 August 2023

36372915R10368